BORN TO ROCK
HEAVY DRINKERS AND THINKERS
ESSAYS AND INTERVIEWS BY
TODD TAYLOR

GORSKY PRESS
LOS ANGELES • CALIFORNIA
2004

BORN TO ROCK

copyright © Todd Taylor, 2004

All photographs in *Born to Rock* by Todd Taylor,
unless specifically noted
Cover photo taken by Dan Monick
Cover design by Todd Taylor
Tattoo work by Dr. Julian and Dave Guthrie

ISBN 0-9668185-8-X

Gorsky Press
PO Box 42024
LA, CA 90042
www.gorskypress.com

THANK YOU

Megan Bentzel and Sean Carswell for both of their tireless friendships and editing prowess. Josh Lane for the final edit. Mom, Pops, Andy, Jen, and Trevor Taylor.

This book is dedicated to the memory of Esther Olympia Doman

The entire *Razorcake* and Gorsky Press crew, 4th Street San Pedro, Al Quint, Andy Harris, The Arrivals Cabal, Art Fuentes, Avail, Ayn Imperato, Ben White, Bill Dr. Strange, Billy Morrisette, Blaze James, Bob MacPherson, Bradley Williams, Brian Archer, Brian Forrester, Bruce Bartels, The entire Carswell family, Dale Drazan, Dan Monick, Danny and Katy Clarke, Darren Walters, Dave Crider, Dave Guthrie, Davey Quinn, Don Seki, Doug Barker, Dr. Julian, Erik Funk, Erika Pinedo, Fuck You, Dale, Gabe Hart, Gary and Katie Hornberger, George Orwell, George Seldes, Glenn Byron, Grabass Charlestons, Haruki Murakami, Holly Connor, Hot Dog Boy, Howard Zinn, Jack Rabid, James Jay, Jason Willis, Jean Luc, Jeff Fox, Jessica Thiringer, Jim Kaa, Jim Munroe, Jim Ruland, Jimmy Alvarado, John The Miner, Julia Kelly, Julie Drazan, Karen Air, Land, and Sea, Karla Pérez-Villalta, Kat Jetson, Ken Cheppaikode, Knockout Pills, Kristin Wilson, Lane Pederson, Larry Genetic, Leatherface, Liz Ohanesian, Maddy Baran, Matt Average, Mike Beer, Mike Faloon, Mike Plante, Murtaw and Casmo, Namella J. Kim, Nancy Meck, Nardwuar the Human Serviette, Nelson Algren, Oscar Zeta Acosta, P. Edwin Letcher, Paddy Costello, Paul Wanish, Pete Menchetti, Radon, Rainer Fronz, Ray Hoskinson, Rev Nørb, Rich Mackin, Richard Brautigan, Rick Bain, Rick Hall, Roger Mena, Russ Lichter, Ryan Henry, Sara Isett, Scott Stanton-Cox, Sean Cole, Seth Swaaley, Spontaneous Disgust, Stan Korza, Super Chinchilla Rescue Mission, Thomas Pynchon, *Thrasher*, Tim Kerr, The TimVersion, Tito, Toby Tober, Todd Congelliere, Tony Reflex, Turbonegro, Upton Sinclair, Vanessa Burt, Var and Jen Thelin, and Yoichi Emori.

THE REZILLOS

TABLE OF CONTENTS

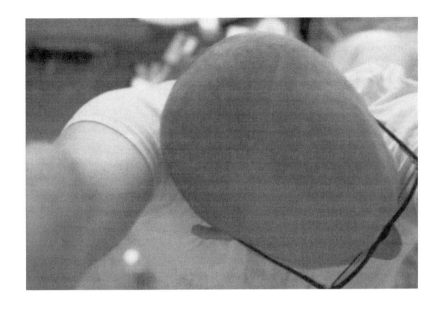

Over the next several days, I'd learned that I hadn't broken a single bone, but had hundreds of stitches in the three layers of skin over my skull and scores in both hands and knees. Reflex had saved me. When I impacted the windshield, my head was down, saving my eyes, nose, lips, and chin. My thick skull had done its job.

My first tattoo was a doozy. Realizing that I'd have it for the rest of my life, I wanted it to get funnier the fatter and older I got. I thought about it for a good three years before it began to get inked. It stretches from hip to hip across my stomach. It came down to this image: me on a Lay-Z-Boy, beer on belly, shirt hiked up from my gut. My nephew comes bounding up and lands on my stomach. Distracted by the colors, he looks at Crazy Uncle Todd's stomach, traces the letters, and mouths them to make sure he's reading them right: "b-o-r-n-t-o-r-o-c-k. What does that mean?"

This is how I'll respond. "First off, do you see the flames coming off the words? Look at them closely. They spell 'MOM.' Always be good to your mom. She's a nice lady." Then I'd turn to the task at hand. "Have your parents told you about punk rock? Do you know about it?"

I'm expecting a shake of the head or a big shrug.

I won't tell him the exact same story I'm about to tell you and it'll probably include his learning how to respect vinyl records and operate a turntable, but the message will essentially be the same. Punk's made by a ton of people who either feel discarded by a larger culture or they, themselves, actively try to discard the worst parts of that bigger culture in the hopes of making something better or at least livable. These people make lots of noises and share ideas to the best of their abilities. One has to look beyond the television, the radio with endless commercials, and magazines with ads for cars to find them. Why do these people do it? No one knows for sure, since everyone's story is a little different.

Here is mine.

*   *   *

When I was fifteen and returning from Boy Scout camp, the front right tire of the car I was a passenger in blew out. The car flipped seven or eight times. I was ejected through a hole in the windshield and flew a considerable distance away from the car. As I tried to stand up, to see if anyone was hurt, I remember not being able to see. I remember not being able to stand up. I remember my brother, who had been sitting next to me in the back seat, crying. I went to wipe what I thought was sweat off of my brow with the back of my hand, so I could go back and help. It was blood that had pooled into my eye sockets. I could feel it coagulating. Growing up, blood was no big deal. Being an active kid, I was always nicked or bruised. I was used to the sharp, iron taste of blood. The back of my hand wasn't getting the job done, so I used my palm. It was then that I realized a good chunk of my scalp had been cut and it was hanging in a flap over my eyes. I gingerly pushed it back into place, then laid back down. It was getting harder to move.

The rest of the afternoon came in snapshots as the pain began to surge. I had felt surprisingly little pain from the time when I was sitting in the back seat until I stopped trying to get up. That would change with every passing second.

My older brother, Andy, and I, both Eagle Scouts, had volunteered as counselors-in-training for a ten-week session Camp Del Webb, outside of Cedar City, Utah. For twenty-five dollars a week, we dug fire lanes, dredged a lake, and set up activities for a total of six hundred scouts. The Boy Scouts of America were supposed to provide us a ride back with the regular campers, but they wanted us to stay just a little bit longer. We arranged a ride home with our good friend, Pasqual DeLuca, a funny, irreverent seventeen-year-old counselor. Everyone called him Pat. He drove a 1967 Buick Apollo. He liked Queen, pulled elaborate pranks, and was a big, hearty guy. Right before leaving Cedar City, Pat had stolen a Nazareth tape, *Hair of the Dog,* from a big drugstore that smelled vaguely of candy corn. He never stole from mom and pop operations. That damn tape kept playing even after the car had stopped rolling and remained on its roof.

I remember that we'd eaten pizza that afternoon, something I'd been craving after a month of camp food. It had burned the roof of my mouth. My tongue kept on probing the swelled ridges.

Being a '67 Buick, there were no factory seatbelts in the back.

I remember how good the air smelled. It was July 28. Mid-summer. Juniper, creosote, clear air and a real blue sky. It was the type of air that even though it was bordering on hot, the windows were fully rolled down and I couldn't help but stick my arms out into it as the car accelerated. That's why the stereo was cranked. So we could hear it above the rush of air at sixty miles per hour.

That's all that happened. The front right tire blew. No over-correction, no swerving, no speeding, no intoxication, no inattentiveness.

I didn't know then, when I was laying down in the Utah dirt with shards of glass jutting out of both legs, both arms, and my head, that Pat had saved my life. I just wanted a couple of really simple things. I wanted my brother, who I still couldn't see, to stop crying. He was a tough guy and if he was crying, things weren't going so well. I wanted the pain to stop getting worse. I wanted the Nazareth tape to quit playing.

I smelled raw gas.

Travelers stopped. A man in a semi blocked traffic with his truck so that the cars wouldn't come to close to me. I had flown over the median and landed near oncoming traffic. A complete stranger covered me with a blanket, up to my neck. The trucker kept whispering in my ear, "You're going to be okay. I called. An ambulance is coming. You're going to be okay. The ambulance is coming. Don't fall asleep."

"What's your name, sport?" someone asked.

I couldn't tell them.

"How many fingers am I holding up?"

I couldn't really tell.

I could barely talk. I remember my throat being dry and blood coming out in bubbles until it started clotting in my mouth, and when I swallowed it, it choked my throat. Someone gently held my wrists. Glass and rocks were embedded in my hands and I had already scratched my face a little, but I had no way of telling. I wanted to know how everyone else was, but the words just didn't come out, no matter how loud I yelled them out in my mind. Words didn't catch up to my thoughts. All I said was, "Thank you." "Thank you." I was an extremely polite kid.

When the tire blew, all I remember is being shot through darkness. I felt like I'd been placed in a black box and thrown down a garbage chute with a lot of sharp stuff. I remember lots of different impacts. It didn't hurt when it was happening. I truly thought it was a dream, one that I'd had many times.

About half an hour later, the ambulance came. The white of their uniforms matched their calm, methodical movements. There's something to be said about being wrapped up tight. The confinement, the immobility was the most secure I'd felt that day. My head was covered in a towel, broad cuts were made into my clothing, my neck was locked up tight, and my arms were secured. I was put on a board, then in an ambulance. The air conditioning felt good. The EMT sure was nice. She kept on saying, "Sweetie, we need you to stay awake, okay?" All I could do was smile back at her. I remember her being very pretty, very calm. "You're lucky to be here," she said.

The pain had become all consuming. They had cleaned the blood from my eye sockets so I could see. I really didn't want to look at myself. Wincing, I could see pebbles, which had been impacted, but not gone in, popping out of my skin. There was a shard of glass at the base of my neck. My whole body felt like it was being crushed by rocks then etched by salt. Every time I moved, new nerves seemed to explode.

When they rolled the gurney into the hospital, I smiled despite myself. It was all too familiar—going into a hospital, on my back, watching the ceiling tile quietly go by. I was an accident-prone kid.

The hospital didn't know who I was right off the bat. My wallet wasn't in my shorts. It was getting hard to move, and it wasn't just the restraints. My body began puffing up, attacking all of the foreign materials in it. At that moment, I thought really hard—"I don't care if I die. It's okay. Being dead can't be this painful. I either want to be back at home in my own bed, or I want to die. Right now. Either would feel real good." It wasn't a maudlin thought or a tough guy thought, I just thought, "Enough's enough. Time to bow out."

Then my brother came up to me. Although he wasn't crying then, there were two clear paths down his dirty face. He gave me a kiss on the cheek, in the only place that wasn't heavily bandaged. "Stay in there, buddy. I know it hurts. You need to stay awake. They're trying to reach Mom and Pops now." Andy's eyebrow was covered with gauze. "I just got a nick." He looked at me longer. "I wish I could be you right now and take your pain."

My parents were contacted. The decision had been made to helicopter me to Las Vegas.

I didn't say a word to the paramedic lady, but my eyes seemed to ask the questions I was thinking. "You'll be in good hands shortly. I'm sorry. We're not allowed to give you any anesthetic. We're going to give you a CATscan. You must be very still."

If I said anything then, it was "Thank you."

The next several hours are still the most excruciating of my entire life. I thought I'd go crazy from the pain and not return the same. I swear to this day that my body would have to be three times larger to feel that much pain. Places I've never felt since were in absolute agony.

When I arrived in Las Vegas, before I was operated on, I mentioned to a nurse that my legs really hurt, too. Understandably, the Cedar City hospital had been more concerned with my head. By the time I was being prepped for the operating table in Las Vegas, attendants removed a dirty, blood-soaked towel that had been pristine when it was put on me in Cedar City. There were twigs and grit in my hair. My chart hadn't made special mention of any other trauma. That's when a nurse noticed deep shard of glass around both knees.

I didn't fall asleep until the anesthesiologist put the mask over my face, over ten hours after the accident.

I woke up the next day in a Las Vegas hospital bed with bandages over my head, hands, and legs. Over the next several days, I'd learned that I hadn't broken a single bone, but had hundreds of stitches in the three layers of skin over my skull and scores in both hands and knees. Reflex had saved me. When I impacted the windshield, my head was down, saving my eyes, nose, lips, and chin. My thick skull had done its job.

At first, when Mom and Dad showed me the picture, it didn't make sense. There were Boy Scouts and people in suits in front of what looked like a huge marble wall. It was a week or so after the accident. The accident was Monday. The funeral was Thursday. I would be in the hospital until Friday.

"Honey," my Mom said. "I'm sorry you couldn't make it. You can't be moved yet."

I looked at the picture some more. It was a funeral.

"Pat saved your life. He was ejected before you and made a hole in the windshield. You followed through that hole. He died on impact when he hit the steering wheel. We didn't want to upset you when you were in critical condition." My Mom and Dad and brother gave me long hugs. I cried so much the next couple of days that it took me over a decade to cry again.

The next several months were difficult. More glass and rocks, which had tunneled deep inside of me, would work their way out. I remember having a pain at the base of my neck, feeling a little barb, picking at it, then blood pouring out as I pulled out a quarter-inch sliver of glass from my flesh when I was sitting and watching TV. It was horrible and demoralizing. My Mom kept a sheet on a comfortable chair in the living room for me to sit in. At the end of the day, she would shake out debris that had worked itself out.

I had a scar that circumnavigated the top of my head. A good friend was dead. If it weren't for my loving family, I would have become a terror.

During my convalescence, since I couldn't run around and be the active kid I always was, I took to drawing, reading more, and writing. I could stop when I got tired. I took an extreme liking to all three activities.

About a month later, Mom sat me down for a talk. "Todd, you were under the guardianship of the Boy Scouts of America when the accident happened. Do you understand that?"

I nodded.

"Well, we contacted the BSA headquarters and we made photocopies of the release Dad and I signed. It's a form that said our fourteen and sixteen-year-olds were not to be in a vehicle driven by any one under twenty-one from the time you left Las Vegas to the time you returned. We're asking that they help pay for your medical bills. We're not asking for any pain and suffering, just to help pay what we owe the hospital because they were in charge of you when the accident happened."

I continued nodding.

"They have declined our request. They said that you could have returned on the bus but decided to ride with Pat instead." My Mom paused and became visibly angry. "Not only that, they've 'strongly suggested' that we sue Pat's family for negligence." She paused again. "I'm not going to do that. They just put their son to rest. We'll have to figure something else out. I just wanted to let you know what's going on."

The next several months, I experienced an almost complete recovery. My mind was a little rattled, I had scars I wanted to hide, but, all things considered, I was lucky. My parents continued battling with the Boy

Scouts of America while still encouraging my brother and me to remain in the organization. I must admit, I liked camping, making knots, shooting guns, and learning how to be self-sufficient, but there was a nagging suspicion in me, at fifteen, that all was not right. On one hand, the Boy Scouts were espousing duty to god and county, to "help other people at all times," to be trustworthy and loyal. Yet, they did their best to wipe their hands clean of the blood of Pat's death and my severe injuries. They wanted to act like neither of us had ever existed. A part of me felt like it was missing, much like my Boy Scout book that had recorded my progress as a scout which had been lost in the accident.

I wanted Pat to live forever. I still miss him greatly.

Although not fully formed at that time, I realized that putting faith, time, and energy into an official organization was one thing. To have that organization recognize me as an individual, to help one of its devoted members out in a time of need, was another equation. It seemed unfair and antithetical. I felt betrayed.

I don't remember the exact first time I heard punk rock, nor do I remember what band it was, but it was later that year. I seethed anger, and love them as I did at the time, The Kingston Trio on Dad's reel-to-reel wasn't cutting it any more.

My family lived in a small town. Boulder City's about twenty miles outside of Las Vegas, but at the time before any of my friends had a car, Vegas could have been adjacent to Bali. There was no record store in Boulder City. I didn't even fully understand what a punk rocker was. I found a community radio station that played music I'd never heard before. It was fast, angry, noisy, and exciting. KUNV was that station and the program was called "The Rock Avenue." (Unfortunately, in recent years, KUNV has become an adult contemporary jazz station.) Punk was played at night and I'd often pop a cassette in my boom box and have it record for the full ninety minutes, station breaks and all, and listen to that cassette over and over and over again.

It's not the most impressive statement to make, but I found an affinity for The Circle Jerks. I, too, felt like the world was up my ass. Minor Threat sounded like a cannon was blasting the speaker out of the ghetto blaster. Crass was the closest sound of all that confusing pain in my brain. On trips into Vegas, I'd try to pick up used cassettes—ones with the least incriminating covers and band names like Agent Orange, Red Cross, Articles of Faith, the Avengers—and play over them over and over until they broke. It would be a couple years, by their names alone, to actually buying the Dead Kennedys, Millions of Dead Cops, Buzzcocks, the Dead Boys, or Cock Sparrer. I saw very few photos of bands. I still had no concept of the scope or even what a punk looked like. I just craved that sound.

It was this easy. On one side was the severely sanitized version of the world that the Boy Scouts had portrayed. And I still believe in being good, honest, upstanding, and respectful—even more so when someone is in dire need—yet, the Boy Scouts lied to me and dropped me off at the curb when asked to stand up to their own ethical code.

On the other side: music and lyrics that explored the grittier side of life, that wasn't scared to check out the bodies buried underneath the carpet. It felt more real, more legitimate. Even amongst all that anger, it seemed so fair. I liked the music a lot because it counterbalanced what I was learning in school. It made me start a line of questioning that is still in use today.

Later on that year, the accident litigation met a settlement. It was found out that the retread tire that had blown out was defective. An out-of-court settlement was made with the DeLuca's insurance company. We received money to cover my hospital costs.

I have the most supportive, proud parents in the world and for that I'm eternally grateful. They have never second-guessed my biggest decisions, which I don't think many people can say.

*   *   *

Over the next several years, my quest for more punk rock evolved from a hobby to a full-blown obsession. I started collecting albums and seven inches. I started reading fanzines. Even in an isolated town of 10,000, I felt connected in some small way to something much larger. More importantly, it was something meaningful and something that spoke to me directly. I didn't have to conform to anything. I just had to look inside myself a bit longer. I would go to the library and read books that mentioned punk.

Also, I can't pinpoint the first time I saw a self-proclaimed punk rocker. It might have been Louie the Letch, who ran The Record Exchange. He looked more like a greaser in a leopard print vest, and would always give me a music suggestion. Maybe it was on microfilm, when I saw an old cover of a national newsmagazine, describing English punk's "tribes." Spiked hair, torn fishnets, safety pin earrings, sneers, combat boots, and leather jackets seemed to be what it was all about. It looked like fun stuff. It also looked like a whole world away.

Unhappy with the yearbook for high school, I made an open solicitation for students to turn in pictures, drawings, essays, and poems. I assembled everything together, photocopied and stapled them. Surprisingly, it was a success. The administration forbade me to sell it on campus. I did so anyway and it sold very well. When I graduated high school and was to give a valedictorian speech, the principal had talked to my mother during the State track meet in Reno, asking her rat me out and to give him a copy of the speech to possibly censor it. Mom told him to go fly a kite. My speech wasn't nasty or mean-spirited, and at the time I still didn't fully realize it, but I wanted people to understand the power of doing stuff yourself. Of looking beyond organizations, beyond institutions, beyond experts. Schools are tricky. They often pull the slight of hand of saying "Think for yourself," but the underlying statement is, "but don't contradict or directly challenge us."

I then went to college in northern Arizona and I met my first friends who were into punk as much as I was—mostly from small towns, too—and we shared tapes, listened to albums, got drunk, and got into varying amounts of trouble. There were punk rock bands in Northern Arizona, like RN and Primitive Tribes. It wasn't a big scene, but it was still nice to see that I wasn't the only one affected by it. It was cool to hear bands I'd never even knew existed. I started snapping together the bigger pieces of the puzzle. Even in 1990, punk was still largely an anomaly. It was really patchy in smaller towns. Since five years old, I'd never lived in a town of more than 40,000. It didn't—and still doesn't—bother me that most people weren't into it.

Six years passed, my vinyl selection grew, as did my zine library. I dyed my hair blue and green, yet finally figured out that I'm a low maintenance dude who would rather spend money and time on the music itself than spending it on hair and clothes. I continued to work hard both at school and part time jobs, and graduated at the top of my class with a master's in literature.

As I was filling out the forms to get my doctorate, I got hung up on the essay section. What did I want to do? I was good at school, but I didn't want to just plug right back into it and become a teacher. I felt I was missing something. I couldn't put my finger on it. I wanted to write—that I was sure of. But ever since my brush with the Boy Scouts, I had a palpable anger towards authority. I probably wouldn't fare well in a large corporation. I had no illusions that I'd live off of novels. I entertained fleeting thoughts about working for a small town newspaper, but that didn't seem quite right, either. Looking back, I can't remember what I wrote in that essay. I just knew I felt a little hollow inside.

To this day, I'm still not fully convinced of the power of a degree. Sure, it'll be nice to have that piece of paper if my current way of living crashes so I could fill in as a substitute teacher instead of collecting carts in a supermarket parking lot. Yet, down deep, I know I've learned more out of school than when I was in it. Perhaps it fueled me with the desire to not want to return to it. That's not a slag on my teachers—many of whom I still greatly admire—but when I was in school, I had the feeling that I was doing work for someone else. To fill a criteria. To study a writer or a time period I wasn't terribly interested in. To do an exercise for the sake of the exercise. What did I get out of it? A solid work ethic, heaps of patience, the tools and mindset for research, the desire to thrive outside of purely academic confines, and the ever-growing love of libraries. I also, unexpectedly, found a group of writers my age who still inspire and challenge me.

I still wanted punk to continue to electrify me, not to put it in a glass box for further examination, as many academics tend to do. The problem was I didn't have a better plan, so at the end of my master's program, I applied to ten different writing schools. I was accepted to a doctoral program in Mississippi.

It was a good excuse for a road trip, so my good friend Roger and I drove across country. We arrived in Mississippi intentionally a little early after driving two thousand miles. I spent a spell of time in their school's library so I could read and be familiar with all of my potential mentors' published work. I'd also written a new story to show them my progress since applying.

The meeting with my potential mentors was disappointing. After a couple direct tries, I realized they didn't care to read what I'd brought. I was already accepted to the program. What was the point? Why would they want more work, dissecting a new student's story? It rubbed me the wrong way. Once again, I felt like a number or a tool or a gear in a machine much bigger than myself.

I was at another crossroads, so after drinking some beer to get some outside perspective on myself and sharing a pizza with Roger, I called my mom. On one hand, I had a Ph.D. degree within grasp. The degree would pay for itself while I taught college English. On the other hand... I had nothing, except a whole bunch of doubts. I dialed. I don't know how many people's parents would back them—without guilt or grief—when they had a gut feeling that a full-ride higher education wasn't for them. And I was just going to walk away from it with no Plan B. My mom listened to what was rattling around in my head. She said something along the lines of, "Honey, do what you feel is right. Dad and I won't be disappointed." I'd pretty much talked myself out of continuing school. Winding down on the conversation, Mom took a breath and said, "Grandma Kelly, she's not doing so well. If you're free, what do you think about staying with her for a bit in Camarillo?"

I don't know if this is an accident, but in most of society's eyes, it probably looks, at best, like self-sabotage. One shouldn't veer off the road to an assured Ph.D. on a gut feeling. But that feeling, coupled with the fact that my grandma was one extremely cool lady who I could repay some of my gratitude to, solidified my decision. After my road trip, I moved to California.

Grandma Kelly wasn't feeling that well but didn't want to be left in the care of someone she didn't know, and she refused to go into a home. It's not completely true that I took care of my grandma. We took care of each other. While I may have replaced a faucet, done some painting, and installed fluorescent lights in the kitchen, she patched holes and shed an incredible amount of light on our shared history, daily making us both laugh.

Curiously, she always said she never amounted to much in this world and considered herself "just a navy wife" who then worked directly for the navy for over thirty years. But if not being capable of guile, of not being capable of vindictiveness, of creating and nurturing two wonderful children is nothing, then I wish the universe was full of nothingness, that more people would treat each other in "nothing" ways. It would be better for it. She talked softly but acted with such strength. She was good. And that was her ultimate strength.

To realize, at twenty-three, that I had more in common with a seventy-nine-year-old lady than I did with most people my age was a powerful realization that went beyond the crude outline of genetics or a vague description of "family." I could, and can, see so much of myself in her that it would have been scary if it wasn't so great, so reassuring, that if I could be only a fraction of her, I'd turn out okay. I enjoyed a great, real break.

She told me a story that has stuck with me ever since. It's another accident.

It was in Philadelphia, snowing like crazy. Grandpa John was driving and Grandma Kelly was in the passenger seat, in her new fur coat, pregnant with Mom. A hard left ejected Kelly into a snow bank. The door never locked quite right and Kelly was leaning against it. John continued to drive for a couple of miles. He realized in mid-sentence that his wife was no longer sitting beside him. He slammed on the brakes, pulled a U-turn, and found Kelly, basically where she'd been ejected, except that she was standing in the middle of the snow bank so she wouldn't get hit by the sparse traffic. I have no idea what Grandpa was thinking as he drove up, but Grandma, in her uncanny ability to understate everything involving her said, "I think you lost something." Then she got back into the car, remembered not to lean against the door, and rebundled herself. The snow was soft enough that she didn't get hurt. My uncle, Mike, yelled, "Do it again, Mommy."

Grandma was bulletproof and that came from being so good.

After three months, Grandma's health stabilized and she encouraged me to do whatever I wanted to do. She never wanted to be considered a bother or a burden. She never was. Even when she was in great pain, I could hardly tell.

I migrated down to Los Angeles, partially because there were some people I knew down there, partially to see how I'd fare in the world outside of academics. I worked a series of odd temp jobs and then began working steadily at an independent coffee roaster in the mornings. I used the afternoons getting acquainted to the fact that I was now surrounded by eleven million people instead of thousands of trees or hundreds of square miles of desert. It took some getting used to.

Almost every weekend, I'd go visit Grandma for a day, do some grocery shopping, and hang out some more.

Out of the blue, Blaze James of *Flipside* called me. I'd contacted *Flipside* six months prior, along with several other zines I'd read over the years, with no response. I lived about three miles away from the office and they needed someone to do mail. *Flipside* was one of the long tethers that connected me to punk rock, almost right from when I discovered it. It was large enough that it was carried at the Record Exchange in Las Vegas on a semi-regular basis, and I'd kept a subscription to it, on and off, for almost a decade. It had begun in the summer of 1977 and was still coming out. At the time, it was the longest-running fanzine in the world. I was stoked, even if I was just the mail guy. Al Flipside seemed nice enough. He was very mild mannered and he looked like a hybrid between Charlie Brown and Spock. Although we'd have long talks and discuss the minutia that helps make a magazine work, we didn't have that much in common. We hung out, outside of Flipside HQ, a grand total of five times in as many years.

I worked several months of getting up at five AM, working six hours, driving down to Flipside, and working five more hours. It didn't matter. I was charged up. I watched videos of bands I'd only read about. I got to flip through thousands upon thousands of gig posters. For the first extended period ever, I felt like more than just a witness to my own life. It felt like I was living it how I really wanted to and it felt great.

Sometimes, when I was in the office, looking for a back issue to send in the mail, I'd just sit and look at the original paste-ups—some twenty years old—yellowed and de-gluing and dimpled from the impact of typewriter keys onto the paper and just be in awe. Punk rock history fascinated me and here was the longest running source text for the West Coast of the United States. The geek in me was mightily pleased.

As a bonus, if I wrote about them, I could see shows for free. If I wrote reviews, I could have virtually any album that came through the mailbox. One thing hadn't wavered since I was fourteen—I still unabashedly loved the music. I no longer had to buy used cassettes to affordably discover new music. I got more thirsty for it the more I soaked it in.

Why had I gravitated towards a fanzine and not just been in a punk band? I don't have any musical talent. I know this. I haven't lamented that fact since my fifth grade music teacher wouldn't even let me play the recorder and I was put on block duty.

Over time, I slowly did more and more at Flipside. I began proofing and editing, began answering the phones. It was during my time there that I started feeling like an active, full-time participant in the punk rock underground. I had been on the sidelines—actively listening, reading, and going to shows—long enough. It was time to put theory into practice.

Although I had prepared for it mentally, it still struck me hard when my Grandma was in the hospital for the last time. When the tubes of the respirator were taken from the corners of her mouth and the remnants of the tape's adhesive washed from her face, when Mom and Dad and my uncle and my cousin Lorrie took turns holding her hands and touching her arms… she smiled. She knew where she was going and it was a good place. I don't know if I'm committing a sin by saying this, but when the priest came in minutes before she died to absolve her sins, I couldn't help but think—that unless she lived a diabolical second life that matched her blatant regard of care—that she had no sin. That she could start casting stones. As many as she wanted. It was Grandma's Roman Catholic belief that purgatory's a place to wait for one's soul to enter heaven. Grandma did her waiting on earth. When her body stopped functioning, she stepped into a great, pain-free, wonderful place. I can only hope so because if she's having a hard time in the afterlife, I'd hate to think how the rest of us will fare. I'd like to think that she's happier that she doesn't have to answer to her failing body, but is floating around with ease and comfort—sitting on her gardening wagon or gently rocking in her Lay-Z-Boy, doing a crossword puzzle.

By January of 2000, four years after starting with Flipside, I was Al Flipside's right hand man. Although there were no titles, I acted as the general manager. I helped make sure that everything ran smoothly, made sure that all supplies were stocked, learned graphic design, coordinated distributors and contributors, dumped the trash, everything. It wasn't glamorous and it surely didn't pay well, but I was happy. By that time, I had become comfortable with interviewing bands and writing columns. Many are included in this book.

The whole shebang began unraveling then, too. Rotz Distribution was putting Flipside through the ringer. Rotz's owner, Kai, owed Flipside a bunch of money. It's really very simple. They sold a lot of Flipside's stuff and then failed to pay us. We waited a full eight months before consulting a lawyer.

We eventually took them to court and won the settlement. Instead of paying Flipside a dime, Rotz declared bankruptcy and Kai disappeared. I didn't see a cent from the settlement. I doubt Al did, either. When the mess with Rotz started going down, Al and I had long talks. I finally mustered up the courage to ask him for an equal partnership. I essentially wanted to start Flipside again as two people, and not just under his real name, Aloysius Kowalweski. It should be noted here that Al hadn't paid me for the better part of the last two years I worked there. As a matter of fact, I made that suggestion because I knew we were in the right with Rotz and I wanted to keep Flipside afloat at all costs. I kept all of my time cards, so when the day came to get paid, it'd all be easy as one, two, three.

How'd I live? It wasn't easy. I lived in a windowless basement room and the rent was cheap. I didn't have a commute because I lived three doors down from the office. Doing stuff for the magazine paid for all of my entertainment. All I had to do was pay rent, pay for gas once in awhile, and I lost twenty pounds by eating mostly tuna fish. I lived off what little money I'd saved from the years prior, working at six dollars an hour.

I wanted to prove to Al beyond any shadow of a doubt that I was serious and I wanted to make Flipside the best magazine we could. I didn't want anything more in the world. It felt like my whole life—ever since my head impacted with that windshield—was leading up to what I was doing with that magazine. It wasn't about scene cred, respectability, or even recognition (I even make it a point to not have my face in the magazine). It was because I knew that not only was I good at making a magazine, but that I loved it. It made me feel that my head finally found what my gut had been missing all those years.

Roughly in this timeframe, Dillinger Four became my favorite band of all time. They're of the rarest breeds of bands that'll make you want to dance, riot, laugh, drink, and sing along all at once. One of their songs is titled, "It's a Fine Line between a Monkey and the Robot." Like all meaningful punk rock, it has a tendency to wiggle directly into my life and put a spotlight where it once was dim. There's no monkeys or robots in the D4 song itself, but goddamn if I hadn't started feeling like a monkey made out of nuts and bolts. I had been working like a machine for five years straight. I had begun to feel like someone else's pet. It was sobering to think that the worst of it was that I had done it to myself. I had given Al the leash. It was completely his game, his magazine, and his decision.

In October 2000, I laid it all on the table with Al. I wanted an equal partnership with full financial disclosure or I'd get another job. Al didn't bat a lash. He told me it would be better if I got another job until things blew over. I asked him, point blank, if there were any hard feelings. He said there weren't. I drove out to Tucson for a week to work on beefing up a computer. When I got back to Pasadena, the Flipside locks had been changed. I went to Al's house and asked him why they were changed. His answer was four words. "I don't trust you." When I pressed him as to how or why, he replied, "It's just a feeling." It was uncomfortably silent. He then asked for his camera bag back, which I had been borrowing. I asked for the twenty-four thousand dollars he owed me for two years of work. He was angry that I'd told people he owed me money. Neither of us got what we asked for.

In my head, I freaked. I felt mental bolts loosen and sheer off. I felt exactly like I had when I was tumbling though dark space after the tire had blown, except this time it was completely in my head. My skin was fine. There was no blood but I couldn't distinguish very well from when I was awake and when I was asleep. That lasted about eight weeks. I wrote Al three times. He never replied. Our last brush with one another was when I started doing freelance work and a check was accidentally sent to the Flipside PO Box instead of my apartment. Al cashed that check.

I seethed. I skated. I wrote. I didn't sleep well. Twelve packs would disappear from the fridge nightly. I was so lazy, I'd pee in bottles instead of walking upstairs to piss. Then forget to take them out to the dumpster. I'd hit a low.

My parents invited me to fly along to visit my brother, who was living in North Carolina at the time. When I was in the South, I hooked up with Sean Carswell, a longtime friend who I'd met in Flagstaff. We hung out for a week. We watched large tankers filled with sand dump their cargo along the eroding shoreline. The shoreline was disappearing due to the placement of a naval base, which pushed all the sand off shore. The base is where Trident nuclear submarines were first launched. Disney was currently leasing it so their cruise ships could visit the island the Mouseketeers owned. It was surreal.

One of the many things I like about Sean is that he's easy-going but defiant. He's also one of the most articulate people I know. He can focus like a laser beam to cut through layers of absolute shit to illuminate how things really work. And he makes me laugh when he does it.

During my visit, we met a stripper who used the monkey bars at her kid's preschool to practice her pole moves, which were considerable. We were virtually the only two in the bar, so she sat down and talked to us. She wasn't buttering us up. She knew we were in for the drink specials.

After she walked off, Sean began talking, seemingly out of nowhere: "Tribesmen would make a hole in a rock." I was waiting for the punch line. I knew how he operated. "At the end of the hole, a little less deep than a monkey's arm, they'd place some salt. Monkeys love salt. They smell it, crave it. They lock their paws around it. When that happens, they can't get their paws out of the hole. They're stuck. They won't let go of the salt. The tribesmen, who made the holes and put the salt in them, all they do is go beat the monkeys to death. The monkeys won't let go of the salt. They're easy prey. An arm's stuck in a rock… don't you see?"

I was still waiting for the punch line or waiting for him to somehow tie it into the stripper. He's good at making abstract associations.

"We're all monkeys going after the salt."

I nodded along. As with most things that change my perspective on life, I had to pause, reflect, and down a couple of beers to establish the right frame of mind. I don't remember responding directly. Maybe I was distracted by AC/DC blaring over the blown-out PA. Maybe it was the disco ball with missing bits of mirror revolving over our heads. What Sean was talking about was me, you, everybody. I knew what the big hunk of salt was in my life. It was the thing I thought I couldn't live without. I gave everything I had to it for five years straight with too many fourteen-hour days and six-day weeks to count. Nobody else forced me to keep a hold of that salt. For better and for worse, one of my enduring talents in life is the ability to sustain severe mental and physical beatings.

Like distinct scenes slapped down one by one, I realized things I hadn't before. I mistook my job for my life. My passion was music. Flipside was the vehicle. While the music and the very real culture it's steeped in kept me fixed and resolute, I mistook Flipside for my passion. At twenty-eight, I was so sure that Flipside was my life—and would remain so for literally decades more. I could see no alternative. I'd finished as much school as I could tolerate. I'd worked enough jobs to know that being a tow truck driver or set painter had their limitations for me. I really didn't want to work for anyone else.

As with any type of drug, what had made me feel superhuman for awhile also became my wrecking ball. That rock of salt got bigger and I had squeezed that fucker harder and harder, trying to either make it crumble or compress it like coal, trying to make it a diamond. Sean made me realize I was crushing myself, not the salt. Although I had been mistreated, my resentment to Al was sinking me. I had to drop the salt. I had to get along with my life. That's a tough pill to swallow.

I believe my answer to Sean was, "Fuck you. Damnit." Then I looked at our more-empty-than-full glasses. "Want another beer?" I'd be lying if I didn't say we drank some more.

At the end of our week hanging out, Sean mentioned that he'd move all the way from Florida to Los Angeles to start a print magazine with me, from scratch. And he did.

Two months later, even after his transmission failed in Alabama and he read about bow hunting because his books were in his truck on a lift, we moved in together and started *Razorcake*, a punk zine that we both equally own and operate, in January, 2001.

This book, a collection of essays and interviews from the last eight years, is a chapter of my life that's opposite to the ending of any major motion picture that deals with punk rock. Instead of being a future professional with a funny haircut, who mistakes that being an asshole is the only form of rebellion, sees the errors of his childish ways, and slips back into the shackles that society has slated for him all the more readily because he'd "tested its boundaries," this book is about a struggle that continues through today. It's about how, accidentally, but with purpose, I'm where I'm at: co-editing, co-publishing a magazine, completely independently. This book is about what I love about a subculture—its bands, artists, activists—and what I hate about culture at large—its homogenization, intentional governmental deception, the irresponsibility of major corporations, and the alienation of its citizens.

What this book is not is a definitive statement on punk rock. No book can be. There are far too many bands, far too many contributors, far too much going on. The list of people I still want to interview is longer than my arm. Due to time, place, or money, there are scads of bands that I'd have loved to talked to on tape, but never had the proper opportunity to. To say they're any less important because they're not in this book is absurd. That said, the number of interviews I've conducted over the years is over three times the number of what's in this book.

What I hope *Born to Rock* conveys is a glimpse into some of the minds and energy of a culture that is often dismissed as being stupid, purely nihilistic, and reactionary. I also want to show that DIY punk is very far from being completely co-opted by the mainstream. For every band that makes it big and uses bus bench ads to sell albums or bands that get their videos played on a cable station I can't afford to see, there are astronomically more that are rocking the hell out of a house party, a dive bar, or have slept on my apartment floor. The type of punk that means the most to me doesn't work solely by soundbites. It isn't restricted to a scene. It takes years and years to get a good grasp on. It's so strong that I don't have strangle it or run up like a banner to know that it's firmly inside of me. Punk means something good—and thrilling—to thousands of people.

While punk has its share of glorified fuckups, black eyes, and dismal failures, that's not the whole story. It's an entire spectrum from obsessive sex with blowup dolls and punching through roofs of fast food restaurants to guys who have earned their Ph.D.s in psychology and people who have made durable, real-life forms of resistance from opening bookstores to community spaces to zines.

It bums me out, though, that so many literary stabs at capturing a certain era or subgenre of punk laud that a specific time or a specific place so often end by stating, "It's over. If you weren't there, you can be nothing more than a poseur." To say punk's over is absolutely ridiculous. To say that no bands can top those of the past is just as silly. What has always encouraged me in punk is that sense of rare discovery that hasn't left me for sixteen years straight. I'm still stoked. I still think some of the best stuff ever is just being created and I've yet to hear it.

All in all, what's the point of continuing? Aren't these just accidents strung together? It's my hope that I can give something back to an art form and lifestyle that has kept me not only living, but alive, since that fateful day on a barren stretch of Utah highway when it all came crashing down around me. It came to my aide. It didn't pass judgement. It hasn't left my side. Like the scars that the fatal accident left on me, I feel like punk—and its series of endless questions—are going to be with me through the end.

That's what this is all about.

• • •

"It's my right to say that the government's shit and it's my right to say I deserve an honest wage and make that a law. It's my right. I'm not going to stand apart from you and act as if I'm the stepchild, because I'm not. I was born here, too."

—Paddy

ANTI-ROBOT MUSIC SINCE 1994:
AN INTERVIEW WITH DILLINGER FOUR

I sound like a stalker when talking about Minneapolis's Dillinger Four. They've been my favorite band for several years now. Let's cut down to the simplest of facts. D4 has nailed the idea that the culture that kills us is—without irony—the very culture that gives us life. They understand that we may hate banks, but have to use them to cash checks. We may hate our bosses, hate work, and hate that the taxes taken out of our paychecks make nuclear warheads possible, but we have to live, earn a wage, and try not to go abso-fucking-lutely crazy. Along with their non-dogmatic and smart-as-hell ethic, they've recorded a catalog of one of the most ballistically compelling galleries of songs ever set to a 4/4 beat. They've made many once-coveted sections of my record collection very lonely places.

I admit, I've probably spent too much time thinking about the band. Fuck it. They're so dead on. What gets me about D4 is how clear they are. Even when they think they're jumbled, drunk, or out of sleep, these bastards are more insightful than most and just seem to have a deeper understanding of what it's like to be honest, funny, hard-working, and hard-playing members of society. Their songs are steamrollers and so are the individual members who make up the Four.

What do they sound like? Everything in punk rock, compressed and energized, and nothing you've ever heard all in one place. They've got melodies but aren't saccharine. They've got hardcore speed and agility, but they hit every note and tweak the sonics. They can all-out scream, but rarely do. Topically, think along the lines of political and personal punk that hasn't lost its sense of humanity, its sense of durability. They pervade a sense that everyone is included in a revolution, even if that revolution is of sound and lasts the length of an album when you're driving to work or going to do your laundry.

Lane: drums
Billy: guitar, backing vocals
Erik: guitar, vocals
Paddy: bass, vocals

Todd: You came in your shoe?
Paddy: [rabid laughter] Woah! What are you bringing up? Who have you been talking to? Did I tell you that?

26 *Dillinger Four*

Todd: No.

Paddy: Holy shit. Yeah. But which time? Holy cow. Yeah, quite a few times. I think I have them somewhere, too. They're an old pair of Converse One Stars. Well, you know, you've got to come somewhere. I didn't necessarily fuck my shoe.

Todd: I've read in a couple places where people are purporting Dillinger Four as the saviors of punk rock. [laughter]

Erik: I think you wrote that.

Todd: No [laughing, then thinking]... I didn't. I'm a little bit smarter than that. I can see the context that you're working in. It's not a vacuum. There are bands that are your peers: The Thumbs, Super Chinchilla Rescue Mission, Toys That Kill, The Arrivals, Tiltwheel, Panthro UK United 13.

Paddy: I don't think there's any sort of savior anything. I think every couple years, something pops up. At the same time, I don't want to think of it as a renaissance because punk is no one definitive thing. It's not like anybody's going to save it. It's kind of the same way, a couple years ago, pretty much ninety-nine percent of what I bought was thousand-mile-an-hour thrash because there was a brilliant period of three years where there was just phenomenal records coming out, but that didn't necessarily mean that there weren't great things like Panthro UK and The Beltones, stuff like that. There was this one genre that really honed down and had this great stretch. No one can save it. That's all I really wanted to say. There's nothing to save. It ain't dying. And if it is dying, it's usually better when it's dying anyway.

Erik: The places or people who seem to write that usually tend to be in larger publications, where I'm sure a lot of what they tend to cover is the larger labels, the larger package tours, the larger bands, and a lot of those bands can be great, but there is a certain amount of more of the same. A lot of those bands tend to operate the same way.

Paddy: And sound the same. Look the same.

Erik: Right. And then we come in, and to them, we are on the same type of record label and all that, but we have sort of a contrary attitude to what they're used to. The not touring so much thing. The not tuning so much thing. All those things. We probably stick out.

Paddy: Even the bands I've mentioned—including the High Stepping Nickel Kids from Boston—people doing something different, none of us really sound the same. I think it's more of an attitude thing. You know what I mean? You don't really want to be pro. You just want to play the music that you want to play, even if doesn't sound like everything else that everybody else is doing.

Todd: But not fall into a lot of the same traps that earlier bands fell into.

Paddy: Right.

Todd: Becoming a little savvier, business-wise, doesn't mean you have to adopt the asshole, cutthroat attitude.

Paddy: Right, and just because you enjoy a beer or twelve doesn't necessarily mean that you're a dirtbag, and by the same token, it shouldn't be your schtick. It's kind of weird. We've met a lot of bands that we see eye-to-eye with. It's kind of hard to explain. I see what you mean. I think there is kind of a renaissance of catchy punk that isn't pop punk, per se, and I would put us in there with that. I like to call it aggro pop. Shit, like I've said before, if the Clash's debut record or Sham 69 came out today, they'd be pop punk bands.

Lane: It's all quasi-social, semi-political, semi-melodic beer punk.

Todd: How do you actively avoid becoming what you hate?

Lane: Change your standards.

Paddy: Honestly, follow your gut.

Erik: Everybody goes through periods where they realize—it's that thing that you're becoming your parents. Everyone, whether it's just bands or people, go through that. Ben Weasel wrote it in a song: "we become what we hate." He wasn't talking about bands. He was talking about people.

Billy: You don't have to be so dogmatic, where you're afraid to change your position from five years ago.

Paddy: Even in more of a scene or music sense, we have a tendency to buy a lot more records and go to a lot more shows than most people I know in bands. It tends to be a trend, especially people in punk bands, if they get any sort of notoriety, any sort of popularity, they become bigger fans of jazz or more sort of—some may say experimental music. I would just say anything opposite of punk. Then they get removed from it and then weird decisions start getting made because they view themselves in this broader world and I don't really think we tend to do that. We know what we like and we're comfortable existing within it.

Lane: In a weird way, it's a trick question because—Billy used the word dogmatic—the more you're pigeonholed, the more opportunity you have to become what you hate. You're stuck within a narrow definition of what you accept, but if you accept a broader range of ideas and different legitimacies, then there's less fear of that happening to you. There are still things that you absolutely wouldn't do and you would hate to be, but those things are probably always going be off limits. You just have a wider range that you're able to operate within.

Erik: There are things that we do now that we probably didn't think we ever would. That's just reality, but that doesn't mean that I hate myself or we hate ourselves because of that. It's just that you live and learn things, essentially. There are things that are universal truths within this group of four people that will probably never change.

Lane: In my definition, there are a couple things that I would never want to become. There aren't many things that I hate, but one has to do with work. If you're ever in the position of being a manager or a boss, never forgetting what it's like to be the person doing the shitwork. The other thing, as far as the band goes is, hopefully, you're successful in an ethical way and don't forget what it's like to play to ten people or try to scrape together gas money or try to do those things that bands do to struggle to get their music out there.

Paddy: That's the funny thing in the punk scene that everybody says and it's totally true, but nobody will say it in front of certain people, is you will see a band play to twelve people who should be playing to five thousand and you'll see a band playing to two thousand who shouldn't be playing to anybody. We tend to be really good at looking at something for what it is. You're the little band that might not necessarily draw a ton of people, but we're going to offer you a bunch of money to play with us because we like you and we want you to play with us. If we have that opportunity, we'll take advantage of it just because we want to see you and we know our friends will like you. But the flip side is also, too, this may be the big, ritzy venue, but, hey, fuck you, your sound sucked and your bouncers were dicks. And, yeah, maybe it's a notch in our belt that we got to play here, but we don't have to.

Todd: What do you do, personally, to avoid becoming a novelty act?

Paddy: Wow, that's a really good question. I've got kind of a beef with that now and I have for about the last two years. Well, first of all, the funny thing is that straight-up, as a policy, I do try to not take my clothes off ever when we play. Also, sometimes, I don't worry about the novelty thing because there still are lyric sheets. So, no matter what, there's going to be plenty of people out there who are going to know that whatever we're doing on the stage or acting like, that's like half of the deal and I think we've always been pretty clear with that. Hey, look, there's a whole other side to who we are, but standing up on stage at a show is not the place for it. I don't want to bum anybody out.

I mean, you know, there's differences. If you just played a show right after September 11, it makes sense to bring it up. If your mother died two weeks earlier and you want to talk about that on the mic, that's your fucking prerogative because that's going on in your life and there's no point to pretend that there aren't serious things going on. But, at the same time, it's like I don't want to get up every night on tour and gripe about how shitty minimum wage is or gripe about my job. It's a show. That's the time for celebration. We're a community. Let's have fun. Maybe there's a lot of knuckleheads and ditzes who only get half the deal and think that we're just drunk dudes pounding on our guitars, but I think there's plenty of people, too, who know we have something else going on.

Todd: Lane, please cover the incidents leading up to meeting the security personnel of the Sahara Hotel in Las Vegas.

Lane: When I was first out there a few years ago for the Punk Rock Bowling Tournament, my friends and I had an enormous amount of acid. We brought a pretty significant amount with us. The first thing we did as soon as we got off the plane was drop some acid and hit the bar. We're drinking all night and everything, and sooner or later, someone says, "Man, I can't believe it's daylight out. It's morning." It was incomprehensible to me. You know what it's like to be in a casino. It's dark. You're not supposed to know what time it is. So my friend Aaron and I go to investigate and, sure enough, we walk outside and the sun is shining. It's beautiful. He and I feel like we're in our own world, and I walk into the oasis at the center of the traffic circle at the Sahara, and I kind of think, well, as long as I'm here, I might as well take a piss.

Todd: Since you're in the jungle.

Lane: That's right. Since I'm at the oasis, looking for relief. So, I put my beer down on the pillar and let loose. It was no small piss. About halfway through, I suddenly realized I wasn't the only one in the world with my friend. In fact, there were people unloading their luggage and milling around everywhere and I was in a very, very public place. Luckily, I was able to finish up. I grabbed my beer. I run back inside and go back to talking to people, which were my girlfriend and some of her friends who I had just met at that time. Didn't know 'em. Suddenly, about a minute later, I'm surrounded by about five or six armed security guys, and this guy says, "Do you think what you just did was funny?" In my state of mind, I knew he was trying to trick me into saying something wrong, something that could lead to a little jail stay or something like that. So I'm trying to think of a reasonable way to answer that question. I want to put my beer back on the bar to address this guy and grab a breath. My depth perception was off and, thinking that I'm letting my bottle go over the bar, I actually let it go over the tile floor and it falls. It bounces once and there's this collective gasp, and then it shatters. That was, effectively, my answer to that question. I just turned to him. I said, "You know, I have a room at this hotel, and I believe I'm calling it a night." They escorted me all the way up to the room with a couple of friends I was with. So, I went up and sat down for a couple hours. By noon, I was back down drinking beer by the pool. It was no big deal. All's well that ends well.

Todd: Lane, you grew up in the rural Midwest. How far away was the biggest city?

Lane: About sixty miles. Sioux Falls, South Dakota.

Todd: In the long run, do you think that's a benefit? Do you think you're more resistant to trends—like pop punk and emo—because there's more of a foundation set of starting off in isolation?

Lane: I think, across the board, it's because Erik and Paddy and Billy listen to pretty diverse things in punk. They're not listening to the same sorts of bands. I come from something that's probably completely different from the three of them, but yet connected in some ways, too, because it's not like those guys never listened to metal or classic rock or some of the other things, too. We probably bring a more diverse range of influences, so it's harder, maybe, to see where the influences are coming from.

Erik: Bands that really fit, that are card-carrying members of their specific genre—for example, when you have four guys who are all the biggest into screamo in the entire town, and they get together and start a screamo band, you're not going to get much else than what you've heard before. I think we're lucky with that. Within or without of the punk scene, we all had kind of different tastes, so we weren't going to be, automatically, anything. It was very up in the air to what kind of sound we would eventually have because we weren't going for any sort of specific thing and the few influences that we all could kind of could agree on, things that we were into, were pretty diverse right from the start.

Todd: Almost all of your friends think you're lazy bastards. How did you gain this reputation while putting out such high quality music?

Paddy: Well, people like you live so far away from where we are and I'm sure we do look like lazy bastards. A lot of people—especially nowadays—their band is their entire life; that's it. And I don't necessarily mean that people don't have boyfriends and girlfriends and wives and husbands, what have you, but it's their job. I know a lot of bands try to spend upwards of six months on the road or put out a record a year, at least. We've kinda never done that style. I think that kind of mentality only came around when punk rock—and underground music in general—got huge, and you could do it as a living. Most of us had been in bands since before that, so we never slipped into that mindset. We all have jobs. Erik has a bar and restaurant that he's also building a venue on to it and I'm going to work there and help book shows as well. Lane just became a doctor. And on top of that, there are a lot of important hot dogs to eat and video games to play, when you get down to it. We've always got a bunch of things cooking. I'm sure, from a far perspective, it looks like we're a lazy-assed band. I just think it's a prejudice against fat people.

Todd: So, how much does Otis Redding have on the direction of your sound?

Erik: Direction of the sound? Sometimes, I wish more. I think soul music, in particular, when it's incorporated into punk well, it's so fucking good, but it's really hard to do it. Rocket From The Crypt is one of the few bands that really has—as far as bands that aren't total garage bands that come much more directly from that—done it well. There's times where we're like, "Let's sorta have one of those beats, sorta like an Otis

Redding song." But when you translate that through the four of us, no one would probably ever get that. But that's how we see it.

Lane: It's an intangible quality and it comes down to whether you think a band has depth of influence or not. Those things translate in ways that probably, even being a member of the band, you don't really understand, but it's one of those extra little things that pins you down in another area.

Todd: Did any of you ever go to camp?

Lane: Erik, I think you need to tell the loading your underpants at camp story.

Erik: It was my first night at one of the Boy Scout camps, which just had tents, not cabins, but they were kind of like permanent tents on a platform. It was storming like crazy. It's the first night there. I was pretty young. I was probably like ten or something.

Weebo (the driver and all-around nice guy): He's probably like fifteen.

Erik: Yeah. Storming. I woke up in the middle of the night. It was probably four thirty in the morning. I have to shit like crazy. I have no idea where the outhouse is, but I know it's storming everywhere and it's off in the woods somewhere. I wasn't entirely afraid of the dark, but reasonably freaked out, just with the thunder. I kind of do the "lay there and pretend that it will go away," forever. Finally, I'm at that point where I'm like, fuck it. I gotta go. I make a mad dash for it and I fuckin' just load my pants—piss and shit them completely. So, I duck into—I don't remember if I went back into the outhouse. I had a bunkmate in my tent, so I'm sure I didn't go in there to take care of it. I was fairly embarrassed. So I pulled my underpants off and fuckin' winged them off into the woods, just figuring no one will ever know it was me. I came back. The guy who was in my tent hadn't woken up, so I figured I was pretty much in the clear. The next day, one of the old campers is poking around in the woods and finds this loaded up, nasty fuckin' piece of underwear. "What the fuck is this?" Right there, in fuckin' magic marker: "Erik Funk" written right on.

Todd: I'm sorry... Is it true that Dillinger Four started as a three piece? (Paddy, Erik, and Lane have always been in the band.)

Paddy: Yes. And we had this guy Sloan, who played guitar, and he never sang and we never thought about it. It was never an issue. When Billy joined, it was, "Of course, Billy will sing." Billy used to be in Scooby Don't and do a lot of backup vocals.

Billy: Those jokers had their eyes on me for years.

Lane: He's a lot to look at. Maybe not so much in other ways, but just a lot of him... I think part of it was, it fills out the sound to have two guitar players. I think it gives the band more options as far as what the guitar parts are because I think that Erik's an excellent guitar player, as is Billy.

Todd: So, Paddy, your dad was a longshoreman. What kind of ethics did he instill in you?

Paddy: It's funny because the things he instilled in me are almost cliché nowadays and I'm almost embarrassed to say them. Songs, like "Superpowers Enable Me to Blend in with the Machinery," and "The Great American Going Out of Business Sale," that's all my dad's influence; very much a working man's view of the world. You can hate the country, but you don't necessarily hate the people, you know what I mean?

Todd: Did he hate the country?

Paddy: Oh, yeah. I think he was a pretty good example of that '50s/'60s period of Jersey City/New York City. He didn't have a racist bone in him, but he hated rich people. If anything, his worldview is a little distorted to what degree he hated rich people. He was very distrustful. That entire side of my family is nothing but longshoremen, and at one time, a lot of them were cops. A lot of that side of my family, there was also a lot of involvement in organized crime and all sorts of stuff. But, I'd say mostly not being embarrassed if someone's got to work for a living, which I think came in really handy for me, somewhere around early junior high. When fashion, style, and "toys" come into play, I was being very solidified with not being obsessed with that. I got that from my dad.

Todd: Why is an American flag put so predominantly on the cover of *Situationist Comedy*?

Billy: We've always flirted with Americana.

Paddy: It's kind of like, "Fuck you, we'll take it back." It's almost a spite thing, like it's so predictable to be punk and hate the American flag, but it's weird, because it represents everything you hate, but on the other hand, it represents what we are. A lot of people who have never left America, I don't think they realize that.

Lane: You can hate a lot about the government, but you don't necessarily hate the people or hate aspects of the culture.

Paddy: There's this thing in *Easy Rider* where he talks about that. He's got the American flag on his jacket. He talks about it like, "I'm American. This is my country as much as anybody else's."

Billy: Hell yeah.

Paddy: It's my right to say that the government's shit and it's my right to say I deserve an honest wage and make that a law. It's my right. I'm not going to stand apart from you and act as if I'm the stepchild, because I'm not. I was born here, too. There is no other American who can tell me what America should be and have their opinion be any more valid than mine, 'cause I am American. Fuck you. We're a punk band. We gonna sing the lyrics we do and this is a flag. It's not patriotic. It's very unpatriotic, but it's very American-ly unpatriotic. We're a country based on revolution. It's a fact. Why should it shock you? Fuck you. I hate the government, but I'm American. This is my flag more than it's yours.

Lane: The founding fathers did not mean for the American flag to be held up in back of a gorilla (as it appears on the cover of the album). That's not proper etiquette. And it was probably dropped at least once during that photo shoot.

Paddy: It's kind of also like the same way where a conservative politician can say, "How can you spite the American flag? It means more than you'll ever know." Yep. It means more than you even know, and not in a patriotic sense at all. Purely, if this is a symbol of freedom, then I have a freedom to use it and say what I want. It's flippin' the bird. Let's call it what it is.

Todd: [to Billy] When did you find your inner Lemmy Kilmister (lead singer of Motörhead)?

Billy: That was pure accident, man. It was hella freaky. I don't know. We talked about doing the show (where D4 played an all-Motörhead set, three of them dressed as Lemmy) so I went to the Halloween store. Everyone was getting wigs. I got the warts and, I don't know, man, no glasses and that wart.

Paddy: It was also the black shirt, half undone. That was fuckin' weird. He didn't even put the entire costume on until I was already drunk and when I saw him, I was like, "Holy shit." He's even got a chest like Lemmy's.

Todd: The same height and sort of the same build.

Billy: It was pretty terrifying. It was a surprise to me, too.

Todd: And your voice, when you gravel it up a little.

Billy: I don't know. I think Paddy's got a better...

Paddy: I think we've got a double-barrel Lemmy going on.

Billy: That was pretty shocking to everyone. After that show, we went down to a nightclub in Minneapolis and I rocked the Lemmy there, too, and got a couple weird stares.

Paddy: We went to go see Motörhead a little while ago and I was trying to get Billy to dress up like Lemmy to go to the show but he brought up a good point. "That won't be any fun." You'd have three hundred people, at least, going, "Hey Lemmy, hi Lemmy, hey Lemmy, Lemmy will you sign my cock?"

Lane: The funny thing is my understanding of Lemmy, is that he's actually not that tall and he's not that big of a guy. I've never actually stood face to face with him, but from people I know who have, apparently he's fairly short and he's fairly diminutive, but on stage he looks like he's fucking ten feet tall.

Paddy: I like to subscribe to the theory that Lemmy's as tall as he wants to be.

Todd: With this band, there were two members who had a hard time getting through high school, but you comprise of one of the most intelligent and politically informed bands I've ever heard. I'll quote Paddy here, you're political, "Not in a late-period Crass sensibility, but in a Bruce Springsteen sensibility." How did that come about? It's not completely bookish. It's not a bad photocopy of a half-assed political pamphlet. Where did those well-formed ideas come from?

Erik: I know that I didn't really start to pay attention to politics, and in particular start becoming interested in leftist politics and not mainstream politics, until middle high school, and around the era of Born Against. There were bands that were starting to pique my interest in that kind of stuff. It really came from punk bands.

Todd: I have to admit that the first time I came across the writer Nelson Algren was because you mentioned him in your song, "Doublewhiskeycokenoice."

Erik: There's a lot of people who've said that.

Todd: And I was kind of ashamed, because literature was what I got my master's in and his name never came up. It's amazing that he's taken out of the canon altogether. Here's a guy who sold 500,000 copies of *Walk on the Wild Side* less than fifty years ago and he's basically forgotten.

Paddy: And it's kind of ironic, too, because you have Hemmingway, who never swayed in popularity or respect, and he said that Algren was the second greatest American writer of his generation, because, of course, Hemmingway thought he was the first. That's the stuff that blows my mind.

Todd: Why is it important that you guys are anti-robot?

Lane: I'm not the guy who came up with it—but, to me, what it means is robots in all sorts of ways, replace humanism, replace people, replace all those things that make life worthwhile. Who wants to be an automaton? Who wants their art to be robotic? Fucking dance music? You put me in a fucking room with dance music, I guarantee you in two hours, I'll hang myself. Put me on drugs and it'll happen in a half hour. To me, monkeys are so real and visceral.

Billy: Robots have one or two tricks. Monkeys fuckin' swing through trees and throw shit. You don't know what's going to happen with a monkey. With the robot, you know he's going to go this way.

Paddy: Because robots don't make decisions but they're efficient, so people love 'em, but monkeys make a lot of decisions and a lot of them aren't very good, but damn it, they're funny.

Billy: Sometimes they ride cute little bikes, wearing costumes.

Todd: For the laymen, what is situationism, in a nutshell?

Billy: One of the biggest things that I always got out of it was not only a very strict anti-government stance, but also a very pro-individual stance. We don't need this government, but we do need artists, we do need musicians. You should get fucking crazy and follow your calling.

Paddy: The pursuit of happiness. I had reservations about actually using the term "situationist" on the record. It isn't just the situationists that we're into. It was also the Motherfuckers. There were a lot of radically political but very artistic "statement groups" of the late '60s through the late '70s that I get a lot of inspiration from and a lot of it's still going on today.

I can't remember what they call it, but it's an art form in and of itself where people modify billboards to have political statements. It's a creative, fun way to get across a very serious political message, which brings it down to a grassroots level that is almost *Common Sense* in its own right, like Thomas Paine. It's easier to mentally digest. Too often, I think political groups get too heady and the thing is, you may be trying to effect the life of the janitor, but if you're going to get grad school on 'em, it might not register and it's not 'cause he's dumb—he's probably really smart or she's really smart—but it's in a different way and it's not going to register. Whereas, I think what we got with situationism was that it brought it down to a very grassroots level, where it was: we're not going to get intellectual about this shit. It's just like this: the rights you have should be stronger.

Lane: That's a good point, that idea of bringing it down to a level where not only can people understand it more across the board, but where people don't feel like they're being talked down to or condescended to. Even people who are very intelligent don't enjoy people talking to them in a way that could be interpreted as condescending.

Paddy: It's funny, because you could probably find a college professor who can possibly give you a really articulate speech on the crime of minimum wage history in America, but shit, no one's going to put it in its place better than a sixty-year-old man or woman who has lived it their whole life. It's one thing on paper. It's one thing in life. If you want to try to affect anybody, you gotta talk like you talk. Just like Muddy Waters.

Todd: Is it true that you guys brought about the reincarnation of The Arrivals?

Erik: According to them.

Billy: That's a feel-good moment.

Paddy: I think that's the thing I'm the most proud of as far as that whole relationship with other bands. We all loved the CD and called them up and we said, "Who is this band that nobody we know in Chicago knows?" We just got a message to them, saying, "Can you come up and do these two shows?" And we found out later, they were already basically broken up. Isaac and his wife, Sue, were joining the Peace Corps. They decided to come up and do the shows. Little Dave from The Arrivals had come to see us for years. We'd kind of met him before.

Erik: His first show was a Dillinger Four show, when there were only three people in Dillinger Four.

Paddy: They came up to do the shows and they went so well, they were kind of, "Huh, well, maybe we should keep on doing this." It's funny. It's great. Now, we've taken them out east with us, we've taken them out west, and all of our friends whose taste we respect have all walked away going, "God damn. That's a motherfuckin' band." It's funny, too, because it sucks that they ever broke up, but they're that kind of band. They're too good of guys. It makes sense that they'd broken up at the point that they did. They'd never think, "Man, things aren't going right. We better get a manager. Let's shop around." It was kind of like, "Hey, things aren't going well. I'm going to join the Peace Corps." "Well, that's cool. I'm going to pick up a couple extra shifts at the bar." It's just kind of cool to look at them now. In San Francisco, they tore shit up.

Todd: How many beers do you drink a year?

Lane: I was told there'd be no math, Todd.

Todd: Give me a week and I'll just multiply it by fifty-two, or just give me a day.

Paddy: Okay. We're flying over to Japan. We're on Korean Air and it's free drinks. The stewardesses went back and forth non-stop between the four of us—this is where the math is starting—it eventually got to the point where when we ordered one beer, they brought us four. I don't mean four for the four of us, I mean four for each of us. My guess is that the four of us, at least, drank a case each. I think that's safe to assume.

Lane: I'm pretty sure I was over the twenty mark. When I got off in Japan to go through customs, I was tired from staying up almost that whole time on the plane, drinking solid, just pounding them, and I looked fucking nuts. Alcohol was coming out of my pores. Standing a foot away from me would be like you were taking a couple of shots of liquor. When I went up to customs, they took one look at me and figured "This motherfucker ain't got nothing to lose," and I went right through.

Paddy: Experts would agree that it would be somewhere over one million beers.

Lane: It's a ludicrous amount, Todd. That's all you need to know.

Todd: What's the "other side of the story," as you allude to in the song "It's a Fine Line Between the Monkey and the Robot?"

Erik: There's a media-driven consensus about what life is like and people try—to be a happy person or citizen—to believe some of these lies. In a way, you have to believe these lies because the alternative is unthinkable. And there's all this sort of misinformation that everybody had to agree upon and the "other side of the story" is exactly that: it's all the stuff that individuals have to dig out. Real information. One side of the story is obvious—every time you read a newspaper or watch a TV broadcast or everyone's telling you something and there's always something else there and that "something else there" is usually less desirable and that's why it's not in those newscasts and that's why it's not in those things.

Todd: You say that people are fitting into the structure of what would be the obvious side of the story. What would be the opposite of that? Are you saying that people shouldn't have shiny rims to their cars but should seek a more difficult knowledge, is that right?

Erik: Yeah. I think the easiest thing to do is not to think creatively for yourself. I won't say that's what most people do, but I think that's the easiest way to live. I don't think it's the best way to live. It's important to try to look at things objectively.

Paddy: Well, you see, it gets really hard. I write songs to other people. Erik writes songs to himself. Does that make any sense? Not to get all corny-emo, or anything, but a lot of times when Erik's writing, he's writing about things, he's thinking about himself. If he's critiquing something, it's usually something he thinks he has going on, so it's kinda hard. When you're talking about "the other side of the story," Todd, I tell you the truth, in any given time during the day, Lord only knows what Erik thinks the other side of the story is.

Todd: You've tackled pretty strong gender issues several times in songs. It's often through how advertising affects both women and men. I'm thinking of both the songs, "Super Models Don't Drink Colt 45," and "Fuzzy Pink Handcuffs," which has the line, "She's got a catalog, it's full of hopes and dreams. It makes her hate herself. It's what she wants to be."

Paddy: Especially now more than ever. It's more and more like that.

Erik: That's something we've written about a couple of times. It's something we, obviously, don't have first-hand experience with, but every woman in our lives does. One thing that has been interesting to me is direct marketing, be it children or minorities or the ways companies can almost, to a point, invent products then convince entire groups of society that they somehow actually need them and actually have to have them.

Lane: Advertising has become so shrewd in terms of subdividing and dissecting people into finding niches to exploit. It's kind of unreal in ways, sociologically.

Paddy: It's kind of weird, because even in a pop culture sense, things are so ridiculous at this point. People think Destiny's Child are feminists. It's so ironic. "She's so strong. She's willing to be this sexy."

Lane: It's interesting: feminism with consumerism. "This fancy car, I bought it. This very fancy ring, I bought it. All this stuff that I own, I bought it all." It's sort of a strange idea to me.

Paddy: It's pretty fucking terrible. Shit, look at the two opposite sides of the spectrum of what's going on in punk rock right now as far as the consumer cultures. On one end, you've got these emo kids who are buying these borderline designer clothing that's so insanely expensive, but they'll couple that with Dickies pants, so then it's cool. On the other side, you have these chaos punks who are going and dropping $140 on bondage pants.

Lane: [to Paddy] You probably bought your fuckin' pants for ten bucks and got your t-shirt for free. Collectively, with what the four of us are wearing now, you could do that for the price of one chaos punk's outfit.

Paddy: I think that's sad in and of its own right, too. But it's weird. Supposedly, the economy's good, so that's what happens. We're living in kooky times.

Todd: That goes off another recurring theme in your songs—that the image of the rebel is up for purchase is powerful. Merchandise doesn't make rebellion. The leather jacket didn't make Fonzie an anarchist.

Lane: And, at the end of the day, Fonzie wasn't that rebellious. He was the good-hearted guy with an edge that people just didn't quite understand until they saw his heart of gold. Fonzie is all about doing the right thing. Let's not kid anyone.

Todd: Paddy, did your interest in underground music start with hip hop?

Paddy: I got into punk and hip hop at almost exactly the same time. For Erik and I, we were lucky enough that we grew up in Evanston, Illinois, and WNUR, which is Northwestern's college station, around 1984 was awesome. The hip hop shows were phenomenally great hip hop shows and there was a punk show that was called "Fast and Loud," that was fucking great. A lot of record collectors would probably know, because they're the people who put out the *Big Hits of Mid-America* comp, so I got into them at the same time, but that's why, to me—Billy and I talk about this a lot—underground hip hop and punk rock go hand in hand. That's why I hated it in the '90s, when they'd say, "Hip hop is the punk of the '90s." No. Hip hop is the hip hop of the '90s and punk is the punk of the '90s. But, technically, and I'm not being racist when I say this because I've read it though other hip hop journalists, and I think it's still true: "Hip hop is the black kid's punk and punk is white kid's hip hop." It's cool because there's a big crossover there, at the same time. I remember having comp tapes that were Sugar Hill Gang and the early Run DMC records on one side and Battalion of Saints, and the *Somebody Got Their Head Kicked In* comp on the other.

Erik: I got into hip hop first, break dancing and stuff like that, and I kind of got out of it again before I got into punk and back into hip hop again.

Paddy: Especially when hip hop became more political, we got really into it. When Eric B. and Rakim got really hard, and when Public Enemy came around, that's when I remember a ton of punks and hardcore kids getting into it.

Erik: I remember when I was first getting into punk was around the time I was first hearing *Fear of a Black Planet*. Then *It Takes a Nation of Millions to Hold Us Back* came out. PDP. All this political hip hop when I was first hearing political rock.

Paddy: Paris.

Erik: So fuckin' bad ass.

Todd: Has anybody ever tried to push an angle on you, like you should try to be sexy?

Lane: Sexy and Dillinger Four are not usually words to be used in the same sentence. In our private lives, maybe, but it would be a colossal failure there, too.

Paddy: Push the angle? That's why we live in Minnesota. There is no need to push angles. We are not even within a thousand miles of anyone pushing angles.

Lane: You see me behind that snow blower? Was that fuckin' hot or what? You can't see any of my fat under that parka. I look like a real man out there, snowblowin'. Goddamn, that thing's an extension of my dick.

Billy: When I came out of the bar, slipped on some ice, and busted up my lip? Yeah, that's pretty sexy.

Todd: Are there any band-wide policies? Any unwritten codes?

Paddy: We won't play a show if it wasn't one we'd go pay and see in the first place. That tends to be more things that are going on in Chicago, Green Bay, Milwaukee or here—somewhere within driving distance. Even if there's a show we know 1,200 people will be at, if we don't have any plans of watching any other bands we're playing with or if we never had any plans of going to the place we're going to play at, why would you want to do it? Kinda lame.

We never made it a rule, but we have long discussions about how much things cost. For a while now the records are tending to come out on labels where they're dictating how much they cost, which we're fine with because I don't think we've done anything on a label that was particularly expensive. But we get in pretty extensive conversation/debates about how much shirts should cost. We got in a huge argument for the cost of the shirts in Japan because everything is so expensive in Japan and it's pretty much par for the course that a t-shirt is fifteen dollars. We got in a band debate. "Should we be those guys who actually charge ten?"

We also get in those debate/arguments about that stuff when it comes to beer for the practice room. It's not all these good guy things. Some of them are also dirty, fat Midwestern dude arguments. We have a lot of drinking rules. You have to have at least two beers before you play because nobody wants a stiff guy up there bumming the rest of them out. At the same time, if you get way too trashed and you can't even play, then you're kind of in the penalty box. You can only have two beers for a couple shows.

Todd: Paddy, pretend Lane's not here. This is a three-part question and you have to answer the first two with one-word answers.

Paddy: Oh, shit.

Todd: Lane has a Ph.D. What is it in?

Paddy: Psychology.

Todd: Has Lane ever gotten shit-ass drunk?

Paddy: [laughing] Absolutely.

Todd: What astute and alarming professional advice has he offered to any of the band when he's been pickled?

Paddy: The only really good advice Lane has given me—professional or otherwise when he's drunk—is, "You probably shouldn't talk to me right now because I'm really fucking drunk." If Dr. Monkey Hustle is loaded, he is no fountain of advice at all. He did at one point—I don't know how you'll translate this—in the middle of a desert in New Mexico with a bunch of people from Yuma, Arizona, he told us all, "Nine dying ding doo wha hah." We're not too sure what it means. He doesn't really know, either, but he was pretty adamant about it. He said it to us a couple of times.

Todd: Not to get too heavy, but is there any social message or any underlying theme for Dillinger Four?

Paddy: As far as undercurrents that took effort—it seemed kinda silly to us at one point you had political bands and you had fun bands and they were two very distinct, different kinds of things—like you had to be some sort of rocket scientist to have a political opinion or be aware of anything that was going on. It was funny because there were bands that we knew who were supposedly apolitical, but when you talked to them behind closed doors, they knew what was going on and totally had opinions too and they were totally as frustrated as anybody else was. On the same token, there were some political bands that were some of the funniest, nicest guys ever, off stage, but for some reason, when they're on stage, they won't let that show. If I went to see MK Ultra and Frank just started to do bad standup jokes, I'd be disappointed. At one point, we took effort to mix both of them. You can be just a regular guy or gal and be a political punk band. They're not mutually exclusive. In my opinion, they shouldn't be.

Todd: What's the kick-off soundbite on *Situationist Comedy*, before "Noble Stabbings!"?

Paddy: That's a friend of ours, Takashi, from a band here called Sweet J.A.P. There was... well... there's no beating around the bush here. I was shit-faced and on the way home. This is so stupid. I was really fucking loaded and I'd taken a bunch of Ativan—they're supposed to be anti-anxiety—and I'd taken a bunch of those and I had drank a lot of Jack Daniels. I was kind of having this daydream—you're kind of dreaming but you're not really passed out yet. I was just thinking about how great it would be—if we were the kind of band that made a video—to make some super crazy cheap video of robots attacking Tokyo and then we showed up with an army of monkeys. That just ended up sticking in my head the whole time and then when were making the record, I thought it would be cool to put that at the beginning. So I talked to Takashi—he is from Tokyo; he is Japanese—and that's what he's yelling over and over again, "Where are these robots from? What are these robots doing? Send in the monkeys. Dillinger Four. We need Dillinger Four! Get the monkeys!" Hopefully that's just laying the foundation down for the concept of the video we'll make some day.

Todd: If you could have one of the following, which would it be? A truckload of stolen Jim Beam and a warehouse full of Lone Star or a cultural revolution? Basically, get loaded for a long time or social change?

Paddy: Cultural revolutions go on anyway.

Todd: Do you think?

Paddy: Oh, I know.

Todd: How so?

Paddy: How do you think they don't? Times change. I mean, I'm not a big fan of the fat pant but it exists. You know what I mean? They happen anyway, but a truckload of stolen Jim Beam.

Todd: Full...

Paddy: That never happens. At least not to me. I'm part of a cultural revolution all the fuckin' time—cultural revolutions you can just make personal but how often do you get to have a truckload of stolen Beam be personal? That's what I'm going for. An economic revolution, on the other hand, then we'd all have truckloads of stolen Beam, not to get too rhetorical.

Todd: What's the involvement with Skeletor (shown prominently on the album art of *Midwestern Songs of the Americas* in a hot tub)?

Billy: He's master of the universe. Oh, that's me. That whole idea was Patrick's.

Paddy: Just because it's a clashing image and I thought that it'd be cool. The luxury of a hot tub...

Lane: With the discomfort of being a Skeletor...

Paddy: People want something to look at—all the time, whether you're playing live or on a record, and the things that make you look twice are the things that aren't exactly right and a fella in a skull mask sitting in a hot tub with a bunch of beers ain't exactly right and if you can throw in an upside down American flag with a slogan on it on the background too, that's all the better. If you want to get crazy and have meanings, we could.

Todd: Using that, for the front cover of *Midwestern Songs*, I don't see it. What double meaning would that have?

Paddy: It's a nice image but, okay, I'm going to get all emo on your ass right about now. It's not a nice image, but it's an involved and lonely image—like the cover photo.

Todd: How so?

Paddy: The photo was taken by our friend Dan Monick and it wasn't just one of us morons with a polaroid. It's very comfortable looking. It's obviously someone's room. It's not something we set up. That was Dan's room, but at the same time, that's sort of like the Midwest to us. You've got the turntable there and there's a record on it, not a CD player, but a record being played, beat-up ass American flag hanging out in the window that's not from being a patriot, it's just something you had to keep the light out, and you got some Christmas lights up there because you're kinda social. You like to have people over. There's some beer cans and there's a bottle in there, you're not like some sort of hermit or weirdo, but on the same token, everything's kind of beat up and it isn't exactly right and it's kinda dirty, too. It just seemed really fitting. That is very Midwestern punk. And a lot of it is a mix of down homey-ness, sure, but it's also—we are in the corn fields of America. There's a feel to it. You're in the middle of nowhere but you're not 'cause everything that you're about is going on there, if that makes any sense at all. But that's what ties in with the black and white pictures though. The bar and the urinal with the Jack Daniels in it, the factory that's closed down. Everything's tied in. It's kinda lonely but it's a microcosm all the same. The album art's comfortable but it's lonely, much like us.

Most of what goes on in punkdom, although it has changed in the last several years—I'm not going to say it hasn't—is really geared towards coasts. It just is. New York, San Francisco—it isn't that simple, but it is geared towards the coastal things and it isn't like the Midwest kids aren't hip to what's going on, it's just a lot of times that's why people from the Midwest tie into Midwestern bands quicker. And some times people don't get it. I remember Endpoint. People on the coasts didn't get it. It wasn't like I was a diehard Endpoint fan, but they were from Louisville and they were doing what they did and they were so into it and that was rad. MK Ultra was on the tip of everybody's tongues for fucking ever before a year ago. I saw their name everywhere. They've been ruling the Midwest for, Jesus, two and a half, three years now.

Lane: Todd, it's like having to be the lone star.

Todd: What is your "Unifying Theory of Indie Rock"?

Paddy: Oh, god, it's just fucking boring. It's funny because even now, that kind of pseudo underground shit is filtering into mainstream shit because when I'm at work, I have to hear stuff like Hoobastank and Incubus, shit like that. Elliot Smith. At the end of the day, it is just music. It's not like I want anybody to die just because they play music that I don't like, but, man, do I fuckin' hate it. It's not heavy. It's not catchy. It's not especially insightful. All I can tell about a lot of these singer/song-writer people is that to certain people they look really cool and apparently their records are really well produced and I should like them and that's something I hate.

The '90s were a period of ironic music. Beck: he's fun, he's goofy. It's novelty music. It's Doctor Demento on the top forty, which is like, fine. But somehow the hangover cure of ironic music turned out to be the golden age of the PR person—music you were supposed to like. "Elliot Smith will tear at your heart strings." It's like, aaahh! No he doesn't. He's annoying. He's really fucking boring to me. But, like, whatever, everybody has different tastes. I know that, but, to me, that whole genre of indie rock—there's some stuff that people call indie rock that I fuckin' love. I really like Guided By Voices. I really like Wedding Present, but these bands are also kind of aggro and at least catchy. The stuff I don't get is kind of atonal mumbling singer looking down at his shoes, like "I'm shopping at a thrift store, heyyy."

The other thing I want to know: indie rock women. What the fuck is up with this thing with cats? I'm not just talking about Cat Power calling herself Cat Power, I'm talking about this Mary Timony lady just put out a record and she's also on the cover in a cat mask but it's almost like a fuckin' rule that if you're in indie rock and you're female, you have to have some sort of cat themed thing in every fucking thing you're doing. I wish I was female. I'd start an indie rock band and it would be based all around rhinos. I would take a different kind of animal. It's really fucking irritating to me. To me, it seems like really self-indulgent stuff where the music takes a back seat to what your intention is supposed to be. To some degree, intention plays a role, but goddamn, can you just give me a fucking seven inch record that I want to listen to eighty times in a row in an hour? What's wrong with that?

Even before when that shit became really in vogue, I could tell—it's considered this division in punk rock because a lot of the people apparently used to play in punk rock bands—but I don't get it. They have more to do with bands like Air Supply and shit than with anything that has to do with rock'n'roll or whatever. And the funny thing is that bands like that get brought up in the same context as a modern Elton John, but at least Elton John was catchy. Yuck. Gross. The whole thing's gross. It's not as bad as yo metal, though. Even for as much as I can't stand Elliot Smith's music, I'm at least willing to wager that he's at least probably a really,

really good guy. So, if I had to be stuck in a room either watching him or Godsmack, fuck, dude, I will be up front for Elliot Smith, fucking cheering him and waving my arms and blowing kisses at him.

Todd: What's the longest ruse you've ever pulled on anyone?

Paddy: The band.

Todd: How is the Midwest the center of the universe?

Paddy: [laughing] Oh shit. Oh man. It's funny. I wouldn't even call it the center of the universe. I would say that the reason I love it is because it is definitely not and nobody wants it to be. No offense, but if you hang around a very cliché Los Angeles person, "LA's the greatest city in the whole world." It's the same with New York and San Francisco, and I'll even admit with Chicago, whatever, and that's in the Midwest, but I don't even think that most Midwestern people think of that kind of shit. "I got a good job. The house is kind of pretty and I think I'm going to have a barbecue this afternoon." I'm not saying that there aren't other people with that mentality on either of the coasts, but if they have it, that's way more of a Midwestern thing than anything else.

It's the kind of thing that drives me nuts when I see an interview with somebody like Moby or Barbara Walters, people will make comments if they're trying to reference an idiot or a hick, like, "That movie was great. I don't know how it will be received in the Midwest." The Wu Tang Clan will make jokes about people from Iowa. The way I look at it, fuck that. That's who I'm down with. Fuck that shit. That's where I'm from. I understand them. It's more laid back. I think it's a little more loyal. I fuckin' love the Midwest. It's just kind of chill. Everybody's just waiting to die and are having a good time before it happens. The funniest point of this conversation, in general, hanging around in LA, San Francisco, and New York and places like that, most people I meet aren't from there. That's the joke my friends say, who live in New York City, "There's more people from Omaha in New York City than there are in Omaha."

Midwest is just fine by me. Maybe people gripe about how the weather sucks, that it's all flat here, so when it snows, it really snows hardcore, but hey, you know what? I love it 'cause that means at least once a year all the fuckin' assholes are leaving, you know what I mean? Los Angeles, it can get really hot, but it's pretty fucking mild year round so if you get somebody who sucks, the odds are more than likely they're going to be staying there forever. Assholes can't make it through the winter. Even if they're bugging you for six months, just wait 'til November. They'll be gone.

•   •   •

AVAIL

"'Dude, what happened?' They were like, 'We thought you were going to throw up and choke on your puke or something. You were acting really weird and out of control. We had to lay you face down and tie you down and you passed out that way.' And that's the last time I think I hit anyone."

—Chavez

FUHRERS OF THE SWITCHBLADE NEW WAVE: AN INTERVIEW WITH SMOGTOWN

Interview by Todd and Rick Bain

We sat on a grassy knoll overlooking kids on skateboards constantly running into one another. This part, deep inside Orange County, has suburbia so perfected, so distilled, that it's apparent that the American Dream is clearly what I consider a nightmare. You can almost see a great big pair of hands come from the sky and choke people who don't belong. Homeowners' associations run supreme. You get the feeling people pay more attention to their lawns and the color of their mailboxes than their kids. Almost everyone looks like they've leapt out of TV show.

But below all of this is this seeping fungus. Maybe technology isn't the answer. Maybe we shouldn't all be put in boxes. Maybe sanitation and predictability aren't solutions.

Enter Smogtown. Products of all this? Yeah. But like any good antidote, they've got part of the disease. If you inject them in the right dose, it'll help make you immune, too. Somewhat. You'll go crazy in the right ways. Smogtown's Southern California's secret weapon. Firmly lightning bolted to the region's past, they've got detectable strains of the Crowd, The Clan, Black Flag, TSOL, and The Weirdos spreading throughout their musical cancer. The amazing thing is that they not only reanimate the past like kids playing with musical DNA and dynamite, they pick up where others dropped the baton and squeal away into the future, pot smoke billowing out the windows, barren landscape ahead, dragging muffler sparking behind them.

They're this stucco culture's remedy. They're the cure to planned communities and cell phone mommies running through red lights in their SUVs late for tanning sessions. They're the electricity that charges the little, invisible nodes inside of us all who crave that pulse of loud, bouncing, melodic music.

Melt that brain to your headphones. Here's Smogtown.

Idea brilliant. Idea perfect.

Chavez: singer
Chip Beef: bass
Guitardo: take a guess. It's not a tambourine.
Tim: drums
Special appearance by **Mike Lohrman** of The Stitches

Todd: Would you say that you're your own favorite band—without sounding like a pretentious asshole?

Chavez: Of the punk scene, I'd say yeah. But not completely, I wouldn't say that. As far as bands go now, sure.

[pause]

Chavez: Yeah, I'm a dick, pretty much. I'll admit it.

Tim: You've got to believe in what you're selling, right?

Chavez: Exactly right. You've got to stand behind your band.

Chip: We play what we want to hear.

Todd: Guitardo, when you play naked, why do you keep your boots on?

Guitardo: Because it's cold up there on stage. You know, if some guy comes up and says, "I'm going to beat you up, fag," at least I've got some motorcycle boots on to defend myself.

Mike: I don't fight anybody with my feet. I'd fight them with my fucking nuts hanging out but I wouldn't fight them with no shoes.

Todd: I can understand the boots. Broken beer bottles. That shit hurts.

Guitardo: Fuck yeah it does.

Chavez: In your defense, I don't think anybody would like to fight a naked guy. What would happen if he tackled you?

Guitardo: I got naked only when I had to do PC 1,000. It was the only time I was sober in the band. It was my only escape to feel normal was to get naked… publicly. I couldn't smoke weed, I couldn't drink. You know, you get in those little phases. Find yourself drinking the same brand of beer for a month straight.

Todd: You guys wrote...

Chavez: A concept album (*Führers of the New Wave*), which is very uncool. That's why we did it; because everyone's got these rules about what a punk album is supposed to be and what your songs are supposed to sound like and we just went against that and made our own concept album. It's this story of this band, actually these teenage kids, that are bored of school, bored of living in the suburbs, and start this band and there is so much police, parental, and neighborhood pressure and watch over these kids that they're really treated like criminals and therefore this vigilante group, called Bodie 601, comes. And the kids are actually treated like a cancer in their society. Bodie 601 has a way to treat the cancer, and that's radiation. And that's where all the radiation in the album comes from— Bodie 601... So does it all make sense, now?

Todd: Very much so. Okay, is the album in order?

Chavez: No, actually, when we recorded it, it was in order but songs get switched around because the label needs to switch them around for some reason.

Tim: Because they know what a punk album should sound like.

Rick: Is there an order that the songs should run?

Chavez: No, not necessarily. Actually, you can take the story all from the way it's run (how it's on the LP).

Rick: I heard the rumor that record was a mixed-up puzzle. Is that not true or true?

Chavez: It's not really a mixed-up puzzle, no. It ends exactly like it's supposed to and all the information is there, you just have to put it together. And any order it was in in the first place, it was almost undecipherable, unless you kind of knew it. Because everybody was asking, "What the heck?"

Tim: Unless you see the movie.

Chavez: Yeah, when the movie comes out, everyone will completely understand.

Todd: Chavez, when's the last time you shot a slab of meat?

Chavez: That was a pellet gun. 550 feet per second, whatever that thing is, it goes fast.

Guitardo: It'll break your skin.

Chavez: I shot Guitardo's steak, just on Wednesday. I asked him to hold it up and he wouldn't hold it up. He said, "Just shoot it on the cutting board." I was all surprised that he even let me do that. But, you know what? A couple months before, I almost shot Chip with the same gun, thinking, "This is rad. What is this thing?" [makes gun sound]

Todd: Did it break the skin?

Chip: [non-plussed] No. It came close to me, though.

Guitardo: He gave us the look of, "fuck," like he heard it go by his head.

Tim: That's the same mentality; Chavez put a staple gun to his hand once, and went, "Oh, it won't stick." [makes staple gun sound] Then it stuck in. "Well, it sticks in wood, what'd you think? It wasn't going to stick in your hand?"

Chavez: It was buried in my hand. I was like, "Ooooooh." Tim's like, "People put up fucking Christmas lights with those," and I'm like, "Bing! I'm an idiot." I was going to put to my temple.

Mike: Imagine pulling that thing out of bones.

Chavez: Dude, it took awhile to get it out of there. I was, "Oh my god." It hurt so bad. Bam! I like shooting things, though.

Todd: Name one record in your collection that you're embarrassed to admit that you like and explain why you like it.

Chavez: *Jesus Christ Superstar.*

Rick: Another fine concept album.

Chavez: I like it because of that. It's a concept. The emotion of all the characters is put in and it's just about something like Jesus, but in the album it's so fucking rock that they make it that Jesus isn't this savior that your parents are cramming into your head. He's just this dude who's got these ideas and everyone's freaked out about his ideas. It's the same exact concept as the Führers. Everyone treats him as this crazy man, and he himself is saying, "Why are you guys freaking out over this? All I'm telling you are these ideas and you guys are freaking out, and now I'm getting crucified." It's all the people, their stories that lead up to this guy's crucifixion. That is fucking hot. It's a pretty fucking rad album.

Guitardo: Probably, I'm embarrassed, I like Extreme Noise Terror. All my friends hate that shit. I just think they do a good job of controlling the chaotic speed that they put out.

Chip: I'm going to embarrass this band totally. Lynyrd Skynyrd's *Street Survivors* because I grew up in Nebraska and I just like that old, get drunk, fucking drive a tractor and shoot-'em-up type band. That, and I liked the album cover.

Todd: So what did Pete Moss, Smog City Waver #86, do to piss you off enough to list him on *domesticviolenceland* (The second LP)?

Chavez: He never did anything. Okay, Pete Moss, Waver #86…

Guitardo: He weighed out his eighths at 3.3 grams…

Chavez: He was our band manager. He'd collect all the money, and basically do the accounting for us, but at the same time, he was a weed dealer and we came to find out that he was taking the money that we made from the shows, buying weed with it, and then selling it back to us at inflated prices. And then he'd make the money back for our account and no one knew it was missing.

Todd: So, do you guys have a new manager?

Chavez: Now we're self-mismanaged.

Guitardo: Now we manage to just get along.

Todd: Could your albums come out of anywhere except Orange County, California?

Chavez: I think it couldn't have come out of anywhere but south Orange County, nowadays.

Todd: Explain yourself.

Chavez: Because, northern Orange County's poisoned now. It's no longer this suburban revolution. Now, it's like—they've all got kids who are growing up into punk rockers who are sixteen now. Now it's all bred into 'em, and again, it's becoming the same old thing, just like the metal thing was before. They already have it. They own it up there. And to fucking really charge and make a rebellious album, you have to be down here where you have fucking bands that sound like... hell.

Todd: What exactly is being "middle class high" as opposed to, say, "high class high"?

Guitardo: Better weed.

Chavez: That's the basis of the song. No matter what they say, Americans spend millions and millions of dollars on weed and we keep talking about these recessions and all we've got to do is legalize weed and, you know, we'll be buying it at grocery stores and shit.

Todd: Lots of high school kids would be gainfully employed.

Chavez: Exactly. You could go down to "Bud's buds" and get some buds. It'd be cool and that's middle class high. If they'd legalize it, they'd be stimulating the economy.

Todd: [in Kent Brockman voice] An economy on the grow.

Chavez: It would be. It's totally true.

Todd: Why don't you guys tour?

Chip: We've got great paying jobs.

Guitardo: Now, we all make $10,000 a year. Smogtown hasn't made that in six years.

Chip: We don't want to tour. We've got everything here.

Chavez: We do want to tour.

Tim: We've got to work for a living. People think, "Oh, you've got a record out," or whatever. They think about making money off of it.

Chip: But you've still got to survive.

Chavez: You look at the bands that really do put an effort into it—getting their name out there.

Guitardo: We've all seen *Another State of Mind* and how it ends up in the end. The tour's called off.

Tim: One of the punk clichés is once you start doing it to make money and make a living, you kinda—maybe—lose anger. I'd like to make a living at it—I'm not saying that. We'd probably end up hating each other just to make ends meet, to sell our label some more records or whatever. We're still making a mark and that's all we want to do. Some people like what we do.

Chip: We never thought we'd get this far anyway. We're lucky to have a record. We all skateboard together. We all surf together. We're different from most bands, you know what I mean?

Chavez: To me, I'd rather quit than have a new guy replace Chip or Tim because it wouldn't be the same anymore. You'd have a whole different sound. You'd have to adapt to that. Maybe if it was years ago and they wanted to quit, it would have been a different story. Tuesday and Thursday we go to the practice room, get drunk and stoned and play punk music. Or don't. Or just sit there, making fun of Guitardo.

Guitardo: Or play three songs and go, "Yeah, we're good."

Chavez: "Let's go to Jack in the Box."

Todd: [to Chip] Were you in any other California bands?

Chip: I was in Fag Rabbit and this band Mud Knuckle, a long time ago.

Todd: Any Nebraska bands?

Chip: No, no Nebraska bands. Just a lot of obscure music.

Todd: Ray, what band were you in before?

Chavez: White Knuckle Driver. It was just some hardcore band I was in in my late teens, early twenties. And that's all I'll comment on that. That's my most embarrassing show.

Rick: Ray, that story's actually better than that. It was just a bunch of metally guys with a punk ass singer and the metal guys couldn't figure out what the fuck he was doing.

Chavez: Here is how it was. There was this metal band down the street from my house and me and Guitardo would just cruise down there. We'd hear them playing. They'd have all this fast music. And at the time—it was the late '80s—I was into The Accused, Septic Death, and all of this crazy, ass-fucking, hardcore shit, and I'd just go down there and yell all this shit into the mic and basically make a mockery of what they were doing, 'cause I knew they were metal heads. And then this one day, the one guitar player came up to me and said, "Dude, why don't you join our band?" And one by one they all got haircuts except for the last guy... but we were called White Knuckle Driver. It was funny.

Chip: Ray was famous, though, as we'd come to find out.

Todd: Really, how so?

Rick: He fudge packed some stripper the first night they played.

Guitardo: On the hood of his Impala. They were great.

Tim: I was in a band called Vader's Crank that was around here for a short period of time.

Chavez: We stole Tim from Vader's Crank.

Todd: How long did you play for them?

Tim: Maybe like a year or so. They never did anything. One guy kind of lost his mind and moved away and then I don't know what happened to the rest of them, so yeah, they're not around, actually.

Todd: I would say that, for Smogtown, although you borrow from the past, you are very progressive. You can say I hear, for instance, The Crowd, The Clan, Stiff Little Fingers, Undertones, but I don't hear any direct rip-offs. And if someone's pressed when you ask, "Tell me, smart-guy, where is it coming from?" everyone gives a different answer.

Guitardo: We're striving to be Rage Against The Nine Inch Korn Hole.

Todd: What was the first punk band that you listened to that really affected the way you view the world—not just specifically sound-wise, but made other types of impact?

Guitardo: Adolescents.

Chavez: I'd say the same thing. That first Adolescents album (self-titled, often called The Blue Album) was the soundtrack to my juvenile delinquency because it had that same feel—that suburban revolution thing going on again. It's like, you're not poisoned by all this big city badness—the gangs and all. It's less than that. It's the overwhelming...

Tim: You're just crying because you're bored.

Chavez: Exactly. And that's where punk kind of lost it is that everyone kind of pisses on that type of thing when they're saying, "They're an Orange County band. They live in the fucking suburbs." Well, that's what punk's about—a revolution. What are you rebelling against in the big city dressed as a punker? You're just another freak living in the big fucking city where you're supposed to live and act like a freak in this club. That's expected of you. So, it's just kind of lost it, like the big rock scene after twenty years. It's the same thing, over and over again, and nothing really good to say is coming from the city. It seems like there's a lot of leftovers.

Tim: It seems like you've got a lot of hatred over there.

Chavez: I do. I hate a lot of things. I hate, therefore I am.

Tim: This guy speaks for himself, not for all of us.

Chavez: All that I'm saying is that's why we sound the way we do and that's why I liked that album.

Tim: What was the question, anyway?

Todd: Punk album that changed your view of the world.

Chip: Devo. Everybody started cropping their hair and looking totally different from the jocks in high school.

Todd: Do you think it opened up a lot of people, too?

Chip: Yeah.

Todd: Put in context, Devo's really strange.

Chip: Where I lived, in high school in the '80s, it was different. It was really jock oriented. I dunno, Devo really did it for a lot for people. It changed your view. You could be different, you know.

Todd: The thing I really like about Devo is that it's really hard to be a tough guy listening to them. But you can be very, very strange.

Tim: "Jocko Homo." Loved it.

Todd: [to Guitardo] Is there anything in your life that you're limited from because you wear leather pants all the time? Will you not hop over a fence because of them, due to restriction?

Tim: I think he performs better in his leather pants.

Guitardo: No, you can pretty much do anything in these. See, I've got a rip in the butt and I don't really fucking care.

Todd: Do you wear them all the time?

Guitardo: Yeah, a lot.

Chavez: Actually, that costume, if you go into his closet, it's all the same shirts, same pants, same boots. Just rows of them. Except for there's rotating shirts. The other one says "Smoke Marijuana."

Guitardo: Ray likes that one.

Todd: I think about this type of stuff way too much. I have a Smogtown theory. It comes from the songs "Audiophile" and "Neutron Blonde." It's basically, the suburbs create this monster, but the monster doesn't get activated until the music comes. And the music is Smogtown or punk rock music. You're putting all these parts together, "Rotting with my head-phones on / they're bolted to my skull." Does that work?

Chavez: That is true. And remember in *Führers of the New Wave*, the Führers, weren't just some gang, they were a rock'n'roll band, so that definitely is part of it. Wow, that's a pretty good theory.

Todd: What is the new wave? You mention it in almost every one, if not all, of your releases.

Chavez: This new suburban punk attack. This beach punk attack is the new wave.

Todd: So, you're setting D-Day. Who's in your battalions, then—or is it just a battalion of one?

Chavez: They are all the bands that are down here. The Stitches, Bonecrusher, Pushers, Smut Peddlers, Le Shok, The Numbers. I guess they can be in it.

Todd: Are there any bands from other areas that can be honorary members?

Chavez: Of course. Any band from any city. You've got to take over your beach. You've got to own your beach. You've got to rule this Teen-age. It's the new beach invasion. It can happen in any city.

Todd: When's the last time you hit somebody for a really, really bad reason?

Chavez: You know, I just thought about this yesterday, too. Remember that huge guy, Fester? And I took all those pills and got super drunk on gin and tonics on my birthday.

Guitardo: Yeah.

Chavez: I reached out and started punching the biggest guy. When people told me what I was doing, I didn't believe them myself. He basically just laughed and flicked me off. I woke up the next day around noon with, like, a shirt tied around my back, behind me, faced down on a couch with my pants pulled down, and when I woke up, I asked them why I was like that. That wasn't happening. I asked Guido's girlfriend at the time, "Dude, what happened?" They were like, "We thought you were going to throw up and choke on your puke or something. You were acting really weird and out of control. We had to lay you face down and tie you down and you passed out that way. And that's the last time I think I hit anyone.

Chip: I haven't hit anyone in a long time. I want to hit every member of this band about every fucking night.

Tim: Yeah, I think we need to start hitting each other some more.

Chip: That's where my next hit's going to be, for sure.

Todd: Do you think *Führers* could have been made in the '80s?

Chavez: No, because we would have been way too young to play those instruments.

Todd: Do you think it's time specific, though?

Chavez: Yeah, it's totally time specific.

Tim: It kind of sounds like it is, but I don't think so. I think it could have been made in the '80s, 'cause I listen to some of my old records and they sound just as good... punk.

Chavez: Sure, if we were all that age and knew each other.

Chip: I was that age.

Chavez: Some of those songs were written in the '80s. Those really nice, melodic songs were from Guitardo's old band.

Guitardo: My death rock band.

Todd: Which was?

Guitardo: Ceiling Zero. We only played in garages, at each other's houses for people, and they would video us and tape-record us and that's about as big as we ever got.

Chavez: And that was "Ode to Street Violence," "Führers of the New Wave," those two.

Todd: Guitardo, give me your thought process of going to play a show and forgetting your guitar.

Guitardo: Oh, don't smoke speed.

Todd: Anything else?

Guitardo: About forgetting the guitar?

Todd: Yeah.

Guitardo: Did you say, "thought process." I think there was a lack of. Hey, I was having a good time.

Todd: When did you realize you didn't have your guitar?

Guitardo: When they said that the PA finally showed up. We were already two and half hours late for the show. And they're all, "Get your guitar." And I just went to the van and there was no guitar. And I'm, "That's right. That guy gave me a rip off the glass dick and I just left the house." We were at Vinyl Solution (Huntington Beach's best record store), and someone said, "Get a guitar for him," and no one would let me borrow a guitar. They're all, "I've seen him throw a guitar." And everyone's all, "I don't have a guitar." That was our best show ever.

Rick: I have a question, going back to the record. You had a whole shit-load of songs that you had already done that had nothing to do with the concept of the record—like "Judy Is a Model" was not really a part of the record. It was an old song. What did you do to incorporate the old songs into the new theme? What was the stuff that was not really part of the concept record that you worked into it?

Chavez: The only thing that's worked into there is "Replay." That's not part of the concept, but that's just their obsession with pinball. Our—my, excuse me—obsession with pinball that's interjected in there.

Rick: But "Judy Is a Model," wasn't that an old song that was written way before the new stuff?

Chavez: It's an older song but it was written way before the new stuff, but then again, so is "Neighborhood Brat," which was our very first song. And it all just ties together. You can relate the same experiences—that's basically the theme of the band. It's what the *Führers of the New Wave* is about. All of the songs that we've ever done can be incorporated into the story. If you pick a song, I can incorporate it into the story.

Rick: Okay, "Judy Is a Model."

Chavez: Judy is the girl who ends up dying and they finally end up saying, "We need to get rid of the Führers" because this girl, this model girl, this girl who really does have a bad side and does all those bad things that all of the community and all her parents don't even believe that she would do, is out doing those bad things and ends up dead and they don't blame Judy, who's doing the bad things, they blame the Führers, who Judy is with. And it comes down to that.

Todd: How is your self-image and the image of the band changed since you've started?

Chavez: I have to have this band. I would go into deep depression. I would have no outlet. I could go surfing and all that stuff, but then again, I would just be one of these guys—I don't mean these guys—beyond them, beyond the wall.

Tim: Welcome to the Chavez Experience.

Chavez: I don't mean that. You know what I mean. I'd just be one of those guys just out there.

Rick: Todd, what do you think their image is? Because if everyone thinks of their image from photos they've seen, what do you perceive the image is?

Todd: I come from a very graphic point of view, laying out a magazine, and some people are very, very intentional on how they want to be portrayed. That's fine, but for some people, their image projects and overshadows other things like their talent and their capability.

Tim: So our image sucks?

Todd: No, because, more basically...

Chavez: Check this out. We just started out playing the music that we wanted to play and everyone told us that we were "beach punk." And "You guys sing about the beach." Except we never really thought about it. It was like, "I guess we kinda do."

Guitardo: It's what we live and what we played. And we were living those lives.

Chavez: The New Beach Invasion didn't come until after all the beach punk hype started around Orange County. Then we just went with it. The New Beach Alliance caught right on. Basically, there was one member from each band who would all meet at the same beach on Saturday and we'd all surf and we basically created The New Beach Alliance right there and took over this beach break, paddled right out there and said, "Yeah, we own this place. We're taking over."

Todd: Did you beat other people up?

Chavez: No. You don't have to do that. Just take their wave. They know better.

Guitardo: Nobody wanted to challenge.

Chavez: If you have enough people, you don't have to beat anyone up. I would never beat anyone up over a wave. I almost did get beat up over a wave, though.

Rick: Who's in the New Beach Invasion and who is The New Beach Coalition?

Chavez: The New Beach Coalition is actually Northern Orange County. Down here, the Beach City Butchers, that's basically us. The Führers is just a nickname, fantasy type thing to protect the innocent in the movie.

Chip: All the bands will unite in The Coalition and The Alliance.

Chavez: The New Beach Coalition is part of the New Beach Alliance.

Chip: It's like different chapters of the Hells Angels, but it's the beach.

Todd: Do you get pissed off if people write your name wrong?

Chavez: Yes. Smogtown is one fucking word.

Todd: Why is that?

Tim: Should it be two words technically?

Todd: Yeah, because it's an adjective and a noun.

Chavez: Yeah, that would represent a town that is smoggy. Smogtown is a specific place that starts in Tijuana and stretches all the way to Ventura, eastward to the San Bernardino Mountains. It's fucking paved, the whole area, and you know what? Everyone tries to tell you, "Smogtown is this place, Smogtown is Burbank, Smogtown is San Fernando." Smogtown is the whole fucking place.

Todd: Southern California.

Chavez: Exactly. And everything that happens in that whole place is what's represented in the songs that we make. That's what they're about. Every single one of them.

Todd: So you're under this umbrella?

Chavez: Basically. Because it's a place.

Tim: So that's why it's one word.

Todd: What do you skate and how long have you skated?

Chavez: I skate an Alva deck with these Independent trucks. I've been skating since I was eight years old.

Todd: What was the first trick you learned?

Chavez: Power slide.

Todd: The last trick you learned?

Chavez: Power slide.

Todd: Chavez, how much weed do you have to smoke to get a master's? (Directly referring to the lyrics in "Teenage") [laughter]

Chip: That's good that you picked that line up. I'm impressed.

Chavez: He comes right back with what we were just talking about... a lot of weed. I forgot.

Tim: He doesn't get high, he smokes so much.

Guitardo: You can apply that to every day.

Tim: He doesn't get high. He just keeps smoking it and smoking it.

Todd: How large a factor is that in touring? What percentage of your preparations are around that?

Chavez: Actually, the problem isn't around marijuana. We just like to say that. We judge how much pot is it going to take for us to get us from Portland to Seattle or San Francisco to Portland. Do you know what I mean?

Chip: These guys, they've got to have pot.

Chavez: Otherwise we wouldn't be able to deal with Chip.

Chip: I can't deal with them. They're bad. They're like women on the rag. It's pathetic.

Todd: So, what are your day jobs?

Chip: Computers. Telling people how to put modems and memory in their computer. Customer support.

Tim: UPS driver.

Guitardo: I work in a tainted grocery warehouse. We sell market food.

Todd: Do people know they're damaged?

Guitardo: Oh yeah.

Todd: Do the people who they sell it to know it's damaged?

Guitardo: Yeah. We sell to white trash and rich people. No one in between.

Chip: It's a rad store.

Chavez: I work in a molecular biology lab. It's true. We clone human parts and ship them to neutral countries where it's legal to put them together and make an actual cloned human.

Todd: What's a plasmid wash? (It's mentioned in their song, "Neutron Blonde")

Tim: Are you grilling him to make sure that he does work there?

Todd: Yeah.

Chavez: A plasmid wash is basically just like, you've got these five steps to purifying the DNA and that's just the fourth step. The first step is buffing the cell. And basically, you're weakening the cell wall so you can open it up.

Guitardo: It sounds really phallic.

Chavez: It is all super phallic. All the jokes that go with it are all sex jokes. The second one is that you lysate the cell, which is just breaking it down even more. The third step is… fuck, I can't remember. You know? The fourth step is the plasmid wash. It's just basically part of this making a solution to do the DNA.

Todd: So, how does that make a neutron blonde?

Chavez: It really doesn't. All the fancy terms are just thrown into a song. I was trying to make a story out of them and that was it. "Treat your heart like a plasmid wash," to wash away the outer walls. It's kinda goofy.

Tim: Those are the lyrics?

Chavez: They don't pay attention to that shit.

Tim: It's the song about his girlfriend.

Chip: His girlfriend's a scientist.

Chavez: She's twenty-three.

Tim: He sweeps the floors. He's lying.

Chavez: No. I build DNA purification kits [laughter]... it's true. I fill solutions in little beakers and put nitric acid on things and shake them and put things in the centrifuge...

Guitardo: Makes a good martini...

Tim: He smokes a lot of pot.

Todd: So, Chip, why the beret?

Chip: The truth?

Guitardo: [sing-songy] Balding.

Chip: No. That's not the truth. I just totally like the hat deal. Always have. Ever since D.I. and those all days.

Todd: So, it's not a French thing?

Chip: No, it's not a French thing. It's just my image. I've always worn hats. Now you see more and more people wearing them.

Todd: Hats in general?

Chip: No. Berets. Because of me. I've got the influence now. [laughter]

Chavez: It's been picked up by a lot of the military.

Chip: I just like it. It just makes me look more fierce. [laughter]

Guitardo: You need the help.

Chip: I need the help, definitely.

Guitardo: It balances out the bag above the belt.

Todd: What's the most memorable thing you've hit with your car?

Chavez: I've never hit... oh, a possum. I had a Volkswagen bug and it went underneath the wheel, underneath the tire, into the wheel well and was so big that it just slowed my bug down to a stop. I had to put it in reverse and kick him out of there.

Guitardo: I had this '70 Dodge Dart, hit this berm jump off of the Ortega Highway, went thirty feet through a barbed wire fence, into some guy's nursery where he grew plants for the agriculture around buildings and stuff. And it trashed a hundred bushes. He didn't press any charges and the engine was still running and DRI was still on the stereo. I thought we could drive away but it wasn't going. I got out of the car and the entire bottom chassis had fallen from the bottom of the car. It was crazy.

Tim: A dog. A big dog named Duke. I was more torn up about the dog than the car. The lady tried to sue UPS and didn't get shit, but the dog died right there and blood and piss and shit was coming out of it and children were crying. It wasn't my fault. The dog jumped right over a fence when I was driving by.

Guitardo: Oh, a sacrifice.

Tim: Even the lady who stopped behind me said it wasn't my fault.

Chavez: Maybe it was sick.

Todd: Where did you get the cover for *The Führers*? I've seen it before.

Chavez: We got it out of this Time Life magazine type thing. It started with the 1900s, and it was out of the 1960s and it was just some picture in there. I think it's Kent State. It said the guy had a broken hand. That's what it says in the caption.

Todd: He's a protester, right?

Chavez: Throwing back a smoke grenade that people had lobbed at him.

Todd: Assuming there is a god, what would be the first thing you asked him if he ended up riding shotgun in your car?

Guitardo: "Can I sit at your left hand?"

Chavez: I would say, "What were you thinking with Pope Pious?"

Todd: Why would you ask that question?

Chavez: Just because, my dad's a Catholic, and he wanted to know why I wasn't a Catholic and that was my reason. Pope Pious joining up with Hitler and shit—that's kind of bad and people just sort of just blow it off and it was just sort of weird to me. That would be my question to god: "If Catholicism is right and the Popes do know what your will is, what were you thinking with Pope Pious?"

Tim: Oh man, you can't follow that up.

Guitardo: "If you made it, why can't we smoke it?"

Tim: "Why didn't I win the lottery all those times I prayed to you?"

Chavez: I might be a lottery winner right now. I played.

Chip: "Why did you let my best friend die, god?"

Chavez: It's just like Chip to bring things down.

Chip: Fuck yeah. That's what I'm going to ask him.

Todd: Is it true you recorded songs prior to your first 7", *Smog on 45*, that haven't been released?

Tim: About twenty-two songs. Demos. I had them remastered. (This collection of early songs, *Tales of Gross Pollution*, was released in late 2003.)

Todd: Holy shit.

Chavez: Some of them you'll recognize. "Suicide," "Berlin Girls."

Tim: Some of them are re-recordings. "No More Waves."

Chavez: Some of them, you're going to laugh.

Todd: Who's going to release it?
Guitardo: [joking] Epitaph.
Tim: Ray wants to make it elaborate—make it look like a 7", put it in 7" plastic, and a bunch of artwork.
Chavez: I have over 1,000 photos of us from 1995 to now.
Todd: According to the *Audiophile* 7" liner notes, it said that it was rumored that you guys had broken up.
Chavez: We did.
Chip: Guitardo had a nervous breakdown.
Guitardo: I asked for another amp and no one would help me out. Everyone's standing there, looking at us, so Chavez said, "Guitardo's having guitar problems, as usual." And I'm all, "Oh yeah? Well, watch this." I kicked the amp.
Chavez: His guitar was broken, so he kicks the amp? There was two weeks of limbo there.
Todd: So, Guitardo, why did you decide to come back?
Chavez: Because the chicks didn't dig him anymore. They're really stoked on him now.
Guitardo: Because I started smoking pot again. It only lasted for three days. They (the band) came to my house every day. I was moving.
Chavez: He was freaking out.
Guitardo: I was living with a crack addict with a girlfriend who was too overweight.
Todd: What does one thing have to do with the other?
Guitardo: Crack and gaining weight? That shouldn't happen. His girlfriend came home with a new boyfriend.
Todd: What was the last thing you threw up on that you really, really wished you didn't?
Chavez: The last time I threw up was driving home from the Sierra Mountains. I threw up in Bishop because I was all hung over.
Mike: I've seen you on all fours, all green and sweaty, barfing for twelve hours straight.
Guitardo: He had his head on the toilet seat like it was a pillow. It looked so uncomfortable. We were like, "You broke the bong, Chavez." And you were like, "Uuunnnghhh."
Chavez: I don't remember that but from eyewitness accounts, I think I did a Baretta roll after the bong broke, and I held it up, saying, "Arrggghh, I saved it," and it was a fucking shard of glass. And then I threw… ohh, that's right.
Guitardo: We just dragged you to the bathroom because you just started puking.
Chavez: I puked on myself and on the couch [points to Mike] at your house. You were in rehab.

Mike: That's how I missed it. I was thinking, "Where was I?"

Chavez: We were at the Stack, playing with Bonecrusher, and you were there drinking Shirley Temples, remember, and Duane Peters fell over and hit his head.

Mike: He came over all hammered and tripped over the cord, and clacked his jar so hard right on the bar. I see his eyeballs roll back and he hits the floor. Everyone's like, "Fuck, Mike, help him. Bring him to Raybo's." Raybo's all, "Grab an end." And I'm all, "Fuck you, man. Not again."

Chavez: It was that night. I was at your house. I had a hangover for two more days.

Mike: That was a gin and tonic problem, huh?

Chavez: Yep.

Todd: What's the biggest compliment anyone's ever given your band. [long silence]

Chavez: "Underneath all Smogtown's pick slides and tsunami rhythm lies an incongruously aesthetic agenda."

Chip: Some guy called us poseurs. That was really nice. That was in the newspaper.

Todd: Why does that give you joy, Chip?

Chavez: Because they commented on his beret.

Tim: I can't really think of anything.

Chip: "You brought a tear to my eye." Some guy said that at The Doll Hut.

Todd: This is the last question. Look to the person to the right, who's in the band, and tell me what you like most about them.

Chavez: I'll tell you what I like most about Chip. Chip is the most generous, father-like person that I've ever met. Seriously. He lent me two hundred bucks. I haven't paid him back for that. And I've gone sleepless for the last five years for it. Seriously, and I will pay you back, Chip. Swear to god.

Tim: Chip doesn't like anything about me.

Chip: Tim's a cool person and he fucking just plays the drums so tight that I feel like I just fit right in with him. It feels like I belong with him when I'm on stage. He's so tight I don't even have to worry. There's no stress. It's weird. It feels like I've known him forever.

Tim: Guitardo, I like. He's got a great personality. He doesn't say too much but he's very easy going. He's a pushover. That's what I like about him.

Guitardo: Chavez, 'cause he's got this Latino charm thing going. All the girls thinks he looks like some Latin lover.

Chavez: Erik Estrada.

Guitardo: Yeah.

Tim: That's what you like about him?

• • •

THE REAL MCKENZIES

THE BRIEFS

"The point of ideals and ideology - you're always falling short, but it's a compass point, something you aim towards. So when people point the finger and yell at you for not living up to your ideals, I say fuck you. That's how I steer myself morally. I miss all the time, I'm constantly correcting my course, but that's what you shoot for."

–Dan Yemin

WE'LL CARRY THE TORCH YOU FUCKIN' DROPPED: AN INTERVIEW WITH KID DYNAMITE

by Todd and Matt Average

The mile markers are there. If you've ever been a fan of this stretch of road, the bands that warn you of sharp curves ahead are well known. Early Bad Brains. 7 Seconds. Gorilla Biscuits. SS Decontrol. All made unrepentant hardcore that, if you listen to closely enough, is positive as all hell—urging its listeners to grow, to question, and to live with integrity intact. Somewhere after 1988, the posicore van launched off the side of the road seemingly forever and blew apart in a depressing reign of bad, floor-punching metal. Somewhere around that time—and I won't boast I know the answer—the fun of retards, geeks, and misfits playing as hard and fast as they possibly could was replaced by punk's version of sports teams in matching jerseys. Leagues of vein-bulging dudes cleared dance floors with moves that looked like they were starting invisible lawnmowers then becoming human windmills. That confused the hell out of me. Minor Threat made perfect sense. Angry metal that looked like it was taking place in a weight gym didn't.

The rub? When done right, hardcore is the world's best catharsis. Bundle all the bad shit in a tight little ball and have it crumple in a world of shouts and sounds. Cheap therapy.

In 1998, when I put Kid Dynamite's self-titled CD in the player, I had to pull over, turn off the engine. I listened to it in its entirety three times in a row right there before I returned home. I'd found it. That missing link between the first, incredible charge of early '80s hardcore to being twenty-six and not wanting to live solely in the past. Here was a band that flew the flag unrepentantly but also brought a modern twist and humanity to the proceedings. Their lyrics were smart. They were tough but not thugs. Their vocalist was snotty but clear. The guitar crunched like it was etching songs into concrete. Their drummer—one of my all-time favorite punk drummers—didn't get trapped in monkey beats as he sped up. The bassist knew how to play the area between invention and convention perfectly. Amid all that power, they were melodic and could play the shit out of a sing-a-long. Dan Yemin and Dave Wagenschutz were previously in another excellent band, Lifetime. Lifetime's latest work has more than a passing blush to Kid Dynamite, but Kid Dynamite definitely used explosives of their own.

Matt and I were able to sit down and chat with Dan, the guitarist of
Kid Dynamite. We found out that Dan not only had earned his Ph.D.,
he had some of the most insightful, intelligent ideas concerning punk and
the power of idealism in one's thirties.

Dr. Dan Yemin: guitar
Jason Shevchuk: vocals
Dave Wagenschutz: drums
Michael Cotterman: bass

Todd: None of you guys are kids. Why Kid Dynamite and not like Middle
Aged C-4? [laughter]
Dan: You guys know where the name comes from. You guys have been
around the block, c'mon.
Todd: Where did it come from?
Dan: It's a Squirrel Bait song. It's the first song on the second Squirrel Bait
record. I always thought it'd be a cool name for a band.
M.Avrg: I thought maybe you guys had a boxing interest or something.
Dan: We were just talking about different names. I think I'm over the idea
of a band name having some huge weighty significance. My friend said to
me—he's another old, jaded cynical punk rocker—and he said Kid
Dynamite is the best name because it doesn't mean anything. The image it
conjures is one of youthful explosiveness.
Todd: I get lightning and wrestling out of it.
Dan: No matter how old you are, hardcore or punk is youthful, explosive
music. The part of me that writes and plays that stuff is like a kid who's
still banging around in my head. He's still running around and he's still like
that picture of that Circle Jerks guy, the skanking guy. He's sixteen and he
has bruises all over him. That's the part of me that drives me to play this
kind of music. The part of me that's actually interested in song craft is the
thirty-one-year-old guy who has been writing songs for ten years. So you
combine that guy with the circle pit sixteen-year-old and you get Kid
Dynamite.
M.Avrg: When you were auditioning singers, what type of singer had the
least appeal to you guys?
Dan: So many people had no grasp of what I meant when I talk about
anthemic hardcore –punk with melody. So many people were like, "Oh, like
NOFX, right?" I'd be like, "That's about—I like NOFX, but—the farthest
thing from what I mean." So people had a hard time grasping what I was
going for. Largely because most of the people trying out were pretty young
and didn't really have much in the way of roots. Everything we're doing, I
think of it as just an amalgam of all the good influences from '76 to '83. If

you're not in touch with that vein of inspiration you're going to miss the point, I think, or at least in terms of people who wanted to be in the band.
Todd: What's the difference between straight edge and being sober? The only thing I've got is the bats and youth groups.
Dan: I don't know anything about being sober or being straight edge. I can't comment. There are people in this band who are straight edge. I'm not one of them. We're about half and half, I guess. It really has nothing to do with the band outside of the fact that, perhaps, as a lifestyle that's what keeps some people in this band safe and healthy, and whatever, but I know nothing about sobriety. [laughter]
Todd: What's been the largest show of dedication from a fan?
Dan: This band? God, I gotta think back. It's hard for me to keep anecdotes straight from band to band. People have gotten the skull that we use on one of our shirts tattooed on them. That's always heavy for me, when people tattoo something of your band on them. That's permanent. So right there and then that's when you know you've touched or moved people.
Todd: When they're getting prune juice at eighty years old, that skull's going to be there. [laughter]
Dan: Either you've really touched somebody's life, or they just have really bad decision-making skills. But I like to think that we've made an impact on people. People will send you things; they'll draw things for you and make things for you. I'm always just blown away and in awe when people get something tattooed on them that has something to do with my band.
M.Avrg: What's the song "Ph.Decontrol" aimed at?
Dan: That's one of two songs on the record that I wrote the lyrics to. It's just about people. It's pretty much autobiographical. I know you guys have been around the block a few times—it's not because you look old and haggard [laughter]—I've seen your names around for a while. A generation of punk and hardcore is maybe two or three years. We've seen people come and go and come and go, and it's like, "What are we still doing here, why are we still involved in this, and why do people burn out on it when they get older?"

A lot of times people figure out somewhere in their early twenties that the world isn't going to change just because you scream it at it. And they're like, "Wow, all this hardcore and punk stuff really doesn't mean anything. It just isn't working." And that's when I'm like, "You missed the point. You didn't connect. What the fuck did you expect? Was all that screaming a waste of breath?" My answer to that is no. It's like a rhetorical question posed to the person who abandons all this stuff that composes so much of what our lives are about: the energy behind the music and the ideology that goes hand in hand with it, too.
Todd: The tenets of faith, dealing with it, too. You have to have that faith tested a lot.

Dan: You have to be able to take major leaps of faith.

M.Avrg: What keeps you interested in it? Being thirty, and a lot of things bands sing about, or zines write about, I'm just like, "Who fuckin' cares?"

Dan: The end of that song is a promise: "We'll carry the torch you fuckin' dropped." That was pretty much the birth of this band. It was all about, "I'm thirty and I'm launching a brand new band and I plan on taking it really seriously."

M.Avrg: My whole thing is to bring something in that appeals to my age group.

Dan: That's what I hope to be doing. It seems that a lot of older punks can really relate to the band. Even though our singer is twenty-three, we have two old, haggard guys and two wide-eyed idealists.

M.Avrg: But in the big picture, thirty is not old.

Dan: No, it's not. But in punk rock years.

Todd: What has Kid Dynamite been able to achieve that Lifetime wasn't able to? Have specific doors opened up or certain things become easier?

Dan: I just have a little more leeway song writing wise. We have plenty of stuff that's infused with pop and melody, but I can also go full-on thrash without a hint of melody, which is a place I couldn't go with Lifetime. We're also much more interactive band.

Todd: There seems to be a lot of forces melding.

Dan: People were intimidated to cross that stage line with Lifetime for one reason or another. Maybe it was because early on we took such a hard stance towards violent dancing and people assumed they weren't supposed to dance at all. Maybe it was because Ari didn't really feel comfortable with handing the mic out, which is part of what defines the music for me. Jason's a lot different. He's more comfortable about it and I think the music is a lot more geared to suck people into the experience with us, right there in the live setting. In Lifetime, the power of the music definitely sucked people in. But in this band, in the live setting, it really sucks people in.

Todd: What do you think are some of the natural inhibitors in this band? What are some of the things you will not do?

Dan: We will not play an age-restricted show. That's not such a big deal. That's not such a hard stance. We turned down a very tempting show back on the east coast. It was very flattering to be invited to do, and something that will probably be pretty immense, but it was at a club in New York that made it clear that they were going to enforce a sixteen and up age policy. That's always been important to all of us. Plus, I was kind of happy when we talked about it as a band there was no hesitation not to do it. No, "Maybe we should do it," no, "Maybe blah, blah, blah." Everybody was just like, "No." With that, there's a song on the new record that's called, "The Cheapshot Youth Anthem," because it's such a fuckin' sucker punch.

The chorus is "All ages" and it's got a big "who-ohoh" part. The song is about saying fuck you to age-restricted shows and why that's important. There's no way we could write that song, and record that song, and put it out on a record and then play a sixteen-and-over show. When it gets to the point you're contradicting the things you sing about, you gotta really just draw a firm line there.

M.Avrg: Do you think punk rock is getting older or is it getting younger?

Dan: In terms of the demographic that's attracted to it?

M.Avrg: Yeah.

Dan: I don't know. It's hard to say. It seems like it's getting younger, but there's a lot of old guys and girls sticking around and doing good stuff—writing, doing film, doing record labels. I found it much more important in the past couple of years in my life to make a deliberate effort to connect with the older folks, just so I don't lose perspective. So many people, they really give away to feeling alienated. They get to a show and they're like, "God, I'm twice as old as some of these people here," and they panic. For some reason, that's an issue.

M.Avrg: I think when you get like that you're looking for an excuse to leave… Who's Ronald Miller?

Dan: It's from a movie, I think: *Can't Buy Me Love*. All of Jason's song titles are kind of these obtuse references to lines from movies and sitcoms. He's very, very grounded in that stuff. The names are never gibberish. They're always something having to do with...

Todd: Some reference.

M.Avrg: So you're like the Beastie Boys of hardcore. [laughter]

Todd: If you could put shape to the flame that burns inside of you, what shape would it take?

Dan: Good god almighty, that's a good question. I have no idea how to answer that. Can I give the flip comic answer, or should I give the overly sincere wide-eyed idealist punker answer?

Todd: Give both.

Dan: I don't know what either would be. [laughter] The serious answer is it would probably be like kind of formless, like an actual flame because I'm never quite that clear about the direction for my passion and my energy. One direction it takes might be the shape of, like, music, and that's definitely a direction. That's a hard question. Have you ever gotten a good answer from a question like that?

Todd: I just thought of it yesterday. [laughter]

Dan: What shape? It would probably be a fist clenching and unclenching, because I'm so furious about things and I want to just smash stuff, and sometimes I'm so committed to the idea of solving things with an open hand as opposed to a fist. That's one of my major conflicts. I'm so conflicted about aggression and confrontation. On one hand, I just want to fuckin' destroy things that piss me off, and on the other hand, I don't really believe that that ends up being a constructive solution. I'm always back and forth—like walking away from conflict and kicking myself for not taking a harder stand.

M.Avrg: What's one thing you felt strongly about when you were younger, but as you get older you feel it really isn't that way anymore? Like you see it for what it is, and you feel good about the change.

Dan: I'm just a lot more comfortable with people running their mouths off, the real core of the English punk rock element, the "fuck you." I used to be so serious about my convictions that I could not listen to, or abide by, people listening to Slapshot, because they made fun of vegetarians, and I'm so serious about my vegetarianism. Now I'm even more serious. I've been vegan for seven or eight years, but I listen to Slapshot. [laughter] They're a good band, and I think it's important to stir shit up. I'm much more comfortable with that. Even if you're stirring shit up just to stir shit up, sometimes that's important. Sometimes the people who get their feathers ruffled easily need to have their feathers ruffled the most. The people that are that uptight really need to be tweaked frequently. Now I'm a lot more comfortable with being really opinionated and obnoxious. Everything out of my mouth doesn't have to be constructive. It can just be what I'm honestly thinking. If you've got something to say, if you've got an opinion, you should fuckin' voice it.

Not to hurt people, but with record reviews, a perfect example would be, "I couldn't say this sucks or this is a waste of precious natural resources." I would say, "This isn't really my thing but they're really good at what they do." I'll try to describe it. Now, if I think it sucks, I'll just say, "This is regurgitated pap. I wouldn't even rest my beer on this." [laughter] And I'm comfortable with saying that. It makes a little more of an impression, and it certainly provokes a response. Hardcore is about dialog, and you can't have dialog if everybody's being polite all the time.

M.Avrg: There's a couple of songs you have that have a Gorilla Biscuits influence. Was that purposely done, or did it just happen that way?

Dan: I didn't start out to sound like the Gorilla Biscuits. I love the Gorilla Biscuits. The Gorilla Biscuits were the one band in the late '80s that really embodied what I'm trying to do with this band, which is make the most out of a really wide range of influences. They didn't sound like every other fuckin' youth crew band out there. They sounded like a band that listened to the Buzzcocks, and The Clash, Bad Brains, and Minor Threat, and the best bands of the current day as well.

M.Avrg: At the end of "Bench Warmer," it sort of sounds like "Start Today."

Dan: Actually, it's more of a Bad Brains lift. But that's the thing. GB lifted those chunky parts from Bad Brains. The last thing I aspire to do is something wholly original. What we intend to do in this band is pay tribute to a musical form that raised us and raised us well. There are a lot of bands that are trying to do this style of music we play. I just want to do it well.

M.Avrg: There's all these bands coming out, and the thing I keep reading about them is they all point to you guys as starting this whole wave of bands coming up now.

Dan: Really? Wow! Good. A wave of bands that sound like anything particular?

M.Avrg: They say the melodic, uptempo hardcore bands. They say you are the catalyst of all that happening.

Dan: Cool. I don't want to make a big age issue, but I think we have that on our side. I hope we do a fantastic job of what we're doing. That's what I shoot to do. I don't know if we do, but I don't think it's arrogant to aspire to do that. I'm not convinced that you could do a really fabulous job of the style of music we want to do if you don't have some oldsters in the band.

M.Avrg: A lot of young kids think that hardcore started in 1988. Very few of them have heard of Black Flag or Bad Brains.

Dan: I meet kids all the time who come up to us—we've done a lot of tours and shows opening up for bigger bands—and people come and they're like, "I haven't heard you guys, what do you sound like?" I'm like, Minor Threat and 7 Seconds, maybe. [laughter] They're like, "Oh, I don't know those bands." Somebody asked me in an interview yesterday: "If you saw a fifteen-year-old kid in a Warped tour shirt in a record store, and he had a Kid Dynamite CD in one hand and a Minor Threat discography CD in the other hand, and he only money for one, which would you want him to buy?" I said, "Of course, the Minor Threat record. If you're not grounded in context and history you're going to lose a lot of what there is to gain from the present."

M.Avrg: A lot of kids I've talked to think that Youth of Today was hardcore and nothing before them was hardcore.

Dan: Kevin Seconds was on stage a few nights ago in Vancouver and said, "Who knows where the term hardcore came from?" We were in Vancouver. He claims Joey from DOA was the first person to use the term hardcore in the sense that we use it today. He said, "Those guys came down from Vancouver and kicked our asses, and that's when we decided we're a hardcore band!"

M.Avrg: There's also stuff like Middle Class.

Dan: I'd like to get Kevin's opinion on who was the first band to play thrash beats.

M.Avrg: Some people say Bad Brains or Middle Class.

Dan: If you can make me a tape of Middle Class, I've never heard them.

Todd: Really? I've got a CD of the stuff. Mike Atta put it out, who was in the Middle Class, but his label went under.

Dan: When people don't have access to it—that's why I think it's really important to pay tribute to your influences, but not necessarily wear them on your sleeve. I've been thanking 7 Seconds on the west coast dates we've been playing. They really did set the precedent for uplifting, positive hardcore punk.

M.Avrg: They were one of the only really true positive hardcore bands. There were other bands who were called hardcore bands but were lyrically negative.

Dan: I met the drummer from Negative FX in a bar right before tour. How weird is that?

M.Avrg: What's he up to now?

Dan: I don't know. He's was friend of a friend. Do you know any record collectors, not punk record collectors, but people who collect old soul records where all the hip hop samples come from? These guys leave at five in the morning to go to flea markets and buy these records. My friend is one of these guys, and he introduced me to a friend, and we happened to be talking about going away for the weekend to play and the guy said, "You have a band? What kind of music do you play?" I said. "We're a hardcore punk band," and he said, "Man, people are still playing that? I was in band a long time ago in Boston called Negative FX." I was like, "Oh, Choke's old band." He said, "You heard of us? Fuckin'-A. Yeah, I have the CD. Unfortunately, I don't have the vinyl." [laughter]

Todd: Where was the last time you saw an animal and it made you smile?

Dan: This morning. I love animals. I don't have pets. I'm not a PC warrior, although I act like one sometimes. I get mad when people use sexist language and homophobic language, even if they're doing it ironically. If you're with the band, you're representing the band, and people who overhear you don't know you're being ironic. So I act like a PC cop sometimes. I'm not that uptight. But I think it's fucked up when people have pets and they don't have a yard, or at least they're not home to walk the animal. I know people who have big dogs in an apartment, but they work around the corner and they come home a lot. That's cool. Me and my fiancée, we're gone from the morning until sometimes ten at night. But I love animals. We stayed with a friend in Berkeley last night, and they have four little dogs. I woke up this morning with them all jumping on me.

Todd: Where does the doctor come in?

Dan: I have a doctorate in psychology.

Todd: Do you know of any other Ph.D.s in punk rock?

Dan: I know of a few, but I don't know any personally. I think one of the guys in Bad Religion has a doctorate.

Todd: Yeah, Greg Gaffin does.

Dan: Dave Smalley (singer of DYS, Down By Law). I don't know if he has a doctorate. I know he has a graduate degree.

Todd: He has a master's.

Dan: Vic Bondi (Articles of Faith). Dr. Frank from MTX isn't actually a doctor. Timmy, the drummer from Snapcase, has been working on his dissertation. It's history or political science. I can't remember, but he's teaching at the university up in Buffalo. He finished his masters, and he's working on his dissertation. The drummer from the best band in the world, in my opinion, Dillinger Four, has gotten the same degree that I got.

Todd: I'm glad you said Dillinger Four, because I see a lot of similarities between you guys and those guys in your approach.

Dan: Spirit!

Todd: Total spirit. It seems not only are you honoring the past, but you're burning the bad parts away.

Dan: Wow, that's cool! Doesn't that record (*Midwestern Songs of the Americas*) totally kick ass? The spirit of what we're doing comes from the same place. It's angry, but catchy. People ask me what they sound like, and obviously you really can't call them hardcore, but you can't call them pop punk. There are poppy elements, but it's fuckin' punk. To call them pop punk would do them extreme disservice.

Todd: What was the last club you were a member of?

Dan: I was a member of the Association for Graduate Students. I'm a member of the American Psychological Association. [laughter]

Todd: Who's the rock star in "Shiner" that the protagonist won't run away from?

Dan: The songs that are written toward a second person, a "you." I talked to Jason about this before. They may be inspired by a specific incident, but they're intended to be intended generally.

Todd: Archetypes?

Dan: Yeah. I couldn't comfortably say the song is about anybody. It's quite possible it was inspired by a specific incident or individual behavior, but it's meant as a general fuck you to that kind of attitude and to the people who imagine that they're above their audience or above other bands they play with. Punk rock rock stars, basically. But it's also a cautionary tale aimed at ourselves and our peers to remember to break down barriers between audience and the band, which might be me and my little hardcore fantasy world, but it's important to strive for.

Todd: It's good to reaffirm. I totally agree with that.

Dan: The point of ideals and ideology—you're always falling short, but it's a compass point, something you aim towards. So when people point the finger and yell at you for not living up to your ideals, I say fuck you. That's how I steer myself morally. I miss all the time, I'm constantly correcting my course, but that's what you shoot for.

•   •   •

"*I believe that reading is truly punk rock and I believe that it's truly punk rock to teach yourself through reading. If you think it's punk to be ignorant, you're wrong. It's punk to learn and it's punk to know and be wiser than those who are supposedly in control.*"

—Jeff

READING IS... FUUUUUCK YOU:
AN INTERVIEW WITH BLOODHAG

Bloodhag are real. It makes me happy that they're not just a really lucid dream I've been having for a couple of years. It's a bitchin' idea. Dress up in ties and nice shirts, attach paperbacks to chains, play some powerviolence/death metal songs that don't clock in too long, and have every song be a mini-biography about a science fiction author. And although they write songs solely about science fiction authors, they don't reek of weak schtick. Not only does it sound great to me on paper, they deliver both live and on record. Hyperfast and hyper-literate, they play libraries and dive bars alike. Not only are they "Hooked on Demonics," they make some of the heaviest snuggie-underwear-soiling sounds this side of Demon System 13, Spazz, Hellnation, and Brujeria, but they're as nice as a grandma that knits huggies for your tea pot. They're the progenitors of Northwest EduCore, and in Bloodhag's hands, literacy becomes a paper cut. Strap on that barbed wire thinking cap, get out your library card, and prepare for a slashing.

Zach(ery) Orgel: bass
Ambassador Brent Carpenter: drums
Professor J.B. Stratton (aka Jake): vocals
Dr. J.M. McNulty (aka Jeff)—guitar

Parentheticals—( )—provided by the band
Squiggles—{ }—provided by Todd

Todd: Where are the fucking codpieces?
Jake: Yeah. My skills at clothing crafting are pretty limited. I was kinda hoping that by this time I'd be hooked up with some sort of fashion model. When we do the *R**d Like a Beast* album {a la W*A*S*P's *F**k Like a Beast*}, I'll be wearing a bloody book codpiece on the cover of that.
Todd: Break your name down into the Latin root.
Zach: Zachary Orgel and I'm Logos the Rhythmatist. Logos is actually Greek. It's "the word made flesh." The living knowledge, or "gnosis," as they say.
Todd: Could it also be construed as "The word of god"?
Zach: In a way. Some people thought it actually resided in the library at Alexandria and that's why it got sacked—they were trying to destroy the logos. That was Philip K. Dick's take on it. (See especially the *Valis*

trilogy. Dick viewed the "logos" as perhaps a symbiote virus [perhaps extra-terrestrial] that when contacted/contracted produced gnosis.)

Jeff: A lot of that could deal with the actual, written word of god. You know how that gets freaked out and twisted around.

Zach: Rhythmatist is a gross derivation of rhythm. (e.g. One who is rhythmic in nature. One who produces rhythm.)

Jake: I am Professor J.B. Stratton and I'm also known as Grimoire the Expectorator. Grimoire meaning the huge volume of complete works, some giant tome.

Zach: It's Germanic, grimoire.

Jake: And expectorator is because of the... spitting.

Todd: In German, expectorate is "ausspucken."

Jake: I could use a good ausspucken.

Jeff: And I'm Deux Ex Libris, the Plagiarazor, Dr. J.M. McNulty. My name is the grossest bastardization of any root words of all of the band names. It's a stupid pun on "Deus Ex Libris" and "Deus Ex Machina."

Jake: "Ex Libris," which would be on book plates, which would mean "from the library of..." so it would be "from the library of god."

Jeff: And then the Plagiarazor is because I steal riffs from everyone? [instantly throaty] And I tear through your skull with brutal dispensation.

Jake: [in falsetto whisper] Sharp as a knife, yow!

Todd: So, why metal?

Jake: Pretty straightforward one. The fact that we all love heavy metal. The general gist is we want to show heavy metal and hardcore music fans the literary inspirations for the music they're currently listening to. The majority of the bands they listen to borrowed imagery and titles from science fiction authors with little actual acknowledgement. What we do is show these people where it comes from. Straight across.

Jeff: We skip the middleman when it comes to hardcore metal.

Jake: I was quite the metalhead coming up and it's the most fun thing to play.

Jake: It's not just about the authors. It's mutated since then. We've realized that a lot of people don't appreciate reading at all, which I kind of did not want to admit to myself at first, but it's the truth. That's really, really troublesome to all of us. They were forced to do it in high school, they didn't respond to it then, and as soon as they got out of high school, they were like, "Phew, I never have to read again."

Jeff: How many people have said to us, "Oh, the book that you threw at us is the first book I've read all year?"

[nods of agreement]

Jake: It's saddening but it shows us the other path we have to go down, which is teaching people to read. If we can't work with them one on one and teach them how to decipher the symbols and read a frickin' sentence, we're going to try to inspire their imaginations to the point where they're like, "Well, maybe we like this song to the point where I recognize who this author is. Maybe I'll buy the book or check it out of the library and start to read it." It's a gateway to wilder ideas—anything other than what the media feeds us, what the government wants us to think. If all you get is from television, you're a real sucker. The best part about this has been Harry Potter. It's an awesome fad. Bring it on.

Jeff: The kids who are dedicated to Harry Potter, those kids are sharp as a fucking tack. I'm like, okay, I have some faith in the future of humanity.

Zach: It's cool to see people excited about a book, no matter what it is.

Jake: Jeff and myself originally conceived the band as a recording project while we were actually doing something else entirely.

Todd: Were bong hits involved? (Possible reference to "reefer cigarettes"? Interview might be "stoned." Colloquial.)

Jeff: It was one of those things; "Wouldn't it be funny if we..." We wrote a song, "Edgar Rice Burroughs," when him and me were doing some other indie rock duo thing. And then we were like, "Wouldn't it be funny if we had a whole band that played heavy metal songs about science fiction writers?"

Todd: So, is it funny?

Jeff: The first demo (*Swords Against Deviltry*, copyright, Bloodhag, 1996) is hilariously funny, in my opinion.

Todd: Who was Robert A. Heinlein's roommate in college?

Zach: I knew that one at one point.

Jeff: That's a rough one.

Jake: Let me think about it.

Todd: Which science fiction writer of the past had the most exacting vision of their future, our present?

Zach: I say John Brunner.

Jeff: I say Brunner and William Gibson but Gibson didn't have to look ahead that far. And if you discount Philip K. Dick's goofiness of the future, I think he was really damn close. Because if you look in all of his books, he talks about people wearing goofy clothes and weird, retro things that would happen and that's exactly what's going on. It's just not the way that he said it.

Jake: He would have in *Ubik* (Dick, Philip K., 1969), where the main character has to pay for everything in his apartment. From the toaster to his shower, he has to constantly put in dimes, which isn't actually, currently going on, but the underlying thing was he was projecting that you would have to pay to do everything, which, more or less, you do now.

Jeff: But John Brunner, he was absolutely correct. He does a thing where he leaves out some of those details that other Sci-Fi writers might put in, like exactly what the people are wearing—that sort of thing—to the point where it's very easy just to picture it going on right now. If you read *Shockwave Rider* right now, you could easily re-write that book with the right references and make it today. It could have happened two years ago.

Zach: And he wrote it in '73 or '74.

Todd: Is science fiction dead now?

Everyone: No.

Jeff: Absolutely not. In fact, I thought that it was and there's this William Browning Spencer who writes for Aborealis Books, which is a total indie book publisher. He is great.

Zach: And then there's Michael Swanwick, Neil Stephenson. Octavia Butler is still going strong.

Jeff: In fact, she's reached her Renaissance point right now.

Zach: Jack Womack.

Jeff: He wrote kind of a geeky story that was sort of cyberpunk, right, and then it turned into this amazing series that was just so right on. It just got better.

Zach: It's changed a bit. Since Gibson, especially, people are really dealing with computers as where computers before hadn't invaded our lives so much. Authors always had computers in their books, but I don't think back then they were thinking personal computer, they were still thinking institutional computer.

Todd: Mainframes in faraway buildings.

Zach: Yeah. So that's really changed.

Jeff: And there's Kim Stanley Robinson (aka "Spider" Robinson), who writes those hard Sci-Fi novels about the colonization of Mars and stuff, takes our actual technology that we have right now, that we could very well make—although it would cost way too much money—and terraforms Mars in a book. The hard Sci-Fi factor, you know, it's getting hard for me to write that sort of thing because I practically have to update my Ph.D. (Biochemistry—Harvard, Applied Physics—MIT)

Todd: All you guys are all published writers, right?

Everyone: Of course. Absolutely.

Zach: Who was Heinlein's college roommate?

Jake: No, no, let me come up with it. I should have brought my book.

Zach: They have cheat sheets.

Jake: The thing I wish would die off right now is the current media Sci-Fi—TV and movies—all the new, original programs, the Sci-Fi Channel and shit, I just wish that would just drop off. The more product there is, the more crap there's going to be and so I wish that it would go down and get back to where it was.

Jeff: It's just because *Star Trek: The Next Generation* was cool and they might have had another hit with *Red Dwarf*, so the next thing, you've got crap.

Jake: Like water down the flood line.

Jeff: Which is what the media does to everything, but it sickens me.

Jake: And then good stuff that comes through, you don't want to see it because you're afraid it's going to suck.

Jeff: It's like you're lucky if there's a halfway decent Sci-Fi movie. Usually, you'd have to put up with some crap in the movie, and say "I like Sci-Fi movies," just to say that you liked it.

Todd: So, how can someone {Harlan Ellison} win eight and a half Hugo Awards?

Zach: Well, it was a technicality, really.

Jake: It was like Milli Vanilli.

Zach: It was given. It was taken away. There were some questions of who wrote what first. That's all I really want to say. {Zach sounds a little pissed at the mention of Ellison, due to his smear campaign against Bloodhag's chum Forrest J. Ackerman.}

Todd: I know this is a really obscure question, but in the 1959 Hugo Awards, where the "Best New Writer" category wasn't won, but Brian W. Aldiss got a plaque for second place. How's that happen?

Zach: That's the fan-based one, right? That just must have been fans getting huffy.

Todd: Does Bloodhag feel that way?

Zach: I'm all about science fiction appreciation in general, any form. Some fans get real ticklish.

Jake: I think science fiction fans are the most rabid, dedicated fans to any sort of general genre than any other fan.

Todd: More than sports and porno?

Zach: More than porn. Sports would be second. Sci-Fi fans are completely dedicated. We've caught flack for what we've done.

Jeff: Sometimes, we go for the humor in the song as opposed to maybe just getting the facts in. Sometimes we do some biographical stuff that's actually a little bit editorial, so we've gotten called on that.

Todd: {roughly quoting a song} "Heinlein, misogynist, fascist"?

Jeff: Yeah.

Jake: There was a guy who did a Frank Herbert website. We told him about the song and gave him the lyrics. He just basically picked it apart.

Zach: On his bulletin board, he posted: "This is wrong."

Jeff: "'Wrote *Destination Void* too soon,' I think not." He didn't explain it.

Jake: It was actually our drummer at the time, Rodd, who went ahead and did it so I didn't have a chance to explain my lyrics to him to give any sort of backup, but I thought I summed up Frank Herbert. It is one of our shorter songs, so I don't say a lot of stuff I could have said.

Jeff: It's an earlier song. If you go back to our earlier songs, Jake and I were writing more for the corn factor—not with a K—which is a couple of our new songs. Since we've actually started doing it professionally, instead of just as a recording project, we realized, well, people would start calling us on our bullshit, basically. We had to do some research, albeit a little bit of research, and you're not going to see me at a convention unless I'm book signing.

Todd: So what happened to Philthy?

Jake: Philthy "Drum Machine" Taylor?

Todd: Is he playing Pong in the afterlife?

Jake: Well, see, what happened was...

Zach: He was a drunk.

Jake: Philthy left. For awhile, we were summoning the spirit of Frank Herbert to play the drums for us.

Jeff: Towards the end.

Jake: He wouldn't show up. We'd have his equipment. We would just channel Frank.

Jeff: We had an autograph and a picture and a candle and it worked. And the problem with that was he would leave his chords laying out all over the place and Jake and I would trip and we wouldn't be able to pull it back together.

Jake: That, and all the blown PAs.

Jeff: Lots of blown PA heads and PA speakers, that sort of thing.

Zach: He loved to blow PA systems.

Jeff: On our first show, he was not even nearly loud enough and we came out sounding like a Japanese noise band and people didn't even know it was metal. They just thought it was three guys with some distorted drum machine playing. All we could hear were his start-up notes and after that, forget about it.

Zach: But he had that great pause in that one song that we did every time.

Jeff: We were so tight.

Jake: And then we had the chance to practice with Lieutenant Governor Rodd Karp (TX), who recently retired and began writing his great stuff.

Zach: It just gelled.

Jake: It was fun.

Jeff: The first practice came together fairly well.

Jake: Rodd was constantly off stumping for something if he wasn't chaining himself to a tree. He was out, generally lobbying. Constantly late to practice. The entourage he brought with him on the road, his personal secretary, it was rough.

Zach: He was pretty hardcore.

Jake: So, we had to let him go.

Zach: Well, he's running that book militia up in the woods now.

Jeff: Armed book militia.

Zach: Yeah, he's pretty hardcore, so we got Master Carpenter (Master Carpenter, aka Codex 23. First appeared in print with *P.T.O.L.—Tales of the Elder Gods,* a manuscript unearthed with the Dead Sea Scrolls and subsequently suppressed by the Vatican. Alternately said to be a hoax perpetrated by the equally mysterious "Eternal 13," winner of the Marduk Award for best misrepresentation of a false idol.) to take his place and it's been even better.

Todd: What's the Codex 23?

Zach: Well, codex is just a gathering of knowledge. Twenty-three is Robert Anton Wilson's synchronous number. Chronomaster is time. (From the Greek, "kronus.")

Jeff: You realize that although you're allowed to print pictures of him playing, I'd rather that you did not describe him as he is in the band because he likes to preserve his anonymity.

Todd: Okay.

Zach: The man's got enemies. (Specifically for his movement "Psionetics—The Psychology of Psionics," opposed by several groups patently lacking in a sense of humor.)

Todd: Short quiz. What's the short story title of *Total Recall*?

Jake: *We Can Remember It for You Wholesale.*

Jeff: Are we allowed to consult our notes on these?

Todd: No. Did science fiction authors always have a predilection for girls with huge hooters or did that just come about since the first *Heavy Metal* movie?

Jake: That's the artists.

Zach: Except for Samuel R. Delany.

Jeff: Yeah, he's gay. Boris Vallejo and Frank Franzetta—the women they wrote about didn't have that big of tits, but man, did they have nice asses and thighs.

Zach: Heinlein had very strong, very intelligent, and big-breasted women.

Jeff: Redheads mostly.

Zach: And related. He's got the whole incest thing going.

Jeff: Piers Anthony, over the last ten years.

Zach: *The Tarot Series*, ever read that?

Jeff: *Tarot*'s nasty.

Zach: That's porn.

Jeff: After that, he gets into this dirty old man thing, where his characters are screwing these young, young girls. It's like the older you get as a Sci-Fi geek, the less action you get, I guess.

Todd: The more *Lolita* you get.

Jeff: We were just in Forrest J. Ackerman's (Ackerman, Forest J. Sci-Fi fan extraordinaire, coined the term "Sci-Fi." Editor *Famous Monsters of Filmland*. Largest Sci-Fi collection in the world. All around groovy guy.

Predilection for bad puns.) house and he asked us if we were all twenty-one and took us into his "bad room."

Zach: It was a picture of him with these two people dressed up like Vampirella.

Jeff: Babes! And all these rad pictures of Marlene Dietrich, all these hot chicks, a big-assed picture of Madonna.

Zach: He said he spent New Years at the Playboy Mansion with Hef. That was great, going to meet the man himself.

Jeff: He's a swinger. He's hot stuff.

Todd: Who wrote *The Glass Teat*?

Jeff: Harlan Ellison.

Todd: This is sort of a throwaway question for other bands, but I know you guys spend a lot of time thinking about stuff like this. What superhero or character in a book do you want to be and why?

Jeff: My thing is Fantastic Four, original Superheros. My two favorite superhero powers would be either to stretch, like Mr. Fantastic, 'cause you can imagine all the things you could do with that [snickering in the van] not only in the sack, but any other manner. I mean, you're perfect after that. And to become invisible. That harks back to my high school days when I wished I could be invisible and walk around in the girl's locker room.

Zach: Did you want to be an invisible woman?

Jeff: No, and you know the thing in Dungeons and Dragons (copyright Gary Gygax), where if you're invisible and you strike someone, you become visible, I didn't want that to happen either.

Jake: I'll go on The Fantastic Four. It would be the Human Torch, for me. Being able to catch on fire, or rather make random parts of my body burst into flame. And then, other than that, it would be The Incredible Hulk. That is basically me wanting to beat people up.

Zach: As far as comic books, I'm a big fan of Dr. Doom, but I wouldn't want really want to be scalded and wear an iron mask. I was big into the Arthurian legends.

Todd: Lancelot?

Zach: Lancelot was a pip. Galahad was worse. I always liked Perceval, and Arthur was pretty cool.

Todd: I've also heard that one of you has three nuts, that you guys just have a little bit more balls than your average geek heavy metal band. True?

Jake: We share the third nut. [laugher]

Zach: It's like the witches who share the one eye. (possible reference to early Science Fiction pioneer Will M. Shockspore.)

Jake: If you notice one of us rocking a little harder than the other, he would be the one in possession of the nut.

Jeff: Last night, I think Master Carpenter had the third nut, because he was forcing me to channel Kerry King from the grave, and he's not even dead yet. Like, I had to go into the future and channel him from the grave and come back with the power.

Todd: The answer to the question that Jake is struggling with: which science fiction writer has the largest religion going right now?

Everyone: It's got to be L. Ron Hubbard.

Todd: And that was Heinlein's roommate in college.

Zach: I don't think he was the one he made the bet with, though.

Todd: I thought it was.

Jake: I thought it was Campbell.

Zach: Campbell published it. First non-science fiction ever published in *Astounding*, John Campbell's magazine, was a Dianetics article.

Jake: I actually have the second publishing. A month later, he published an updated version of it.

Jeff: I've got the hardbound version of *Dianetics* from 1954 or whenever it came out.

Jake: It's pretty cool. The whole, big preface is John W. Campbell saying, "This is going to change the world. This is the new, future thing." He was completely sold on the whole deal.

Zach: Did you read the article, the whole thing?

Jake: Yeah, well, I'm trying to. It bugs me.

Zach: This is the closest I've ever gotten to Dianetics—except for filling out their survey because someone handed it to me on the street—was that, you read it along, and it would all be common sense, actually kinda modern for the time, like general self-help, new age-y kind of stuff, and then there'd be one little paragraph at the end of a section, and you'd be, "What the hell are you talking about?" Right now, it seems really tame, but I suppose in 1950 it was pretty revolutionary. I don't know. I just can't deal with it.

Jake: John W. Campbell, who was such a great proponent of Dianetics at the time, had a big falling out with Alfred Bester, whose *Demolished Man* book we gave you, because Bester was opposed to the whole thing because he saw how ridiculous it was. They were close pals for years.

Jeff: Interesting thing about that pal-dom is Heinlein—there was this bar where the geeky Sci-Fi writers would hook up, the ones who were the real deal, we're talking about Heinlein and such—and he actually liked Bester and brought him along and brought him into the thing.

Zach: Their own version of The Round Table. (reference to the Algonquin Round Table, taken up as a literary tradition. Heinlein et. al. Second or third science fiction version. Originally a group initiated by H.P. Lovecraft.)

Jeff: Yeah, basically. I was wondering about Forrest J. Ackerman. I know he was friends with A.E. VanVogt: great writer, early seventies. We were trying to pull some stories out of him. He was like, "Hmm, mmm." He knew but wouldn't tell us.

Jake: He went back to the raygun era and was talking about some really cool stuff. I am such a huge A.E. VanVogt fan.

Zach: With Ackerman, the same thing with Ray Bradbury. He was like, "Oh yeah, I'm going to go see Ray next week." And we're like, "Do tell."

Todd: Are you guys going to mass-produce the book chain? {Think of a chain wallet for a book.}

Jake: I'm trying to develop the technology. Currently, you have to poke the hole in the book. I'm trying to develop a thing that you can actually clamp on the end of the book so you can switch out the book easily. That's the only thing that's holding me back. This last tour, I actually sold a couple when we were on the road but I handmade them all from parts at the hardware store. I made bookmarks this tour, instead.

Todd: Have you hit up any science fiction authors to come and play at your shows or do a hootenanny?

Jake: No. My current plan is to get Ursula K. Le Guin to come to one of our shows in Portland, 'cause I love her.

Jeff: He's got a thing for her.

Jake: I need to talk to her.

Zach: She won't return any of his phone calls and he calls all the time.

Todd: Are there any science fiction authors you know who are in bands? They don't have to be good bands.

Zach: Does Steven fucking King count?

Jeff: I guess he does.

Jake: Kurt Danielson, who was the guitar player for Tad, I talked to him one time—he was a big Philip K. Dick fan—said that he was currently writing a SF book, so whether or not that's ever going to see the light of day is another question.

Zach: So, it's just us, really.

Jeff: And he's actually in a band called Valis.

Jake: Which is another Philip K. Dick title.

Jeff: *Valis* and *Ubik* are part of the trilogy

Zach: *Ubik*'s not part of the trilogy.

Jeff: It's not?

Zach: No, it's by itself.

Jeff: *Valis* and *Ubik* are two books I think that should be taught in high school along with that Frank Zappa autobiography we've got floating around in the van.

Zach: It's funny.

Jeff: It's not just funny, it's illuminating.

Todd: Take this as you will. Who's the most "metal" science fiction author?

Jeff: Michael Moorcock.

Zach: As far as being just full-on metal, yeah.

Todd: Qualify that.

Jake: His direct relation to Hawkwind, Blue Oyster Cult.

Todd: Rolling Stones.

Jake: The Rolling Stones did a song called "2,000 Light-years from Home."

Zach and Jeff: Which is James Tiptree Jr.'s song title. {Tiptree has a collection of short stories called *Ten Thousand Light-years from Home*}

Todd: With the Rolling Stones, I'm thinking of Harlan Ellison, who wrote *Spider Kiss*.

Zach: Just the guys with the big swords and a lot of killing.

Jeff: Elric is the possibly the most metal Sci-Fi, and Corum, plus there's Jerry Cornelius. (All references to Moorcock's multi-dimensional uber-epic of the "eternal champion." In moments of wry humor, Bloodhag like to refer to themselves as "eternal librarians.")

Zach: He was a hippie.

Jeff: Yeah, but he played guitar.

Zach: That's true.

Jeff: He was a guitar player in every book of the Jerry Cornelius series. At least once or twice, he ended up jamming with this psychedelic blues band. He'd just sit in with them.

Jake: Michael Moorcock did write lyrics for Blue Oyster Cult, and especially Hawkwind.

Jeff: I have a Nik Turner album on Cleopatra that has Michael Moorcock on it reading a poem. He flew to Texas and read the poem live at a Hawkwind show.

Zach: "Veteran of a Thousand Psychic Wars," that one in *Heavy Metal*, he wrote that.

Jake: Moorcock wins "most metal," hands down.

Jeff: What about Philip K. Dick and Frank Herbert?

Zach: For influence on metal, Tolkien.

Todd: No shit. Burzum, the Nordic death metal band, the name's from Hobbit-speak meaning "complete darkness."

Jeff: He's almost tied.

Zach: For influence, Tolkien. Obviously from Zeppelin, on—the elves.

Jeff: Everyone says Zeppelin started heavy metal.

Zach: I don't, but they're part of the whole thing.

Jake: There's a great website called The Tolkien Music List. This guy had researched everything that even mentioned Tolkien: song title, content, live music. We're listed on there.

Todd: Which science fiction author would make the best president?

Jeff: I'd say Octavia Butler because she's brilliant, she's got really good politics, she's a woman, and she's black.

Jake: Any president who would get the fucking Scientologists off our asses.

Todd: How in the hell did you guys score an actual library tour?

Zach: Well, we played the Seattle library and the guy who set it up really liked it, and I schmoozed, because he loved it. I told him to talk us up and he went to a library conference, and that's exactly what he did. He started emailing these people back and forth and sent them a tape so they're quite aware; they have fair warning.

Jeff: He warned them that we were brutal.

Zach: My big goal is to do the National Teen Read Week.

Jake: Which is another tour, which has been possibly sort of dangled out there.

Zach: I think we need to do this tour, and if it works out, maybe word will get around.

Todd: Are you going to get government funding?

Zach: That would be government funded.

Jeff: Our next record will be sponsored in part, if not largely, by the Timberland Regional Library District.

Zach: Yeah, because they're paying us and that's going to put out our next record.

Jake: We're going to contact the National Literacy Council at some point. I'd like to talk to them but I don't think, necessarily, they're going to be too keen on it.

Jeff: I think our choice of musical genres, at times, alienates us. We also end up on shows—if we play a brutal metal show, they're grim and they don't understand. And if we play a punk show, we're metal.

Zach: I get in a book conversation every show, at least once.

Jeff: I've had nothing but positive feedback, except from the drunken asshole. I've never had anybody come up and have someone say, "You know what? You guys suck."

Jake: We kind of make the cream rise to the top, because I guarantee you, whoever out there that reads books is going to come up and talk to us at the end of the show, which is gratifying.

Jeff: At least the people who book the shows know we're going to throw books and yet it comes as a large surprise to a lot of people, except in Seattle, where they know and it's greeted with open arms.

Todd: Zach, how much do you bleed when you floss with the E string? {Otherwise known as doing bass slides with his teeth.}

Zach: Well, I've been known to lose chunks of teeth and I learned my lesson with that one—not to do the solo to "Phillip K. Dick" with my teeth.

Luckily, my mother works at a dental clinic and I got that fixed on the cheap.

Jake: He earned the name, "Notch."

Zach: I did lose a good chunk of the tooth.

Todd: Jake, have you ever faced litigation for throwing books and inflicting severe paper wounds?

Jake: No litigation yet. That would have really scared me.

Jeff: You wasted a dude right in the face and broke his fucked-up Mongoose-style glasses.

Jake: That was a straight head bash. He was up by the side of the stage and I hit him on the head. I didn't know he had his sunglasses across the top of his head, and I split them right in half. He's all, "These were eighty dollar sunglasses." Then there was this really big straightedge kid. He and his friend were threatening me. We finished the song up, and he said, "You hit me in the face with the book." And his friend goes, "He's going to kick your ass." And I'm like, "You're not going to kick my ass." And he's like, "What do you mean?" And I'm like, "Well, you can't kick my ass. How about that, motherfucker?" The worst part was after the show, I went up to him and tried to apologize. He wouldn't take my apology. "You marked my face." He had this little, tiny blue mark under his eye.

Jeff: The biggest pussy on the planet.

Jake: The guy was a foot and a half taller than me. "Dude, I meant no disrespect. I was aiming towards you but I wasn't aiming at your head." He just turned away and walked off. That's cool that he didn't go through with his urge to crack me in half. The first book I ever threw out, hit a really, really cute girl right in the face.

Jeff: It hit Brent's girlfriend right between the eyes.

Brent: Pretty much point blank from five feet away.

Jeff: And she was such a trooper, man. She fuckin' went for it.

Jake: That was the curse. I was always going to hit the biggest guy and the smallest girl in the head.

Todd: What makes what you do above and beyond being just a schtick? Because I think it's actually really good music, insightful lyrics, and a great time. Isn't that the point?

Jake: I think that's what it is. At one point, we became serious about the metal and crossed over from being a joke band into being, "Okay, we're the real deal." And then also our lyrics, although some of them are funny, Jake's always clever with the lyrics.

Jake: I really do try to get some information in there. Beyond that, it was conceived in humor, but the deal with promoting literacy is legitimate.

Todd: Do all you guys read vigorously?

Zach: Copiously.

Jeff: This is probably one of the quietest tour vans you're ever going to be in because at least three of the people—nose in a book.

Zach: The other thing about schtick—from the Yiddish—all schtick means is that we have an angle. And it actually helps us keep really focused. We've tapped a rich enough vein so we'll be able to do this forever. I've sat down and written down all the science fiction authors I could think of off the top of my head one day and I got a hundred and then I went and cross referenced through all my big collection of short stories. I now have a hundred and fifty and I know I missed people.

Jeff: And that's, like, two CDs worth of songs? [laughter]

Zach: And the metal is just 'cause of the resonant themes.

Jake: Heavy metal owes a debt to science fiction thematically. Titles, everything like that. Black Sabbath.

Zach: That Queen cover that uses The Astounding Robot. (*Astounding Science Fiction*, ed. John Campbell.)

Jeff: I would seriously like to go on record as saying that I believe that reading is truly punk rock and I believe that it's truly punk rock to teach yourself through reading, and I'm totally into that and I've gone off on tirades on stage, and if you think it's punk to be ignorant, you're wrong. Because it's punk to teach yourself. It's not punk to go to school. Go to school, have fun. I'm just saying it's punk to learn and it's punk to know and be wiser than those who are supposedly in control.

Jake: If you're a punk surrounded by jocks, every day in your school, I know that you think you're smarter than the jocks, so you better read.

Jeff: You've gotta be smarter than them, and to a large degree—half the dudes I knew in high school were metal dudes with their nose in a Tolkien book or any sort of fantasy book, and I'd be sitting there with Arthur C. Clarke, and we'd be sitting right next to each other. They'd be like, "You're a freak," and I'd be like, "You're a dirtbag." But, at the same time, we were both smarter than everyone else in the class.

Jake: That's the real crossover. Literacy.

Todd: Are you guys going to open your lyrical aperture up a little bit to get people like Vonnegut and Orwell?

Jeff: Vonnegut is absolutely a Sci-Fi writer, as is J.G. Ballard.

Zach: Vonnegut, any statement he's ever made about what type of writer he is—he's a Sci-Fi writer. He just gets stuck in literature.

Todd: There's a lot of sociology, humanity, and politics to him.

Jake: That's why I absolutely love Vonnegut, man. Not only does it make you think about things socially, his use of science fiction is a frame, and that explains everything else—just like every writer who's written SF and is taken as serious literature. He also manages to evoke all sorts of emotional things out of you because you can really relate to a lot of his characters. I know I can.

Jeff: He tickles your funny bone, too.

Jake: Yeah, he makes you laugh. It's got everything I want. He's so straightforward.

Todd: He's so insightful.

Jake: Absolutely. He can say more in just a little sentence than most people get tangled up in huge books.

Zach: Orwell is in literature; well, his essays aren't Sci-Fi, but his main novel is. (*1984*, duh.)

Jeff: Aldous Huxley.

Zach: Aldous Huxley wrote a lot of Sci-Fi. Doris Lessing writes a lot. She got nominated for the Nobel Prize.

Jake: William S. Burroughs.

Jeff: And that will be on a forthcoming record. There will be an album called *Appetite for Deconstruction*.

Jake: We're currently writing songs for those authors. Vonnegut is almost done. Ballard has been done for awhile. And we've still got to do Orwell, Huxley, and Lessing.

Jake: We've conceived other—not concept albums in the classic term...

Jeff: Theme albums.

Jake: Grouping albums.

Jeff: Another single of child Sci-Fi writers. Madeline L'Engle.

Everyone: John Christopher, Lloyd Alexander, Daniel Mathis Pinkwater, Roald Dahl, C.S. Lewis, L. Frank Baum.

Jake: And that's going to be called *Reading Rainbow Bridge*.

Jeff: A little Norse.

Jake: We're going to try to get full, furry boot, Man-o-war outfits for that.

Todd: Who's the most anarchic science fiction writer?

Jake: Ursula K. LeGuin. She did write *The Dispossessed*.

Zach: Doris Lessing was a hardcore Communist and then got disillusioned. That's not really anarchy.

Jeff: But George Orwell definitely teaches you some things that every anarchist should learn.

Zach: Burroughs.

Jeff: Burroughs has got to be it. And even J.G. Ballard to a certain degree.

Zach: *The Dispossessed* is a study of what happens when you have one planet that are anarchists and one planet that are capitalists.

Jeff: And the melding of the two and how they kind of end up being the same.

Zach: They meet each other, sort of.

Todd: Do you think that women science fiction writers have been marginalized?

Jeff: Throughout the '60s and early '70s they were, but not so much now. Absolutely not.

Zach: There's a lot of female science fiction authors and a lot of credit is being given to the earlier ones.

Jake: There are a lot of women Sci-Fi writers who do a lot of the popular Sci-Fi, like *Dragonlance* kind of stuff.

Todd: Like Anne McCaffery?

Jake: Yeah, and those great, big thick ones with princesses on the cover. Books like that are always in the store. They are selling huge amounts. It's not like they're bad. I don't read them myself.

Jeff: Honestly, some of the best science fiction writers of the '60s were Joanna Russ and Ursula K. LeGuin. Joanna Russ is a god. James Tiptree Jr. {a woman writing as a man} is amazing.

Zach: Some of the first Sci-Fi I ever read was Ursula K. LeGuin, Anne McCaffery, and Madeline L'Engle.

Jeff: *A Wrinkle in Time* blew my little mind away. I read that in second grade.

Zach: I was like, "Oh my god, a big, pulsing brain."

Jake: Currently, the field is wide open. I think at one point, especially Heinlein and those guys, it was all boys and when the women came in, they were like, "Get out of our club."

Zach: I think it's Theodore Surgeon. There was a big thing with James Tiptree Jr. He wrote this huge essay about he was sure that James Tiptree Jr. was a man, for sure. "There's no way James Tiptree Jr. is a woman."

Jeff: And Ursula Le Guin the whole time was like, "Nuh uh."

Zach: I actually have a series of Tiptree stories where that's the introduction and then in the postscript, he's like, "I was wrong. Sorry."

Todd: Who was Charles Manson's favorite science fiction author?

Jake: Robert A. Heinlein.

Todd: Absolutely correct. Have you ever stalked a Sci-Fi writer?

Jake: We stalked them in our store.

Zach: Well, Jake stalked Ursula.

Jake: Yeah.

Zach: He's really harmless, Ursula.

Jake: My problem is when I sing her song, I get so choked up thinking about her, and my glasses fog up and I get all misty. I sorta lose track of what I'm doing.

Todd: Did any of you cry when they took out the card catalog at the library?

Jeff: I fucking hated card catalogs.

Jake: I like card catalogs. I just knew how to use one really well. I'm not a proponent of complete computer takeover. Although I don't think that people should read them this way, I think that all books should be transferred to digital media for posterity's sake.

Jeff: I think they should be sealed as books, in vaults, forever. 'Cause you can read a book and translate cryptology of any language on earth. Someone with a brain could very easily do that. But there's no fucking way that you're going to find a book—microfiche, you can see it, it's there—but when it's in a computer, and I think you're right. The whole Library of Congress should be digitized. I'm just saying that that's not what's going to last.

Todd: And you have to couple that with you can't take a computer to a shitter and if you lose a book, you're out some bucks, not hundreds or thousands.

Jeff: And if you do, you're such a geek. Those are strong words coming from a guy like me.

Zach: Actually, I'm reading a book by this guy Stanislaw Lem which is all about way in the future they're digging up the ruins of civilization—the full earth—which is supposed to be a little in the future from now. And in the destroyed civilization, there was a pathogen brought in from space from a shuttle or something that destroyed all of the paper in the world in the course of two weeks and it destroyed civilization.

Jeff: There goes my theory.

Zach: Money, books, everything was lost. In the book, there was this thing called The Third Pentagon, which was buried in The Rocky Mountains, and they found this sealed chamber that had this one guy's memoirs. Aside from that, it's like *The Trial* by Kafka.

Todd: Is there a line from a book you can quote that changed your way of thinking permanently? Mine is, "The Dark Ages. They aren't over yet." That's a paraphrase of Vonnegut.

Jeff: I've never had any one line, but I have to admit, the first time I read my first science fiction, when I read J.R.R. Tolkien and moved on from there, it just made me a different person from who I was before. When I was a little kid, when I went from dinosaurs to Sci-Fi and I read a lot of mysteries. I know this is stupid, but growing up in the '80s when I read *Stranger in a Strange Land*, it actually made me think in a different fashion. *Lathe of Heaven* is another. There are Sci-Fi books. *Cat's Cradle*. And also a lot of Philip K. Dick's books—*Ubik*—and I read that when I was already fully grown. *Ubik* changed my mental attitude completely. It made me take stock of the world around me. It actually made me sit there for awhile and go, "Holy shit, my idea of the world is not true and possibly I might be all wrong." And I don't know of any other genre of popular literature that can do that to a person.

Zach: Speculative fiction is really where it's at.

Jake: The one line I like in *The Hobbit* is, "There are Moonletters here." [laughter, lots of it.]

Jeff: Only we would laugh at that joke.

Jake: That, and the little speech that the Lakeman makes, "Black arrow..."
Jeff: What about in *Dune*, "Even my name is a killing word."
Jake: That's not in the book.
Zach: He actually does say that. He's in his spice trance.
Jeff: "Usul no longer needs the weirding module."
Todd: Quick association. Canadian border patrol.
Jake: Abridged version.
Jeff: We're run afoul of the Americans on the Canadian side.
Jake: Dirty Americans.
Jeff: Glock-wearing, swagging losers.
Jake: I must put something off. It just comes out of my skin, so we get pulled over every time.
Zach: We were all in shirts and ties. I was driving and they said, "What do you do?" And I said I owned my own pinball arcade and toy store. And they're like, "Pull over." [laughter]
Jeff: They're like, "What do you do?" "I'm an audio engineer." "Pull over."
Jake: The last time we went there, it was pretty funny. We had been given pot by the band we played with—called Drugstore—so we did our best to demolish all of it before we had to leave the next day. We even ate it to make sure there was nothing left as we drove across the border. They make us pull over, as usual. We get out. They search the van. They come out and go, "Well, we found a roach down in the driver's seat cushion.
Zach: Jeff was, "I do not know what to say to that."
Jeff: 'Cause I didn't. We'd already been searched and given the full-ball, up against the "uuugggg." They didn't break out the gloves.
Todd: That was going to be my next question. Did you hear the unnerving snap of rubber?
Jeff: No, he didn't. I was so sweaty and disgusting from playing the night before and I wouldn't put my hands down there, to be honest, until I took a shower, and I wouldn't recommend anyone else do it and he had to. And he was washing his hands and he hadn't been wearing rubber gloves, and I saw the look on his face and I kind of smirked, and he's was all like, "You think I like doing this?!" I just shrugged. That's what you get, motherfucker.
Jake: He grabbed mine and I was like, "It's all real." [laughter] The funny thing is that he wanted me to stick my leg out straight while I was sitting down and turn down the cuff of my pants. And I couldn't do it. I'm like, "Dude, I'm fat." The last time we went up there, they found a roach in the seat cushion—this wasn't the ball touching time—they bust us on it and they go, "But we can tell it's really old, so you guys get out of here."
Jeff: He throws our IDs on the counter and says, "You boys get out of here."

Jake: They let us go, right, and we go back out and the roach is sitting on the seat. He gave it back to us.

Jeff: It was so old and decrepit. There was no way you could do anything with it.

Jake: It was probably from the previous owner of the van.

Todd: Jake, how often do you rip your pants?

Jake: Lately, I've been trying to get pants that fit me a little bit better, but I would say—there's no wood to knock on—every third show I rip out my pants.

Jeff: I've ripped out my pants on numerous occasions.

Zach: I've never ripped out my pants.

Todd: Okay, final words—give me some inspiration for America's youth.

Zach: Read to live. Live to read.

Jake and Jeff: And there's R.I.F. Reading is... fuuuuck you.

•   •   •

"I'd rather be poor and live like shit and do what I love to do than be rich or even make a sufficient amount of money and be miserable at what I'm doing."

—Sean

WHAT'S A TRIP WITHOUT A LITTLE DANGER? AN INTERVIEW WITH TOYS THAT KILL

Although we live about thirty miles away from one another on opposite sides of Los Angeles, as the crow flies, I first saw and hung out with Toys That Kill at a show in Erie, Pennsylvania in the summer of 2001. Attendance was sparse, which gave me time for reflection. Was I vaguely interested in them before they plugged in because of the FYP pedigree? Did I secretly wish to join the many who have seen Todd Congelliere piss his pants? Did I have ulterior motives? Perhaps. Tours converged and I got to see them about ten times in row.

They rock, and I dare say more so than their previous band. They're loud and fast, to be sure, while remaining tight and crunching and producing music as sparkley as the hood of a flipped-over van on asphalt (more on van accidents in the interview). Think bombastic and playful without getting too arty. What strikes me, after listing to their debut album, *The Citizen Abortion*, for over the hundredth time, is how well they make songs. I know, I know, songcraft is usually a dispersion heaped on bands like Foreigner, and shouldn't be used when you like a punk band, but I say it's true. There's something more than your basic 1-2-3-4-go! attack that keeps me coming back.

If the pain of getting cracked in the nutsack could be turned into a good, good sound, it'd be Toys That Kill. They're instantly likeable without being genre-locked ball lickers and chart slaves.

Todd Congelliere (Cong): guitar, vocals
Sean Cole: guitar, vocals
Casey: bass, backup vocals
Dennis: drums

Todd: So, a little background for clarification's sake. You were in a band called FYP, which stood for...
Cong: Five Year Plan.
Todd: And you were together for...
Cong: Ten years.
Todd: So, the five year plan didn't work out?
Cong: We wanted overtime, for the kids.
Sean: You can't take us, or the things we say or do, too literally.

Cong: That's a bad, bad maneuver.

Sean: They're sort of shrouded in metaphors and cynicism and jokes.

Todd: What would be the cynical joke of Five Year Plan, then?

Cong: That it existed.

Todd: So, the last FYP album was called *Toys That Kill*.

Cong: Yeah.

Todd: And then, you broke up and the next day, you played as...

Sean: It wasn't that condensed.

Cong: It was sort of planned.

Todd: Then, why? Why change your name when people know it?

Cong: That was one of the things. To get rid of all the FYP sensibilities. That was one of the things that was bumming me out. I hate it when people ask us to play "Bring It On." It's the stupidest thing I've ever heard in my life.

Sean: Kind of like cleaning the slate. I think the thing is a lot of bands will sacrifice having a good time and sacrifice loving what they're doing just so they can keep the name and they will play songs that they hate just because their whole motive is making money or sustaining popularity, where we just couldn't deal with that. We didn't want to go that route. We wanted to start a new, fresh concept that we'd be proud of and enjoy doing.

Cong: It's funner to start over, too. The first Toys That Kill tour was the best thing in the world compared to the last FYP tour. Sean and I like the music better. We had Chachi in there.

Todd: Thematically, then, what's changed over the years? Did you get too mature for toilet tard (i.e. "tardcore") music? Did you just learn how to play your instruments?

Cong: Neither.

Sean: Not to toot my own horn here...

Todd: Toot it. Be honest.

Sean: I think that after the first 7"s and the early line-up, a big problem was there was always a constant revolving door of members and it didn't really matter how musically talented you were. You just kind of went for it and there was a charm to it, but I think once Todd and I were a more steady lineup, if you listen to FYP's last record, it's not virtuoso music, but it's pretty musically proficient. It's simple music, but it's tight and not all over the place like the early stuff and I think even with *My Man Grumpy*, the same thing—a pretty well put together record. *Toilet Kids Bread* was kind of pivotal and shaky in that department, but a lot of people, when they think of FYP, they think of some early stuff.

Cong: Yeah. *Dance My Dunce* and before. It's just like a joke that you keep on saying. It's an all right joke. You keep telling it. The more you say it, everyone's like, "Shut up" and rolling their eyes, but there's new people coming in and they want you to play songs that you were playing eight years ago and it just got to a point where, "Ummm, that's not funny anymore." To us. If it was still funny to us, we'd still be doing FYP.

Todd: What's the law of three for you guys? Why is every album three words?

Sean: I think it's just fun.

Cong: I think it's just coincidence.

Todd: Coincidence?

Cong: *My Man Grumpy* was when we actually figured it out. It definitely wasn't planned.

Todd: Is it planned now?

Cong: No. Toys That Kill, *The Citizen Abortion*, I had no idea. I mean, I knew those were three words. I didn't think about it.

Sean: Autism.

Cong: Yeah. I didn't even think about that until the record was out. Then I was like, "Oh, man." Me, personally, I don't want to continue with things, even though we did the Descendents thing where we called our last record the new band that we were going to be and that was all planned. (The last Descendents album was called All. Milo, their singer, split to get a higher education. The rest of the band continued as the band, All.)

Sean: I think, too, using the *Toys That Kill* title and then into the band name, it's kind of reflective of bands that do that. We're continuing on a cycle. Some of the Toys That Kill songs were going to be new FYP songs. And Todd and I are two-thirds of FYP and, in a sense, we wanted to have a clean slate but it's not like we're playing prog metal all of a sudden. We wanted there to be some relation.

Todd: So, how did these two guys find you, Casey?

Casey: I don't know. They moved to San Pedro and they couldn't get rid of me, pretty much.

Todd: When was the first time they started calling you Chachi?

Casey: That must have been Hal. A couple years ago.

Sean: A real trendsetter, that guy.

Todd: Do you really look like Scott Baio?

Casey: I don't think so. Maybe a couple years ago.

Cong: He has the aura of Chachi. He used to wear the sleeveless shirts.

Sean: He's an amalgamation of Ralph Macchio and Scott Baio. Originally, it was Chachi-o.

Todd: How do you feel about that?

Casey: I don't care. Whatever. I used to be Chachi-o Viagra.

Cong: Now it's Chachi Ferrari.

Todd: Casey, have you ever misinterpreted and lyrics to a Toys That Kill song?

Casey: Actually, the first tour, I sang the backups wrong every night. In "Amphetamine Street," I would sing "when the scream…" I got it wrong.
Sean: "When the scream MU330."
Casey: Todd had the lyrics printed up so I could practice, and I was, like, "What?" "Where the scream mutes the sound"?
Todd: Everyone has to answer this question. What does your dad do?
Sean: My real dad? [laughter] He works at a mental hospital driving medical supplies. My latest stepdad is a sales representative for an optical lens company and the stepdad who raised me works at an oil refinery.
Casey: My dad's a longshoreman down on the docks and he's been doing that for almost twenty years now.
Cong: My dad's a teacher, but he really wants to be a football coach because he used to be a football coach.
Todd: What does he teach?
Cong: English, P.E., any sport.
Sean: And he wears those short coach shorts.
[laughter]
Cong: I don't want to talk about my dad's balls, all right? I'll talk about anything else except my dad's balls. They're fantastic balls, obviously.
Sean: [in Todd voice] They made me.
Todd: Todd or Sean, what's the worst mangling of a lyric screamed back at you?
Cong: I've actually heard on the last FYP album, where it goes, "Wherever the creeps go at night, I'll be there with my fork and knife." Someone emailed me, "'Where ever the creeps go at night, I'll be there stabbing you with my fucking knife.' That song's badass, holmes." I almost believed it.
Todd: The song, "Bullet from the Sky." Where'd that come from? Are there a lot of people in San Pedro on the Fourth of July getting really happy and shooting their guns into the air?
Cong: San Pedro is probably the capital of shooting in the air. In the news before New Years, there were billboards and signs everywhere.
Todd: Yeah, there was one down the street from me. "Save your love ones. Don't shoot your firearms in celebration," all in Spanish.
Cong: Last year I actually saw a couple of news reports or little station IDs saying that, but this year, I saw probably fifteen. I think it was the thing to do.
Sean: In San Pedro, I've never had any problems with violence and I like living there, but it's gotten to the point where you're kicking back in your house and these shots ring out, "bap, bap, bap, bap" and I look over to my roommate. "Is that a gun?" He's like, "Yeah." I'm, "Oh." Then you go about your business. If my mom heard four gunshots, she'd be on the phone, calling the police. It's, you know, whatever.

Todd: For people who couldn't know, how does San Pedro infuse itself into your band? There are very few places in America where people are extremely proud of where they live. I can think, right off the bat, Austin and Boston.

Cong: There's definitely thick Pedro pride going on. I love the city. I'm glad I live there.

Sean: We're not skinheads about it. We don't have the Pedro patch.

Cong: There's definitely some Gestapo Pedro guys who will lay you flat if you talk shit about Pedro.

Sean: Really. It's totally true. There's this old story. A friend of mine's band played and there was this one person in question, during this set, they're playing at Sacred Grounds (a local coffee shop) and he's like, "It's great being here in Pedro. I'd rather be in Temecula right now." This guy comes up to him; "Talking shit about Pedro, bro?"

Casey: There are a lot of people like that.

Sean: I don't give a shit. Living in San Pedro, it's a nice little town. There's a lot of mom and pop businesses. Lots of cool scenery. It's not all hyped up with malls and crap like that. It feels like you're living in an old city. The rent's cheap. Can't beat it. That's it.

Cong: I think the biggest thing is the Rite Aid. That's the Burger Barn coming to town. When I first moved there, I thought the whole pride thing was just stupid. So what? It's a city. Now, I understand it more, what they're talking about.

Casey: I grew up wearing San Pedro sweatshirts as a little kid. I got one this Christmas from my dad. "Thanks, Dad. I'm not going to wear this."

Sean: A lot of these lunkheads aren't trying to preserve any sort of ethic. It just seems like a reason to gang up and be a dick. It's not like, "We've got to save our little city."

Cong: There are those people who stand up for, always talk about, and love the background and history of Pedro. Mike Watt (Minutemen, Firehose, Dos, Madonabees) is one of them.

Sean: You can tell the difference between almost gang mentality and people who are down to preserve—we're all down to preserve—the things that exist. When they tried to build a Taco Bell and wreck our houses, we all went to the city council meeting.

Todd: Isn't there a Taco Bell several blocks from your house?

All: There's two.

Cong: They wanted one every two blocks, pretty much.

Sean: They were calling it the Taj Mahal of Taco Bells.

Todd: Wouldn't it be more like the *menage a trois* of Taco Bells?

Sean: As a side note, good old Bob Congelliere…

Cong: There were fifteen of our friends at this hearing and there was one guy who was for Taco Bell that was a citizen who lived in San Pedro. It was my crazy uncle that I didn't even know existed. [in uncle voice] "My name's Bob Congelliere and I love Taco Bell."

Casey: And that was his only defense.

Cong: [still in uncle voice] "It's supposed to be the Taj Mahal of Taco Bells."

Sean: [in goofy voice] "I love Taco Bell."

Cong: And there's a fucking Taco Bell on 10th Street and on 1st. So they need one on 4th Street? I don't know. Poor Uncle Bob. He's a championship swimmer, I hear.

Sean: He probably gets a six pack of tacos and starts doing the backstroke.

Todd: There's a lot of anti-establishmentarianism in your lyrics. Is that intentional?

Cong: I don't think anything's intentional.

Todd: But there's a definite recurring theme. In "50 Geniuses," you say "they only wanna raise you only if you get them high," and in "String," it's "Sometimes a string's just a fucking string."

Sean: It's not like a super-acute attack on anything in particular, but I think for all of us it's an inherent thing. It's just something that just kind of exists. I think we're all here and we all believe what we believe for a reason. And getting into punk rock and stuff like that has an effect on how you view the world. We never use rhetoric.

Cong: I don't want to ever get accused of sloganeering or anything like that.

Sean: Everything's always very personal, but there is an underlying anti-establishment vibe underneath.

Cong: Even saying that bugs me, but at the same time, only because, if you're in a punk band, you're lumped in with all the other punk bands and then, all of a sudden, you're lumped in with all the bands that are lumped in with the punk bands that will listen to Propagandhi and go, "I'm gonna write about this, too." And they just have no idea what they're talking about, for one thing. They have no idea on how to write a song and that's the worst thing.

Sean: You have to talk about what you know. Real feelings. Even some of the greatest rock bands have that air of rebellion. It's not necessarily like Crass but it's like, "My Generation." We're fucked up but who cares.

Todd: Sean, do you have a flamboyantly gay hip hop side project?

Sean: There was a time where I borrowed this guy's four track before I had my own. The idea originally came up was when we were on tour in Canada. Me and Greg from The Grumpies were bored out of our fucking minds and thought it would be a funny idea to make a fake band compilation and so we're writing all these names in a notebook and the idea was his part would be all these fake Huntsville, Alabama bands and I'd be all the fake Pedro bands. The whole concept behind it was you get whatever small group of friends and you get all these fake bands spanning all these genres—emo, death metal—whatever you could conjure up. The Pink MCs was one of the names I came up for a flamboyantly gay hip-hop thing. So, I got back—it was something you just say on a whim and it just stuck with me—so I decided to buckle down and do it. That was one of the bands that I recorded. I got a couple of friends to do that.

Todd: Can you give us a sample lyric?

Sean: [smiling, embarrassed]

Cong: "Sperm don't burn unless it's got the germ in it."

Sean: "I'm a cum clucker. I'm a cocksucker. Who needs a pussy when I make a man's butt pucker."… so, it wasn't really a side project. We never performed.

Casey: There was almost a performance, though.

Sean: I think the other guys got cold feet. It's a commitment.

Cong: Even Hal had his second thoughts about it, actually playing live. He's like, "Dude, once it gets serious and we're actually singing these lyrics. We're not gay, but…"

Sean: The only worry I had was that you're—if you're a homophobe, you're not going to sing these lyrics, not even in jest. I was kind of worried if we became a real band, would we be offending people who were really gay? I don't know. It seems kind of silly. It was all in good humor.

Todd: Individually, you have to answer this question. In which way do you feel obsolete?

Cong: Computers are taking everybody's jobs away. That's one reason. That song, "Playdough," that *Twilight Zone* part (the sound bite) was actually inserted into that song afterwards. The lyrics are pretty much about Silicon Valley and how they work people into doing the grind, man. And the next thing you know, you're in a job that's an internet startup and it's totally bountiful and you're making six figures a year, and the next thing you know, you're not. Because they're just going to find parts to replace everything.

Casey: Lately, I've been having a hard time coming to grips with reality. [lots of laughter] Trying to work and make rent and stuff. It's been really hard for me since our last tour.

Cong: Tour makes you hate work.

Casey: Yeah.

Cong: I'm into it now, when I'm getting to a point where I want to work more hours because I'll get paid more hours and I actually like the job that I'm at. But, when you go on tour, when you get back, you're just not into that mode. It takes at least a month. It's just like the whole drug thing. If you do drugs, you're pretty much a loser, right? But, when you're sitting there actually on drugs, you're like, "Hmm. This is good. This is how I want to live. I don't want to wake up in the morning and have to work for somebody who I don't really like." But when you're off drugs, you're like, "What are those losers doing?" I don't know if that makes sense. But when you're actually on tour, you get into the mode that you can't really break out of until being back home for a few months and you're actually settled and you're content and you're always thinking, "Is somebody else making me feel content about this job or am I making myself feel content about it?" You just get to a point of questioning your head. Especially on weed, man.

Casey: Paranoid.

Sean: How do I feel obsolete? I'd have to say that the biggest thing is that I don't understand or enjoy pop culture after 1985. Everyone's all into these shitty TV programs. What's that one that everyone watches on Thursday? *Dawson's Creek*? Friends who I value, friends who I think are intelligent get into these lame TV shows and these lame pop references. If I watch TV, I'll watch *The Simpsons*. I do like new movies. Movies are coming out all right, more or less. I don't give two shits about—everyone loves Christina Aguilera—people I know. People I sit down and try to have a conversation with and they'll bring that up. Their whole lives are surrounded by reading shitty magazines and watching crappy TV and I just can't relate to it.

Cong: It's weird because when Nirvana was huge and all these bands were coming out, I actually liked the mainstream, sorta. I could look back at it now and say that that's way better than what's going on now or before that, because before that, it was New Kids on the Block and Michael Jackson ruled for ten years and now he's back. What the fuck is all that about? People totally destroyed New Kids on the Block and they tore down their posters of Joey McIntyre. The next thing you know, their daughters are into the Backstreet Boys. I know new babies are born every day and they don't know about New Kids on the Block, and they're going to like something like New Kids on the Block, but I just don't know how history can repeat itself so badly. Seriously, it's like Hitler.

Sean: The band that you like shows up in a shitty magazine like *Spin*. Like, if Nirvana—I love reading about Nirvana. I loved Nirvana. I thought they were a great band. In pop culture, per se, just because something is popular, just because it's something everyone else is into, doesn't negate the fact that I can get into to it. That was a time for the mainstream where I had some interest in it, where Nirvana was peaking.

Cong: When they were on top of the whole fuckin' world, you actually sorta wanted to watch the American Music Awards or the MTV Music Awards just out of curiosity's sake.

Sean: Just to see the wacky shit they might do or the sarcasm or the cynicism.

Casey: At least they were a rock band.

Cong: A rock band that was good. No matter what, they were great.

Sean: They wore shitty clothes, had fucked up hair.

Cong: Nowadays, the American Music Awards were on two days ago and last night I found out because I saw a billboard. There's no way in hell. What's going to be on there? Shit you've never even heard of. I seriously always think about that and I think, "What if Limp Bizkit is the Nirvana for nowadays? What if Limp Bizkit is as good as Nirvana? If I was ten years younger, would I like Limp Bizkit the same way as I like Nirvana?" Fuck no. No way in hell.

Sean: The thing is, too, we're in an active band. We go see bands a lot. We read fanzines. We buy records. We listen to not as much new stuff, sure, but we're definitely very exposed to it.

Cong: We definitely—and I can say "we" because these guys are my brothers—we all have listened to a band that either we know or they're a band that started just like us, as an underground punk band, and I know we listen to that at least three times a week. A lot of people call me jaded because I hate a lot new shit that's coming out, but in my mind, I think I'm hopeful. I'm actually worried that there's not going to be new shit.

Sean: There's great bands out there. You talk about being in touch. How more in touch can you be than going on tour and seeing a young band that kicks ass, like The Arrivals. You stumble upon a band like that and they're guys just like us. They're as underground as you get. Who's heard of them?

Cong: I feel fully out of touch and I do a record label and I work at a distribution company that pretty much specializes in small bands, small labels. Nothing's a Lookout or an Alternative Tentacles, even. When I first started working there, I looked at all the bands, and I'm like, "Who is this?" and everyone's calling, "Oh, we need that record really bad. This is flying out the store." And I felt like this old, bitter fool who just didn't know what was going on and I listen to the records. A lot of them I just don't get. All it is, is that you come up with a name that's really long, like We Will Show Up at Your House and Kill Your Mother and that's the name of the band and that's pretty much what's going on, and you put on the record and it doesn't sound anything like we're going to come to your house to kill your mother. There's sort of a pattern of that and I'm not really interested in it. I don't think of myself as being jaded. I'm just not interested in that. I think it's whack and they should give it up.

Todd: On that tip, you guys opened for AFI.

Cong: Speaking of whack.

[laughter]

Sean: That Son of Sam, boy, wooosh.

Todd: To put this into perspective, how much did you guys get paid to play The Palace, which holds about 1,000 people, plus or minus?

Sean: They gave us fifty bucks. [serious] And the singer's pants. [joking]
Todd: For the entire band?
Cong: Yeah.
Todd: AFI's rationale behind that is? I'm just postulating here, but they must have made $10,000 off that show. Couldn't they kick down some love? (After these two shows, on the strength that the shows were sold out, AFI penned a deal with Dreamworks, Disney's record label.)
Cong: That's the thing I don't want to ever understand. We're not pulling in all these people. I was actually making jokes on stage. "Okay, you guys are going to leave after we play, but make sure you see AFI. They're great." It's not like that. I wish it was.
Sean: Unfortunately, we're not going to be sucking any of their assholes in the recent future.
Cong: It puts us in a weird position, 'cause we're not a fan of the band. Their booking agent wanted us to play. If they call us up and they want us to play a show, it's "Yeah, thanks." They're doing us a favor. We play for free all the time and sometimes we get paid a lot of money but we don't really have that much money to be crying about. We could easily pull, "We used to pack this place in our last band," and blah, blah, blah, but that's just stupid. At the same time, we should have gotten two hundred bucks for those two shows.
Sean: And the thing is, too, we got asked to play these shows. It's not like we're like, "Come on, man, we just got done eating milk and cookies and we want to play with AFI." Kick the old guys a couple hundred. We're willing to work for our dollar. We have no delusions of what we are. We just like what we do and we try to put on a good show and try to do good songs. We don't walk around with an attitude. We don't demand too much. It's kind of a double-edged sword. We're not out there going, "We were in FYP and we deserve this much money." On the reciprocal, sometimes we're a little too lax. We're not businessmen. That's not what we're in a band for.
Cong: I don't want to get into the position where people will say of us, "Yeah, they'll do it for fifty bucks."
Sean: "We can do them for fifty bucks."
Cong: We know the difference between earning the money and just getting paid that amount of money because if we play a show where pretty much two-thousand kids are waiting to see Davey with his… I'm not going to get into that. They're pretty much there to see AFI. We didn't earn the money. Probably five people came to see us, maybe. So, we got half of those five people's ticket price. It was probably twenty bucks. But, if we play a place that we're headlining and a hundred people show up then I would hope to get one hundred, two hundred bucks. If you break it down like that and actually get a business sense of that, you'll be all right. A lot

of bands like to take a lot more than they earned. Just because they're headlining doesn't mean shit.

Todd: So, Casey, how did Todd mutilate your ear?

Cong: Aw, man. I was starting to feel good here.

Casey: Well, in New Orleans this last tour, Todd does this thing where he flips the guitar around his body. His guitar's flying around his body and he smacks me on the side of the head. My ear busts open blood and stuff.

Cong: What sucks about that…

Casey: I don't think he's done it since.

Cong: I did. I won't do it now when it's, "This show's rad. I'm all fucked up." It was a great show and it went "tonk." The thing of it is was that the first week of tour was really, really bad playing-wise. We just barely get to the show. The first couple songs are great. We're playing good. People are into it. So, I'm, "Yeahh!" Hits him in the ear. He just goes down. Troy (former drummer) fucking stops playing drums, jumping out from his kit like he's going to beat me up or something. "What happened to Chachi?"

Sean: "You were hitting him."

Casey: It's better now. It's just a little scar. It was tender for a good couple weeks on tour.

Sean: There's a bit of an emotional scar.

Casey: I think Todd was a little bit more freaked out than me. I couldn't sleep for two weeks on my left side. There was definitely blood running down my neck.

Cong: It was definitely a gruesome scene.

Casey: It was the fourth song we were playing so it was really early in the set. It just totally knocked me. "Whoa, what's going on? Are we still playing? I'm standing. Okay, that's good."

Cong: The crowd was pissed at me. They all wanted my blood. "You got Chachi." Everyone likes Chachi. Nobody likes me. Nobody likes the old men in the band.

Casey: Yeah, they chant for me sometimes.

Todd: So, Todd, you were a professional skater, were you not?

Cong: [lying] No.

Todd: Is it true that you left one of the last messages on the skater Mark "Gator" Anthony's machine?

Cong: The night before he turned himself in.

Todd: For what?

Cong: For raping and killing a girl and stuffing her into a surfboard bag.

Casey: It was his girlfriend, right?

Cong: No. It was his girlfriend's friend. She was coming over to console him.

Sean: This is just in reflection. Your message was, "Did you kill that bitch yet?" [laughter]

Cong: No. We used to go down to San Diego a lot and stay with our friend and crank call people and skateboard and just do boy things and went to Tony Hawk's ramp to skate it and Gator was there and was like, "So, what's going on?" I'm all, "Nothing. What are you doing?" He's like, "Nothing." I'm like, "Who are you riding for now?" because he was off of a company. And he's all, "Jesus Christ." I'm all, "Is that a new company?" I seriously thought he was talking about a new skateboard company. He's like, "You know what I mean. You should ride for Him. I know you like the punk rock music and shit like that, but that's going to lead you to the devil." I was, "Yeah, whatever." So, of course we found our new victim to crank call that night. We called him, "This is Satan. We know what you've done." And he really did something and we didn't know. I swear we didn't know.

Todd: So, the next day the cops visited you?

Cong: No, no. His outgoing message was like this: "Hey, this is Mark. I'm not going to be around. You can leave a message but I'm not going to get back to you. Praise the Lord." The reason he was leaving that message was because he was going to jump in front of a train and his friend found out what he was going to do and talked him out of it. The next day he turned himself in because he'd already killed that girl. His girlfriend dumped him. This girl, her best friend, came over to console him and he just went crazy on her.

Todd: And all of those events affected the skate video you were working on, didn't it?

Cong: Yeah. We were doing what I think was the first-ever skate/horror movie. It was crazy because at the time of it, our company—it was me and Mike Smith, pretty much—two guys who didn't really attract too many kids who really wanted to buy boards, so it was pretty much the rugged, bearded vert guys would buy our boards and we were looking for new riders and Gator was one of them. I think he was born again because of what he did, but I could be totally wrong. "I've got to find a way out of this. I must look for Christ. He's going to lead me out of this wreck I've made for myself." I was doing this horror video, just skaters chopping people's heads off, as a joke, you know? The video was almost totally edited. All I had to do was put the credits on and I found out this happened so I had to put a disclaimer: "We didn't really do this, like that other guy."

Todd: Sean, what happened the last time you inadvertently played a skinhead's birthday?

Sean: It was out in Pacoima. The show sounded okay. We didn't know what to expect, except it was a birthday party for this guy, pretty cool dude. He was going to give us a hundred bucks and there was going to be beer and one of them little blow-up bouncy rooms.

Todd: Woo!

Sean: We get there and say, "Where the fuck are we going?" Pacoima? Who goes here? It's a place you get dropped off." We show up to the house. The guy whose birthday it was was kind of skinhead-ish. He wasn't wearing a Skrewdriver t-shirt. He was really nice, a real cordial dude, really stoked on us playing. More people started showing up. A majority of the people showing up were Mexican guys with white pride hats, swastika tattoos, and they looked like gangsters. They didn't have flight jackets and shaved heads but they were all totally down for being a nazi and shit. It was really weird. So, we set up and we start playing and are kind of skeptical and we're kinda freaking out, thinking we should just get out of here. But we go play our set anyway. There's a song, "Ian Stuart," that Todd wrote about the guy from Skrewdriver and how he died. He introduced the song, "How many of you out here know who Ian Stuart is?" The crowd roared, "Yeah!" He's like, "How many of you are big Skrewdriver fans?" More cheering. Todd's all, "This song's about how he died in a car accident and we're pretty happy it happened." Just blatantly, fuck you. It was commendable, but dangerous.

Cong: You know what happens when I get beer in me.

Sean: Let's just say that the most pit started in towards the band. We're playing the entire song and the audience is, "Grrrrh," like *Day of the Dead* or something and Jed (FYP's bassist at the time) is looking really scared, standing right in front of his amp and some guy feigned to punch him, pulled it back, and Jed fell over the amp. And the guy's all, "That pussy fell over the amp and I didn't even hit him."

Cong: He flinched over his amp.

Sean: We stopped the song. It was crazy. Some people seemed to be coming towards us. Some people seemed like they were going to fight each other. Next thing you know, it's this huge, confusing scene. We're like, "Let's get our shit in the van. Let's get the fuck out of here." Opened the van door and we're just throwing our shit in the van. Tossing it. Not taking apart the drums or anything. We all get in the van and people are punching the van and rocking the van. Gun shots fire out and we peeled the fuck out of there.

Cong: We were doing weird body counts. "Everybody here? Everybody here?" We had a lot of skinhead incidents. That's something that totally amazes me when I look back. The most retarded, stupidest punk band could get a rise out of the most retarded, stupidest people.

Casey: I remember going to see you guys a few times and Jed getting chased by a bunch of skinheads.

Cong: Because he would always try to make out with their girlfriends. Even the ones with the chelseas.

Todd: The colander cut?

Cong: Yup.

Todd: Switching gears altogether, you have a song called "Hare Ruya." I have no idea who or what that is.

Cong: It's this guy in Japan. His business went down, he had a family, the economy was really bad. He went and bought some boxing gloves and at two in the morning, stood out by the bars and charged people ten dollars to box the shit out of him. He'd tell people, "I can put my dukes up this high," [at cheek level] but you can hit me as much as you want." He would just sit there and take it. He made money, got out of debt.

Todd: He wouldn't fight back?

Cong: No, he couldn't fight back. He would guard his face. For a minute or two. He's probably still doing it.

Todd: What's the most endearing expression of fandom that you've seen in any of the bands you've been in?

Casey: There's this kid I brought backstage at the Palace. He was at one of our last shows and he was talking to me. I knew I knew him from somewhere, but he was just some kid I'd met somewhere. He wanted to get his album signed. I said, "I'll bring you backstage." It's upstairs, behind all of this security. He was so stoked on it. He's like, "Yeah, Chachi, yeah." Pretty cool.

Sean: There's definitely loads of FYP tattoos, and shit like that, but with Toys That Kill, the tattoos are just starting to come out. [laughter] I'm hoping that some guy will come up to me and it'll say "Cole" (Sean's last name) in old English.

Todd: Give me your step-by-step thought process after your van hit the deer.

Cong: My knee was on top of Sean's throat.

Sean: I've got a buff neck.

Cong: That freaked me out because I thought somebody died.

Casey: Because you were sleeping.

Cong: Yeah. I flew off the loft. I woke up in mid-air.

Casey: Flying over me.

Cong: I cleared him and landed on Sean.

Todd: Who was driving?

Cong: Jack. (Their roadie and merch guy.)

Casey: Troy was riding shotgun.

Sean: Troy and Jack were up at the front.

Cong: They liked to hit each other a lot.

Sean: They were playing with their Hello Kitty pencils, listening to this techno music that was giving me nightmares. So, I'm in progress of a nightmare that I'm trapped in machinery or something, just falling through gears and stuff, and I wake up from the nightmare [jerks straight]—you know when you're on the freeway and you're not paying attention for a second and you stop? It feels like you're in control. You skid a little bit. It was this veering and skidding that seemed so out of control that I was like, "I'm going to die."

Casey: I thought we were going to flip.

Sean: "This is it. I'm dead." When I think of death, I always think I'm going to die on tour, I'm going to die in a car. This seems to be my destiny. Destiny unfolds. Jack is fucking freaking out. Todd's flying on my neck. All this shit's flying. And the van comes to a stop. I thought we hit something like another car. I thought we were in a car accident. First, I'm like, somebody's dead. We're alive, that's great, but somebody got mauled. Somebody's dead. Somebody's car flipped over and is on fire. I'm like, "What happened?" "We hit a deer." I'm like, "Oh, okay," thinking the van's totaled and fucked. It all went in this transgression, these steps. And when we looked, just fucking knocked the headlight out.

Cong: Duct taped it right back on.

Casey: Missed the radiator by an inch. I saw the deer first and I was laying down in the back. I kinda look up to see what's going on up front. And I see this deer. "Oh shit!" Jack locks up the brakes and starts swerving.

Todd: Fifteen years ago, name the album you were listening to and playing along with, even in your head.

Cong: Millions of Dead Cops. Either that or *Kings of the Wild Frontier* by Adam and the Ants, but stick with the first one. It sounds cooler.

Casey: Probably, Go-Go's, *Vacation*. I was like ten years old. I was into the Stray Cats, too. Those were the two bands I knew about.

Sean: I definitely have to say *Kill 'Em All*, Metallica.

Todd: Todd, you also own Recess Records. Is that correct?

[long pause]

Sean: He'll sell it to you for eighty bucks.

Cong: I was going to sell it to Sean for eight hundred dollars.

Todd: Does anybody work for you?

Cong: Not any more. Nope.

Todd: Which titles keep you in business?

Cong: The Dwarves do good, all the FYP ones do good. Those are the constant back catalog sellers.

Todd: How long have you been doing it for?

Cong: Since 1989. The first piece of vinyl came out in '90, but I count the demo tapes and shit. Don't let people steer you wrong on that.

Todd: So, Sean and Casey, what do you do for your day jobs?

Casey: I'm a part time dock worker. Everybody from my high school works there, too. It's kinda gross. When I was having trouble dealing with reality—an example is—I go to this place and I pretty much have a number, and a letter, and I have to wait until my number comes up and then I can work. So you just have to hang out. It's just like recess. It's just a bunch of people hanging out. It's a bunch of people who would never talk to me back in high school. Now they're like, "What's up? Cool. Yeah." I went there and I was just standing there, trying not to look at anyone in the eye, hanging out by myself while everyone has all their friends around them. I just ended up leaving. I didn't even care if I got a job that day.

Sean: I used to cook pizzas, man. I moved furniture. Cater. Just a bunch of odd jobs. I recently got a job building amplifiers for Matchless Amplifiers. Haven't started it yet, but if feels pretty good not to have a loser job; something where you're going to learn something. We've always been—through the course of the years—busy enough with the band where I consider that my entire life and it's been a lot slower and I want to work at this place and I think I can save a lot of money and get better stuff. Better music stuff. Not like a year's supply of Cheez Whiz.

Cong: Or a double burger. Going large.

Todd: Someone explain Porch Core.

Cong: No.

Sean: I hate to be the one who breaks this one to the public, but…

Cong: Porch Core is just the figment of you lame cunts' imaginations. It was written on a bathroom wall.

Sean: Porch Core is no more, no less than this batch of stickers we made on tour in '98 or '99 and we made these stickers and slapped them up everywhere and this band called the Jag Offs, my roommate's band, they have a song called "Porch Core," and it just seems magazines and kids think it's some scene. It's not anything. We have porches.

Cong: It's about sitting on a porch, drinking a 40, and shitting your pants and then you go to sleep. Pretty inspiring, huh?

Sean: I think as a group of friends, when we all first started hanging out with each other, it got to a point where things were, as a big group of people, very productive. Not necessarily changing the world or nothing, but we used to do a lot of things. Like building a skate ramp. In the process of making the video, doing skits, the fake band comp. Things, little activities that we'd all do as a group of people. But people move and people fuck each other's girlfriends. [nervous laughing] And they go off in different directions. All the friends are still pretty much intact, but it's not as tight as it used to be. When our old bass player, Joe, died it really got a big group of people in really close.

Cong: Just as fast as it brought everyone close…

Sean: Everything sort of just disintegrated.

Cong: But it took years to do that.

Sean: Yeah. It's not bad. It's just a natural thing. To get to the gist of Porch Core, it's just… nothing.

Todd: What's the biggest obstacle you've overcome to be in this band?

Sean: It's not as pinpointed. I can't think of, "Oh, I flipped my mom off to be in the band," or anything. I think I sacrificed progression in a money sense. I could have gone to school. I could have money and things like that. I'd rather be poor and live like shit and do what I love to do than be rich or even make a sufficient amount of money and be miserable at what I'm doing.

Casey: I had to blow all of my money on a van so we could tour.

Sean: [happily] Right on.

Cong: There are only obstacles *to do* the band.

Sean: Sacrifice is probably a better world.

Cong: There is nothing else that I could possibly do. I have a day job to bring in the rent and I love it and I love the people who work there, but what I really want to do is the label, and especially the band first.

Sean: You have to subsidize. You get to be thirty—not that I'm thirty— you can't help but feel pressure. You're born of something. You're not like some alien with some inhuman concepts of life. You're going to feel pressures, no matter how stout you are in your beliefs. You go to Thanksgiving. "Why aren't you married? Where are my grandkids?" "Mom, I'm not thirty yet." Or like, "Shit, man, I don't have a DVD player."

Cong: I just got one. No pressures here. My parents are cool with me.

Sean: I'm inheriting a computer that has Windows 95 on it. Talk about slow. It was free, man.

Cong: Everyone has pressures, but when you're coming up to thirty. It's a weird thing, but you've got to decimate before you get decimated. That's it.

Sean: Pressure is what keeps everything in perspective. If everything was one-sided, where would you be? You have to weigh and balance your priorities and what means the most to you. It makes your endeavors more important. I'm not giving up, man.

• • •

"It's like you wanna not be obvious but you want people
to know what the fuck you're talking about
and that's the balance."

—Mike

RAISE YOUR BOTTLES TO THE BRUISES: AN INTERVIEW WITH THE THUMBS

The Thumbs' songs sound like they're being played as the band's being pushed out of a moving van, wrapped in a carpet. Immediacy and terror and anxiety bundled tight. There's lots of tumbling around, screaming, and a quick series of nicks and bumps. The Thumbs are wound up with so much velocity, like they're rolling down a hill, picking up speed with every note. The carpet's the thin, protective layer of hooks and choruses that keeps 'em from disintegrating completely. I like that quality in songs. Terminal velocity dirty pop that's energetic, ethical, hard working, sharp thinking, and hard rocking.

The first time I saw them was at the side of a warehouse in Las Vegas. Cold wind howled, which was great for keeping the beer cold and breaking out oversized, furry Communist bloc hats, but tough to play in when your hands feel like pork chops. The Thumbs are great live. Picture good-natured wolverines attacking microphones and instruments. It was a fun time in Vegas, even after someone tripped over a cord and the table lamp that was the only immediate light was smashed to bits. The Thumbs stayed visible by the glow of a not-too-distant glass pyramid with a light shooting into space. The fourth or fifth time I saw them, they played so hard—and sweat so quickly into their set—the cockroaches migrated en masse from the walls. That's power and true dedication, audience be damned.

Songs this ragged are rarely this catchy.

Mike: bass, vocals
Bobby: guitars and vocals
Roman: drums

Todd: What's with the exploding drummer syndrome?
Bobby: We played one or two shows a month for awhile, then we had some lineup changes. Randy was in The Great Unraveling, and they were touring with The Unwound and had all these great opportunities, so we kinda made a choice for him to get out of being the drummer. It's been a lot of different drummers and a lot of different tours.
Todd: What would you do to improve The Thumbs?
Bobby: Well, we had two guitars before and that was pretty cool, but Mark went to New York. I like the direction that we've come. We're evolving.

Roman: It seems to me that all you need to do is keep going and The Thumbs improve themselves.

Bobby: I'll buy that.

Todd: [to Mike] Do the keys that are strapped on your wrist ever get caught on anything when you play?

Mike: No. 'Cause they're always underneath. They wrap around and they bang on the strings sometimes and make cool noises, but they never get stuck or anything. That would be a little embarrassing.

Todd: Roman, you're drummer number what?

Roman: Ten.

Todd: What's going to be your mode of death, like in *Spinal Tap*?

Roman: I will probably choke on someone else's vomit.

Todd: Let me clarify, The Thumbs tours are actually named after the drummer, correct?

Bobby: That's a new thing. We finally realized, "Well, Jesus, we haven't had the same drummer for a different tour."

Mike: It all kind of begins to run together. Roman's the perfect one for a repeat. If he comes back, it can be the "Roman Numeral II Tour."

Roman: That's actually been thought of before.

Todd: Would you guys tour with a drum machine?

Roman: That would be Thumbs 2010.

Bobby: If it was shooting out fire.

Mike: If it was a drum machine that had arms, that would be one thing.

Bobby: They'd be, "Wow, they were great live."

Mike: I totally felt the pressure going from four down to three to be more active and aggressive-looking. Going down to two, you pretty much have to be a monster. It wouldn't be good.

Todd: How was Japan?

Bobby: It was amazing.

Mike: Yoichi from Snuffy Smile Records brought us over. I think we were the first band that he brought over that wasn't already kind of big shit in Japan. He brought Hot Water Music over, Discount, and Dillinger Four. People just went crazy over there for them and for us it was good shows every night but it wasn't like everyone was jumping around and yelling our songs or anything. It was more like playing a really great, solid tour. Hopefully we turned some heads and people liked it.

Todd: At this time in the scheme of things, what makes a good tour for you guys?

Bobby: The beginning of this tour was so good. We played all of these house shows and different, weird places and everybody's in your face, microphones getting knocked down and into your teeth. You're physically not able to play your songs because people are mobbing you. That happens to us a lot. That's why we go to Aberdeen, South Dakota. Chattanooga is

our favorite place. We seek those places out. You go on tour for a month—
"Okay, we've only got this many shows, these actual days we'll be on the
road," so we have to play the best shows we can find and those aren't necessarily the biggest shows. Sometimes they're the shows that make us feel
good about ourselves. I'm sure we can play a lot of huge, huge, big shows
and nobody really gives a shit about us.

Mike: Fireside Bowl comes to mind.

Bobby: We've done that a bunch of times and Brian always hooks us up,
but nobody really cares. There'd be three people there who actually want
to see us. It's cool, it's fun, but it's hard to keep on throwing yourself back
into that with the same enthusiasm when you can go to some place that
nobody's ever heard of. The kids are just so happy and grateful and they
just go so nuts. That's what's fun.

Todd: If your music could be a piece of clothing, what would it be?

Mike: A blue pocket tee.

Bobby: It's starting to get a little worn thin. There's a little hole next to the
corner of the pocket.

Todd: How do you define yourself and how do you define yourself as a
band?

Roman: I define myself by whatever I do. You always try to make it good
but it's not always good and a band is the same thing. It's activity. It's not
that you're out to prove something to anyone, it's about experiencing
things. Right now, it's what's outside of my town and what's outside our
scene at home and trying to get out and seeing who's around and where
people are at. I often define myself by the relationships that I keep and
how they reflect on me—how they make me feel. The same thing goes for
the band. If you've got a band and you enjoy the music and you get to go
around and meet all of your friends, and play just about every night with
someone you know and you enjoy seeing, well then it's relatively successful. If you have financial troubles doing that, actually physically making it
from town to town, that's disappointing but that's rarely the case.

Todd: Do you think of tours as like 50/50 vacations?

Roman: Absolutely.

Bobby: It didn't used to be. We played with The Jack Palance Band in the
beginning of this tour and we got to hang out with those guys and they
were amazing and then we couldn't wait to get here because we get to
hang out with Tiltwheel. When we hit Minneapolis, we get to hang out
with The Dillinger Four and we actually get a couple days with those
Panthro UK United 13 guys and even though they're not together, we're
trying to get a petition going to get them back together. You have all these
people who you love. You can play and show off and you can drive them
to play better and it's not like, "Yeah, fuck them," it's more like "Wow, I
love you."

Roman: I've always thought that tour is part vacation. For me, when we're at home, our time is constantly filled with these tasks, whether you're working—especially before the tour we were doing websites and t-shirts, and I was, personally, just freaked out. I was moving out of my house, selling my car, getting another car, and it was incredible amounts of stuff and it had my stomach tied in knots and I'm just thinking, "Two or three more days and I'm out of town and I don't have to worry about it." And when you get out of town, you just sit back and relax. You've got nothing to do. You're in this car so you sit there and you think for eight hours and it's really nice.

Mike: It is a weird feeling. You sort of know, for example, that we have thirty-six hours before we leave for this fucking tour. We have to get this and this and this done, but you have to get in the van and drive away and once you're in the van, it's like, "All right, whatever didn't get done, fuck it," and it's a great feeling, really.

Bobby: It's weird, too, because as you tour more, you're living your life, you're busting your ass, but then you sort of know, "I'm going on tour in a month." It's like this great escape. It affects your relationships too, because when we get back to town, it will either be exactly the same or it will be completely different. There's no way you can get that back. It's like Rip Van Winkle. "What the fuck happened?" Completely different.

Todd: Bobby, you've said that The Thumbs songs were complex—in a pop context—how so?

Bobby: I think we are very critical of the songs we write. We just wrote a song, one of the first songs we wrote with Roman—and it's totally, quickly written. Mike came with all this stuff and it was, "Yeah, yeah, let's do this." It was so fun. There wasn't a whole lot of deliberation or grueling working on it. And there's other songs that we've sort of pieced together and they're a lot harder but they're complex and they're good, too. People sometimes don't realize what's going on until they actually have to sit down and figure out the songs. There's usually a lot more going on than three chords. Other times, we actually try to balance it out. If there's some really weird thing, we've got to come back with a really catchy thing. Somebody might go, "What the fuck? That's not complex."

Todd: What job did you leave back home?

Bobby: I shrink wrap boats for months. I finished, so I was just dicking around.

Roman: I was a graphic designer at a science museum and I quit to go on tour.

Mike: I'm an administrative assistant for a lobby group in D.C. Just answer the phones and type shit. A little cubical job. It's good.

Todd: You've got a degree in history?

Mike: I kept on changing my area of focus. Basically, twentieth century, U.S.

Todd: Name either a really interesting fact or one thing that most people don't know and should.

Mike: Maybe this is changing now a little bit, but Malcolm X, the actual, real civil rights movement. I remember being in grade school, Black History Month, and it was so fucking bland and tame and we learned about George Washington Carver inventing peanut butter. You got a little bit of Harriet Tubman and a lot of Martin Luther King Jr., and that's great, but there's so much going on. It's a pretty young country and we're still dealing with a lot of problems. You've got Martin Luther King, Gandhi-style pacifism. And Malcolm X. He's a little bit more of an enigma but they were fighting for the same thing. It was avoided conspicuously. If you're going to learn it, you should learn it and start learning when you're six years old instead of when you're twenty or twenty-two or when you're on your own.

Todd: What's the largest reoccurring theme in The Thumbs lyrically?

Bobby: We're usually pissed off at something.

Mike: Anger.

Bobby: Frustration and stuff. You just react to anything that you're dealing with in your life and you take those emotions and then for awhile now, we've been putting it in the context—like historical or some strange metaphor—and you focus all of those emotions and you put them in this other and it's disguised, but it makes it so much more real to us.

Mike: It's like you wanna not be obvious but you want people to know what the fuck you're talking about and that's the balance.

Bobby: We found we have to beat people over the head with it. "Sprague Dawley Rats" is this really cool story. And they're like, "They're singing about rats. Cool." They think it's sort of catchy.

Mike: The Sprague Dawley Rats are a brand of laboratory rats. Basically, these rats are bred for research, mostly in America. I don't know how long this company has been around but they do really well and somebody did an experiment—these are inbred rats, born and raised just to be carved up or rubbed up or whatever. But someone did this experiment where they went to this island and let them go to see if they still had the survival instincts. The rat is a survivor. They've been around for so long. And they wanted to see, "Did this get bred out of them or are they still rats?" They dropped them off and they came back and they found their little skeletons. They got totally devoured by the native rats. They couldn't cut it.

Todd: So they're domestic rats.

Mike: Yeah. Exactly. So that's sort of the song—"What the fuck am I? I'm not what my shell is anymore."

Todd: So why do you guys yell so much when you play? You seem very mild-mannered off stage.

Bobby: We call it crooning and we call it screaming. Sometimes we try to balance the two out. Sometimes stuff's really catchy if we're good. Definitely, when we're on tour, it's all like "rraarrrgghh." Sometimes we need to make a part tough because it's too catchy or too pretty. Sometimes we make a weird part. We calm it down a little bit by making this catchy, crooning part over it.

Mike: We're about energy, at the shows especially. Hopefully, on the records, too. I like the way I sound better when I'm singing kind of high and really loud. I love Joe Strummer but I don't have the voice to do that. I just try to what sounds good.

Todd: What's the estimated average of people who attend your shows—smooth it all out.

Bobby: Twenty, twenty-five people. That's at home, too. That's a good night for us.

Todd: Why does your album *Make America Strong* sound so poppy and you guys, live, don't sound that way?

Roman: I think that has a lot to do with time. It was a long time ago, that last CD.

Bobby: On one hand, we probably sounded poppier with Mark. That's his style. He was just an amazing bass player and when he left to do animation stuff, Mike jumped back and Mike's style is distorted bass. The Karl Alvarez (Descendents/All), cool bass lines; that changed right after Mark left.

Mike: It was just mixed really poppy, too.

Bobby: We didn't fully realize how far up front our vocals were on that CD, which is cool. It's one of those things. I like Dillinger Four. Those guys, too, bury their vocals for the most part. You're straining to hear it, some of that stuff, but it fucking rocks, it's so good. But it helps because it's pulled back just a little bit, whereas our stuff was pushed up a little bit. It was still really good but you can hear the imperfections a little bit better. I think that this stuff that's out now (*All Lesser Devils* EP, *Last Match* LP) is our favorite stuff so far just because it was on a lot less of a budget, fewer tracks, and just tougher and done back just a little bit.

Todd: What's the dirtiest, most disgusting place you've ever stayed at?

Mike: The Kirby House in Chattanooga, Tennessee.

Bobby: It was during the summer and we'd been touring for nine weeks. We were in over 100 degree heat in the South. They were like, "You can stay at the house that we're going to, go to bed and there's no air conditioning, and you can go to sleep or you can go to the Kirby House and they're up all hours of the night. It's a party house. You can get drunk and pass out." We thought, "If we went to sleep we'd be dreading the heat, so we'll go to the Kirby House, drink, and go crazy." They didn't have running water. You had to go to the bathroom in a bucket. They had these rats that had tumors and were just nasty. Basically, all these people lived in this one house, total squalor. We brought some beer in and they were totally respectful of all our stuff. They had nothing and opened themselves up to us. It was a really cool thing. Dirty place. It was also a blast.

Todd: What's a Baltimore colloquialism?

Bobby: "Hey hon." A waitress would be like "Hey you'se hons."

Mike: "I'm as tired as a chicken" is another one.

Roman: I've never heard of that.

Mike: What? You've never heard of that?

Roman: That's ridiculous.

Bobby: He's just trying to start that. He's been doing it for five years.

Mike: Everybody's saying it down there.

Todd: Name the two musicians who are fighting it out in your head when you're playing a song.

Roman: Mine is Rob Oswald (Karma to Burn, Charm City, Queens of the Stone Age) versus Lyle Kissack. Lyle's a drummer from Candy Machine, a band in Baltimore who is really smooth, technically adept. His beats are just so groovy and kick ass. And Rob is the best drummer I've ever seen in my life. He's just a monster and he's incredible. His skill is out of this world. Just his enthusiasm is amazing and what he brings to any band he's ever played with is just amazing. So, I'm trying to get a match between that sort of energy and focus and appropriateness verses the kind of smoothness and the style.

Bobby: Greg Ginn and Bob Mould.

Mike: I'll go with Mark (former bassist) and the guy from NoMeansNo (Rob Wright). I don't know his name but I like the way he fucking plays. This fucking huge sound. That's what I want to sound like, not as a band, but the same bass sound. I think we're a guitar band. Every time I try to get that sound—I used to be in a band a long time ago—and played bass and the recordings were always murky and if you turned it up, it kind of sounded like shit. When you're more of a guitar band, it sounds better the louder you turn it up and that's kind of what I want.

Todd: Okay, final question. Look to the left, to the person sitting next to you, and ask them one thing that you don't know about them and would like to know.

Mike: All right Bobby, what was it like when your mom married your stepdad?

Bobby: It wasn't a big deal, really. Worlds just sort of opened up. I think I'd be a different person if I stayed in Norfolk and I've been really lucky to do all the things I've done. I've got to see a lot of different things and I've slept on the floor of the Kirby House, I've seen billionaires piss in the sink, and I've done lots of things in between and it couldn't have happened without that. I'm sure I'd be a big music fan. I don't know if I would be in a band. I'm just totally like my dad.

Roman: Mike, you have a family life now and you have a strong determination towards the band. You have a good mix of the two. I don't want to ask if one's a priority over the other, but how do you envision balancing that in the future with, hopefully, more success for the band.

Mike: I got married last May. It's obviously really important to me. I love her to death. We've been together for nine years now. However you say "everything stays the same," it doesn't quite. It feels better to be with her but it's still a little bit of added responsibility even though everything before the marriage was totally shared and the same. Still, there's something a little bit different. It's great. I think if I had a kid, that would definitely change things. It's in the plans for the future. I don't want to be out, cruising around, and call back home; "Yeah, he walked today," or, "'He said his first word." Maybe in five years, if we're still playing, we may be making enough money, hopefully, to make the accommodations to bring my wife and the kid. And if not, I'll probably be done by then. Right now, it's great. Heather's got her life and I've got mine and there's points where they match up and there's points where they don't. And that's great. I think it makes us both a lot stronger. It's going really well.

Bobby: I've known Roman for a little bit, but the layers keep getting peeled off the onion a little bit. He blows my mind because he's got all of these ideas all the time. I'm totally like that, too. He's got all of these Spanish songs [in Roman voice]—"It's a soundtrack to this movie I've conceived," and I was like, what the fuck is he talking about? And he actually started whipping them out. And he's like, "I've got five or six or ten of them." I just wonder where he gets so much art and energy. You produce these things and ideas, and where does that come from?

Roman: I don't know. I wish I could bottle it up. I'd sell it. I'm trying to think if it's always been natural for me to do that. I haven't been playing music for very long and I haven't been listening to music—especially rock music—for more than eight or so years. When I was in high school, I was into rap music and things like that. I got into rock later and the way I got into it was kind of in the underground way. I wasn't so into anything that's been on the radio, almost ever. I got into the indie scene and there were bands that were coming into my house and I saw these people coming through, and I thought, "Wow, these are schmucks just like me. If they can do it, I can do it." And so I decided, first of all, I'd like to play an instrument.

I guess I've always been compelled to create something. So I pick up an instrument and start to play and my instinct is not to play something else. It's to start something new and have something that I can call my own and I don't know why that is. I don't know if I could play any song, start to finish, that's not mine, just because I've never really been able to do it. I've always almost been plagued by creativity to a certain extent because, in one sense, it's great and you're making all these things, but in the sense of *The Banditos*, which is my Spanish movie, this is an idea I've had for some time. I've always made plans to do something with it, and I've gone as so far as trying to get a screenplay together and get these ideas together but it always kinda grinds to a halt when something else overtakes it. I'm in four bands. I just don't have time to do that and this and this and this and this. It goes on and on. To a certain extent, I do all this stuff and it's great. But to a certain extent, I can be like, "I did all this stuff but look at all the stuff I didn't do." It's a blessing and a curse. For now, I changed my position on it. Whereas it used to bum me out that I wasn't doing things, what I've done recently is trying to get more control of my product and my output by saying, "What are the things I personally can control and how can I get them done? A lot of things depend on other people. For the most part, it's hard to depend on other people.

Todd: Any final words?

Mike: Come to our show and be the twenty-sixth person. Raise our average up.

• • •

photo by Kat Jetson

"Even though it seems ritualized from a distance, when you're in it, it's not. It could never be. I think that for a lot of people who detract from punk, and think that it's just a processed, consumer-driven, artificial thing, I don't think it's possible because there's so much creativity in this connection."

–Thomas

IN DEFIANCE OF EMPTY TIMES:
AN INTERVIEW WITH STRIKE ANYWHERE

When I really think about punk rock and what it truly means at its core, it quickly gets pared down to this: this music keeps me alive and living a life I want. It's naked. It can't have a uniform. It's my pep talk. My meditation. My close family. Partly, my rage. The fact that others—with much larger media megaphones and fancier pants—have acquisitioned parts of it doesn't bother me that much. Perhaps, in the seventeen years I've been involved with it, I've developed an instinct. I can smell shit a mile away, no matter the dress code or the raping of its most obvious rituals. To be sure, at times, it's tough to see through the gauze of advertising that would have worked on me even a year ago. Our own clever weapons—even our very own words—have been used repeatedly against us to sell punk's skin and appearance over and over again. Two things usually happen. We either get smarter with each turn and learn from our mistakes or we give up, give in, and tie our own hands behind our backs because we're already so very fucked.

All's far from lost. It helps to think in these terms. If there wasn't something real and vital—an earnest intimacy—punk would dissipate completely. It's not all falsely manufactured. If it were, we'd all be talking in the past tense, purely as historians, picking at the parts with sterilized tweezers. That's far from the case.

Strike Anywhere is the compression and ignition of a long tradition of hard, melodic bands. Start with the swelling compassion of Avail and the kinetic explosiveness of Kid Dynamite's ability to make an active yet kindly pit. Lead it with clear, acerbic, and thoughtful political lyrics. Steep it in over a century of Southern heritage. Instead of a photocopied miasma that zings off in too many directions, their sound is amazingly clear and directed, sieved and distilled into something that can be simultaneously as hard as straight shots of bourbon and as easy to gulp down as sweet tea. It's been a long time since I've heard a band sound so contemporary and so traditional at the same time.

If you think punk's been long dead and buried, look again. The coffin's been resurrected and been built into another stage for an all-ages show when you weren't paying attention.

Thomas: vocals
Eric: drums
Garth: bass
Matt Smith: guitar
Matt Sherwood: guitar

Todd: Strike Anywhere, the name, does it mean you're ready to ignite at any time or that you'll encourage people to exercise their right to fair treatment?

Thomas: Probably the latter, more like joyously inhabiting a parallel media to the actions of folks and putting our voices in everywhere that we can.

Todd: Being that you are both from Richmond, if there was ever such a thing as a GWAR karaoke, what song would you like to perform?

Thomas: I only have their first record, which is called *Hell-o*. It was on Metal Blade Records, very pre their explosion as the cultural artifact that they are. The only song I remember was the "We are GWAR" anthem ("GWAR Theme"). It just had some guy running around with a battle axe, going "GWAR, GWAR, GWAR, GWAR!" and some exploding, flatulent, pustulant alien sculpture out of foam and plasticine formed by two people who they'd have on the stage. The early GWAR shows were insane. You'd get drenched in juices. It was strictly for punks and psychotic art students in the late '80s in Richmond and really didn't have the cultural breadth that it has right now.

Matt: That's an unanswerable question to me. I'm probably more familiar with Death Piggy and the few, obscure, and possibly not-so-great bands that proceeded GWAR. You're just sitting there, getting sprayed with fake blood in a reverie. I never learned any song titles. I can't understand the point of listening to a GWAR record, actually.

Thomas: But we love them.

Todd: I was talking to Chuck from Hot Water Music a while back, and I noticed that he had a symbol tattooed on his arm of three arrows going in the same direction in a circle. To be honest with you, the reason I first listened to your EP, *Chorus of One*, was that symbol was on your CD. What does it represent?

Thomas: It was a symbol that was used several different times in history. The earliest that was known of it—and I'm sure there are people who have researched it better—it was the anti-fascist movement. It was the Berlin progressive paper that was an organ against the lies of the Nazi party and the street violence. They got shut down right around, before or after, the Kristallnacht ("Night of Broken Glass"—was the organized anti-Jewish riots in Germany and Austria, November 9 and 10, 1938) and were destroyed and taken to camps. They were the anti-Fascist resisters of that terror and they were also in places and cities all over Europe. And then, in Moscow, there was a plaque I saw of the Jewish Anti-Fascist International and they were there from the '30s until '46/'47, when Stalin came to power and really took everybody to the gulag and said, "Alright all y'all, there's no more bullshit. It's time to die." That's on the part of the radial streets in Moscow named for Peter Kropotkin, the anarchist, and that's where the Jewish Anti-Fascist International met. The Redskins, the anti-fascist Communist skins in New York City in the '80s used that symbol a lot, too. And Chumbawamba, in their anarchist days—they're still in their anarchist days—but in their pre-radio-friendly anarchist days...

Todd: The pre-"soundtrack for the trailer promoting *Home Alone 3*" anarchist days...

Thomas: They used that motherfucker. My friend, Joe, got to see them in the early '90s when he lived in London for awhile. He brought me back a t-shirt that had that symbol on it. So, it is everybody's symbol. We definitely wanted to bring it State-side and I think we want it to be known. I think that we either inferred or figured out through the cultural ether what the arrows mean.

Matt: Liberty, equality, and solidarity.

Thomas: And I don't know where we got that from.

Matt: It's kind of loose research online and looking through what historical documents we could find. That's actually a French slogan translated into English that's ancient as hell, too, by some socialists.

Todd: Liberty, equality, and fraternity.

Thomas: I think Chuck has that tattoo because we all met when I was in my old band, Inquisition, and Inquisition used that symbol a little and Chuck just got that tattoo in a passionate frenzy and I plan to get it too—same one, same place, eventually. Hot Water Music always has an understated identification with the working class and the roots of folk music, especially with the research that they do and their side project bands, like Rumbleseat.

Todd: And The Blacktop Cadence.

Thomas: We hold a lot in common with that—that aggressive underground hardcore and punk, and rock music in general—has to have a populist base. As artists, you create because of the voices all around you. It's not just some kind of abstracted inner artistic vision—that's a part of it, too, but it has a lot more to do with claiming the vitality of everyone around you and talking about issues in your community and just communicating.

Todd: Going off of that, I'm going to give you a date and you're going to tell me what happened on that date. April 2, 1864.

Thomas: That's the bread riot.

Todd: What has not fundamentally changed in those 138 years since a woman lead a protest by saying, "As soon as enough of us get together, we are going to the bakeries and each of us will take a loaf of bread"? What are some historic parallels that are still viable in Richmond in 2002?

Thomas: I would say that the bread riots were about a lot of different things. They included the Confederate army burning Richmond so the Union couldn't have it and hoarding the food from the rest of the people:

the Africans who were still in the slavery system, the freedmen, the dissenters, and all the women—all over Richmond. There were so many people in Richmond, and the South in general, who did not agree with the war, with either side. Or switched sides. Or were terrorized. My great, great, great uncle was one of them. He died in the Chimborazo Military Hospital, which is now a park in the old part of the city of Richmond. I would say that the rich have a lot of shit and they manipulate it really well. They keep their business completely secret and somehow legal—but it gets caught up every now and then and found out. There's still a lot of voices and a lot of people who are trying to organize and crack it open and get the wealth and the food and life back.

Todd: Food that otherwise would be feeding the city's residents was being commandeered by the military.

Thomas: We even develop cultural channels to encourage high demand in this or to discourage people learning how to fuckin' feed themselves or take care of each other. Everyone stays isolated. I helped start, with some friends, a community garden right before I left for this tour. In Church Hill, which is an old neighborhood in Richmond, which has been burned several times, we're applying the same ethic to the Food Not Bombs we have in Richmond, radicalizing it, and moving it into low income neighborhoods and historically African American neighborhoods. We get people to remember about nutrition and about food just coming out of the ground and sharing it with each other.

Matt: And even just about cooking. About making food at home, preparing it. The rituals that go along with that and family and being involved in your neighborhood. All that good stuff, so that you just don't go down to the corner store and buy some crap and eat it.

Thomas: Or drive fifteen miles to a suburban strip mall to get some shit that's filled with pesticide and gives you cancer. It's just strange that people lose touch with that and I think that's one of the first steps in people becoming machines, to work their treadmill, and remain isolated from each other.

Matt: The beautiful thing about the community garden, you don't even have to go to the over-the-top, gourmet health food store, either, and give them the money. You can just pull it out of the ground and go cook.

Thomas: The community garden is this tax-delinquent, abandoned property that's just been staring at me hungrily since I've moved into the part of the ghetto that I live in. Me and my friend Mark, who's in the band River City High—we were home for a weekend and we went to the Home Depot and the Richmond straight edgers work at this Home Depot and our bass player, Garth, is kind of like their overlord.

Matt: Tom just made that up.

Thomas: That's a bit of an exaggeration. Anyway, they let us use this fuckin' tiller. As long as we got it back by six, they wouldn't tell their manager, so we tilled up this ground. The last thing that had happened on this earth, aside from a lot of forty-ounce bottles being tossed in the weeds, was the houses burned down twenty years ago. It was very rich soil.

Todd: Another interesting thing I found out about the bread riot is that a lot of the troops from the Public Guard who were called in, their own wives were among the rioters.

Thomas: I think, a year later, when the war ended, April 4, 1865, Lincoln walked through the town with his son, like the day after Richmond was liberated. It was a jubilee. All the freed Black folks were singing and dancing and it had to be the best day of Lincoln's life because seven days later he was killed. But he was in Richmond and there's nothing in Richmond that talks about that, to commemorate his walk. He walked past the Devil's Half Acre—that was where all the enslaved Africans came to the South, through Richmond, right at the Manchester slave docks, walked through the night, and were put up on the blocks. There was a jail there. They were bought and sold and all that.

Matt: The cobblestones on our streets were used for the ballast in the ships, when they sailed away and were sailing in from inland.

Thomas: We played shows in Richmond at this place called Alley Katz, which is six and a half blocks southeast of the Devil's Half Acre. To finish the story, the war ended. Everybody was emancipated. The day after that, Lincoln and his son, Tad, marched through the town. The man who was the overseer/ businessman of the slave trade in Richmond turned to an African woman who had been his property for her entire lifetime, realizing he'd been very much in love with her for that whole time, and married her in a fit of joy and powerful cultural defiance. That woman, after he passed away, turned that place into a school for Blacks in Richmond, during the Reconstruction, right before the Reconstruction went sour. Obviously, that is what informs us—whether it's subconsciously or whether it's right in the song. That's why we're a punk band from Richmond and why that matters and why it's different than being a punk band from anywhere else.

Todd: A lot of people forget that Richmond was the capital of the Confederacy.

Thomas: And there was so much misery and so much dissent on both sides of that. Nobody thinks about that shit. The people who go to schools in the North talk about the righteousness of the Union, holding itself together, freeing the slaves, Confederate pride, the confusion about heritage, the need to think that our great, great grandfathers weren't manipulated and they weren't fighting for a rich man's cause, which, essentially, they were. It's horrible to think about. I have several histories of different

great, great grandfathers leaving the war, getting hunted down by merce-
naries. One of them went out to Texas. The other one was shipped back
up to Richmond after being captured and recaptured by the Union. He
died. It's insane.

Matt: They actually just found a really complete diary of a captured
Union soldier. He spent a lot of time in Confederate camps, did a bunch
of watercolor paintings, and has insanely complete diaries, so it's a really
nice picture of everyday life of a prisoner. It's not glamorous, but it's
really interesting. Apparently, he was a really gifted illustrator, so he was
tapped to do that.

Thomas: There's this island in the James River that we all go to, it's
called Belle Island. It was actually called The Isle of Misery. It was a
prison for captured Union officers.

Matt: They starved them to death.

Thomas: They also starved the city to death. Then they burned the fucking city. At the same time, there's a lot of manipulation and bullshit on
both sides and I don't think Abraham Lincoln was the clear-cut hero of it,
either. A lot of people contend that it was the Fourteenth Amendment
("No state shall make or enforce any law which shall abridge the privi-
leges or immunities of citizens of the United States; nor shall any state
deprive any person of life, liberty, or property, without due process of
law; nor deny to any person within its jurisdiction the equal protection of
the laws.") that freed the slaves and not the Emancipation Proclamation.
It's frustrating.

Todd: How does the sleeping cop inside of you force you to do something almost against your will? (This is in reference to the song, "Chorus
of One": "I will try everything to kill the sleeping cop in me.")

Matt: It doesn't let me relax properly. The sleeping cop, to me—I didn't
write the words—there is an aspect of that. It's this abject perfectionism
that you can't escape. It's kind of a more personal thing. We don't really
think a lot about adhering to rules, but you kind of naturally do. You've
got rituals that don't really make sense but you function within them and
if you don't do them exactly correctly, it can cause a lot of mental
anguish.

Thomas: Every aspect of our society, including its economy and the way
we think we're organized, it's all about keeping us isolated and hateful of
our emotions instead of embracing them and trying to work with them,
like art. I think the sleeping cop is also the parts of me that feel too
exhausted and don't let go of negative shit, but lies to myself so that I
can't embrace really positive things. It goes through it like that. There are
also aspects of the sleeping cop that are a lot more ideological. They
have to do with standing on the treadmill and believing a lot of the myths
about if you work hard, the system can work for you and will take care

of you and all that shit and it doesn't work for millions and millions of Americans. It's like playing a lottery. That's how I feel, politically, the sleeping cop works in this country and this age.

Todd: The converse to that, what's the last fearless thing you've done?

Matt: I study kung fu. My instructor, we were doing applications where you actually pretend to be in a fight, which is sort of weird and I'm really terrible at fighting. Accidentally, I ended up kicking my older brother, who can beat the hell out of me if he wants to, right in the balls. And I just kind of looked at him and I felt really sorry, but I actually didn't feel afraid of retribution. Maybe I was just confident there wouldn't be any.

Thomas: I always feel painfully aware of my fears. Sometimes playing shows, even though we've played over 250 times.

Matt: Oh, playing as a four piece was the last fearless thing.

Thomas: We had to wait for Matt Smith to get off tour with his other band, Liar's Academy, and meet us in Sacramento. We'd never played live as a four piece and it worked out much better than we thought and it was an incredible time.

Todd: Did you feel extremely exposed, not to have the fifth member?

Thomas: We had to not just play our songs minus a second guitar, we had to reconstruct our identity as a band instantly. Almost like this version of ourselves. Not a version in an artificial way, but really embrace the idea of it to retain a wholeness and not be just, "We're missing a dude. Fuck it. As long as y'all mosh, it's cool." If it's a great show and there's something that I feel is fearless, it happens—where you walk right up to the middle of the maelstrom or maybe jump on someone's head who wants it. Or just singing along with people and just connecting in a way that is vulnerable and intense. And even though it seems ritualized from a distance, when you're in it, it's not. It could never be. I think that for a lot of people who detract from punk, and think that it's just a processed, consumer-driven, artificial thing, I don't think it's possible because there's so much creativity in this connection.

Todd: I hate to sound cheesy about it, but getting a hug from a good friend—someone you really care about—that's a ritual. You can see it on TV and in movies ten thousand times, but just because of that, it doesn't take away from the power of your personal relationships with people. If you mean it, that's what counts.

Thomas: Meaning is being taken away from all art and all culture because meaning gets in the way of profit and commerce on a gut level. Meaning makes people hold on to something. Meaning makes people go home with whatever tools they have and create something for themselves and not just consume the next product. That's fearless. That's why aspects of this are still frightening and when I can get through that and do it, it makes me happy and makes me feel like there's courage left.

Matt: People make those criticisms and they're totally legitimate—that you're going through a ritual, you're going through a cycle, you're participating in something that is a consumer culture and it seems that way. "We're an anti-consumer band. We've got merch in the back, bling, bling."
Thomas: We said that in a political basement show and everyone laughed. 'Cause we try to bring it both ways. You have to have the self-awareness and self-analysis, but there's still hope, you know… I got married in February. That was probably the biggest leap of faith I've ever taken in my life. It's good. It's intense, emotionally, and I don't know why it is because we had this marriage that was devoid of any of the patriarchal rituals and had a very earthy, elemental, sacramental fabric. It was definitely something that we crafted ourselves, was casual, and was in our own home. That was probably the real, fearless thing I've done recently.
Todd: Do you work at a stained glass place?
Thomas: I did. My wife is a manager at a stained glass art studio. I worked shipping out art paper. Her boss was the owner of two separate companies. He owned an old warehouse, seven-and-a-half blocks away from the Devil's Half Acre. It's our focal point, subconsciously. We also practice there. It started getting to where we were getting all of our mail there. We wrote most of *Change Is a Sound* there. I'd work there forty, fifty, fifty-five hours a week for years and years and years, but right before we left for tour, we moved all the glass to a proper art studio and we had to move all of our stuff into the van. Now we don't have a practice space. We're homeless as of right now. Every now and then, I will work for the stained glass studio, but not so often any more.
Todd: Matt, you have a degree in engineering?
Matt: Yeah.
Todd: Have you ever used those skills in this band?
Matt: I fix all of our equipment.
Todd: Electrical engineer?
Matt: Yeah. I'm expected to fix all of our equipment free of charge and fast.
Thomas: We started making him bill the band. It worked better, emotionally.
Matt: I'm allowed to charge a little bit. Ten bucks apiece now, which is awesome.
Thomas: We could give you a raise.
Matt: No, no, I don't need a raise.
Todd: Do you bring your solder gun along on tour?
Matt: I do.
Thomas: Other bands are like, "We wanna tour with Strike Anywhere. We can get Matt to fix our shit. We really don't like that band, but Matt's in it."

Matt: Every now and then I'll over-extend myself and break something for somebody and they won't ever ask again. You'll definitely see me before shows, with stuff taken apart, with a soldering iron out, plumes of lead smoke rising up and out. I'm the dude when there's math to be done or something scientific to be explained. I worked in Northern Virginia a little over a year before the beginning of the band and I was actually designing spy gadgets. I was working for the intelligence community. I quit that to be in this band. All this stuff with Donald Rumsfeld and the fuckin' (Department of) Homeland Security. There are so many institutional problems. I can tell you first-hand that they have not a hope in hell of pulling this together. They need to just scrap it all and start over because everyone involved with it is so self-interested, Rumsfeld can't possibly be successful. No information will be collected or assimilated in the interest of stopping innocent Americans from being killed, and that's their stated goal. They can try, but I don't think it'll happen, 'cause people would come to my work and they'd be all, "We want a death beam."

Thomas: No bullshit.

Matt: "We'll give you twenty million dollars if you build us a death beam." The senior engineers would be like, "Sure. Just give us twenty million." Of course, they knew it was totally unreasonable, but they needed the money to stay in business. The intelligence community operates that way. They're asked for these devices and they'll contract these research and development companies to build this specialized equipment. A legitimate outcome of research is the fact you can't realize the entire object that was contracted for. So, that'd be like, "Take this scientific principle and build us something that can drill through walls without actually touching them, with water."

Thomas: Or using microwaves at riots.

Todd: Really?

Matt: Yeah. That's a new riot control device. I never had anything to do with that, but that's some new shit they're pulling out. They're going to start cooking protesters. It was just ridiculous and people's attitudes were so bad and people's politics were terrible. They had no compassion. They were utterly self-interested to the exclusion of everything else, even future generations, their own children. Nobody had any compassion. It was bizarre.

Thomas: That shit's cold.

Matt: I was sitting there, getting made fun of because I had this spirulina. "You eating that green shit again?" I'm like, "Dude, I'm just listening to music and working on CAD (computer-assisted design). Leave me alone."

Thomas: And they're interested in something that automatically spikes the tires of someone going over the border.

Matt: Technology's crazy. People don't even know. It sounds like *X Files*, but it's not. It was actually a really interesting job, but I'm glad that I left.

Thomas: My uncle repairs the innards of a nuclear power plant. He's a steamfitter. My grandfather, supposedly, was a master sergeant in the Army Corps of Engineers who organized some aspects of the Manhattan Project in the Tennessee Valley and he wasn't told. He died horribly of cancer. There were a lot of other health-related things that occurred in that side of my family because of that.

Todd: What was the first show you realized a bunch of people began pointing back at the lead singer when there was a breakdown?

Matt: Four Walls Falling—all I remember was Taylor in the middle of this big heap of people clamoring for the mic. He would hold it out. He's a spindly little vegan dude with a powerful voice, but he would just get mobbed constantly. Every song, people would sing along.

Thomas: Most of those things are true for some of our DC and Richmond shows. For me, I seem to have inherited his style. We had a really interesting, home-grown version of the '88 straight edge scene in Richmond that had a lot of heart and a lot of political awareness that went further—not to disrespect our elders—than the New York straight edge bands, beyond just the "go vegetarian" and "stay positive," but discussions of capitalism in 1988 in a hardcore band were amazing. Four Walls Falling went to Europe, and then we heard about bands from the Netherlands like Man Lifting Banner, a communist straight edge band. And I was never straight edge. I was always one of the punk kids, sneaking beers in the back alley behind the club, but it still meant so much to all of us. And now, me and those punk kids who were in Inquisition together are now in Ann Beretta, River City High, and Sixer. I'm in a band that sonically and ideologically resembles the stuff we grew up on in Richmond, particularly, but it's still a part of the fabric of each of us.

Todd: Has anybody threatened to cut your hair?

Thomas: Like jackasses at a show? No. My band mates sometimes have. Jesus, my mother-in-law always does, but she's kind of a wacky lady. I've had dreads for ten years. My cousin, from Gambia, she came in 1991. She put them in my hair.

Todd: What is your direct connection with The Black Crowes? You have met and worked with some person who has worked with them.

Thomas: John Morand, the producer for *A Chorus of One*. He also made Inquisition records. They're the studio that Avail's recording their new record in. It's the Richmond studio that David Lowery from Cracker came down and started in an old warehouse with vintage equipment and gifted engineers. John Morand's the producer of The Black Crowes, us, the solo record for the woman who sings for the Cardigans, and other really obscure, talented people rolling through Richmond. He was one of the first generations of punk rockers from Richmond in '77. There's a picture of him in the paper from Freeman High School, "Punks! What is this!?" A picture of him with a trench coat. Just a trench coat. But back then it didn't matter, you could have just a trench coat and it was scary. So, he knew where we were coming from on that shit.

Todd: Do you have the nickname Fangy?

Thomas: How the fuck do you know these things? There's a lot of different nicknames for me. Fangy T is one of them. Our friend Max was recording a 7" for us. When I was recording vocals, he would turn the mic off, so everyone in the control room could hear them, but not me, and he said, "Thomas is just fangin' in there." Everyone's like, "Tom, stop fangin'." And I never knew what it meant. It must be the stupid way I make my face when I scream.

Todd: What's the story behind the song "Sunset on 32nd"?

Thomas: They were doing a racial profiled drug dragnet shakedown. Any black male between the ages of twelve to thirty who's riding a bicycle, they assume is a runner for the corners—for the drug trade. There are corners in our neighborhood. There are runners. Maybe some of them are on bikes. Many, many of the kids got arrested for these arcane bike violations that would never have been applied to anyone in any other neighborhood, or any white kid riding a bike, anywhere. It was horrible. Harold, our neighbor from across the street, had to get diapers for one of his kids. They have two daughters. He went and came back. His bike's brakes were fucked. It was a pretty old bike. The police, I guess, had followed him back to his house and he went into his home and they broke down the door, ran into his house, flashed their weapons in front of Chanté and their kids, Tiosha and Niasia. They went into the back, where he was, and pulled him onto the carpet in the hallway and beat him and then dragged him out of the house. Six or seven cops. He's a big man. He works at Lowe's. We would hang out with them all the time. We'd have them over. They were great neighbors. We would take care of the kids sometimes, too. They'd come over and play with our dogs.

We heard this because we were taking a nap in the back room at my house. We heard them—from inside their house from across the street to inside our house—he's screaming, "I'm not resisting you. Please stop beating me." It was the most horrible thing to hear someone say that. Ever. Here's a strong, kind, intelligent, proud man. Proud of his family. They were filled with life, this whole family was. We were good friends with them for about a year and a half.

The police saw me and Leslie come out of the house and they kind of stopped kicking him a little. They had three cop cars, about six or seven police, including the sergeant, who is the head of that district in Church Hill. He's an unbelievable racist, who's gone to the local bar in our neighborhood and said, "We've been pushin' 'em back North ever since the '60s," referring to the collusion between real estate investment in the historic neighborhood and racist police practices, driving people of color out of the neighborhoods that their grandfathers and grandmothers have lived in. It's horrible. Because of our skin color, I'm assuming, and the shock that there were Caucasian folks in the neighborhood watching them beat down a citizen, they stopped. We walked right through them with the most intense disgust and rage I've probably ever felt and contained in my life. We went over and picked up their kids. How do you call the cops on the cops? So, we called the media and we tried a program called "Channel 12: On Your Side." We called the newspaper. We called our city councilwoman and we left a couple messages. We got a few callbacks. Nobody was interested. It happens all the goddamn time. Our heroic police force is doing a great job on the war on drugs. This is just collateral damage. One of the cops said, "I thought he had a gun. I thought he was running into this house to take these people hostage." It's his fucking home. They said the most worthless excuses.

Todd: And I'm assuming that if you're getting some Pampers, the package is pretty big.

Thomas: Groceries and diapers. Anyway, the police had a lot of fabricated shit about the incident. They took him to the hospital first. They cleaned him up. They took him to jail. He stayed there overnight for resisting arrest. Chanté had to testify in court. It destroyed their life because they didn't have the money to fix the door before the landlords came. The landlords kicked them out because the door was broken off the hinges. They had to move North to the projects, which is the intention of police actions like this in every neighborhood in America. Me and Leslie would take their kids to the park and take them to work when we could. We got Chanté a job.

They broke up. Harold actually started getting into fights. There was gunplay in the neighborhood. He went to jail. She found another boyfriend, and I don't know what happened. The drug trade got in their lives, where once, it wasn't. Where once, they were a nuclear family, working and filled with happiness and potential. The last thing we heard, the kids ended up in a foster home. Those kids who were like our godkids. They're gone. We can never find them. It's insane. It just breaks our heart. We helped them financially and with our friendship for a long time, and we tried to get local activist groups involved, and all it basically turned into was a song that we sang and a warning and that is the most frustrating thing. And the line in that song about, "holding your family close to your heart," is the most critical therapy for this event for me.

I can't begin to imagine what it meant for them to go through this. We just saw this. We're across the street. And we hate those fucking cops with our guts. We see them at the Church Hill diner and just look the other way. There are a lot of people in Richmond who are curious about this event and we've talked to so many people about it, and there's awareness building. The councilwoman was generous with us and there's a sense that maybe with incidents like this—there was another shooting of a man, Levester Carter Jr., was shot to death by a police woman in Richmond. Actually, the Southern Christian Leadership Conference came in and rallied there the week before we left for tour and he was shot. He was a man who had some outstanding warrants in DC. The police pulled him over and he ran and as he ran, they emptied a clip into him and when he was on the ground, she emptied another clip into him. This woman, a police officer, was awarded a medal for heroism for shooting a man in the back. And he was armed and he had outstanding warrants, but he was running. One shot or a warning, whatever, it's understandable in this context. So, that's what we're faced with and what every community's faced with. This is just our experience in Richmond in particular.

Todd: What are you going to do, as a band, from becoming your own parody or cliché? What are you doing internally in keeping the band vital?

Thomas: We talk about this a lot. We have a self-awareness. We make fun of ourselves to ourselves constantly. We are the first band to joke on our own songs. We make crazy fun of our songs. We know that there is a lot of vitriol and aggression and love for humanity that drives us—and a love for how flawed and stupid and silly punk still needs to be. It has to be something that is self-aware and it has to be something that has ideals, but isn't just a humorless political movement or a backdrop to a bunch of people mimicking a political movement. We are really aware of those potentials and it's conflicting and strange and we write songs that we give our hearts, trying to diffuse any sense of musical tactics or the hidden aspects of being a product. We try to get that out of music and still play what we love and tell the stories that we have to. That catharsis is what punk's really about and it has to start from a personal level. I think we're still trying to do that—and learning from each other and making this a part of our lives, not just like a business or artistic venture or some combination of either. We're making it a part of our lives, our adventure in the world, and still retaining our humility about it and to know that we're just a small part of it and we're happy to add whatever momentum we can because it meant so much to us.

· · ·

"*People who don't change their views aren't smart people. Some people have a way with words and others have... not... way.*"

–Fat Mike

THINGS WERE AWFUL
AND IT WAS GREAT:
AN INTERVIEW WITH NOFX

It's one of the longest overnight success stories ever told. The band toiled in Los Angeles's underground for the better part of a decade, toured constantly, and barely broke even. They often got panned as a derivative blend of RKL, metal, and stilted humor. But they stuck it out far longer than lesser bands. Fat Mike's lyrics transformed from pretty obvious with easy targets to truly witty. Eric and Erik—guitarist and drummer—were able to transcend the Nardcore musical headlock they started in and not only came into their own, but, not to their fault, they spawned a cloning process which convinced literally thousands of bands to cop, note for note, the style they developed. With the addition of El Hefe's trumpet and humor in the early '90s, the band took off. Sort of.

There was nothing meteoric about their ascent. Each record continued to improve in sales a bit. 1994's *Punk in Drublic* sold steadily. In 2000, it went gold. 500,000 isn't too shabby for a band that was stoked to sell 10,000 copies of *Ribbed*.

While this was happening, Fat Mike, along with his wife, Erin, started a label, Fat Wreck Chords. Mirroring NOFX's success, the label continued to grow in increments. Instead of going for an easy brass ring by opting to be purchased by a major label, both the band and the label were constantly reinvested into. By the end of the '90s, Fat had grown to become one of most respected, fairest, most artist-friendly, and strongest labels that punk rock had ever produced. In no small part, NOFX made it possible.

Herein lies great beauty. There is an underground in America and NOFX is one of its stalwarts. Access to that underground is less difficult than getting a driver's license, but it does take some effort. You have to learn how to tune into and collect songs that don't get played often on the radio or the television. (NOFX has never been on MTV.) NOFX are no strangers to punk rock, will never be the next big thing, and don't adhere to a complicated marketing scheme. This one's all about a band that bought in instead of selling out.

They rarely give interviews.

Fat Mike: vocals, bass
Erik Ghint: drums
Eric Melvin: guitar
El Hefe: trumpet, guitar, vocals

Todd: What was with all the shoes thrown up on stage? How many shoes did you collect?

Fat Mike: Probably twenty.

Eric: I caught one on my mouth.

Todd: Oh no.

Fat Mike: It happens in the LA, Phoenix, San Diego areas. Once we start going east, people hold on to their shoes.

Todd: They've got to walk home. It's cold.

Fat Mike: That's right.

Todd: Who had the fight back stage last night? Was that Fletcher?

Fat Mike: Yeah, Fletcher from Pennywise. Five guys were on him.

Eric: A guy from the Palladium grabbed our tech by the neck.

Todd: That's not good.

Eric: It wasn't cool.

Fat Mike: And I think Fletcher broke some guy's jaw. Pretty rough.

Todd: Why the hesitancy to give interviews?

El Hefe: Because every time we give interviews, people have been mean to us and rude and it hurts our feelings.

Fat Mike: No. That's not it at all. There's two reasons. First of all, we did a lot of interviews and somehow they filtered into major magazines and they were just lies, a bunch of bullshit. The other reason is we have nothing to say really.

El Hefe: Can I say one thing? [He takes the microphone and farts into it.]

Fat Mike: The other thing is, we just started lying all the time, making up stories because our interviews were so boring. So then we thought, "What's the point of lying?" And then now, we don't like doing them because we're not looking for publicity anymore. We're just looking to play and have fun. We don't need to get any bigger. We don't want to get any bigger. I saw a friend of mine's band. They did an interview and a photo—some punk band—and it was in *Spin* and it looked so dumb. And I thought, I don't want to be there.

Todd: What didn't you like? What didn't you want to see?

Fat Mike: I didn't want to see them in that magazine. That photo of them—it was like—god. 'Cause they're cool guys, they're friends of mine but they looked like fucking idiots in *Spin*.

Todd: Gel and mousse. They look pretty.

Fat Mike: Yeah. I don't want to be involved in that, you know? We're really lucky. We're in a great place. We have a lot of fans and we're not trying to fool anybody. We're just putting out records, having a good time.

Todd: Do you mind telling how many records you've sold? The last couple albums, are they selling better or worse?

Fat Mike: Our last couple albums have pretty much plateaued and that's fine. We're all making a good living. No problems. The three punk bands that signed and got real big, they have nowhere to go but down. And they all are going down. You know what? We're staying right where we are and we're totally happy.

Todd: Technical question. NoFX or NOFX?

Fat Mike: All big. That was a Doug Moody (owner of Mystic Records) thing and somehow we got a small "o."

Todd: What does it stand for?

Fat Mike: Well, it's stupid, but when we started, the other guys in the band were straight edge. I wasn't. So, NOFX.

Todd: Did some of the original members come from La Cresenta, Montrose area (A little north of Los Angeles.)?

Fat Mike: Yeah. Our drummer. We were a three piece and we still have those three original members. Thirteen years now.

Todd: Wow. You, Melvin, and... Erik?

Fat Mike: Erik.

Todd: I got confused because I thought his name was Herb for some reason.

Fat Mike: He changes his name on all the albums.

Todd: There we go. That's why I didn't recognize it.

Fat Mike: Herb Reath Stinks—"her breath stinks." All our old names were like that. Mine was Mike Rackhabit—"my crack habit."

Todd: I don't want to ask this question, but where did the name Fat Mike come from? El Hefe's bigger than you are.

Fat Mike: You know, I want to get this out because I'm tired of that fucking question. Don't ever ask me this question again. I was a hundred and thirty pounds when I went to college and they gave me this little food card.

Todd: Ahh, the thirty meal plan.

Fat Mike: You could eat whatever you want and I gained thirty-five pounds in one school year. I went on tour the next year and every city we went to, people went, "Fuck, you put on some pounds, didn't ya?" Everywhere we went, everybody started calling me Fat Mike.

Todd: Who has the biggest tits in the band right now?

Fat Mike: El Hefe.

Todd: Know his measurements?

Fat Mike: No, but he's getting pretty big. People who have never seen us before, they go up to him and say, "Are you Fat Mike?"

Todd: I bet... has he always played the horn? Does he have any training with that?

Fat Mike: Yeah. He plays horn, piano, skin flute, hanging sax, the male organ, all types of stuff.

Todd: Where do you guys get your ska influences and your reggae stuff?

Fat Mike: Operation Ivy. The Clash. All the good ska and reggae comes from punk bands, if you ask me. Bad Brains. I got this *Bob Marley's*

Greatest Hits and I like one song, you know. It has a nice feel to it but the melodies aren't so great.

Todd: Can you give me, to the nearest thousand, the number of bands that have spawned to sound like you?

Fat Mike: I dunno.

Todd: How did NOFX come across this sound?

Fat Mike: I'll tell you exactly how we got this sound. It's pretty simple. When we first started, we wanted to sound like RKL. So we started playing songs like RKL. Then Bad Religion. They've always been my favorite band. *Suffer* came out. We were, "Shoot, maybe we should put some melodies in our stuff." So we're a cross between RKL and Bad Religion. That was all that it was. And all our reviewers used to say, "Sounds like RKL," "Sounds like RKL." So now, I guess it's our sound. And D.I., too. We got the octave chords from D.I.

Todd: Where'd you get the humor?

Fat Mike: Us. But, you know, humor didn't pay our rent. The first six years were really terrible. People always say, "You've gotta tour. The more you tour, the more popular you're going to become," but we toured every year for five years straight and we still had forty people at our shows. It was when our albums started getting better.

Todd: What's changed the most for you, for being in NOFX for so long? When you wake up in the morning, what do you realize has changed the most?

Fat Mike: I'm just stoked all the time.

Todd: I would be, too.

Fat Mike: I don't have many worries.

Todd: [to Eric Melvin] You own a coffee store?

Eric: Um hmm. A coffee store. I call it a cafè.

Todd: I roast coffee.

Eric: Do you really?

Fat Mike: He's got a coffee yard in the back.

Todd: Do you know any interesting coffee facts?

Eric: No.

Todd: None whatsoever?

Eric: You mix it with water and it gets really interesting. Yeah, it was something I wanted to do. I thought it would be fun. God, everybody's got record labels so I thought I'd try something different like *not* make money. I like it a lot because everyone's there and everyone comes in and is hanging out and everyone has to eat and drink something so that's where I get my bucks. People come in everyday and I've got a lot of friends who work there.

Fat Mike: It's just a nice place to hang out.

Eric: See if it's going to work, you know.

Todd: How long has it been open for?

Eric: Two years. And it's getting better and better and I'm learning how to really do it.

Fat Mike: How to really pour the milk in and...

Eric: Foam it.

Todd: Nozzle control.

Eric: There's such a skill.

Fat Mike: When was the last time you did it?

Eric: Never. But when you get it just right, the foam stands above the cup.

Todd: It's like meringue.

Eric: It's really good.

Fat Mike: Not me, I don't like that foam stuff. Straight, no milk, unless it's rice milk.

Todd: At the coffee shop I work at, I took an informal poll. Most people who come in are thirty-five or over. About half of them had heard of either Green Day or the Offspring but none one of them had heard of NOFX.

Fat Mike: Good.

Todd: Why do you think that is? Is that intentional or a really nice by-product?

Fat Mike: You see, it's our job to keep punk rock elite. It's not for every one.

Todd: Do you think punk rock's dying?

Fat Mike: No. I went to that Dickies show last night. It was awesome. It was pure punk rock.

Todd: Yeah, it's alive and well.

Fat Mike: We were playing at the non punk rock show.

Todd: How were your teeth? I heard you got hit by the mic.

Fat Mike: A chip here, a chip there. I can take it.

Todd: Do you think there's still a high level of resentment towards punk rock bands that make more than five dollars a head at a show? Do you think there's people who think you've sold out?

Fat Mike: Sure.

Todd: Why do you think it's so prevalent?

Fat Mike: It's kind of a punk rock thing. I don't know. It's just an elitist thing.

Todd: Elitist?

Fat Mike: Yeah, but I like that about punk rock. I felt the same way when I was a kid. It's our scene and when some band tries to get a bigger following, well fuck you, you know. We like it small. We like how it is. But, you know, you can't have it both ways and we chose to make a living at it and not work in a factory. Fat supports about ten people. I don't think any of the musicians have to work other jobs. I'm a vegetarian now.

Todd: Seriously?

Fat Mike: Yeah.

Todd: What brought that about?

Fat Mike: I used to sing songs about how dumb vegetarians were. "Vegetarian Mumbo Jumbo," but it has something to do about a cruelty free existence.

Todd: Do you feel any remorse about hurting vegetarian's feelings?

Fat Mike: No, I just think people change.

Todd: It's all personal choice.

Fat Mike: It's all part of being human. Intelligent people, they...

Todd: Cut you a little slack?

Fat Mike: Well, no, you just change. People who don't change their views aren't smart people. Some people have a way with words and others have... not... way. [laughter]

Todd: What's the last book you've read?

Fat Mike: My favorite author is a woman called Pat Califia. She's this S&M lesbian in San Francisco who writes gnarly bondage stuff. It's pretty rad.

Eric: I used to read fantasy and science fiction. That's what I always read.

Fat Mike: We're all big fans of what's his name.

Eric: Douglas Adams.

Fat Mike: In fact, he's got a tattoo from it on his neck.

Eric: *Hitchhiker's Guide to the Galaxy*, *Restaurant at the End of the Universe*.

Todd: Who's got the stinkiest ass?

Fat Mike: Our drummer. His nickname is Smelly.

Todd: Who has a hidden talent?

Eric: I'm good in bed.

Todd: Somehow that doesn't surprise me.

Eric: I'm learning to play the ukulele. I'm learning to play the banjo as well.

Fat Mike: I have one, I just don't play it.

Todd: Are you thinking about using more horns in future albums?

Fat Mike: Probably not. We're going to use less. Take out the guitars probably.

Todd: All drumming.

Fat Mike: Basically. Come on.

Todd: How do you come across ideas for songs? They don't seem as arbitrary as others bands' stuff, but the song "Johnny Appleseed," for instance, is kinda weird because it deals with an Appalachian folk hero.

Fat Mike: Well, it's not because what it is actually about is our drummer, right. Because we'd go on tour and he'd go around and he'd be fucking these girls everywhere. So, it's not actual apple seeds, it's him fucking chicks. Planting seeds. So there you go.

Eric: Then it gets twisted around and El Hefe sings it like...

Fat Mike: See, if you notice all the words in there, they're all referring to sex.

Todd: Where did "Liza and Louise" come from?

Fat Mike: Liza and Louise? That's directly from Pat Califia and Liza. There are references in Liza that absolutely no one will understand unless you read her book, *Macho Sluts*.

Todd: Who did you masturbate to when you were kids?

Fat Mike: Absolutely, Becky Bondage (Vice Squad), all the way.

Eric: Just about anything.

Fat Mike: Wendy O. Williams.

Todd: Plasmatics. Did you know she married Richard Dean Anderson of MacGyver fame? I shit you not.

Fat Mike: You shit me so.

Todd: No I don't. Honest truth.

Fat Mike: Wow.

Todd: So are you guys happy all the time? Not happy happy, but satisfied with what you're doing?

Eric: Yeah. Things are definitely getting better.

Fat Mike: I cannot think of anything I'd rather do in any way.

Todd: That's the perfect answer. Do you think people are trying to get the wrong things out of life? Do you see that a lot?

Fat Mike: Totally. But, you know, there's not too much choice. You get sucked in.

Todd: Where did Me First and the Gimme Gimmes come from?

Fat Mike: San Francisco.

Todd: Is that one of your side projects?

Fat Mike: No. Sorta.

Todd: Is anybody interested in doing any other side projects? Are you worried about that?

Eric: I am. I'm very interested. One question at a time, okay.

Todd: Okay.

Eric: I'm interested. My friend Kelly is a drummer. He plays in a band called Failure and we did a song for an Amnesty comp. Good time for the tape recorder to stop.

Todd: Do you want me to?

Eric: No. We did this for an Amnesty International benefit comp that's going to be released soon. I think and we're going to do some more stuff in the future. Less pop, more experimental or something.

Fat Mike: We have a lot of spare time now because NOFX; we only tour three or four months a year now. We used to do it eight or nine months. We don't do it so much any more. We feel more fresh. When you play two months in a row, it starts to become kind of a job. We do two-week tours now and it's fun. The whole tour is fun and you can tell. When we're on stage we're having a fucking great time.

Todd: It's fun to watch you guys interact. What's the coolest shirt you've ever got thrown at you?

Fat Mike: I got this shirt that said "Drug Dependent" (in the style of Independent skateboard trucks) but that's not very interesting. Got some cool bras.

Todd: Do you get a lot of boob shots when you've playing?

Fat Mike: Boob shots?

Todd: Girls flashing you.

Eric: It happened once, I think, from what I can remember.

Todd: That's it? You guys aren't the Allman Brothers? Happens to them all the time.

Eric: Once Mike yelled, "Gimme all your clothes," and kids were throwing...

Fat Mike: Once, in Seattle, I said, "Gimme your grunge clothes, man." I got so many clothes and I put them all on.

Eric: And he put them all on. Bras and panties, too.

Fat Mike: I had a panty on my head.

Todd: Did you guys get any flack for sending out the Love Ewes, the promotional inflatable sheep for *Heavy Petting Zoo*?

Fat Mike: Two stores got sued for the posters.

Todd: The art is so well drawn. You don't see any of the bad parts of the sheep. It's all suggestion.

Fat Mike: That's right.

Eric: That's the funny part. It's all suggestion, so anybody who takes offense at it, it's their own imagination that's like... well, I guess you don't need too much imagination for what he's doing to that sheep.

Todd: Did MTV offer you a lot of money to do a video?

Fat Mike: MTV didn't offer it. They were bugging Epitaph a lot to send them the video because they really wanted to play us. It really started getting ugly when we kept on saying no. We had No Use For A Name on Fat Wreck Chords. They had a video and MTV started to play it because they had a lot of radio play and one of the lead guys there, Kurt Steffic, the leader of *120 Minutes*, he talked to me one day and was like, "Well, you know, we'd really like to play you guys. Will you please give us your video because we're going to push the shit out of it. We really want it." I go, "We're really not into it." He said, "Well, we're going to drop the No Use For A Name video." So they blackmailed us. Give us NOFX. We'll keep playing No Use For A Name. Right then is when my philosophy became straight. I'm not fucking dealing with any of these assholes.

Todd: Can you name one punk band that made a good move to the majors?

Fat Mike: Green Day. They're the only punk band I know of that was successful switching from an indie to a major. Punk band, we're talking about. How many did bad on major labels? Bad Religion, Offspring...

Todd: The only one I can think of that is doing okay is Social Distortion.

Fat Mike: Yeah, but that's kinda weird. They've been a major for a long time.

Todd: The Dickies were one of the first on a major. A&M.

Fat Mike: Yes they were. I really didn't have anything wrong with major labels. Whatever. Do what you want. I've just seen so many of my friends' bands get flushed down the toilet. Jawbreaker. Samiam. The list is huge. They've all got fucked by major labels.

Todd: What is your guys' association with snowboard and shoe companies? I see Vans and Airwalk all over the place. You're on quite a few snowboard comps.

Fat Mike: Well, we all snowboard. Morrow started giving us free snowboards. We all walk, so Airwalk started giving us shoes.

Todd: Where was your worst tour experience? Was there ever any time you said, "This is no fucking good. I'm going to make peanut brittle the rest of my life," or something like that?

Fat Mike: Well, no. When we were a small band, things were awful, and it was great. We had to siphon gas and sell acid on tour to get by, but it was so fun. The worst thing was just recently, I think. I was so pissed. We had a show in Moscow and they wouldn't let us into the city. We flew up there and they wouldn't let us play. They wouldn't let us out of the airport. First they said, "You have to pay eight hundred dollars each," and there were eight of us. We said, "Okay, we'll do that because we just want to fucking play." Then the head chief guy said no and we fly all the way back. So that was pretty lame.

Todd: Was it just for one show?

Fat Mike: Yeah.

Todd: What's the worst mis-billing you've ever been on?

Fat Mike: Whitesnake.

Todd: No shit?

Eric: That was some German festival. Our largest show. 200,000 people.

Todd: As a kid, did you know what you wanted to do when you grew up?

Fat Mike: No. There was not even the slightest hope of ever making money playing punk rock. So, none of us had any idea. In fact, I remember I had a goal and that was to make a hundred dollars a night. I thought if we could make a hundred dollars a night, we'd be set, we could all make a living. That was my big goal and we just about reached it.

Todd: I've got sort of a philosophical question. Why is punk rock so fervently protected and so fervently attacked? For the mainstream press, punk rock is something to grow out of. If you're young, it's okay. Bjork will say,

"Yeah, back when I was in the Sugarcubes, I was punk," but it's not okay when you "mature." Why do you think that is?

Fat Mike: It's just the big anarchy thing when you were a kid. The big rebellion thing. You don't get into punk rock when you're old so I think you just grow out of it because you get into it when you're a kid.

Todd: You think you're less angry about it now?

Fat Mike: I was never too angry. I thought it was cool and fun.

Todd: Still do?

Fat Mike: Yeah.

Todd: Who do you think is the paradigm of punk?

Eric: AJ, the singer of Das Klown. He loves that in-your-face shit—shouts at the crowd, puts people down.

Fat Mike: Paradigm of punk. I know what paradigm means.

Eric: I don't.

Todd: Are your parents happy with you?

Fat Mike: Yeah, well both sets of our parents were, "When are you going to grow out of this fucking shit?" His mom wanted him to be a psychiatrist and my mom wanted me to be a real estate agent and they kept on saying, "When are you going to start your life?" and then we started making money.

Eric: Now they're proud of us.

Todd: Why did you change the original name from *White Trash, Two Kikes and a Spic* to *White Trash, Two Heebs and a Bean*? [Silence]

Fat Mike: Tell him.

Eric: 'Cause my mom had heard about it and she told my grandma and my grandma became very upset and I just couldn't live with that.

Fat Mike: Jewish guilt is pretty tough.

Todd: What are you going to say to the kids who want to do an interview with you and you won't let them do it?

Fat Mike: Well, we do interviews with some small zines sometimes but we don't want publicity. We don't need it. That's it. We've fucking told our story a million fucking times. We're not that interesting. If you want to learn something about us, read our lyrics.

Todd: What are the most Fat Mike-esque lyrics you've written?

Fat Mike: ...fuck.

Todd: Quite a few bands try to distance themselves from their lyrics and say they're just words so they don't get clumped as an instrumental band.

Fat Mike: I don't know if I could pick one song but I've got some advice. Join a punk band and see the world.

•   •   •

MAN... OR ASTRO-MAN?

"I'd rather have punk actions than punk fashions."
                                                    —Fletcher

BLOWING CHOWDER ALL OVER THE PLACE: AN INTERVIEW WITH FLETCHER DRAGGE OF PENNYWISE

It's difficult to deny. Part of what makes punk rock tick is that it liberates a few souls to do what they want to do, physically. Sometimes there's too much thinkin' and not enough drinkin'. It comes down to practical jokes and acts of petty larceny pulled off with style, two often overlooked and important elements that prevent the entire enterprise from becoming stale. Fletcher is an imposing man. He's just big and strong. Not particularly muscular or sculpted, he's built more like a bear and has the strength of someone who's worked their entire life in manual labor.

Fletcher plays guitar in Los Angeles's South Bay, politically conscious punk rock band, Pennywise. He's infamous for stunts: ripping the roofs off of burger joints, crashing golf carts, going through parties and water-pistoling people with guns filled with his pee. He does this trick where he snorts a ball chain through his nose and pulls it through his mouth, inducing a gag reflex of puke—usually on his friends.

Dusk has fallen on the previous era of physical embodiments of punk rock. GG Allin passed on with a whisper instead of bang. El Duce of the Mentors died under suspicious circumstances and was hit by a train. Fletcher's a fine example of one of the strong hopes for the music I adore, and the culture it spawns, remaining nice and fucked up. It's important, solely by the fact that what he did and does can never be bought and sold as commodity in a mall next to eighty-dollar sunglasses. What he's done is criminal. Funny and ballsy, yet criminal. The actual act of the crime can't be canned, labeled, and put up for sale. People like him partially negate one of the most common complaints leveled at punk rock. Perhaps the music itself isn't seen as the widespread threat as when it first came out, but that doesn't mean that the people involved in it can't be as potentially dangerous as anyone who preceded them. When Fletcher charges, fear registers pretty quickly.

All that said, Fletcher isn't a sociopath. He's a man who understands the importance of timing and placement. He doesn't wake up and go punch the mailman, set fire to a hillside, then dump nuclear waste into the ocean to get his destruction quota in for the day. He waits. He understands how cops operate and what the term "statute of limitations" means. At the time of this interview, he was calm, articulate, expressed animals as sacred ground, and he offered me a soda. No blood was spilt, no teeth were lost.

Todd: Okay, fact or fiction? Did you beat a hole in the top of a Burger King?

Fletcher: Oh man, you're asking these kinds of questions.

Todd: Well these are the stories I've heard so I want verify...

Fletcher: It wasn't a Burger King but we'll leave the name of the fast food chain out.

Todd: For retribution?

Fletcher: Yeah.

Todd: In the ceiling?

Fletcher: We wanted to get some food after a show at the Anti-Club and my friend's house has a balcony that overlooks... the buildings were close enough to be able to jump from the roof. So, we got on the roof and ripped open an air conditioning vent or something. It was dark so you couldn't see, but I've done construction my whole life so I know how these things are built. We got this guy to hang down there and he couldn't touch the ceiling and I was trying to step on his fingers to make him fall through. We were having a good time. A couple of my friends were trying to stop me and we were fighting on the roof and he was hanging there 'cause he couldn't pull himself up. We finally got him up and went and got a flashlight. It was about eight feet down from where he was hanging to the end of the ceiling (the inside of the rafter) and so I decided I was gonna go in. I hung down and then I dropped in. There was a little piece of plywood to land on and I kicked a hole through the ceiling and the ceiling fell out and then there was a t-bar ceiling, like an acoustic ceiling below that, about four or five feet. The debris fell through that and the floor was another ten feet down. It was probably a total of fifteen feet. I was like "I'm not doing it. I'm not dropping in there. It's too far. I'm gonna get hurt." They were trying to pull me out. I couldn't pull myself out. It was a tight hatch so my friends would grab my wrists and they'd get me up to my stomach and they'd drop me. They did this three times in a row 'cause they'd start laughing and there was no way for me to catch myself on the way down so I would fall straight back in and land on this little piece of plywood and if I missed it I'd fall through. The third time they were pulling me up, they started laughing again. Then we all started laughing and they let go. I fell straight through the plywood, straight through the one ceiling and straight through the other thing and straight down on the floor. They said it was like... what was that movie called? *High Anxiety.* I've never seen it.

Todd: Me neither.

Fletcher: But there's like this scene in it... they watch me fall through the ceiling and there's all this shit and I'm laying on the ground underneath them and they're lookin' down at me goin' "Goddamn!" We didn't steal any money or anything. We just went back and loaded up a couple of milk crates full of food and a bunch of meat. Burger fixings. Mayonnaise, relish, all that stuff. We found a ladder. You know, they have those ladders for cleaning, and we put it up on the service counter, punched another hole through and climbed back to where that spot was through the attic. They got the food and finally pulled me up and we went and had a big feast and a food fight. I'm trying to mellow out these days because I don't want to go to jail.

Todd: How close are you to going to the pokey? What's the count?

Fletcher: I've been a few times, but I mean... it's hard to say. I just have some problems with some local police. They don't like me. I told some cop that if I ever saw him without his badge again then I would brawl him or maybe a little worse, you know. Then they caught me a month later. They gave me a beating and arrested me for assault on a police officer. It's kind of a long story. Basically, I got two years probation and a fine, so now the cops really don't like me. They all know me around here. I've lived here my whole life. So we'll see what happens. I'm gonna keep kinda mellow around this neighborhood. Save my exploits for out of state and out of the country.

Todd: True or false: you went through a party with squirt guns filled with pee?

Fletcher: Yeah. That's true. That would have been at a girl's birthday party, I believe. I think DFL (Dead Fucking Last) got the worst of that one. Tom Barta got a couple of mouthfuls of urine.

Todd: At what point did you think that was a good idea? Was there any alcohol involved?

Fletcher: Oh yeah, plenty of alcohol involved. For some reason I tend to think that bodily fluids are funny. You know, you watch someone in a movie start puking and everyone starts laughing. Funny stuff.

Todd: What happened at that NOFX show at the Palladium? I was there. I saw the scuffle and I heard that a sound check guy got wrung by the neck and then fifteen people were there all of a sudden.

Fletcher: Oh, I wasn't even at that show.

Todd: Really?

Fletcher: Yeah, it was just Fat Mike fucking around. He knew I wasn't there and he just knew that people would believe that story.

Todd: Mike's good at that.

Fletcher: Yeah, he's a good guy.

Todd: What story do you hear most about yourself that is completely untrue?

Fletcher: Well geez, most of them are true. That's the problem. I've heard a lot of stories get exaggerated but, uh, untrue? I've heard a couple of times that I'm dead. Those are common. Actually, some kid at a cof-feehouse the other day was talking like he knew the band that I'm producing. Someone said that I was producing it and he said, "No, he's in jail. He'll be in jail for two weeks."

Todd: What's the craziest thing you've ever done? When do you think, "Oh man, I fucked up real bad?"

Fletcher: Um, I don't want to talk about it.

Todd: Okay, what's the worst one that you'll share?

Fletcher: The stuff that I think is fun or whatever people would think is crazy. Like something really bad would be... bad, but no animals, man. Animals are sacred ground.

Todd: True or false? You got on a surfboard and paddled out to a cruise ship. You went on to the cruise ship and told people, "Hey, give me beer or I'll beat you up." You then got beer, paddled back, and gave beer to your friends.

Fletcher: Now you see, that's a combination of two stories. I think this is what happened. My friend and I had a boat, an old beat-up boat, years ago and we were in PV (Palos Verdes, California) up off the coast and we needed some beer so I paddled my surf board to the beach and then climbed up a cliff, all filthy and muddy. The houses up there were all nice and I walked onto these people's property and I told the guy there that my boat was out of gas. So he told the kids in Japanese and they got me a gas can and put me in their Mercedes in a pair of trunks that were all muddy. He took me to the gas station and bought me five gallons of gas and then I told him that I needed to stop by the store really quick. They didn't speak English. So they stop by the liquor store and I come out with two cases of Bud tall cans and they were like, "What the fuck is this guy doing?" I went down the cliff and set the gas can down and I go, "Thanks." I walked down and paddled back out to the boat and we continued drinking. And the other story that got crossed with this was kind of incriminating but they can't prove it now. Anyways, there was a barge out at sea and it was like three or four miles out—three times the size of a three-bedroom house. They had a restaurant on it and we were all hammered one night and all the liquor stores were closed so we got in the boat and went out there but no one knew where we were going. I was just driving out to sea, singing "Pirates of the Caribbean." So we get up there and dock onto the boat and the waves were pretty gnarly. There were swells out there so the boat was getting slammed against the barge. We tied it up, got the anchor, and smashed off the... man, if someone reads this I could get in trouble. We smashed off the lock and just went in and pillaged like sixteen cases of beer and got some food. We left all the money. Only food and beverage. So, we loaded the boat with all this beer, went back, and unloaded it in the car. But that wasn't me who did that. It was actually someone else who did it. I just heard the story. But there's the combination of your two stories.

Todd: What's your tolerance level? How many beers can you drink before you pass out?

Fletcher: I pretty much never pass out. It's very rare. Probably a lot of beer. I could drink for twenty-four or forty-eight hours straight. A lot of beer.

Todd: How do you feel about El Duce dying?

Fletcher: I heard about that. That's pretty much a bummer. I've known him a long time and haven't seen him for years. I used to hang out with him at the Anti-Club and the streets of Hollywood and drink beer and wine in the bushes with him. I think a lot of kids these days have no clue who he is. It would be the older, more hardcore people who know who he is. He was a great punk rocker. One of the all-time legends of Hollywood, I would say. Good band, too.

Todd: Yeah, good band.

Fletcher: Good stuff.

Todd: Who do you think will fill in his shoes? I mean El Duce's gone, GG's gone. There's no bad boy anymore.

Fletcher: That's a good question.

Todd: You're waiting for a European tour?

Fletcher: Yeah, to belly up. I don't know, maybe that guy from the Dwarves will have a relapse too. I'll have a relapse. Back to the old days. It could be anybody. There are a lot of crazy, demented people out there who could probably step up and pull it off… I'm really surprised that I'm alive right now. There's been a lot of stuff involving cars—stolen cars, bad car wrecks and jumping off buildings into pools. All really stupid things but you only live once so you might as well have a good time doing it.

Todd: What's your biggest sustained injury?

Fletcher: I don't ever really get hurt that bad for some reason. With all the stuff I do you'd think I'd get hurt a lot worse. Just broken bones and bumps on the head. Nothing fancy. I should be in a wheelchair by now. My body's pretty much getting put through the wringer.

Todd: Scar tissue or anything like that?

Fletcher: Oh yeah, there's a couple scars laying around. I burned "Pennywise" in my arm with a hot knife about six years ago. It's healing up pretty good, though. Overall, I'm in pretty good health. I just feel like I'm sixty.

Todd: How old are you?

Fletcher: I'm thirty-one. Pretty old.

Todd: How tall are you?

Fletcher: 6'5", about 219 lbs.

Todd: Is there anybody you've hit who you wished you hadn't?

Fletcher: I don't really ever hit people.

Todd: What's the biggest misconception about you?

Fletcher: Probably that I'm a bully. But I only fuck around with people I know. People who understand, you know? If you're my friend then you have a lot better chance of getting injured than you do if you're a stranger. I'm really not into violence at all. I hate fights. I always try to break up fights even if I don't know people. It takes a whole lot for me to get mad enough to punch someone, but I might hit somebody out of fun. Not hard. A lot of people think I'm this complete asshole. People have called me a Nazi. They don't see the humor in stuff but if people who didn't like me, took a chance to hang out with me, they would probably like me within an hour. You guys already like me. I'm not as bad as you thought.

Todd: I didn't think you were going to be bad, to tell you the truth.

Fletcher: Yeah, sure you did.

Todd: To be around for such a long time and to have such high profile, you have to temper things. Otherwise it'll self-destruct.

Fletcher: Yeah, a lot of people who don't know us, or me, think we're some jock rock punk band. I played soccer when I was thirteen and stuff. I was into punk rock in 1980 so pretty much I didn't even watch sports on TV except for surfing and skating. We're just a bunch of beach kids and people think that Pennywise is this big jock thing.

Todd: Why do you think that is? That's such a prevalent misconception.

Fletcher: I base punk rock, my existence, on being punk rock and not looking punk rock. For me, it's more of an attitude and a way of life. I know tons of people who look fuckin' hardcore who don't have a punk bone in their body. "What do you do that's punk? You get your mohawk all set up in the morning and walk around." I'd rather have punk actions than punk fashions, and I think a lot of people think the beach scene is all volleyball, surfer type guys and they think our shows are violent with a bunch of football players. We have a lot of different people from skaters and surfers to marines. You go through Germany and we've got five hundred marines showing up.

Todd: My brother went to your show in Frankfurt.

Fletcher: There you go. Is he a marine?

Todd: He's in the army.

Fletcher: I think everybody is entitled to listen to whatever they want and do what they want. When a band starts to get bigger people think... I can understand the mentality that if there's a band that you like and nobody knows about them, you can then turn your friends on to them and it's like this special feeling of...

Todd: Camaraderie.

Fletcher: You're like, "Whoa, these guys rip." You feel like you've turned someone on, and when your favorite band gets huge you start to think, "Fuck these guys," everyone's into it. It's trendy. I'm not into it anymore. I'm gonna go find another underground band. That's totally understandable. We try to keep it low profile and for the fans. It's all just based on kids, not the money or this and that. We try to do the right thing and keep it cool, but you still get people saying, "Oh, fuckin' sell outs." You're probably always going to hear something from somebody and they're probably just misinformed or just have that kind of attitude. They don't like a band that's sold over forty thousand records, and that's cool if people want to be like that. I totally understand. We just try to do what we think is right for the scene and the kids and have a good time while we're doing it.

Todd: Who produced your album, *Full Circle*? There was a definite punch that I hadn't heard before.

Fletcher: Well, the last time around we worked with Brett Gurewitz (owner of Epitaph Records, guitarist in Bad Religion), Jerry Finn and Eddie Ashworth. They engineered that. The time before that I was pretty much behind the controls and before that it was Brett, but this time we didn't want anyone telling us what to do so we were pretty much doing it ourselves. Although, we hired Eddie Ashworth who's a really cool guy who worked on Sublime's last album. We just told him that we're calling the shots but you can put in whatever you feel like, so it was us and him together. The song writing and the background vocals were all us. It's always been like that. Even when Brett was there giving us ideas, we'd pretty much shut him down. So it's just like family, just really close friends. Brett actually helped out a bit but we didn't get along in the studio at all. We're too strong-minded. That only worked for a couple of days. We just wanted it to be what it was 'cause we felt real strong about the album and we worked hard on it and wanted it to come across the way we wanted it to come across.

Todd: Who did the piano solo?

Fletcher: That was Ronnie King from Joykiller. He's awesome. At the beginning of *Unknown Road* I have this little piano part I made up off this thing my mom taught me as a kid. I showed it to him at the studio at like six in the morning and we were at the final step of the album. We had been partying all night as sort of a wrap-up party and I showed him a piece and we put up a mic. I only had a little bit and he went off and played the whole thing in one take and we put up a picture of Jason, our bass player, on the piano and he just went for it. He knew Jason pretty good and he did an awesome job. We got it on tape right before we went into mastering it. We figured it would be good if you're home alone and you just wanna kick back.

Todd: It's very pretty but it's...

Fletcher: It's kind of heavy at the same time.

Todd: Yeah.

Fletcher: And people who knew Jason personally will understand it more. For me, it brings up a lot of memories about him when I listen to it. Each part's very different.

Todd: How did Jason die?

Fletcher: He shot himself. The newspapers, the coroner, and even the cops want to blow it out of proportion and say it was suicide. The thing was, though, that it was a chest wound. It wasn't like he shot himself in the head. He was partying and the neighbors saw him come home. He was hammered, and when we get hammered... all of us are notorious for partying. When Jason got hammered, he got hammered. That's why he'd drink. He'd drink to get drunk. That's why I drink. [Laughter]

So when he got home, he was hammered and playing around with a gun. He didn't just fire one shot. One shot went through his wall into his refrigerator—obviously an accident—and then he wound up shooting himself in the chest. The cops want to say it was this and that but there was no suicide note. He took his bass in for repair that day. He had a new house, a new car, his girlfriend and his family. It just doesn't add up, but the media wants to make something big out of a rock musician... If you knew Jason, his lyrics and the way he lived, then you'd know that there's no way he would do something like that. We all believe that it was just him partying and just a bad combination. A handgun is not a good thing at all to have around the house, period. He's gone but not forgotten. He and I founded the band and it was his PMA (positive mental attitude)—he wrote a lot of lyrics on the first album that gave the band the direction. Instead of being a destructive, negative punk band, he put a positive twist on it. I didn't know a lot of bands that were doing that. There was Minor Threat and stuff, but that was hardcore. I don't even know what you want to call our music. Minor Threat was a huge influence on me in my playing and stuff. Everybody calls it hardcore punk, but it has more of a positive message than that. That was all through Jason's outlook on life that kind of turned me around. I was probably headed for prison and he gave me some hope and shit. He was a rad guy. That's the bottom line. An awesome person all the way around.

Todd: What's the funniest thing you've ever done?

Fletcher: It's hard to remember all the things. There are a lot of them, in my opinion.

Todd: Give me one.

Fletcher: I think one of the funniest things is throwing up on people. I know it sounds stupid because of the KROQ thing and all, but throwing up on people is fun.

Todd: What's the KROQ thing?

Fletcher: When I threw up on Dr. Drew on the Loveline. You've never heard that?

Todd: No.

Fletcher: I might have the tape around here. It's pretty good. It's just one of those things where they ask you to do Loveline but they've never played our music. I don't give a shit about being on the radio. I actually got into punk rock because of Rodney on the ROQ (who started airing his show in 1976). I heard Bad Brains and I was like, "What the fuck is this?" I was hooked. So we were going up there to do Loveline and I was thinking, "You know what? These kids gotta be taught a lesson!" I was just getting pickled at this bar and got some tequila at the liquor store. Actually, the whole session I was obliterated. Me and Byron, our drummer, were just talking shit the whole time. We were cussing and they had to bleep out half the thing.

Eventually, I just got the tequila out and took a shot of it. They were in this U-shaped area so the rest of the band ran. They just hauled ass. I ran around the backside and I got him, the program director, and Ricky Rachtman in the backs and just kept fucking pukin' on 'em. The thing was, Ricky knew. I told Rick beforehand—I was like, "Do you like Dr. Drew?" And he's all, "He's my friend." And I'm like, "Well I'm gonna fuckin' puke on him." He's like, "You can't do that!" And I'm like, "Well, I'm going to, so just be prepared." Ricky was an all right guy and everything. He's pretty cool but a lot of people don't like him. But he's all right when you get to know him so I was like, "If you don't wanna get puked on..." He left it (the entire puke episode) going out over the air so it was pretty classic. The program director was like, "Don't you fuckin' throw up on me!" She was cursing and shit, live on the air.

There was a college couple there doing a magazine piece on Dr. Drew and I got them too. I was just blowin' chowder all over the place, and I was laughing and shit the whole time. Those people tried to run me over in the parking lot. I had to jump up on the hood of a car. I had to fuckin' pay for my friend's hood. The next day the band was goin', "You mother fucker. They're gonna hate us," and I was just like, "Who cares, buddy?" In the end they thought it was pretty funny. A good thing to do to people is, when you're in the car on the freeway, just start fuckin' puking all over everybody. Everyone starts vomiting. It's great. We were in a taxi cab in Hermosa and we were four across the back seat and a couple girls up front and I was just like, "I'm gonna puke." They're like, "What?" Blaaaaa. I was throwing it all over everybody and all over the cab driver. Everyone in the cab started puking and screaming and the guy pulls over and everyone's covered in vomit. We all rolled out of the cab and were puking in the street. It was fuckin' hilarious. I went and took a shower but my friend went to a bar just covered in vomit. He was so ranked. Everyone was like, "What the fuck is that?" And he just smiled. There were other bad things that happened that night too, involving feces, but we won't get into that.

Todd: That was my next question. Any fecal stories?

Fletcher: Fecal stories are kind of hardcore. What if my grandma reads this? Let's just say there's been a couple of fecal mustaches for crewmembers along the road.

Todd: Did you ever meet GG Allin?

Fletcher: No, I've never met him but I've heard plenty of stories. He seemed like a pretty alright guy. Have you ever met him?

Todd: No, I've never met him. He was hospitalized before a show I went to in Phoenix.

Fletcher: He had some good theories, if you ask me. People trip out on stuff, but even if you get the straightest adult to watch someone throwing up on somebody, they think it's funny. They just never think of doing it.

Todd: Any videotapes of this stuff?

Fletcher: There's a videotape of me throwing up on somebody on our home movie. It was some guy in Switzerland giving me shit about something and you know the chain trick? It's when you take a toilet chain and snort it and bring it out your mouth. I usually vomit when I do that. I've got some cool video of me throwing up on this guy. You can see him running with puke all over him. That's why people think I'm a bully and I torture people, but it's all in good fun. I get it back. People give it back to me. People just get completely creative.

Todd: Has anybody taken it just completely wrong? Have you ever been sued by puking on somebody?

Fletcher: No, I haven't been sued.

Todd: Is it true that you're an avid golfer?

Fletcher: Every time I would see golf on TV I always thought those golfers were fucking morons.

Todd: That's what I'm sayin' right now.

Fletcher: I've got a couple of friends who go play golf and I was hung over one morning and was like, "I'm going." They go, "Oh no, you're not allowed to go." I went and forced my way on to the course. You can drink beer out there and drive golf carts. I totally sucked but there's this addiction that comes with it because every time you miss, you wanna try harder to do it better. It's this stupid game but it's really hard. We pretty much get in a fight out there every time. We always piss off people. Old men come back and are like, "You sons of bitches!" You've got Mike playing golf. I know some hardcore criminals who play golf. You go out on to the course and people are like "What the fuck are they doing?"

There's this golf company called Death Sticks. They're the only alternative golf club company and they sponsor a bunch of people. You go up there and there's these golf clubs with skulls and cross bones on them. One day, me and my friend were driving a golf cart. I was driving and I kept heading for trees because I was playing shitty and I was bored. I kept

heading for trees and I'd swerve at the last minute and then eventually he
got behind the wheel and was headed straight for this tree and I thought he
was for sure going to hit it 'cause I thought he was gonna go right but he
actually went left. Right before he was about to hit the tree I thought, "I'm
fuckin' outta here." So I go right out of the cart and he went left so it
pitched me right into the tree while going fifteen miles an hour or something. I hit the tree really hard with my back while I was airborne. He pan-
icked when he saw me jump out and he saw me hit the tree and thought I
was hurt really bad so he went to step on the brake and jump out of the
cart but he was looking over his shoulder and stepped on the gas on accident and hit a tree head-on going, full speed and just got fuckin' pitched.
So we're layin' in the fuckin' mud, injured but just cracking up. All these
people were running towards the golf cart. It was completely totaled. We
were just like, "The steering went out and we heard this popping noise and
we hit a tree and we're not injured." So we didn't have to pay for it or anything. Basically it goes back to the theory of having fun doing whatever
you do whether it's on a golf course or at a punk show. It's life—you can
make it what you want to. You can go out there and be a crabby old man
in plaid pants or you can go out there and crash golf carts.

Todd: Are you married or do you have a girlfriend?

Fletcher: Yeah, I've been engaged for four years.

Todd: How does she feel about the Fletcher experience?

Fletcher: She thinks the stuff is pretty funny.

•   •   •

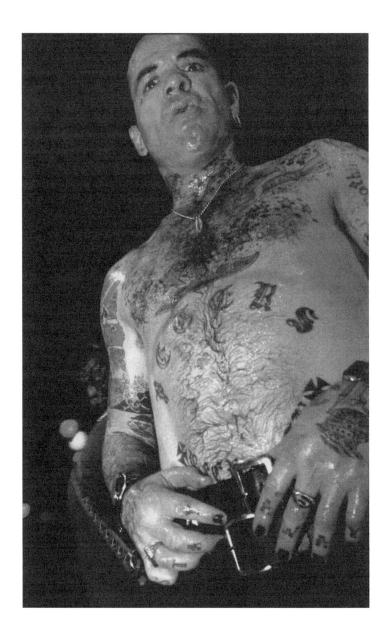

"*I had a seizure on a motorcycle one time. I was doing all of this bad coke or something and I just had a seizure and I guess I just missed a freeway pole. My bike got totaled. I went into some bushes, woke up in an ambulance...*"

—Duane

ALMOST SPIRITUAL, LIKE IN AN ANGRY WAY: AN INTERVIEW WITH DUANE PETERS

Duane Peters is the lead singer of both the U.S. Bombs and Duane Peters and the Hunns. He's also a professional skater. He's forty. By all standards, he's one indestructible motherfucker who should be very, very dead by now.

A lot of people in rock pretend to be a threat. It helps sell records. Sure, with the proper lighting, they can look scary or demented. Sure, they may be insufferable pricks who thrash hotel rooms, get arrested once or twice, or get their master's degrees in Asshole-ishness. But a true rock threat? Folks like Marilyn Manson, Eminem, and Billy Idol are pussies. True threats to this nation's youth don't have movie star girlfriends, don't get Grammies, and usually don't have a great set of teeth. This one doesn't even have clean underwear.

Enter the Master of Disaster, Duane Peters, grinding through the dirty deep end of sex, drugs, and rock'n'roll. It's been said that his influence on skating is as huge Orville and Wilbur Wright's was to flight. Slash and burn, coping-dusting, pool-defying mayhem. He's forgotten all of the tricks he's invented. He's also forgotten all of the bands he's been in. Amongst what he does remember is that he was once fired by his used car salesman dad for shooting speed into his neck during business hours. And that he robbed a 7-11. Twice. In one day. Without completely realizing it.

In the meantime, he's maintained founder and godfather status of the person who connected the positive and negative battery terminals of skateboarding and punk rock, electrocuted a lot of people in the process—including himself—and doesn't look like he's letting go any time soon.

I caught up to a very talkative, extremely nice, and sober Duane and his then long-time girlfriend Trish.

Todd: Did you ever get your high school diploma?
Duane: No. I quit at the end of the ninth grade. I made it almost to the end. I went to sixteen elementary schools, including middle schools, three high schools with the continuation school at the end. The last two weeks is when I quit. There was a guitar-player hippie teacher with his feet up on the table. Everyone was smoking and hanging out. I skated there, sat down for an hour, and left. Nobody noticed. I came back four or five days later, did the same thing, and just went, "fuck it," and skated all day.
Todd: What was band most influenced you to cut your hair in 1978?

Duane: I cut my hair from The Pistols. It was all okay with The Ramones.
I had a candy-striped jacket, pogoing, got a thin tie. We were all crazy,
wearin' 'em, walking around the streets. Me and my friend Barclay. We
had a homosexual friend we were really proud of. One of the loons. Bobby
Shannon. I heard the Pistols. It'd already been out for awhile. I finally got
my hands on an LP, played it at a friend's house, then I took it home. And
I didn't leave my house for three days, I swear to god. I sat there listening
to it over and over and drank, sat there listening to it, smoked some weed.
I knew I had to cut my hair. I had to make a commitment. There was a
really heavy Huntington contingency going on. The Crowd's parties were
starting right then. Then I went up to a skate contest up in Winchester and
the guys in Lakewood were cutting their hair. Pat Brown (Immortalized by
the Vandals in "The Legend of Pat Brown") was one of them. He was skating. Todd Barnes (TSOL's original drummer) was one of them. Then there
was a scene up north. All of the Alotaflex guys had cut their hair and they
were heavy hippies and they got really cool spiked hair. It was a heavy
time. I lost every fucking friend I had except the guy who had his hair cut
with me. He ended up being my first bass player and a very good friend.
Chris Barclay. You left your house and you went to war. Bikers, everything. I started cutting other kids' hair at Big-O Skatepark a year and a half
later.

Todd: Did you ever serve any time in jail?

Duane: Yeah, a lot of county time. I spent most of my twenties going in
and out. I did a lot of thirty, sixty, and ninety days. I had 180 days, but did
104 days, something like that. I got thrown in LA County for fifty-four
days one time from a skate contest. I showed up really loaded. Tony
Hawk's dad—that's why I had a big thing with him.

Todd: Why'd he get you arrested?

Duane: At Carson. I did three days. I'd never seen *Colors* before, the
movie. '86 or something. I'd been in a bathroom, shooting up every day. I
was trying really hard to get off dope and the only time I could clean up
was going to jail. That was the whole issue. Whoever I was hanging out
with at the time, it was like, "When are you going to jail?" I'd try to give
them my last bit of dope money and that would be my big promise. "I'll
go turn myself in." I'd always had warrants. But I hated him, man. It was
the hardest fifty-four. A guy got butt-fucked. It was my first experience
with The Crips and The Bloods. When I left Carson, I guess I was with
one of them—The Crips or The Bloods—I don't know. And I sat down
and they have a cage in-between, in the bus, in the very middle. And you
sat down, right in front of the cage. My nerves were shot. It was three days
without my fucking dose. It was Memorial weekend or something. You sat
on a curb in the county jail. There were no provisions at all. It was horrible
and it was stinky, packed, and then we got to the bus, and the next thing I

know, "Why is half of the bus closed?" They closed the thing. There's a guard guy here and they let one of the other gangs in and these guys were on top of each other. Fuckin' hatred. I had no idea of what was going on. I sat there like I see it every day. My insides were completely shattered.

Then I thought I was black when I got out of there. 'Cause I had to go to Orange County from there; expedited. So, we're on a LA County bus and I was really fucked up in the head, 'cause I didn't sleep for thirty-three days. Twenty-three hour lockdown with three black guys that were trying to teach me how to meditate. One guy had one arm.

And I jumped down the stairs there to try to get some sort of medica-tion. Head first, jumped into the bars. Had them yell, "Man down!" Drew blood, spit everywhere. I dove down the stairs. They just laughed at me. They tied me up, threw me in the infirmary for eight hours, then they wheelchaired me back. Everyone gave me a handclap. Then I had to hock my shoes for ten Kool cigarettes. Finally got some money before I lost my shoes. If you lose your shoes, you're fucked. You're a bitch. I got mugged in front of my cell by the trustees. Threw my money to my guys. It was the smartest thing I did. I got beat down. They got ten bucks out of me. And then when I got to Orange County, I was like, "Yo got butter on yo pan-cakes?" I thought I was this black guy. "Yo, baby," talking to my girl-friend. She'd be like, "What's wrong with you?" 'Cause I was a Mexican the other times, when I was copping dope. I used to tell myself, "Why do I talk Mexican every time I'm copping dope? Stop doing that." [In Mexican-tinged accent] "Pacito, can I get skunky picante?"

Todd: Previous jobs. Who did you roadie for?

Duane: I got asked to road manage Face To Face once but I didn't know what I was going to do. Goldenvoice gave me a biscuit. (Duane-speak for a favor.) 'Cause I was doing all of these shit jobs. I worked at a rehearsal hall. I didn't get my first job until I was thirty. I was just a bum. I'll be forty in a month. I just roadied for Goldenvoice—sound and lights. I've worked at Vinyl Solution. I worked at a rehearsal hall that we used to play in and do movie extras, skateboarding, and keep my band together.

Todd: Did you ever work with your dad as a used car salesman?

Duane: Up in Sacramento. Yeah. And down in San Diego. Got kicked out because I was shooting coke in the bathroom. He made me the manager. He wanted me to work there so bad. I couldn't even write up a contract. And I was shaking because I'd always be shooting up coke in the bath-room. He thought I was really nervous. That's how I'd play it off. "Dad, could you just take this contract?" "Okay, take it easy." Then I got caught. He came in when I had a bloody neck. I wasn't good. I was twenty-two and he wouldn't have nothing to do with me no more. He tried to give me a biscuit, but I didn't want that. These guys were all professional liars. I could never do anything right. I was like, "Dad, why don't you just try fix-

ing the cars and then it would be easier to sell?" He'd say, "That's conden-
sation." "That's a two dollar part." "You want me to fix it? It's going to
cost ten dollars." I'd be, "Have some of this fucking stuff work so I don't
always have to have a story." He'd be, "That's not a good salesman." My
dad's been selling used cars all his life. He's a wreck.
Todd: Is he still?
Duane: Yeah. He's still doing it.
Todd: The teeth. How did you lose your front teeth?
Duane: The first time, microphone. Then I got a fake one when I was a
kid, probably about eighteen. When I was in Political Crap. I lost another
one in the U.S. Bombs. And then I got punched. Some big guy who just
got out of prison. He was just speeded out. I didn't do nothing.
Trish: You were yelling to Baldy.
Duane: I was yelling to my roadie. He thought I was yelling at him. I'm
just walking, "Baldy, take something, blah, blah, blah…" This guy thought
I was talking to him. Big guy. One punch. It wasn't even loose. Took it
right out. God, well, that saved me a hundred bucks.
Trish: And when we ran after him to his car, he pulled out a gun.
Duane: A bunch of people. I was, "Yeah, that guy. That was weird." And
someone said, "Let's get him." We all started running, aaaahhhh. He opens
his door and has a gun. Fuck that. I didn't even care anyway… I just
pulled out two more teeth in Germany. A back molar. I'm going to try to
get some teeth down the road here.
Todd: I've read that once you got sober, you were going to get a couple of
silver teeth, which would definitely up your pirate quotient.
Duane: That's what I wanted—a whole rack of silver teeth, like Jaws in
007. But she doesn't really… she wants to get married.
Trish: One would be all right, but not a whole rack.
Todd: What do you have buried in your back yard right now?
Duane: You know the answer. In my back yard now, I don't have nothing
buried, but you're talking about the fuck doll, right?
Todd: Yeah.
Duane: That was about seven houses and apartments ago. I buried it,
stabbed it, got strung out on it. I had a horrible girlfriend who wouldn't
fuck me because I had all these jobs. She was a suit and she would still
make me take her out to dinner and shit. And then I'd get home at three in
the morning and I'd have to be up at seven. Most of the time I was like
that. And I'd want to fuck, you know? It was like, snooty bitch. We had
two bedrooms. I'd go to my punk room and I had a fuck doll, all tattooed
up with a short dress and I never really thought of fucking one.
Trish: [laughs nervously]
Duane: But I'd go in that room and beat off, then come back to bed
because it was too much of a hassle to romance this thing, you know what

I mean? It was a lot of work. So there I was, whacking off in my punk room and I look up and there's the fuck doll. I went, "It's a fuck doll. You fuck it. I'm fucking this thing." And I went to the bathroom, got some vaseline, stuck it in the puss, and starting fucking it.

Trish: [groans]

Duane: The next thing you know, I got strung out on fucking this thing. It was amazing. I was like, "Hey." [grins] So there I am on this doll, fucking it and choking it, making the ass get harder. I had to stop. I'd unflate it. We were going to move and I didn't want her to know, 'cause she was so weird that she'd act like I was cheating on her. I couldn't even have any mags. She was a freak and I was scared I was going to get caught with her. So I took out the air. "I can't fuck this thing anymore. I'm going to get busted." I stuck it into my closet. And I'd be out on the porch, bored. I'd be like, "Fuck, I wonder how long it is to blow that thing up." That's when I knew I had a problem. I'd be out on the porch blowing this thing up. It took about eighteen minutes. Then I'd take her in the room, fuck it, and then I ended up stabbing it, burying it. It's still there, I'm sure. Haven't fucked one since. It's been about four or five years.

Todd: Where are you now in your sobriety?

Duane: Six and a half months now. I had about seven months. I've been struggling with sobriety for about twelve years and then I just gave up on it about three years ago. Three years back from that, I figured I can't do it, I can't get it. I'm a loser. The demoralization. I went, "Fuck it."

When Chuck (first U.S. Bombs guitarist) died, I was hanging out with him. 'Cause he called me. We didn't talk for a year. When he had AIDS, he didn't let anyone know. And he found out and pretty much just hung out with his girlfriend. Me and Chuck and his girlfriend Donna, and Trish, we were like Ricky, Fred, Lucy, and Ethel. We were very close. They'd fly out to see us. Me and Chuck were roommates in the band. When he left The U.S. Bombs, it was a big blowout. I'd call all the time and maybe once every three months he'd talk to his mom and he'd always be sick. Then, finally, I got a call from his mom. "Chuck wants to see you. He's at the hospital." I dropped everything, went down there, saw him. "Hey Chuck, what are you doing?" "Oh, just sitting here, dying of AIDS." Total sense of humor, but he looked totally thin. It was really good to have my friend back. So I sat down. "Bullshit. Where's your cop shades?" He'd been with his mom and his girlfriend, so surrounded by women, he lost all of his style. "I'm fucking turning into a geek," he said. I said, "I'm fucking getting your creepers, getting you some CDs, I've got some killer new videos." We started hanging out every day. I'd walk him around in the wheelchair in the yard, sneak a cigarette out for him 'cause his mom didn't want him smoking no more. I was feeding him. Then I got him a bootleg Bombs shirt from Cleveland. It was so great. We were best friends.

Then he was going to join the band for this record. We were exercising. He was going to get better. It was the biggest roller coaster. And then something else would go out. His liver, this, that, and the other. And then I had to go to Germany. When I said goodbye to him, I had a feeling that that was it. And when I was in Europe, Chip's daughter died, we got our van broken into, stolen everything—money, my passport, my plane ticket—you name it. None of us could fly back. We wanted to end the fucking tour. I wanted to come home and go to Chuck's funeral. They're Germans. They all just turned us down. Chip can only go back because of a death in the family.

Todd: What happened to Chip's daughter?

Duane: She was born with a really rare disease. There were only two hundred cases ever documented. She was mentally and physically disabled from birth. It was his only daughter. She had already way, way outlived her life expectancy.

Trish: She wasn't supposed to live at all.

Duane: It just kind of hit him for a loop 'cause they didn't expect it at all. They had a nurse over there and it just happened. It was heavy. Everybody went into deep depression. I had seven months sobriety. I threw it away in Amsterdam. My whole world's crumbling. I went to a bar and got some orange skunk. We had a show at a festival with Slayer, Buzzcocks, forty thousand people and this German van driver as our drummer. And all these people are dead. And then they're sneaking me into other countries because my passport's gone. So, I could go to prison. It says right there that, "The U.S. Embassy will not help you," if you do these things and these are the things I'm doing. Fucking sure enough. It was a dramatic nightmare.

So I got home, locked myself up in a room for four months, and then decided I'm tired of being depressed, opened the curtains one day, went, "You know what? I'm going to do it this time. I'm fucking over it. I'm going to do it for Chuck." I saw *Shawshank Redemption*, where it says, "get busy living or get busy dying," I fucking totally held that in. You know what, that's so fucking right. What am I doing? I'm over this. I'm not dying. So let's get busy. That's when I started writing. Skating. This is the first time I'm going to Europe and not fucking up. I don't feel like I'm missing nothing. Something weird's happening. I'm going with it.

Todd: You picked up the name "Master of Disaster" as a skater.

Duane: Yeah, when I was a kid. D. David Morin (at the time, the Associate Producer of *Skateboarder Magazine*) gave me that name during a contest in Marina Del Rey.

Todd: Why?

Duane: Because I used to cause a lot of shit at the contests. I was always getting chased by somebody. The Hobie team was actually pretty rad when

I got on it. Eddie Elguera was the good guy, but me and Darrell Miller would start shit with everybody. We were pissing on George Orton (the first skateboarder in history to do an aerial)—who was his buddy. Some other jocky guy. On the overhang of the hotel we'd get all drunk and think of things to do and knock on their door. We'd see them lifting weights and shit. And they'd come out, "Who the fuck? Huh?" And we'd been up on the roof, going, "Yeahh." Then they came out one time. "We're going to kill you." It was like the third time. We both started pissing on them. And then we had to hide all night long because they were going to kill us. Big guys. Then when we got the Santa Cruz team later— me, Olson, and Alva, and then Orton was our whipping boy. It was pretty cool.

Todd: Is that where the name for your record company, Disaster Records, came from?

Duane: Yeah.

Todd: Name some bands you've been in besides The U.S. Bombs, Duane Peters and the Hunns, Political Crap, The Sharkx, and The Mess.

Duane: *The* Mess, Santa Ana, 1986. Not Mess, from Texas. Probably about fifteen other bands. Horrible bands. I used to join a band to stay in their garage. I went through a period where I built studios and I just got good at grabbing junk plywood and nailing them together. I'm not no carpenter at all, but I actually could build those pretty good and get the carpet. I was a good little thief. I was in a bunch of bands. I don't really know any of their names. I just went from band to band that would last a month or two, and it'd be embarrassing, and I'd steal all of their equipment and run and hide. I moved all over the state.

One of the bands I was in after Political Crap with some guys from The Rayons was called File 17. We supported the Misfits at the Cuckoos Nest their first time through O.C. in '80 or '81 and one of 'em asked if he could borrow my mics that I just bought. I was young and weirdly had my own mics. I would never let anyone use 'em and no one had seen these monsters before and they scared the shit out of me. I said yes, "Of course!" Gave him the mics. My band was like, "You pussy!" Jerry smashed one of my mics the second song with the end of his bat bass and it went flying! My band goes, "What are you gonna do about that?" I go, "Absolutely nothing!" I had never seen a band like that. They were so fucking pissed, huge, and on fire. It was a great show. There were probably thirty-five people there. File 17 got a full page in *Slash* from that show. The Bombs supported the Misfits a couple of years ago in London and in Switzerland. It was my birthday at the Swiss show and me and Jerry smoked some homegrown Swiss bud that would blow away any of our so-called chronic and I mentioned that show. We had a great laugh because he said that so many thousands of people over the years say they were at that show and it's amazing how empty it was. He gave me a pair of Misfit sweats for the mic! And had a great show.

I had a band called Firesports in San Francisco in 1984. We actually got signed. We started shooting up in front of the guys from the studio who were signing our shit. That was Michael Belfer. He was in it from the Sleeper with Ricky Sleeper (also Toiling Midgets).

Trish: The band Cracker.

Duane: Yeah, he ended up in that. Anyways. He's been doing a lot of weird stuff up there. Arty stuff. Make sure—I never was in Cracker. Never even heard it. Make that much clear.

Todd: Who's been your longest band compatriot?

Duane: Kerry (Martinez), by far. Plus, I've known him for twenty-three years. When he was in the first Shattered Faith, Political Crap and Shattered Faith used to play together. And we used to fight side by side. We took out this place in Pomona. Later on, they reaped the benefits. They jumped me, kicked the fuck out of me at Godzillas. But, yeah, me and Kerry go way back.

Todd: You guys are on the same comp with The Cheifs. *Who Cares?*

Duane: Right.

Todd: What's the main difference between The U.S. Bombs and The Hunns?

Duane: Everyone in the Hunns is actually in California. I just wanted to play the clubs again. Kerry lives in New York. Everyone's doing side stuff now. It's good for the band. It makes us get along good. Chip's going to drum, I think, in One Man Army. He's going to do their new record. Kerry's going to do some side thing with some gnarly guy in New York. Then I can be home and I have a label. It's pretty cool.

Todd: Do your bands get along?

Duane: I think so. From afar, probably. I don't think they're fighting over me or nothing.

Todd: Why is it Duane Peters and the Hunns as opposed to just being The Hunns?

Duane: Well, Patrick (who runs Disaster along with Duane) suggested that I do that. He goes, "Do you want to sell records? Nobody's gonna know who The Hunns are." I wanted to call it The Hunns. I was totally down with that. Mark Lee wanted to call it The Hunns. We got in a big argument over it. Then Shane McGowan and the Popes. He was my hero before he did The Dropkick Murphys thing. [laughter]

Todd: The slur-along.

Duane: Yeah, fuckin' okay. But I don't care. It's ego, anyway. That's why I put the Hunns together. To do a single 'cause I was so emotionally torn up. I got kicked out of the Bombs, I just got sent home. The whole Unity Tour didn't want nothing to do with me. "Nobody wants you on this bus!"

I was a nightmare. I was at war with that whole tour the whole time. They thought I was going to be at the next gig. I packed my shit. I was going to work for a German family and work my way back to the States. I was so fucked up. But I had enough money on me to just get back to the States. When I got back, she (Trish) had my bags by the door. She didn't want me around. She wanted me to quit drinking. I'm a fucking nightmare.

Trish: I stood back at the airport to see if he was drunk and I watched him come off because I was going to leave if he was.

Duane: I went to one of those sober places with all of these musicians and I was like, "I wanna write a song about my chick. It'll give me something to do in the studio," and all these guys started intervening and going, "Fuck, let's put a band together." It turned into an album and I wrote the song, with the guitar. The Bombs never let me write (the music to) a song. "I wanna play this," and they're "cool," and they're saying yes to everything. "I want to do one more. Here's another one that I've been fucking around with." God, I talk too much.

Todd: I'm assuming that you have two "n"s on the Hunns because of the Huns from Texas?

Duane: Rob was like, "I think there was a Huns," and Mark was like, "Yeah, but I think they did just a single." Then I went down to Vinyl Solution, saw they did that live record. I liked the name so much, let's just put another "n" on it. Budda bing, done deal.

Todd: Do you know what happened to the lead singer of the Huns, Phil Tolstead (Who once went to jail for kissing a cop)?

Duane: Nope.

Todd: He's an evangelical minister. Someone told me he was on the 700 Club a couple of times. How did the U.S. Bombs end up as the house band on a comedy show?

Duane: They called us. We had no idea. We were in Georgia on tour and we got a phone call. We were beat up. Nancy Severinsen—Doc Severinsen's daughter—she was in charge of the music and saw our record, *War Birth*, and she turned it over and saw the picture. She said [in Hollywood voice], "Very apocalyptic. That's going to be the theme of the new show. Find these guys." Wade goes, "Hey, we're going home for four days. We're going to be on Comedy Central." We had to jump some tour we were on and said, "We'll meet you in four cities." Me and Chuck were going, "Why would we be on Comedy Central? It's not that fucking hard to figure out. They want to fucking laugh at us, but let's do it 'cause we'll get to see our chicks. Let 'em laugh. How much are they payin'?" Seven grand. We had to pay for our own tickets. That was $3,500 and the other $3,500 to get even on our merch.

We met that Jim Bruer guy. He was so fucking cool. I was shaking like a motherfucker when we showed up. We were so beat up and I had to get a bottle really bad. And they were doing sound checks. I first met Jim Bruer at the crap table. He goes, "How're you doing, buddy?" and I go, "Doin' a lot better now" and I had my Captain's bottle. And he said, "Me too," and he had a bottle of Jack Daniels. Talkin' up a storm. Kooky comedians, they're just like us. They thought all the other guys were geeks. It was really cool. Everybody was really hammered.

Todd: Is there any truth to the rumor that Epitaph tried to get you killed by having you play Yugoslavia?

Duane: We thought that, definitely.

Todd: When people were being taken hostage and they didn't give you the courtesy to tell you not to be there…

Duane: Nobody told us a thing. When we were getting out of there, Slapshot was like, "You guys went in and played?" We got held at the Slovenian border eight hours and they took Chip to jail. He'd never been to jail his whole life and he had a bottle of penicillin with two valiums in it. His wife put it in there, "In case he gets sleepy." And he didn't even know. I came back from the duty free with a carton of smokes and went, "Oh fuck." It was like *National Geographic*, when they have the guns. They were taking him away. "Why couldn't they take a roadie?" I thought they were going to execute him. "How am I going to get a drummer?" That's what I was thinking. "Somebody more expendable, please." Then we got back to the next country to where you're free—or somewhat—and they pulled out all of the U.S. bands. "We're going to bomb that place." That's why those countries really hated us. We had "U.S. Bombs" all over our gear. We were standing in a cavity search for fucking hours, going, "They're going to ream us. Get ready. Pucker up." That's where the conspiracy theory came. "The label. They want us fucking dead." We were laughing at that.

Trish: But they made it out.

Duane: Yeah.

Todd: [to Trish] What does Duane smell like?

Trish: Good.

Todd: Does he?

Trish: Even if he doesn't take a shower for a week.

Todd: That's love.

Duane: She loves me. I'll never find another one like her. Even my band guys go, "How does she fuckin' do it?" I won't wash my long underwear. There's shit stains along the back…

Trish: Oh, honey.

Duane: When everyone else does laundry on the road, I won't. My chick will wash 'em when I get home. "You're kidding me." Eh, she loves me. Go figure.

Todd: One thing I've noticed about you, is that you're a style person. The style of the music is definitely '77 punk, but it's not just a copy of it. It's taking the spirit of it and exploring it. Like your skating.

Duane: As far as skating, I made up a lot of tricks. And I used to skate fourteen hours a day. Skating saved my life and got me out of a lot of trouble. I got in a lot of trouble with skating anyway. My whole trip is that I wanted to die without learning any other tricks, but I'll learn a trick every couple years now. It's a little one—like invert roll-in reverts. I used to do those in the clover, but now I can do them on vert, no matter how big. I can still do my old tricks. I still have a good array of shit that keeps me happy. I don't want to go to a gym.

Skateboarding and punk rock are the key to having a good day. Get all your shit out. Almost spiritual, like in an angry way. Whenever I get bundled up, she says, "Go skate. I'll take care of this, that, and the other." I'll come back the happiest fucking little kid. If you get to go to the punk rock show, or play, it's double what I love. I did so much time on junk. All that stuff I used to be doing: shooting up in bathrooms, sitting there or wherever I ended up—in ditches, getting stabbed—so many times low guy at the hospital, getting abscesses cut out. All that shit was gone. It was never going to come back. You get brain dead. Water in the brain. I used to beat myself up. "Can I even skate any more?" Then you get thrown in jail. It's been a long, weird, learning life. That's the style I like. I don't see any rulebook.

Todd: We go skating a lot now and it's great to see old-style skaters skating ditches and banks. It sounds cheesy, but it's very soulful.

Trish: It's better.

Duane: I can't remember this kid's name. I can never remember it, but he's a top half pipe skater. This kid didn't know what to do in a full pipe. This guy could barely hit vert. He was totally mind blown and there was a little rough spot at the bottom. Steve Olson (another lifetime skater, and skater of the year in 1978) would have laughed at him. Olson's like, "Kick flip now, you little fucker!" When you throw these guys in a pool, they're straight up and down, ready to flip, no style at all, and it's like, "Come on, do you know how to carve?" It's amazing.

Todd: What do you account for the number one reason that you're still alive today? You've been through so much shit. You've broken so many bones.

Duane: Every day I wake up, I'm stoked, dude. It's a good day, you know what I mean? Sun's up. My life used to be so full of trauma. Every day something would happen that was life-threatening. I lost track of everything. Seven motorcycles. All totaled. Over seventy miles-per-hour, without helmets, back in the non-helmet days. DOA several times. I had a seizure on a motorcycle one time. Riding with Mike Lohrman (The Stitches). They lost me. I had a really embarrassing Yamaha and him and this other guy on their Triumphs would always be a half a mile ahead and I was all strung out. I was doing all of this bad coke or something and I just had a seizure and I guess I just missed a freeway pole. My bike got totaled. I went into some bushes, woke up in an ambulance, Mike and all those guys are staring, going, "Fuck, man." I don't know, but I'm grateful.

Todd: Do you even need glasses?

Duane: No. Perfect sight. I don't get it.

Todd: You fucker.

Duane: I've got plenty of flaws, plenty of scars.

Todd: When was the day you realized, "Duane, going to a party, knocking on the door, punching the guy who opens the door, and trying to take on the whole party" wasn't such a good idea?

Duane: I've done that several times. I got everyone to stair dive up in San Jose at some guy's house that everybody knows, but I can't think of his name. But I got all of these guys to stair dive. I did all of the stairs in America and Chuck put me into retirement. I was like Evel Knievel. I would run—I did Maritime Hall, Coney Island High—dive, flip, and keep going. I'd slam into doors. I could barely walk. Every day I had a cane. Horrible shit. I did that then all these chicks were mad at me. All these guys broke their arms and shit. I was the last guy left with a big bottle of whiskey.

We were standing in their living room. "Have you ever seen someone do this?" It was one of those old glass-plate doors with the old windows, and just smashed my whole face into it. Did my "Here's Johnny" thing. Half of my nose was left on the thing. My lip was cut completely the other way. [Duane pauses to point out the scars on his face.] I used to take parties on. It had to be ten people or more. Ask Mike Lohrman. He used to have to pick me up. I used to yell at him. "Why don't you help me?" He'd wait until after the beating and then he'd take me back home. I used to hate him for that.

Todd: Did you really rob the same 7-11 twice without realizing it?

Duane: Yeah. And I ended up on the TV up in Sacramento. We dumped a guy out of a truck. We had to leave town.

Todd: How did you not know it was the same 7-11?

Duane: I was with Pat Stratford from Tales of Terror. We were hanging out every day and we were bored. We had such a blast. We ended up doing liquor store runs all of the time. We'd rip off Vivarin, take a bunch of those, and then go into the liquor store, and it was somebody's turn, and somebody drives, and I just got a 502 (a DUI), but it was my turn to drive, and I'd rather drive than run right then. We got a case, went down the street, not even a mile away, sat in the back of the truck, the four of us, and drank it and then went back to the 7-11. "We'll just go get another one." We're just—you know—drunk. Went into the same place. They're completely on to us. The 7-11 worker jumped into the back of the truck. Two of the guys stayed behind. This guy, Mike McCorkendale up there, they had this knockdown, drag-out fight. I guess the guy was hanging by the fingertips and he kicked him. I pulled over down the street. I didn't want to get a 502. I heard a thump, and that's when I took off. "What happened?" Then I didn't believe him. Stole a bottle of vodka 'cause I was like, "This is really fucked up if that guy got dumped." I was going along at fifty to sixty miles per hour. A 7-11 worker? Oh my god. So, yeah, it really happened.

Todd: So, was the guy all right?

Duane: He ended up living. Everything went fine. I don't talk about that shit much. I didn't kick him out. I was just driving.

Todd: You have a son named Chelsea, is that correct?

Duane: One named Chelsea and one named Schulyer.

Todd: No offense, but isn't that like naming a boy Sue?

Duane: Yeah, kinda. I guess. I was really strung out, but I named him after the Chelsea Hotel and at the time I didn't know any kids named Chelsea.

Todd: But that guy Clinton comes along and gives his daughter the same name.

Duane: I thought it was a really cool name. The band, Chelsea. A cool kid. Schulyer. Very German. He went through a little period—his middle name's Dylan—"Dad, I want to go by Dylan." He tried for six months but it didn't fly.

Trish: He's just like him, too. My god. Exactly.

Duane: Pretty cool. Real good skater. He got kicked out of his older brother's band. He's a drummer. They're doing Corrupted Youth in Parker, Arizona.

Todd: What's a skill that you're really, really good at but you'd never want to do again?

Duane: Years ago, me and Darrell Miller in Cherry Hill, put on a pair of roller skates each and when the place was closed, and we could both do it right away. We were getting backside airs, the third time trying, back and forth. I think I could have been a good roller skater. I used to do roller derby as a kid, on the block.

Todd: What percentage of your liver is currently working?

Duane: They say ten percent, but that's all you need to live. Your liver is supposed to be susceptible to things that you give it, but it leaks really bad. When I drink, it burns. The last ten years, every time I drink, especially playing, it burns because it doesn't filter. It goes right to the bloodstream and goes to my inner skin or whatever's underneath the skin, and my blood's boiling when I'm drinking. I don't know if it'll get better or not, but I'm going with it.

Todd: Number of times you've re-broken the same bone?

Duane: Sixteen times. My collarbone. Both of them.

Todd: Number of DUIs?

Duane: Six or seven, total. I just got one when we were doing *The World* record. It was horrible. Five grand. Bunch of classes.

Todd: Number of cars you've wrecked?

Duane: Fourteen that I've counted since I was about thirty-two. I don't think I've been in any since then. Fourteen that I've totaled. I've been in many more.

Todd: Number of cars that you owned that your friends wrecked?

Duane: Two or three. We used to get each other back.

Todd: Didn't you shit on someone's face because of one?

Duane: Barclay… yeah, yeah. In the early, early days we were fucked up. We were like brothers. I'd get in a wreck, he'd get in a wreck, and it was my turn. You know what I mean? We did that for awhile. We had some heavy wrecks.

The last time I broke my nose, Chip, my drummer—in London—his birthday's June 11. Mine's June 12. We passed the buck with shots. He's an inbred, so he's shooting bourbon. We lined up six of them—for the month of June—and I lined up six Jaegermeisters. "Go!" It's twelve o'clock. "Now it's my birthday." "What's you want?" he's all hammered Southern guy. "Break my fucking nose!" He goes boom. On the perfect break on the side of my face. I went, "no." It was really bad.

I'd done two weeks in the hospital before, with tubes to breathe and everything and looked at my face. It was like a faucet. So I went out to the van, "Now or never." Boxers do this. They have to. I totally cranked—I did my own nose job. All the bones, totally hammered, you could hear it like popcorn, backed and forthed it. I had it looking straighter than now, but two nights later, I jumped in the crowd like an idiot and they kinda fucked it up more, but it's still pretty good.

Todd: Number of dead guys you've found at the bottom of a pool?

Duane: Never. Kerry found a dead guy. We used to break into rentals in Newport Beach and there was a dead guy in the bedroom and we left him in there and drank in another room.

Todd: Did you drink his liquor?

Duane: The guy had no liquor. He was just a bum lying in there. He was completely dead.

Todd: What's the number of stories you jumped out of a parking garage to avoid the police?

Duane: Four. And I thought it was two stories. My knee went completely the other way. Hyperextension. Really, really bad. It was the most pain—it took me three years to get that thing healed.

Todd: What's the largest dollar amount of drugs that you've put in your body at one time?

Duane: Probably about two or three hundred bucks, at one shot. When I had a really bad habit, I used to do about five hundred bucks a day, coke and dope. I've OD'd. I've never really intentionally tried to kill myself ever, but I thought I was going to be a dealer one time when I was living in San Francisco. We made a big run to San Jose and came back with all of this gnarly Persian and I shot way too much and my habit was really huge. That's what saved my life is that I had a really big habit. It was pretty pure. There was two times I was DOA officially. Used to get ambulances at my house all the time. They all knew me. I owed ambulance companies in Orange County for a couple years.

Todd: Duane-speak. What's a "verifag"?

Duane: A "veribot," a Veriflex rider. (Veriflex was a skateboard company that isn't very well respected. Maybe it has something to do that the company also makes yo-yos and trampolines.)

Todd: What's "simplexity"?

Duane: Something's that simple, I don't know. I'd have to know what I was saying. I mix my words up all the time. The band knows that.

Todd: What are "tinker toy people"?

Duane: Tonka toy people? Robots, basically, probably.

Todd: "Stub people"?

Duane: What was I talking about?

Todd: You were talking about how few disabled skaters you see nowadays.

Duane: The guys with no legs. They used to skate at Lakewood. "What the fuck?" There they go and they'd be fucking riding the half pipe, using their hands, "Hey, 'scuse me." Those guys were hot. There was like three of them, every day at the skatepark.

Todd: What's a "beat hammer"?

Duane: That must have been awhile ago. Working nine to five or construction and hating their lives. Broken capillaries and kids and nothing but bills.

Todd: How's riding for Beer City?

Duane: Really good. They pay me every month. Mike Beer is true to his shit. He's sending me to Australia. I'm forty years old; I'm still getting paid to skate. He doesn't really ask much of me other than to have new graphics a couple times a year. I skate all the time on the road when I'm sober. I just skated a bunch in Europe. Did some German sports channel thing with a downhill skier guy. Weird shit. It's really cool.

Todd: Have you been pro the whole time or have there been gaps?
Duane: I think I've been pro the whole time. Even when I was strung out, I rode for Circle A, Skull. Think picked me up. Chuck Holtz would make a board for me when I was in-between. I always had a board and always had something going. Independent—because I was one of their first riders—used to give me money. Santa Cruz. I never went more than two years without riding. When I did my knee is the longest. I just started drinking like mad. Started drumming in a band called the Teddy Boys up in Sacramento. We were very Clash. We were a three piece. It just sounded wrong. It was made after the Teds in London. It sounded really rockabilly.
Todd: Not to sound like a commercial, but how is Duane Peters like Independent Trucks?
Duane: Original.
Todd: The design hasn't changed in twenty years.
Duane: I'll go with that.
Todd: What was your first tattoo?
Duane: "Peters" across my stomach. I wasn't going to get one. I got one way late, like '88. From going to jail. Me and Chuck went to parish prison. We got thrown in there for two days and the band had to pay to get us out. That was the oldest, gnarly prison. I think I thought I was Mexican at the time. Got my two kids here, my girl. [points to various parts of his body] Then I met Art and Steve Godoy (identical twin tattooists) when I climbed out of the ditch in 1992, they started Scratch Pad [points to chest]. I figured get a lot or keep none.
Todd: Why did you say that Tony Hawk probably did some really good shit in his last life to get the biscuits he gets because he's a horrible looking skater?
Duane: Oh, he is.
Todd: Explain that to somebody who doesn't know much about skating.
Duane: Well, I've seen him ever since he was a little geek kid with his dad hanging on the fence—no disrespect to his dad any more. I'm over all that shit. I used to tell his dad, "Go get a job." We were all dysfunctional kids. We didn't like seeing some dad caring about his kid.
Todd: Just like soccer moms.
Duane: Yeah. "Go buddy, go in there." And he was padded from toe to fucking head. He was one of those annoying, skinny kids who looked like you could see their veins. Skin's transparent. Can't help but want to punch him. But he was too little to punch. I couldn't believe that he became what he did. I was getting a Slurpee one day. That's when it first started really hitting me. "You've got to be kidding me. This guy's everywhere now." I'm way over it. More power to him. I figured he did a lot of good things because he's a kook. He's done a lot for skating, so whatever. I used to get pissed about The Loop thing and everything else.

Todd: You did The Loop in '78.

Duane: Yeah. I think it's been done backside, forward. A few guys have done it now. They all did it with the same dimensions that I made. Fourteen feet, which I'd made after the Baldy pipeline and a Hot Wheels track. They came up to me when I was sixteen, sitting on a beach, because I was riding for Rad Ramp and there was a show called Skateboard Mania and it was going to do all these gnarly things. Sid and Marty Kroft Productions was backing it. It was going to go on the road. We did Seland Arena, The Forum, The Long Beach Arena, and then it closed. Three nights at The Forum. When I broke my collarbone I was very hammered and I was trying to teach Tony Gitone because he was a good-looking guy, a big muscle guy. He was the star of the show. They ended having Skitch Hitchcock double for him with the track. They wouldn't let me near it when I broke my collarbone. I came back two weeks later with my brace on, doing fakies. "Get that fucking nut off the fucking track." They wouldn't even let me on it. I wanted to do successions. Nobody made that big of a deal out of it at all. I was embarrassed of it because when I started showing up at contests after that show folded, I had to make some money. I was already blowing away a lot of guys. It was like music—you're not getting the coverage because you're not *the guy*. I was, "That's the guy who did The Loop. He can't do nothing else." I was skating better than Weed. I was on Hobie and they would all focus on Mike Weed when we'd be in the van and Jeff Ruis was the team photographer and I'd be blowing that guy away doing all kinds of tricks. That guy had two or three tricks that were nothing, but they would focus on him. Ruis finally started shooting me.

I went through a hard time to win my first one. I should have won contests way before Whittier. I used to have issues. "Now, this guy's won a contest before me because I broke my elbows, both of them, at Del Mar during the bank slalom because I got hammered the night before and didn't tighten my trucks at all. I just showed up, they called my name. I was just trying to get overall points. I was ripping the pool way more than Eddie. I was going to win. My trucks gapped. I went boom, I mean hard. I was riding the train home the next day, got home. Got a phone call. "Eddie won."

Todd: Have you ever lined up the sponsors to do the jump over the thirty-six cars?

Duane: Years ago, when I was going to kill myself. All I wanted to do was get enough money for a lot of dope, some sort of way to jump a bunch of cars, and end my life that way. I could never see landing it, but I would have tried. I thought nobody knew about that. That's hot.

• • •

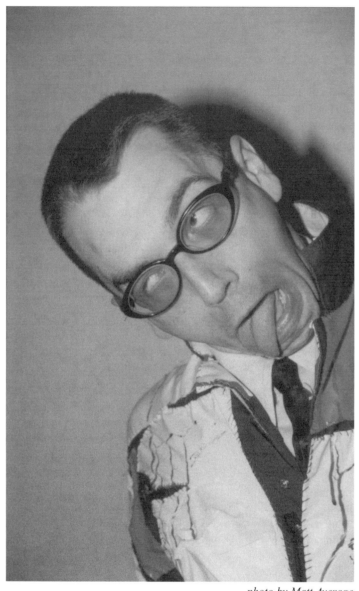

"He got pulled over with a B.A.C. of .10. Mine was .26. You call that Raider tradition? You're nothing, little man, you're nothing."

—Nørb

UNDER NO CIRCUMSTANCES SHOULD ANYONE EVER ADMIT THEY DON'T KNOW WHAT THE FUCK THE OTHER PERSON IS TALKING ABOUT UNLESS THE OTHER PERSON IS A COP OR YOUR MOTHER: AN INTERVIEW WITH REV. NØRB

By Todd and Matt Average

Rev Nørb, ringleader of Boris the Sprinkler, often dons an antlered football helmet that has "GEEK" stickered on the front and "PUNK" stickered on the back. That pretty much distills his entire philosophy.

Boris the Sprinkler is an institution. Many think that Rev. Nørb, should be institutionalized. If '90s pop punk was a Pez dispenser and its head was snapped back, Boris The Sprinkler would be one of the first three candy bricks to be ejected through its throat. As goes with all major religions, varieties of snack foods, and here, with pop punk, people disagree and fall into disparate categories. There's the pious who are wholly converted to the band's hard, sweet candy punk. And there are the naysayers who disregard Boris The Sprinkler's songs with contempt, discounting the band as nothing but Ramones ripper-offer-ers. Beyond such divisions of taste, there is no denying frontman Reverend Nørb's metaphoric nutsack. It's huge. It could tent a rhino if the temperature was warm enough.

What amazes and delights is that he's densely packed like uranium and has the energy of a thousand Super Balls being dropped out of a speeding semi. Like a superhero who was born on a planet with a different gravity, he's capable of tongue movements that would blister a mortal mouth. He also possesses an elasticity that makes his skin look like drawn taffy. He talks like he's announcing a monster truck event at a bingo parlor.

As you'll read in this interview, he's self-referential (see his footnotes) and self-fueled. (The tape recorder was merely set down. He provided all the entertainment.) He reminds me of classic *Mad Magazine*. There's always something written in the margins, always asides.

"Green Bay, motherfucker" is his mating call.

If he had never got a haircut in his life (factoring out such things as split ends and assuming a constant growth rate and good hair care), he surmised that he currently resides that theoretical hair's length away from the hospital where he was born. This being so, the session starts with a Wisconsin über alles quiz.

Todd: Name the 1973 Packer who got his dog shot.

Nørb: I recall Tony Mandarich getting his dog shot in 1992. 1973? Wow. It's one of those things where you can only remember the last Packer dog shooting... Ken Ellis?

Todd: Dan Devine.[1]

Nørb: He wasn't a Packer. He was the coach.

Todd: Wasn't he the coach of the Packers?

Nørb: He was coach of the Packers.

Todd: That's part of the Packers, is it not?

Nørb: I'm not so sure. This is a trick... If you're going to try to entrap me, we should just put the videotape away right now.

Todd: What was the greatest fire...

Nørb: Peshtigo.

Todd: There you go. What year?

Nørb: 1871?[2]

Todd: 1907. Very close. Which notorious U.S. Senator came from Wisconsin?

Nørb: Oh, that would be Joe McCarthy, who was born in Grand Chute, Wisconsin, which is the location of the nearest Hot Topic to my home.

Todd: Which famous cinematographer and moviemaker came from Wisconsin?

Nørb: [silence]

Todd: Fat and guttural.

Nørb: Fat and guttural?

Todd: Well, fat.[3]

Nørb: I don't know much about cinema. It's not Alfred Hitchcock...

Todd: He did one of the most respected movies of all time.

Nørb: Orson Wells.

Todd: There we go. No help from the audience. Which Wisconsin town has the highest per capita bars in America?

Nørb: That would be La Crosse, Wisconsin.

Todd: According to my sources, it's Merrill.

Nørb: Merrill? There's like three people in Merrill and one bar there.[4] I used to work at Wisconsin Public Service, which was the electric utility for our hunk of the state, and whenever we had old equipment that nobody

---

1. I certainly hope this happened *after* the Hadl trade, not before.
2. This is actually the year that the Republic of Germany came into existence. My apologies for the mix-up.
3. Since this adjective describes about 90% of my fellow Wisconsinites, it wasn't much of a hint.
4. Actually, two people, because Wendy Looker was at Las Vegas Grind.

else wanted, we would always have to put it in the store room and prepare it to get shipped out to Merrill.

Todd: Which architect came from Wisconsin?

Nørb: I'm afraid it was Frank Lloyd Wright.

Todd: He was from?

Nørb: He was probably from Madison.

Todd: Spring Green.

Nørb: Oh, that's right. That's where the House on the Rock is. I tried to go to the House on the Rock once with a girl, as sort of a date type thing[5], and my car broke down eight miles from Spring Green[6] and I was forced to suffer the humiliation of having to call my mother who was in Madison; have her pick us up, because I'm thirty-two years old and can't get my car to the House on the Rock at all.

Todd: What kind of car does Reverend Nørb drive?

Nørb: After that one died, I bought a Ford—actually, my last three cars have been Ford Escorts—but the new one is a weird one. It's a Ford Escort Sport SE that doesn't even look like a Ford Escort and it's got a spoiler, 'cause I'm having a mid-life crisis. And because my other Escort died ten feet away from a Ford dealership and I was rather limited in my choices. Wait a minute, let's just try something here. [Nørb jumps up and plunges his thumb repeatedly down on his car alarm and door lock device on his keychain.]

Todd: Does it go?

Nørb: I don't know. We'll see. If I get home and my car horn is on...[7]

Todd: Which mid-to-late eighties band had a hit that was from Wisconsin?

Nørb: A hit? Here's the question. This actually sort of came up today. And if it did, it's an interesting coincidence that we heard a country version of this song. The song I'm thinking of is "The Future's So Bright, I Gotta Wear Shades" by Timbuk 3, who weren't actually from Green Bay or from Wisconsin, but their lead guy, Pat McDonald or whatever, went to Green Bay West High School, which is the evil counterpart to my old alma mater, Green Bay East High School[8], and got thrown out for wearing long hair, but that's apparently not the right answer.

Todd: No.

---

5. Accent on "sort of."

6. Now that I think about it, the House on the Rock is in Dodgeville, which is eight miles from Spring Green, which is where my car broke down.

7. It wasn't; if it had been, I probably wouldn't've spent a half hour searching for it in the O'Hare airport budget lot.

8. East produced Earl "Curly" Lambeau, first coach of the Green Bay Packers, who led the team to six world championships. West's only contribution to the Packers was QB Jerry Tagge, who, now that I think about it, was the entire *reason* for the Hadl trade. I rest my case.

Nørb: Okay, there were the Violent Femmes.

Todd: There you go.

Nørb: But did they have hits?

Todd: They had hits.

Nørb: I saw the Violent Femmes at a frat party[9] when I was sixteen years old before they were signed to Slash.

Todd: Have you ever run for public office, like mayor?

Nørb: Actually, I always want to run for mayor, but then I think if I actually do good enough, people will start to unearth the skeletons in my closet to bring them out to sabotage my campaign. Therefore, I've not yet done it. I have run write-in.

Todd: What country-tinged, REM-esque band came from Wisconsin?

Nørb: Is this counting the BoDeans?

Todd: That is the BoDeans.

Nørb: From Waukesha.

Todd: What Madison band used to be called Spooner and now has a top hit?

Nørb: Well, Garbage were not actually called Spooner, but they had some of the same guys. And, in point of fact, Butch Vig, the big production guy from Smart Studios, who is the big wheel in Garbage and Spooner, once was in a lame band called Firetown. Not to be confused with his current lame band Garbage or his old lame band Spooner, and they once played a place that was approximately eight blocks away from my house and I had some friends who were working at the place where it was and—I was having a party—and some people who I was partying with went down to get the people who were working there and have them back, and in any event, some people from Firetown, including the world-famous Butch Vig himself, came by and apparently partied at my house for a little bit and had one beer and left because nobody would talk to him, but I don't know because I was passed out, face down, in front of my television set by that point in time. So, in a way, I partied, in absentia, with Butch Vig. And Spooner were not good. I don't care what you've heard. They sounded like The Shoes but worse.[10]

Todd: What Supreme Court Justice came from Wisconsin?

Nørb: My goodness. This I do not know. I have no clue.

Todd: Rehnquist.

Nørb: Really? I'll be dipped in shit. He's just saying that to build up his cred.

Todd: A part of a country's rainforest has been cut out and placed in a museum in Milwaukee. Which country is that?

---

9. "Co-op" party, whatever.
10. Or like Big Star minus the three good songs.

Nørb: These questions are becoming progressively more difficult, which is underscoring Wisconsin's reputation as a politically progressive state—and I don't know why it has that. I'm going to say Brazil.

Todd: Costa Rica.

Nørb: Oh, that's where former Packer Travis Jervey used to go surfing.

Todd: Who were the Harvey Wallbangers?

Nørb: The Harvey Wallbangers? They were a political party formed in 1903 by the castoffs, many German immigrants, who lived life by shoveling small, tunnel-like homes in the Wisconsin countryside, much like the badgers, for whom The Badger State is named, though there are no actual badgers, and they basically, ahh, they campaigned on statehood for the Mooselvania issue, which is what I think Bullwinkle did in 1959, and since Mooselvania or even Bullwinkle didn't exist, they were doomed to failure.

Todd: All I have is that they were a baseball team in 1982.[11]

Nørb: Oh, oh, oh. That was the Brewer's nickname or something. I didn't pay attention. I've only paid attention to baseball for the last two years since the Brewers went back to the National League because Mike from the Kung Fu Monkeys (and *Go Metric!* Fanzine)—it's all his fault—happened to bring up that when I was telling him how much I hated baseball and how I hadn't watched it since 1976 and the Cincinnati Reds were really great, that you could listen to baseball games at work. And the stunning logic of that was absolutely correct so now I have paid attention to baseball for the last two years and I'm not exactly sure why.

Todd: Perfect. That's my Wisconsin quiz. And now the interview proper. Reverend Nørb, fact or fiction?

Nørb: Fiction. And intentionally so.

Todd: Act of nature or chain reaction?

Nørb: Hmmm. I'm going to have to say act of quirky god.

Todd: Chemical reaction?

Nørb: Negative reaction coming your way. I'm sorry to quote The Fuck Ups, ruining my skinny tie credibility.

Todd: What are your guilty pleasures?

Nørb: My guilty pleasures include listening to baseball on the radio, which we've covered already because Bob Uecker is the color and the play-by-play announcer for the Milwaukee Brewers. Also, I enjoy heterosexual sex and the missionary position is really excellent. I also enjoy shopping at ladies fashion stores with my girlfriend because that's where all the cool gloves are.[12]

Todd: Why did you stop drinking alcohol?

---

11. Lost the World Series to the Cardinals in seven games.
12. When visiting the Mall of America, Rev. Nørb suggest a trip to Nordstrom's.

Nørb: I got far too good at it and if I got another DWI, they'd put me in jail. I don't feel like breaking rocks for whitey.

Todd: How many years were you drinking for?

Nørb: Gosh, lots, but I don't really remember.

Todd: Do you know anything about Pabst being taken over by Miller?

Nørb: I remember; that was fairly recently. That was two or three years ago. Yeah, because my band had two shows in Milwaukee and two shows nearby or something like that and we were in Milwaukee for the day and we wanted to tour the Pabst brewery for which to tour it, and it was closed because it had been all co-opted and somebody did something weird with the pensions and there was a great furor, but that was after I stopped drinking, so, you know, I didn't really care.

Todd: Vicarious furor?

Nørb: My big disappointment was that the Schlitz brewery, which made Old Milwaukee, was bought out by Stroh's, which was completely screwed.

Todd: "When you're out of Schlitz, you're out of beer."

Nørb: "When you're out of slits, you're out of pier," if you remember that joke. Our priest actually told that in church, sometime in the seventies. But I liked it when Pabst took over the Olympia brewery because I liked Olympia beer.

Todd: "It's in the water," wasn't that their slogan?

Nørb: Yeah, "It's in the water," or it used to be in the water.

Todd: Drug of choice?

Nørb: My drug of choice appears to be caffeine.

Todd: How often, how much?

Nørb: Not very often. I can stop at any time. Two liters at a time. That's the dose.

Todd: If you could skin somebody and then dance around in their skin, who would you want to be inside?

Nørb: Old hat, old hat. Actually, I can't say this. That one guy from Indiana who we saw on the escalator because I need fucking room to boogie, motherfucker.

Todd: In layman's terms, what's the difference between the Revillos and the Rezillos?

Nørb: The Revillos are more towards the cutesy sixties retro pop aspect of things whereas the Rezillos have more of a legitimate punk rock aspect to them. Also, the difference is a "v" and a "z." And I think Revillos is worth six points less if you play it in Scrabble than Rezillos because a "v" is four and a "z" is ten. So, six points would be the difference. But that's a big six points to be paid on triple letter score.

Matt: Signals from the mother ship—what are they saying?

Nørb: They're saying, "If you neglect your face each day, this is what we have to say, Burma Shave." No, they're not saying that anymore. Actually, they aren't saying anything, but it's like that Rocky and Bullwinkle thing where they go [in Bullwinkle voice] "Eenie weenie chili beanie, the spirits are about to speak. Are they friendly spirits?" [in Rocky voice] "I don't know. Let's find out." And then it leads into something different. Whenever someone asks me what the signals from the mother ship are, I say, "I don't know, let's find out," and then we start a cartoon.

Matt: If you could be a cartoon character, who do you most identify with?

Nørb: At present, I most identify with Plastic Man.

Matt: You do kinda look like Plastic Man.

Nørb: I didn't want to be Plastic Man for quite some time, but B-Face of the Queers said I was Plastic Man. I believe Mike Lucas of the Phantom Surfers also said I'd make a damn good Plastic Man because I've been lamenting over the fact that I'm not The Riddler or was not The Riddler in that Batman movie where The Riddler actually showed up. I thought I'd set my sights on Wolverine, so I have a Wolverine costume but I didn't pack it in my bag. Unlike most people, I actually like to have my clothes when I get off the airplane so I try not to bring any luggage that I have to check and I just take my carry-on bags. There wasn't any room for my Wolverine costume and wouldn't you know it, they cast for an X-Men movie and I'm not Wolverine. Now I think I've either got to be Mr. Fantastic or Plastic Man. I think I make a better Mr. Fantastic, who was a cartoon character[13], but was Plastic Man ever on a cartoon?

Matt: Yes he was. There was a cartoon for a little bit in the early to mid eighties.

Nørb: I'll be dipped. Plastic Man, he was sort of a swarthy guy, an ex-gangster, was probably good with the ladies. He had the exposed chest thing but he didn't have any chest hair and he had the curly hair. I don't know. Shouldn't I have to answer this question as a non-humanoid type? I think I should, like a funny, animal-type cartoon character. I've always identified with Bugs Bunny but I don't know why, because he likes carrots and I despise all vegetables. Other than that, I've got big feet and ears, so that's pretty much it.

Matt: Guy Debord, *The Spectacle*, is it still relevant today?

Nørb: No.

---

13. While primarily known as a comic book character, Reed "Mr. Fantastic" Richards has been on Saturday morning cartoons a number of times, first on ABC circa 1966, then later on NBC (I think?) in the mid-to-late seventies. Fuck Herbie the Robot! I don't know if the Fantastic Four were on TV in the nineties, though.

Matt: Why no?

Nørb: Jjjaaahh. 'Cause times have changed, dude.[14]

Matt: What was the most enjoyable chapter of the *Orgone Accumulator*? (A book by natural scientist Wilhelm Reich on biophysical discoveries. Orgone is biological life energy and is such a controversial topic that the Food and Drug Administration burned the book in the '50s and '60s.)

Nørb: I actually did not read the *Orgone Accumulator* thing. However, it was a thing in Madison, oddly enough, built by Frank Lloyd Wright, and it was some sort of center—the Frank Lloyd Wright Center, I think it was called—but it was something they were planning to build for fifty years and they finally built it. They had all these stars on the ground, like the Hollywood Walk of Fame, and people who donated money get a really big star and then, not to be confused with the band Big Star, who provided the theme song to *That '70s Show*, although on *That '70s Show*, they took out the line about smoking pot.

Matt: That same song?

Nørb: Not that recording, but it's actually a Big Star song called "In the Streets" or something like that.

Matt: It sounds a bit like Axl Rose.

Nørb: No. But Cheap Trick have a single version of that called "Rockin' in Wisconsin" that they play in Wisconsin, and it's really rockin'.[15] Where the hell was I? Well, anyway me and my mother were walking across this big Frank Lloyd Wright convention center and out of these millions and millions of these stars with donor's names on them, Wilhelm Reich had his own star in the Frank Lloyd Wright Center.

Todd: Olestra. Have you experienced any anal leakage?

Nørb: Oddly enough, I'm not allowed to have Olestra any more.

Todd: Why?

Nørb: It makes me weird.[16] Actually, I made that up. I've actually not sampled Olestra. It costs more. I like to wait 'til the stuff goes on sale because nobody wants it and then I'll eat away. I'm just thinking that the cancer I'm working on from the saccharine or whatever's in here [jiggles the two-liter of diet soda] is enough strange, non-caloric food additive menace. Actually, doesn't it have aspartame—yeah it does.

Todd: What's the most noticeable consistency difference between full size and mini Reese's Peanut Butter Cups?

---

14. Under no circumstances should anyone ever admit they don't know what the fuck the other person is talking about unless the other person is a cop or your mother.

15. He said sarcastically.

16. Op. cit.

Nørb: The smaller size are given to be more affected by heat. Whereas the bigger, since they're large, absorb heat better, so the small ones are more likely to be all mushed up and gooey and stuck to the tin foil wrapper than the large ones, which, where the heat it absorbs, unless it's subjected to a very large radiator type heating device. Usually it's minimal. Plus, plus, that also has something to do with the fact that the larger ones are packed in a little paper thing that doesn't really adhere to the actual Reese's Peanut Butter Cup itself, whereas the mini ones are actually packed in aluminum foil, which has a tendency to be more form fitting.

Todd: What do you look for in girls besides class rings?

Nørb: Stole my line... Spare change. Um, let's see. A willingness to put up with... I can't say right now. [Putting on a diplomatic air, noticing the earshot of his significant other.] Good personality, brains. What else, honey? Lots of shoes and lots of clothes. I like girls who shop, take a lot of time making up their face, and use a lot of cosmetics and what else? Did I say a lot of shoes? That's mostly it, and I did say nice personality?

Todd: What carnage was wrought on your from the very simple phrase, "The Cadillac of Vaginas"?

Nørb: Well, oddly enough, Cadillac sales have plummeted; vagina sales have sky rocketed. Somehow the phrase, "The Cadillac of Vaginas," somehow—well I would say that it led to me leaving my post at *Maximumrock'n'roll*, but now that I think about it, I don't think that I ever wrote for that magazine and anybody who implies otherwise is guilty of libel and slander, so no consequences whatsoever.

Todd: Who gave you the best answer to what would be "The Cadillac of Vaginas"?

Nørb: Actually, most people seem to read into it a certain amount of roominess and leathery interior, and I can assure you that leathery interior and room for five cigarettes—no, that's not what I meant whatsoever, however, there's been no good answers.[17] And I don't really know what it means because I forgot and I'm deleting all references to that. Maybe.

Todd: Ever gored anybody with your antlers?

Nørb: I've gored myself a lot of times. I gore band mates occasionally and they get really, really pissy when they wind up with that antler through the head, so usually I wind up with stigmata and whatnot going on, just from my flailing and my antlers, so I take the most abuse from my antlers but I'm not adverse to running somebody through on a dare.

Todd: How are the antlers adhered to the helmct?

Nørb: They're actually bolted on but the bolts are a bit loose. The bolts are turning and I can't quite get a wrench in there properly to tighten it in,

---

17. The "Mazda Miata of Vaginas" is an entirely different story.

so they spin. I've got them tethered with duct tape to kinda keep them at a proper angle so I don't have droopy horns, which would seem to imply that I'm impotent, which I hate. I've tried adhesive. I've tried mushy stuff. I've tried hot glue. I've tried chewing gum, but I still can't quite get that bolt. I think, perhaps, I've got the wrong sized bolt for my antler thread and I should have had a qualified hardware handyman type guy take a look at it. They were very helpful when I had to fix the plumbing in my house and the guy pointed out to me that I needed a pipe nipple.

Matt: What's the difference between geek and punk?

Nørb: Three letters. The "k" is the same.

Matt: Have you ever bit the head off of a chicken?

Nørb: Not recently, but I actually used to work, not in a circus, but during my high school years, I worked at a restaurant where we would get these thirty-five gallon tubs of raw chicken parts and it would be my job to rip the fat and the guts off the chicken parts and crack the thighs so they cooked better[18], so I would usually walk home with my Chuck Taylor whatever the hell they were soaked with chicken blood, not unlike some type of satan worshipper Ozzy freak or head biter-offerer chicken geek, but I'm not that type of a geek. I'm not that much into raw poultry because I feel it detracts from the extra crispy aspects of things. And god damn it, man, if your shoes are leakin' with chicken blood, you want to be as crispy as possible to mitigate that sloshing feeling of chicken plasma between your toes. [whispering to recorder] This has no point whatsoever.[19]

Todd: Why should people listen to your music?

Nørb: [silence] Mmmm, boy. Okay, I thought it would be really funny if I just paused and couldn't think of anything. People should listen to our music because the interesting backward messages will, eventually, eventually lead to situations which I, myself, can control with my cybernetic spooky wristwatch, which I'm showing you right now in the computer, tape recorder, whatever that is, probably a computer, and I realized in the last week that no one has ever—no one, ever, ever—has ruled this entire planet. Not once. I mean, there have been presidents, there have been dictators, there have been people trying, but no one has successfully ruled the entire planet. And I usually have pretty humble aspirations for myself, but now that I think about it, why not? Why not me? I don't believe in a lot of kowtowing, but I'll do what it takes to keep the rubes in line. I think that somebody should, at one point in time, be the first guy to completely rule the planet and I guess it's going to be me. But, you didn't hear it here. You can hear it by buying the entire Boris the

---

18. $3.35 an hour. God bless Reaganomics!
19. No *shit*!

Sprinkler catalog and playing it all backwards if you still have a turntable that accommodates backwards play. If not, what can you do?

Todd: Do new turntables accommodate backward play?

Nørb: Mine don't. Mine rarely accommodate forward play. I seem to have bad luck with stereo equipment because it always seems to last two to three months and then it's shit. I blame myself.

Todd: Have you been in any other bands besides Boris the Sprinkler and Suburban Mutilation?

Nørb: Yes. In the interim, I was in a band called Depro Provera. That is the end. Actually, now that I think about it, I actually played drums briefly for a joke band who didn't realize they were a joke band called A Bunch Of Morons, or ABM. I think we only played three shows.

Todd: Has anybody close to you died suddenly?

Nørb: You mean keeled over from sudden, natural causes, or keeled over—rocketed through a windshield and splattered against a telephone pole or something?

Todd: The second.

Nørb: Yes.

Todd: Care to elaborate.

Nørb: Nah, not particularly. You've seen one violent splattering, you've seen them all.

Todd: Did it change your life in any way?

Nørb: Probably so. Less Christmas cards to send. Daddy likes men.

Todd: Does that tie anywhere into the drinking.

Nørb: Uhhh, no. Not mine. I wasn't responsible for anybody's sudden death that I can think of, but I'm willing to learn.

Matt: Do you have a clause like David Lee Roth, for like when you get women pregnant on tour—an insurance clause?[20]

Nørb: Actually, I was at the M & M center. I didn't see any brown M & M's. Uhh, yes. We have this contract stipulation that we need bowls and bowls full of SweeTarts with the orange ones picked out because those taste more like chewable vitamins than actual SweeTarts and you can't have those backstage. Unfortunately, because we've never actually had a backstage area, the contract clause is somewhat moot. However, boy, if it wasn't moot—Leonard of The Dickies likes the orange ones best. I don't like the orange ones at all.

Matt: They all taste the same in the dark.

Nørb: No. Not at all.

Todd: You still have taste. You still lick things in the dark.

---

20. I apologize for not listening to the question. I thought he was talking about the "No brown M and Ms backstage" clause Van Halen used to have in their contracts. I guess this shows you where my mind's at.

Nørb: I mean, all the others are vaguely the same, but the orange ones— someone skimps on the citric power on the orange ones, which I find disheartening.

Todd: Do you think they go as far as remolding Flintstones chewable vitamins?

Nørb: I'm not too sure what they do. They probably, you know, get the orange ones from Canada because if you've ever been to Canada and had Canadian SweeTarts, they are shit. That nation is a nation of like bad SweeTarts and bad, crappy, turnover-infested football.[21]

Matt: Which do you hate worse: Canadians or French Canadians?

Nørb: I've actually never met any French Canadians. But, in theory, like they used to say in *Creem* magazine, you know, "French Canadians, perfume on a moose." I don't understand it.

Todd: Did you start the label Just Add Water?[22]

Nørb: I'm going out with the ex-girlfriend of the guy who started it. Apart from that, no.

Todd: What's the maximum number of variations of a single that you've released?

Nørb: That would be the *Drugs and Masturbation* version and I have absolutely no idea of how many versions are done but I'm sure there's somebody out there—I think our guitar player keeps track of these things—but I don't know.[23] I don't care. I just take the gigantic cash outflux and buy myself crazy extravagances like lavender Hush Puppies and that's about it.

Todd: Who's written you the most threatening letter?

Nørb: I've been threatened with disembowelings before, but they've always been on my answering machine. I think once, a teenage girl threatened to slurp lime Jell-O out of my nostrils or something. I dunno.

Todd: Is that a threat?

Nørb: I think it's a promise.

Todd: Ever thought of changing you name to Cap'n Nørb, Spaceranger?

Nørb: No, actually, when I was an anguished twelve or thirteen year old, and had misgivings at the world for having a strange first name, I wanted to change my name to Johnny Baron or something like that, or Johnny Blitz[24]. I think there already was a Johnny Baron, something stupid like that.

---

21. Their streusel cakes kick ass on Mexico's, though.
22. This was a weird goddamn question!
23. Actually, I think it's eighteen.
24. Then that fuck from the Dead Boys stole my name!

Todd: So Nørb is your given name?

Nørb: Norbert, actually. It's true.

Todd: What do you call the circle with the slash through it in your name?

Nørb: Absolutely nothing. It's an empty set. Sorry. Math humor. It's not a Danish "o." It's an empty set so point at that and go, "What does that mean?" And I can say "Absolutely nothing." Ha ha.

Todd: Where does the "Reverend" come from?

Nørb: I was actually ordained when I was sixteen by the Disciples of Divine Right from Boca Raton, Florida through some sort of classified ad they had in the back of *The Weekly World News* for absolutely free and in 1984 I was ordained by the Church of the Subgenius and the Reverend Ivan Stang waived the ordination fee because I'm so damned weird.

Todd: How much is the fee usually?

Nørb: Twenty bucks. So that's when they actually had money coming in and they weren't bankrupt like they are now or whatever the problem is.

Todd: Have you ever used you reverend status to your advantage?

Nørb: I don't even have any slack. However, who was that, the BC Lions—who's the one with the quarterback Reggie Slack, Dennis Slack? Okay, never mind that. Enough CFL humor. No, no, and I lost my membership card when I decided to swim across the Fox river. No, I lost my wallet. I did something. I swam across the river and I lost my wallet. I lost my Church of the Subgenius identification card, and without my ID card, I'm just pink to Bob, or whatever the hell.

Todd: What's you favorite internet porn site?

Nørb: The one that Jason from the Weird Lovemakers maintains. It's called like "Asian Beauties" or "Asian Poontang," or something brilliant like that, but he sorta made the logo for the site like the Boris the Sprinkler logo. There's also this picture you can click on—it's a free one—that's supposed to entice you to get the real ones, there's a picture of a urinating Asian female and he called it "Asian the Tinkler" or something like that, also in our honor. And I also really want to know why he doesn't have in one of the photos called "Little Yellow Box," after one of our 45s. It's not important right now.

Todd: How is the Lucite cryogenic capsule coming along?

Nørb: Well, I actually haven't been gotten to work on it because I figure it can be mixed posthumously when I'm dead because I don't think you can actually get it ready, you just have to have this stuff in advance and I figure nobody's actually going to do it for me anyway.

Todd: What new technology is so good that you just want to go out and hump it?

Nørb: I really like those little car things where you can open your car door by pushing the little button and I would hump that but it will not accommodate my huge, throbbing member.

Matt: What do the Packers pack?

Nørb: They're a bunch of crazy, psycho, goddamned Vietnam veteran types who get hip boots full of blood and they walk with much more blood squishing between their toes than I did when I worked gutting chickens and whatnot, and they're mean and nasty and it's not fudge, man, they actually run around with those electric cattle prods and meat cleavers and they kill and chop and maim and do all sorts—it's actually sort of an Ed Gein thing.[25]

Todd: What is the last thing you gave a long, satisfying lick to?

Nørb: Honey? I'm going to have to take the fifth right now because there is no partition between me and other people.

Todd: Spell something impressive.

Nørb: S-o-m-e-t-h-i-n-g-i-m-p-r-e-s-s-i-v-e.

Todd: I was hoping you wouldn't do that.

Nørb: I'm sorry. Uhh, uhh, uhh, m-o-l-y-b-d-e-n-u-m. It's element number forty-two. I'm not too sure if that's right, though.

Todd: What's your favorite homonym?

Nørb: I like exorcise and exercise.

Todd: Has punk rock ever gotten you laid?

Nørb: Yes.

Todd: Really? Explain.

Nørb: No. Everyone knows the really hot, desirable females are into punk rock. So though, I myself don't like it, I occasionally play it so I can circulate amongst the great masses of femininity and give long, satisfying licks to that which would otherwise not be mine to longly and satisfyingly lick.

Todd: Any product endorsements you're vying for?

Nørb: I've always been sorta disheartened that after my band recorded the song "Gimme Gimme Grape Juice," we could not get a Welch's grape juice endorsement, so I actually don't really see any kind of endorsements coming my way although if there was some sort of skin elasticity lotion, like you know, some collagen thing, that I could show how stretchy I am, and how I've got baggy elbow skin—you can't really tell 'cause I'm wearing a long sleeved shirt—I'd like to do that, too. There's SweeTarts, too, but they got bought out by Nestle so they've lost their corporate identity as far as I'm concerned.

Todd: Who were SweeTarts owed by before?

Nørb: They were owned by Sunline Brands, based out of St. Louis, Missouri; home to, of course, William S. Burroughs and Chuck Berry.[26]

Matt: Would you want to brag about that—William S. Burroughs?[27]

---

25. I guess "meat" is what I was driving at (please, no roadkill jokes).
26. I own a Rams hat.
27. I dig Burroughs and all, but it *is* sort of hard to talk up someone who would shoot his wife and sleep with James Grauerholz.

Nørb: Eh, good point. Not if you've got SweeTarts. SweeTarts never fucked anybody up the ass, as far as I know.

Matt: So how does it feel that at this moment your whole life has been leading up to this very moment?

Nørb: Better than I bargained for, actually. I thought my entire life was leading up to the moment tonight—what am I going to do tonight? Stand in front of some bands and get my foot stepped on by some drunken slob again, just like last night during Thee Mighty Caesars. I thought my life was leading up to that, that moment, which is like an hour and a half in front of me, but it's lead up to this moment, right here.

Matt: Do you feel like you've been short-changed anywhere?

Nørb: What, you've got a better bruise than I do?

Todd: Who was Boris the Spider?

Nørb: The short-lived character in a John Entwistle rock opera that only lasted about three minutes long. He got squished. He was creepy. He was crawly. He was creepy, creepy, crawly, crawly, creepy, creepy, crawly, crawly, creepy, creepy, crawly, crawly. He came to a sticky end so I don't think that will ever mend.

Todd: Was that where the name Boris The Sprinkler came from?

Nørb: Well, it was a combination of me humming that song coming home from work, and, uh, getting home and playing my tape recording of *The Bullwinkle and Rocky Show*, which I used to tape every day before cable bought the rights to it, as it did with everything.[28] And me singing "Boris the Spider" and me seeing Boris the Secret Agent on the TV, and going "Boris The..." and you can't say "Boris the Secret Agent" because that doesn't sound right, looking out the window and seeing a sprinkler, and you know kismet and stupid things, and I was pretty void of ideas as I still am, and so that had to suffice.

Matt: How much garage rock can one man take?

Nørb: Well, you should have asked me that question a year or two ago when I had already taken as much as I could take, but I guess apparently more than anyone can take. I'm not too sure what that means. That was supposed to be some sort of pithy and insightful comment on the current nature of current quote, unquote garage rock today, but heck, I just love it when all the little kids who were off listening to Fifteen three or four years ago now start bands ripping off the Devil Dogs and play that stuff and have all the snotty attitude like they thought of something really, really great and that they had this epiphany that rock'n'roll is good and that everybody else is, you know, an uncool moron who doesn't realize that pure rock'n'roll such as the stuff they play, is good. I especially like it when you remember members of bands, rock'n'roll bands, and you

28. I don't have cable. Is the Sunday night game ever any good, though?

remember when they used to play Rush covers and stuff.[29] It makes me feel good in here. [Pointing to his heart.]
Todd: Favorite science fiction author?
Nørb: Do comic books count? Probably not. I'm going to be lame and say Ray Bradbury. There you go. That one guy, the *Mona Lisa Overdrive* guy—he sucks. Fuck him.
Todd: William Gibson.
Nørb: I got a hard cover copy of *Mona Lisa Overdrive* for a dollar ninety-nine at a grocery store. When I started seeing all these bands popping up naming themselves after that, I decided that I should start reading him.[30]
Todd: Explain the curious glass partition in our hotel room that on one side is the bedroom, and the other side goes directly into the shower.
Nørb: When your girlfriend is masturbating in the shower and you're still lying in the bed, too tired to screw her in the shower and you want to feel like you're participating, the partition is there so she can open it up and you can hear her scream.
Todd: Are you a computer whiz?
Nørb: No, I suck... Hey, is this on? [Noticing for the first time in the conversation that we're recording this on video.] I've been sitting here, not doing anything. I'm not using the camera. I thought the red light would come on.
Todd: It's been on the whole time.
Nørb: Why? What for? What particular reason could that be? [Starts contorting for the camera] I hate computers. Is it true that the Oakland Raiders field[31] is named after Umax computers? Because if it is, I use a Umax at work and if they play as good as their computers, they fuckin' suck totally. And their coach, John Gruden, Raiders' attitude, what the hell is he thinking. He got pulled over with a B.A.C. of .10. Mine was .26. You call that Raider tradition? You're nothing, little man, you're nothing.
Todd: What is your other job?
Nørb: I work at a newspaper, a cheesy entertainment newspaper with pictures of strippers in the back and things of that nature. I get to type up all the personals. That's how I know about sling back heels. [Starts to get up on the glass table.] Is this connected? It's just a piece of glass on a goddamned piece of stone. That's crazy. The Flintstones designed this hotel. Frank Lloyd Wright has nothing on Fred. Hey, did you know that in that first Batman movie, that guy who's the army general is the guy who plays

29. The Leg Hounds are actually a very good band; this was not in reference to them (but that guy's old band did play a Rush cover).
30. I don't know why; none of the bands named after that book were particularly good.
31. The Oakland-Alameda Coliseum, sorry, I drew a blank on what it was called.

the voice of Fred Flintstone? It's true, absolutely true. Sunday, Sunday, Sunday night! Stop turning the camera upside down. [He attempts a head-stand from the almost-sitting position.]

Todd: How many people have died in ice fishing in Wisconsin lately?

Nørb: People have been dying all summer ice fishing. The ice gets so fucking thin on the lakes during summer in Wisconsin. It's fucking terrible.

Todd: Is there a lot of tension between you, Nørb, and the rest of the people who live in Wisconsin? Or have you formed an assimilation?

Nørb: I apparently can blend in somehow. I don't know how. I don't want to know how. Plus, I let the snowmobilers go over my lawn.

Todd: Do you know any secrets to peacefully coexist?

Nørb: [In thick Wisconsin accent like in the movie *Fargo*] "Well, no, there's no special dialect, so there's no special way to blend in. You know, I don't know, you go to the bubbler and get a drink with the guys. I don't know, you know."

Todd: Have you ever wanted to move out of Green Bay?

Nørb: Yes.

Todd: Did you ever?

Nørb: No. I'm not a very motivated person.

Todd: Have all of the members of Boris The Sprinkler lived in Green Bay?

Nørb: Well, actually, our bass player lived in Appleton, Wisconsin, which is very close to Grand Chute, home to Joe McCarthy. So there you are.

●   ●   ●

photo by Dan Monick

*"I think it would make people really angry if they under-
stood, that government priorities as such, that monsters continued to be made, beasts continued to be built, and all government will offer them is a eulogy at their funeral when
the grown victim turns predator."*

–**Andrew Vachss**

PREYING ON PREDATORS, NOT PRAYING FOR THEIR FORGIVENESS: AN INTERVIEW WITH ANDREW VACHSS

It seems so simple and so right. To protect kids. To nurture them. To want them to become healthy, productive, active parts of society, not sociopaths and killers. It seems so obvious. But when the nuts and bolts of our government's laws and the underpinnings of our society's heritage are scrutinized, some truly horrifying eyes are staring back from that darkness. There has been wonderful P.R. work afoot in America that claims families are first, are valuable, and that no kids will ever be left behind. It simply isn't true. Children, by themselves, have so little leverage. In the national political arena, they can't fight for themselves. They can't vote. They can't hire lobbyists.

Andrew Vachss (rhymes with ax), doesn't talk from a hypothetical point of view. A warrior, he has exposed child abuse for thirty years. In 1969, he traveled to Biafra during its genocidal civil war to try to set up a payment system for foreign aid. Since then, he's been, amongst other jobs, a federal investigator in sexually transmitted diseases, a labor organizer, a director of a maximum security prison for "aggressive-violent" youth, and since 1976, a lawyer who represents children exclusively. In 1993, Vachss helped hasten The National Child Protective Act, which formed a database to track child abusers who move from state to state. He is now lending support to the C.A.R.E. (Child Abuse Reform and Enforcement) Act, which promotes the improvement of information on, and protections against, child sexual abuse. He has also published fourteen novels.

If every human was as driven, focused, and articulate as Andrew Vachss, the world in a generation would, quite literally and pragmatically, become a better place. As trite and as unfocused as the rallying cry of "save the children" may seem as it streams out of a politician's mouth, one gets the diametrically opposite impression when Mr. Vachss talks about how "today's victim is tomorrow's predator" and how children are truly the key to a sustained civilization. What I first approached as an informative exercise and historical context of child abuse also turned into discussions on political leverage and law, the nature of serial killers, the nuances of the death penalty, and the United States' hapless war on drugs.

Special thanks go out to Vanessa Burt for not only raising this to my attention but also her selfless conviction to this cause.

Todd: In layman's terms, what is the legal definition of incest?

Vachss: Well, the actual definition of incest is sexual contact between people who are related within a certain degree of consanguinity—blood or marriage. However, its definition isn't popularly understood, so when people think of incest they think of first cousins having consensual sex in Kentucky in a shack. They don't think in terms of a parent and a small child but the law does cover that. In my opinion, it didn't contemplate such coverage when it was first passed. If you look at the incest laws, they're quite ancient.

Todd: Is there a historic precedence for incest?

Vachss: A precedence supporting it?

Todd: Yes.

Vachss: No. In fact, quite the contrary. Where it came from was through observation of nature, and humans observed that inbreeding was a dangerous thing. So, even people in the earliest forms of animal husbandry understood that inbreeding was guaranteed at some point to produce genetic defectives. Now, if you're talking about the Egyptian kings, for example, who intermarried, sure, it happens. There's no question. There were people in ancient times, and Nazis today who believe that the way you keep a race or a species or a bloodline pure, you don't mix it with outside blood. Ipso facto, you're going to have people having sex with their own kids.

Todd: I was thinking that the historical precedence for the United States would be having the vestige of British rule, which is a monarchy that used incest to keep their bloodlines.

Vachss: That privilege was always reserved for royalty. Look, royalty's always reserved to itself every hideous style or privilege—to torture people who don't agree.

Todd: What is the legal definition of rape?

Vachss: Sex by force. However, it's important to understand that force is implied in certain cases even though no physical violence is used. So, for example, if a child is too young to consent, or if a person is impaired by mental illness or if a person is intoxicated, drugged—all of those would be rape, even if the person did not require physical violence be used to accomplish their end.

Todd: What I want to deal with is the CARE Act. Why is there a legal difference between incest and rape and what are the different penalties?

Vachss: The reason is that it's an anomaly that's hung over. If you stopped any fifty people in the street, I don't believe you'd find one who would understand that, for example, a father having sex with his six-year-old daughter could be called incest. So, it's simply an anachronism in terms of law not having caught up to society. There's no legal justification for it. There's good reason for an incest prohibition, but an incest prohibition is a societal message. For example, there is a law against adultery. How many people do you think go to jail for it?

Todd: Very few.

Vachss: Okay. Never, in my life, have I heard of anybody going to jail for adultery. But, because of the sort of religious underpinning of the country, that law stays on the books as a way of expressing a view. So, it's fine to have a law in the book that expresses the view that first cousins shouldn't interbreed, but in reality, I've never heard of anybody going to jail for what amounts to adult-consensual incest.

Todd: Would there be probation or anything?

Vachss: Oh yeah, I've seen people prosecuted for it, but, again, it's such an after-the-fact thing that nobody expects it to alter the conduct of the party. I've personally been in numerous cases where there've been incest babies, but all of those involved children being sexually accessed, not adults. First of all, the FBI does not break out incest as an index crime. We've attempted to run Bureau of Justice statistics and we don't see any statistics being kept on incest. (The FBI in 1929 implemented standardized crime reporting across the country. Seven major, or index, crime categories were selected and reporting criteria were established for each: murder, forcible rape, robbery, aggravated assault, burglary, larceny/theft, and motor vehicle theft. An eighth category, arson, was added later.)

Todd: Even though there aren't statistical numbers, how widespread would you estimate incest and child abuse to be?

Vachss: You mean adult incest? Or do you mean sexual activity within a family with a child as a victim? Those are really different things to me.

Todd: The second one.

Vachss: First of all, that doesn't get broken out as incest, but in terms of the numbers of children who have been sexually abused each year, obviously they're monstrously significant numbers or you wouldn't have every single state legislating against it. That's not really debatable. What's debatable here is why any human being should get special dispensation from the law for having the good taste to have sex with his own child as opposed to a neighbor's child. And that, if you examine it historically, as you seem to be interested in doing, stems from property rights.

Todd: That's what I was trying to figure out.

Vachss: Sure. Because, look, I have the legal right to burn down my own house. I can't burn down yours. Well, apparently, I have some degree of legal right to have sex with my own kid but not with yours. If you look at the radical disparity in penalty, I think that's true.

Todd: Oprah Winfrey was helpful in passing the National Child Protection Act.

Vachss: I don't think it could have been passed without her. I think justifiably deserves to be called the Oprah Bill, as many do, because without her financing it just couldn't have happened as quickly. Most of these efforts, and even that effort, take years.

Todd: Am I correct in remembering that it passed the House of Representatives 416 to 0?

Vachss: I don't believe there was any opposition.

Todd: My question would be, what would be the opposition to it?

Vachss: Those who would oppose the CARE Act would be very quiet about it. I think there are people who certainly wouldn't want it passed. Certainly, no American thinks any politician is exempt from any form of hideous conduct but I can't see them committing political suicide and standing up on the floor of Congress and saying, "Yeah, I believe people who fuck their own babies should be appealed," and that's, in effect, what they'd be saying.

Todd: What are the largest hurdles for the CARE Act right now? What are the stipulations that people are bugged about?

Vachss: None. Let me be fair. There are "child advocates" who take the position that since, theoretically, if the federal legislation was passed and State X didn't adopt a version, it could lose a percentage of its Child Abuse, Prevention, and Treatment Act funding since that funding is going for [in facetious voice] "the children and I don't want do anything that could possibly negatively impact the children." Bleah. And there are a few prosecutors who treat their discretion as some sort of sacred thing and anything that interferes with their discretion, they're opposed to. They don't care what it could be. It could be three strikes, it could be anything. There will always be prosecutors opposed because they want to be the ones who make that decision. But if you leave that aside, the problem with the CARE Act is its lack of constituency.

Todd: Meaning lack of people trying to push it through?

Vachss: No, no. Let me ask you a question.

Todd: Sure.

Vachss: Why is the NRA so powerful?

Todd: Lobbying?

Vachss: Nope. Don't agree.

Todd: Lots of members?

Vachss: Don't agree.

Todd: One focus?

Vachss: Yes, and that makes them a deliverable block of votes. Take the gun issue. The people on the other side of the gun issue—they haven't got any focus. They don't want people to own handguns but they also want whales protected. They don't want people to smoke cigarettes. The list is a smorgasbord. Therefore, they're unfeared by most politicians. There is no single-issue constituency for children in this country because any jack-ass—NAMBLA bills itself as a child advocacy organization—so, it's a self-awarded title that means nothing. There is no group that could say, "Mr. Senator, here's the deal. If you vote for this act, we're going to have a million people supporting you, voting for you, raising money for you, advocating for you, and if you don't, we don't care if your opponent is Satan, those million votes will go to him." Which is the NRA's position. The NRA is unconcerned about minutia: like taxes, the environment, war, poverty, famine, disease, you see?

Todd: Or specifically who runs the country, as long as they support the NRA.

Vachss: They don't care. That's exactly right. Beelzebub could be running. So, as a result, they're taken deadly seriously. Whereas the people who are "concerned about children" have never formed that focused constituency because, you know what, they spend all of their time either fighting over grants, among each other, fighting over territory, or demanding that they be the spokesperson. In this country, there is not a child protective lobby.

Todd: Interesting.

Vachss: I dare you to find one.

Todd: I did a lot of searching for one, specifically, and I found little to no information. Changing gears, does this fit into the dynamics of abuse? Those who are abusing want to cover their tracks. Those who are abused are scared or ashamed and can't find the vent for the abuse, and those who aren't directly in the cycle don't want to hear about it because it's really ugly stuff.

Vachss: Except for the latter, I agree with you. I think there are plenty of people who have some concern about this issue but they have never—just by nature of the political temperament of that kind of person—they're not fanatics and it the squeaky hinge that gets the oil. See, the NRA's bankrupt. It's not their lobby. It's not their money. It's the deliverable block of votes and I don't know any group—for kids, you see—that can promise that. The Mormons can promise that in Utah. Hell, there's places in this country where the Klan can promise it, but I don't know any place where children can promise it and if you look at any organization involving kids, each of them is setting themselves up as the only game in town. There has never been a coalition. No one's ever willing to say, "I'll drop my personal issues on this long enough to get yours passed and then you can help me with mine."

Todd: Has Oprah tried, since she was successful with the National Child Protection Act, to step into this arena?

Vachss: It's not a question of stepping into the arena. It was much more Oprah's money than it was anything else that was done. The only time she spoke of this is when I was on television with her. And that was several times, sure, but it was really me talking and her saying, "Yeah." I'm not saying she wasn't supportive, but you if have looked at Oprah's shows the last year or so or two years, or three years even, they are not exactly what you'd call issue-oriented. And her constituency—if there was legislation about makeovers, I think maybe. She can certainly get people to write letters, but she's not going to get anybody, who I can see, to be obsessed about the passage of a particular piece of legislation. It's not a referendum system. If it was a referendum system that we had nationally, I believe we could get it passed. I absolutely do.

Todd: Is there any way a grassroots effort can bring this up on a referendum?

Vachss: Not federally, no. There's no legislative process where there can be a national referendum. You're talking about something as big as a plebiscite (a direct vote of the qualified electors of a state in regard to some important question). My goodness, if you look at the history of the ERA, a struggle that you think *couldn't* be lost...

Todd: Is still going on, full throttle...

Vachss: Yeah. Also, you've got to remember, for politicians, you have to offer them some inducement other than, "It's the right thing to do."

Todd: Correct. I think, "It's the right thing to do and we can do it on your term. It can be finished and your name can be on that bill."

Vachss: That's right. The good part about it is the bill really appeals to those who want to see it as an anti-crime measure. It's a "Let's make child molesters do more time" kind of thing, and those who see it as a child protective measure. It has no tax consequences, so you don't have that handicap. But the fact that something's beneficial or valuable or even righteous has never been enough, in and of itself, to move Congress.

Todd: I think the family values platform is really nice to say but it's really vague at the same time.

Vachss: Let me tell you something. Family values is beyond vague. Remember, I've been doing this a long time and I can't tell you how many times I've stood up in court and had some defense attorney talk about the need to keep the family united even though daddy's been raping his daughter.

Todd: Right. So biological dysfunction is better than anything else.

Vachss: That's exactly right. Aberrational biology, the hell with behavior. I did one TV show—I don't remember which—this is probably not the one that got me audited but pretty close. No, it was later on in my career. It was when Reagan was in the White House when I first got audited. Someone asked me about family values, and I said "Who's the biggest spokesperson for family values?" And they said, "Dan Quayle." And I said, "If I was Dan Quayle, I would be for family values, too, because if it wasn't for his family, he'd be flipping burgers." It's family values in the sense of how much money does your family make that it values. Look, the law schools are full of people who are there because of their family. We're

probably in the third or fourth generation of politicians now who are all
connected. Udall's son is in Congress, you see. How many generations of
Kennedy? Yeah, family values, that's nice. Certainly, John Gotti could
have something to say about family values.

Todd: He runs a tight operation.

Vachss: Also, the right to define is the right to control. So, let's say you
and I agree that communism is bad. If we agree to that, all we have to do
is say "This guy's a communist," and we wouldn't have any more dispute.

Todd: And then we could have a trial, and it'll be all right.

Vachss: Sure. But when it comes to something like family values, it's way
too nebulous—I mean, I really consider it a family value that somebody
who sexually assaults his own child is drummed out of the human race. I
don't mean killed but we don't consider him one of us.

Todd: Why wouldn't you want to kill molesters?

Vachss: I'm not in favor of capital punishment for a number of reasons.

Todd: Is it just by the mechanisms that it takes so long in the appeals
process and it creates some kind of celebrities?

Vachss: Or that. You're very well read or else we think alike. All of that's
true, plus, let's face it, there's the ever-looming prospect of a fatal mistake.
But it does, absolutely, make celebrities out of the worst degenerates. It
does cost more to kill somebody than it does to incarcerate them for life.
That whole argument about "Why keep them locked up for life?" is bullshit. It's created an entire industry that shouldn't exist.

Todd: By your own experiences, do you know how child molesters get
treated in prison by other inmates?

Vachss: Let me tell you the truth instead of what you've heard. How you
get treated in prison depends on your size, your coldness, and your connections. I have been in prisons where people with the most reprehensible
crimes you can imagine, everybody treats well. People with high-status
crimes are hurt and abused and even killed. Because in there, it's very
much a jungle mentality and if you bring power to the game, nobody's
really concerned about the status of your crime. Now, it's true that if you
fit the standard predatory pedophile definition and you're sort of a weak,
ineffectual shrinking person, you're going to prison and people are going
to take advantage of that but it's not because you're a child molester.
That's an engrafted-on excuse.

Todd: You don't have a dynamic personality, that type of thing.

Vachss: Well, you could be good with your hands. That could be enough.
Let me give you an example. Do you know who Albert DeSalvo is?

Todd: No, I don't.

Vachss: He was otherwise known as The Boston Strangler. How come he
was never in protective custody? I mean, this is the guy who raped, tor-
tured, and killed, what, fifteen grandmothers. You might check Albert

DeSalvo's record and find out that he was also the light heavyweight boxing champion of Europe when he was in army. Albert was a bad guy. Albert could hurt you.

Todd: Interesting. I've always wanted to know about that.

Vachss: People have this idea that there's this cool prison subculture where the convicts shun...

Todd: That there's a morality...

Vachss: Forty years ago, sure, no question because forty years ago, the lowest thing you could be was not a child molester, it was an informant. People go into prison now, bragging about the other people they brought with them, for god's sakes. I mean, the people who are in protective custody are there because of specific hostility towards them, not because of their crime. And anyway, child molesters can easily be isolated in prison because all they have to do is opt for one of these treatment programs. There's separate housing, separate wing. If you look at the history of people killed in prison, look at prison stabbings, take a state, and you will see that it's Aryan Brotherhood against black Muslims, the Nazi Lowriders against the skinheads. It'll be about territory, it will be about a debt, it'll be about a sexual assault, but about a crime? No.

Todd: You've said that true anger and hatred can be effective tools against abuse. Does this go against the current trend towards forgiveness or do you think that forgiveness by itself is faulty?

Vachss: I think forgiveness by itself—let's face it—any doctrine which teaches forgiveness is probably written by perpetrators.

Todd: Well, yeah, I was thinking of the Bible.

Vachss: Let's just be honest about it—with forgiveness—that it is an individual choice and that the right belongs to the wronged, not society, but to the person actually wronged. Telling people that you can not heal unless you forgive is a pernicious, destructive lie because so many people say, "I can't forgive what they did to me so I'm doomed. I'll never heal." As if you had the obligation not only to be abused but to forgive the abuser. There's nothing about that dynamic that's psychologically correct. Nothing. In a way, it's supporting—I'm the therapist and I'm telling you— "Yeah, look Todd, I did these horrible things to you but you have to forgive them." So who am I advocating for there? Whose side am I on?

Todd: You're advocating for the person who abused.

Vachss: That's exactly right. That may have some religious validity, although I consider that an oxymoron, but I don't see where it has any therapeutic validity. And I'm not saying that everybody has to go kill their abuser or even everybody has to sue their abuser or even everyone has to simply stop any contact with their abuser, but the idea that they have to somehow forgive the person who hurt them, for them to heal, it's just a lie. It's just not true. The healthiest people I know are people who say, "I hate

them for what they did and I'm going to get even. The way I'm going to get even is I'm going to protect other children."
Todd: Excellent.
Vachss: That has been the single-most healing thing. You would not believe the volume of mail I get from people who read the books, who kind of identify with Burke's unrelenting hatred. (Burke is the main character in many of Vachss's novels.) And the result is, "Does this mean that I'm not crazy? Because that's the way I feel."
Todd: Shifting just a little bit again, do you think child abuse and incest haven't reached the main focus in the American conscience due to its impossibility of being televised on national TV? I'm thinking along the lines of the women who got mobbed by a group of men in Central Park, where there are fourteen videos capturing that...
Vachss: There are plenty of videos of children being abused.
Todd: Has it been nationally syndicated?
Vachss: Of course not. Those are videos for commercial sale. They're deliberately made for product. There's no question about that. I think the reason is, first of all, child abuse is an amorphous term, second of all, people operate off of religious belief as opposed to fact, so people say, "I believe there's an epidemic of false allegation." And other people will say, "I believe that no child ever lied about sexual abuse." Those are belief systems. They're not facts. I don't believe this country will ever come to grips with child abuse until they make the obvious, simple connection between today's victim and tomorrow's predator. As long as they believe a Ted Bundy or a John Wayne Gacy is a biogenetic mistake as opposed to a beast that was built and a monster that was made, they'll continue to blithely walk around, saying, "I'm against child abuse," whatever that means. Then there's also the people, who, for example, spanking freaks. "Oh, it's all right to spank children." "Oh, it's the correct thing." "Oh, it's biblically...," you know. Of course, I see these same people posting to boards that are all about spanking but they're spanking between adults and purely for erotic purposes. [facetiously] But, ahh, there's no connection, I'm sure. Never mind that pictures of children being "disciplined" are the hot topic. They're sold and traded all the time. That's not because people are connoisseurs of, you know, correcting children. I don't think America's going to do anything except of that of perceived self-interest. I think it is America's self-interest to really ruthlessly and relentlessly battle child abuse because the ones who are not protected, the ones who are not safe, some percentage of them will turn on us. Most of them will not. Most of them will turn on themselves. But if you don't think the societal cost in mental health services and drug addiction services and alcoholism services is not killing us... and where does that come from?

Todd: It comes from the very beginning, from the seed of it.

Vachss: Of course. The cost of early intervention in child abuse is like a dollar compared to a hundred thousand dollars for intervention in even juvenile violence, never mind adult violence.

Todd: I was trying to parallel this in my mind the other day. I thought it a little weird that there's a long-time, incredibly expensive, dubious war on drugs and there's not even a battalion devoted to child's rights.

Vachss: Amen. The war on drugs; Nancy Reagan has poisoned and ruined this country. Not only is the war absolutely futile—or if it's a war, we're all POWs, but it's poisoned pain management in this country to where people are dying in extraordinary pain because doctors don't want them to be drug addicts.

Todd: There's a stigma attached to it.

Vachss: To the doctor, not to the poor person who's in freakin' pain, but those decisions—doctors are more afraid of the DEA than they are the IRS. There has never been a war on drugs. It's silly. You've got to understand, it's just a question of privilege because there was also a war on booze, remember? The money from Prohibition financed organized crime right to this day. And if you don't think that the war on drugs isn't financing organized crime, you're absolutely crazy. If we had the money that we spent on this utter futility... I don't care if people want to be dope fiends. I care what they do to get their drugs.

Todd: And how they treat other people.

Vachss: If you want to go in your house and shoot up, good for you. I don't give a damn. I really don't. But the cost of drug enforcement and the damage done by addicts and the cost of treating addicts, it's going to bankrupt this country. If we didn't have this bullshit, we could probably fund every single social program in the world times ten. We could feed Ethiopia. But, in this country, there's kids—we don't want kids to be dope fiends, that's very nice—as if there's really pushers hanging around school yards trying to get kids. What a canard. What nonsense.

Todd: I grew up in a very small town and I got into trouble quite a bit. It was a very weird dynamic. The powers that be say, "Don't do anything destructive." And it was little things like skateboarding, but they wouldn't make a skate park. They wouldn't give you something to do, only say "Don't do it and just stand on the corner of the street and stare at something." They didn't provide any activity or anything that was a viable alternative to a young mind.

Vachss: They could do it. The money is certainly there. The money has been squandered on absolute, utter nonsense. It would be fine with me if we had an actual war on drugs. If you want to have a war, I've been in a war and I know what a war is. This isn't one.

Todd: It kind of reminds me of the tactics of the Vietnam War. It's a completely shifting battleground. Battles are fought over non-sequential hills that are overtaken as soon as the forces are pulled out, and you still haven't engaged your enemy directly.

Vachss: The enemy was undefeatable because the territory couldn't be occupied. If United States had "won" that war, what would we be doing? Would we have 175,000 troops in Vietnam now?

Todd: No. I think we'd have cheaper motor scooters, that's about it.

Vachss: The whole trade balance is utter hypocrisy. You can't expect a country to protect its own children when they get on their knees and say, "Oh god, we must have trade with China, ehh, don't worry about the human rights thing."

Todd: I was curious about the current condition of The Domino Theory. Have they said, "This isn't good any more"?

Vachss: I think they must have said that because ask the Russians about Afghanistan. The whole idea was to crank up a war machine. It was to do anything about stopping the spread of godless communism in southeast Asia. You ask yourself why they didn't attack Cuba, if that was their rationale. If the rationale was that this is a fascist government that's controlling the people and, you know, no freedom in this, no freedom in that, why don't they just... Cuba's just sitting over there. And it's another example of American hypocrisy, which is why people don't respect it. I have friends who are Mexican. They say to me, "What the fuck is this? If I'm a Cubano and I make it to the shore, everybody wants to give me a kiss and a job. But when I try to go across the goddamn Rio Grande, they want to shoot me." The rationale is that the Cubans are fleeing oppression. Have you been in Chiapas lately? Mexico's a booming, wonderful democracy because they make Volkswagens?

Todd: Mexico was controlled by the same party since 1929.

Vachss: And by force.

Todd: Prior to Fox, opponents were killed. (Vicente Fox, Mexico's current president, elected in 2000, officially ended the Institutional Revolutionary Party's seventy-one-year-old stranglehold on Mexican political power.)

Vachss: They've killed them in the street. So, when people flee that, they get turned back. I would flee that, I wouldn't want to be there. But if they're Cuban, okay. That's one reason why when people talk about the Hispanic vote in this country, they're idiots. They don't realize that the Mexicans and Cubans are not exactly pals because of the disparity in their treatment by this government. It comes down to what? Deliverable block of votes. The same way Puerto Ricans have been a viable force of New York politics since, my god, the '30s.

Todd: I think there were more Puerto Ricans in New York than Puerto Rico at one time.

Vachss: Certainly more than in San Juan, no question. That's because a politician, Envito Mark Antonio, a long, long time ago got through legislation that Puerto Ricans could vote as Americans. I mean, it's not a state. Any time there's political power, children, by definition, never are going to have political power. What they're going to have is "spokespersons." There is no other group on the face of this earth—I don't care if they're mass murderers—that don't have one of their own as spokespersons.

Todd: Concerning child protection laws, how would you rate America in the grand scheme of the world?

Vachss: We're at the high end as to the law. Let me distinguish between law and law enforcement. We're not where the Scandinavian countries are, for example, which prohibit so-called corporal punishment.

Todd: But we're nowhere near Thailand.

Vachss: Australia's coming up strong. Australia's going to pass laws that are appropriate but I would definitely say America's at the high end in terms of a legislative scheme when it comes to kids. However, our legislative scheme does permit you to kill kids, right? You can be under twenty-one and be executed in the United States. And you can be thirteen and tried as an adult in the United States.

Todd: I think it's getting lower and lower, too.

Vachss: No, no. Every state has a different law but they all have one provision or another by which they can make a child into an adult. In New York, for example, at sixteen you are an adult. There's no judicial process involved. You shoot a guy on your sixteenth birthday, you're an adult. But on your fifteenth birthday, they would have to get permission to treat you as an adult. And they would have no trouble doing that because we have this theory that a thirteen-year-old, obviously couldn't sign a contract, couldn't drive a car, couldn't vote, couldn't drink, but, by virtue of the maturing experience of having killed other human beings, they are old enough for criminal justice purposes.

Todd: Maybe we should just fire guns at people, to get them smarter and instantaneously growing up.

Vachss: I can tell you that having guns fired at you makes you smart for a very brief period of time. It does make you smart for the moment.

Todd: It makes your legs smart, too.

Vachss: The people who are not smart don't have a continued experience of being shot at. Did you know that the United States has not signed a U.N. convention on the rights of the child?

Todd: Really?

Vachss: Because it prohibits the death penalty. [facetiously] We're not going to do that because the death penalty has been proved to be such a potent weapon against crime. We kill more than everybody else but we seem to have more murders than everybody else. Duh.

Todd: And I don't think it's because of drugs.

Vachss: No. It's not because of drugs. It really has a reason. I mean, look, there are a lot of murders that are just, you know, stupid murders, but the sociopathic murders that scare us the most, those people are not born bad. They're just not. There's no isolatable chromosome or gene or combination that produces murderers.

Todd: Do you think that some people are born evil?

Vachss: No, but certainly there are people whose triggers are set differently. On the other hand, lots of those people never grow up to be vicious criminals. There are checks and balances. We're all different in that respect, but born evil—evil's a choice. To be evil, you have to volitionally chose conduct.

Todd: Right, or be exposed to that conduct and not know the difference.

Vachss: Nope, you still have to imitate it before you could be called evil. You could be exposed to it endlessly but doesn't mean that you copy it.

Todd: That's true. I was thinking about that the other day, too. About if you had a serial killer and he had a twin brother or she had a twin sister, what was the difference between the two? One's successful, or definitely not out killing other people, what is that trigger, what is that margin?

Vachss: Remember, too, that some of these twin studies are badly flawed because they say, "Look, there were two twins and they both turned out to be bad, which says something about genetics." And then you say, "Geez, were they separated at birth or were they raised in the same home? If they were raised in the same household, what are you saying?" I, personally, have had families in my caseload who literally, third and forth generation, every goddamn one of them, was a rapist, a murder, a thief, an arsonist, everything you could think of, not because their strain of genes was bad but because their intra-familiar culture was...

Todd: ...systematic, repeated abuse.

Vachss: You have a choice. Look at any juvenile prison. You see a kid come in there. He looks around. He figures it out almost immediately. There's predators and there's prey. The way you can tell the prey is they're forced into sex acts, for example. So if I force somebody into a sex act, therefore, I put myself on a different side of the fence. It's a lot of adaptive, survival-driven behavior that's pretty damn ugly.

Todd: What can you tell me that can make our readers angry? You've said, "Informed, inactive people are just as useless as ignorant people."

Vachss: That's right.

Todd: Can you give me some information that could, possibly, drive people into action.

Vachss: Yeah. The information is, you've been hosed. You don't know that there is a law that permits special, more lenient treatment of people who rape their own kids.

Todd: So, if you can raise them, you can raze them.

Vachss: The ownership of kids to that extent—people don't know this—in people's minds, incest is much older. When people think of incest, they think of a seventeen-year-old girl and her stepfather. They haven't been told the truth, and more importantly, you know I think it would make people really angry if they understood, that government priorities as such, that monsters continued to be made, beasts continued to be built, and all government will offer them is a eulogy at their funeral when the grown victim turns predator. Because all this three strikes stuff, all this "let's lock them up and throw away the key," I mean, that's just so much after the fact.

Todd: That's when the curtain's falling instead of the first act.

Vachss: Sure. What you said before is true. A politician will not support something that won't bear fruit within his term of office and when you're talking about intervening in child abuse, so as to protect one generation removed, no politician wants to touch that.

Todd: No self interest in that.

Vachss: No, because he can't. With the exception of a Strom Thurman, who's going to be around to say, "I can take credit for it."?

Todd: Just for my own curiosity, do you know any famous people who have been convicted as pedophiles or have been up for incest charges?

Vachss: Are you serious?

Todd: Yeah.

Vachss: Roman Polanski. He's sitting in France. An exiled hero to the Hollywood community, but in fact, he was convicted of sex with a twelve-year-old girl and decided to not hang around and go to jail. So there's this great campaign to get poor Roman back into this country. There've been all kinds of people convicted of having sex with their own child but I don't know about famous people. What I would say is there aren't a whole lot of rich and famous people in jail for anything.

Todd: Why are people trying to kill you? Why is there such secrecy around you?

Vachss: I don't know that either of those things are true. Certainly, I've had my share of stupid threats over the years and in the course of my work as an investigator and other things, yeah, you're in violent places, violent things happen. I had a law office in New York City for many years and a day didn't go by without some degenerate simply using the phone lines or using the fax machines for his or her own entertainment. When I practiced law full time, that was just something I had to bear. I don't now because I've switched to sort of a different type of work. I still do courtroom work but they're selective shots not open to business to everybody. My home address has never been public and never would be. I don't know why anybody would make their home address public, to be honest with you.

Todd: No way. On a much smaller scale, I help operate a small magazine. I want to keep the two—home and work—separate. I want to go home and not have to answer the phone.

Vachss: That's right. I don't think that's unique. I take precautions because I teach people to take themselves seriously and I intend to take myself seriously. In other words, I'm proud that I'm on the enemies list of the International Pedophile Liberation Front but I don't dismiss people who send me pictures of myself with my face covered by a crosshair or people who send funeral cards or even people who call up and say, "You're dead." Are they far more likely than not freakish little windbags? Yes. Sure. I pity the fool who would find my house and break into it, unless somebody has a real affection for pitbulls.

Todd: I get the feeling, and I really appreciate this, is that you're not solely there for child's rights because child's rights is a good thing and a wholesome thing to do, but you're going after the predators themselves.

Vachss: I've never pretended that I've got any great, special, unique love for children. That's not me. I hate the people who prey on them, but I'm doing it as a pragmatic warrior. I think the greatest threat to this country's long-term existence is not communism and it's not cocaine. It is that no society can survive if we let too much of it prey on its own young. We just won't survive. The quality of our lives, everything that we hate about our lives is somehow connected to sociopathy and sociopathy is nothing more than ambulatory humans with no sense of empathy. They feel only about their own feelings. They care only about their own pain. And I'm not saying they're all serial killers. Some are selling used cars, some are on Capitol Hill, but they're all pernicious to us because they're not *of* us and the only way you get that is when the socialization process is skewed. When a baby's born, it has no empathy. It just has its own needs.

Todd: It's just receptive.

Vachss: Sure. What else could an infant do? But they learn empathy through socialization. If they get sodomy instead of socialization, some percentage of them are going to get very, very dangerous. And it's not a question of a moral obligation, although it is one. It's pragmatism. We just can't keep building this thing to critical mass.

Todd: That's very interesting. In my line of work, I deal with a lot of racism—counter and pro—and I'm always looking for something that's more elemental than skin color or creed.

Vachss: I know more about that than almost anybody because when I hear the term African American, my hair on the back of my neck stands up because I was in the middle, as you probably know, of a genocidal tribal war in Africa.

Todd: In Biafra, right.

Vachss: Black people, African people, people—you can't even call it a country because it's a war zone not a country—trying to exterminate one another. And if you think that's unique, check Rwanda.

Todd: The Tutsis versus the Hutus.

Vachss: What's happening is that racism isn't the problem. It's tribalism that's the problem.

Todd: My brother was in Bosnia and he said that the Croats and the Serbs hate one another. They live across a river and have hated one another forever.

Vachss: ...And try to wipe each other out. And the Serbs and Croats are, ethnically, highly different. I mean, they're both Caucasian. The reality to racism is that even if each race lives separately, we have proven that that won't bring peace and harmony.

Todd: Definitely not. It'll just give them time to sharpen their weapons.

Vachss: What happens with racism is that it's become a great source for profiteers because you can explain to any inbred moron that the reason his life is so terrible is because of somebody else, and he'll buy it because he's not very smart. He'll not only buy it, but he'll act on it. If you look—and, actually, that's what my book, *Dead and Gone*, is about—the fusion between the extreme left and the extreme right on these issues because if you look really closely at the current Nazi dynamic, you'll notice something really different about their recruiting. You've got young people, say skinheads, right, who are Greek, are Italian.

Todd: I've known Jewish skinheads.

Vachss: Well, that's a psychiatric disturbance. There have always been Jews in the Nazi party and they're just sick humans. But there are people of an ethnicity that's not Aryan, so what they've done to increase recruitment—because they were never about racism, they were about power—is that they say, "Oh, you guys are welcome. You guys are perfectly qualified to be Aryan." Well, Hitler would be spinning in his grave—"Greeks? Are you kidding me? Fucking gypsies? Italians? Mediterraneans? Spaniards?" Look at the Nazi Lowriders. They're Latino. They don't really have any sense of all of this, but it's always been a fact. When I was a kid, when the cops would bust teenagers, the real dark-skinned Puerto Rican kids would only speak Spanish because they didn't want to be mistaken for black, see? Racism's horseshit in this country anyway. For example, if you have a black girlfriend, you're somewhat suspect, but if you have an Asian girlfriend, she's exotic. Racism really isn't an issue because the profiteers at the top of the pyramid are not racist any more than the people at the top of a drug cartel are dope fiends or any more than the people who are running huge kiddie porn rings are pedophiles. They're profiteers.

Todd: They're just dealing in a different material than Microsoft is.

Vachss: Sure.

Todd: Is that what your book, *Dead and Gone*, is about?

Vachss: *Dead and Gone*, the truth is if you look at the one area where the extreme left and the extreme right don't have any dispute with each other is about how children can be used. I mean, Allen Ginsburg, you know who he is, is a member of NAMBLA. Well, I mean he's also a Jew and probably you'd think that the extreme rightists would hate him, and yet when it comes to using children for their own fun, there is no dispute. It's like a Moebius Strip. They're not really separate. I'll give you another example. There's one thing that absolutely unites the extreme left and the extreme right—and although they don't speak to each other, they're united about one thing: fear of registration.

Todd: Can you explain that?

Vachss: Sure. If you look at any of the gun people, what they're always talking about is they don't want to be registered because the government's keeping lists.

Todd: A database.

Vachss: Right. And they're going to move on them some day. Well, it's the exact same thing with the anarchists who are allegedly the extreme left. See? Actually, it's not a line, it really is a spinning continuum and there's points where they intersect. If you scratch a severe enough liberal, you'll always see a fascist. This is very important because you don't combat ideology, you don't combat skin color, you combat conduct and we tend not to look at conduct. We tend to look at trappings: color, things like that.

Todd: Boxes to put things in.

Vachss: Sure, because that makes it simple and that makes it convenient. So when it's put against child abuse, when you ask them to define it, you're going to get different definitions from different people.

Todd: That's helpful.

Vachss: Take a dozen people, and ask, "Define child abuse." And they won't be able to do it and fair enough. That's the fault of our lawmakers who have not been really clear. Child abuse cases, which might be tried in family court, can be any kind of horrible. I've been in homicide cases that were prosecuted as child abuse but there's other people who have been accused for child abuse for slapping their kids.

Todd: Has there ever been child abuse cases for just mental abuse?

Vachss: Oh yeah, and I would never precede mental abuse with the word "just," because it's probably the most damaging of all.

Todd: Right, because scars can heal.

Vachss: That's right, and the other thing is that it doesn't change you as much. The most common—in the people who have studied serial killers— what they're shocked about is what's so prevalent isn't sexual abuse, not even physical abuse, but emotional abuse. Unless the child—and there's a critical period in which this can happen—bonds, he becomes that hypothetical lone wolf, that sociopath. You can't bond when what you're told, "I, the adult, won't bond with you. I won't accept you. You're a worthless piece of crap. I'm sorry I ever gave birth to you. You're fat, you're dumb, you're ugly, you're stupid. You're not mine. I'm ashamed of you." On and on and on. Those detachment disorders have caused more dangerous people than physical abuse or sexual abuse. When I wrote about emotional abuse for *Parade*, I got 6,500 plus letters. We were staggered. This one absolutely hit a nerve, so many people saying, "Thank you, Jesus, for finally recognizing that my pain's just as much as somebody who's suffered from being beaten or being raped.

Todd: A word lashing is even worse that a belt lashing.

Vachss: It's worse when it's systematic. Any kind of kind of outburst in the world can be cured.

Todd: Can you give me some contact information so people can find out more about the stuff we've been talking about today?

Vachss: The best one: <www.vachss.com>. That one, if you ever click on "resources" there, you can spend several hours. It's not like, "Here's some hot links" crap. It's really thorough. It's brilliantly indexed. I had a lot of people work on it. That's the best one-stop shop. If they just want the CARE Act, it's <www.careact.org>.

• • •

DIRT BIKE ANNIE

REAGAN SS

"*I wish that there was a world where a platypus could trundle down the road with a pygmy hippo in the back of a cart and a meteorite would be coming down and a man would be being chased by dinosaurs in the background and a clown would hold a sledgehammer up to the meteor.*"

–Winston Smith

THE HIDDEN ADVANTAGES OF SNIFFING GLUE: AN INTERVIEW WITH ARTIST WINSTON SMITH

Instead of sticking a pair of scissors into a co-worker's neck or dragging the uncrossed blades from pelvis to collarbone as a piece of performance art, Winston Smith works with a steady hand, liberating images from old magazines. He'll, for instance, stick a housewife who looked like she just huffed oven cleaner right into The Apocalypse, or riding a dinosaur, or reviling from a steam shovel, or becoming the queen of Egypt. In effect, he's pulling up the blinds of traditional consumer context, deflating the tires of the American Dream, and stripping back a couple of layers of skin from political beasts. He quietly lacerates and, in the process, gets to a new, darker heart. At first glance, nothing's wrong. Winston captures and re-arranges images from the their original context of old magazines, like *Life*. He crops what he cuts out so close that you can't see the line. His art looks like a photo. For instance, take an idyllic, innocuous scene with a '50s Betty Crocker replicant whipping a meal into place. Look closer. Maybe a dog's peering forlorn from a window in the oven. Or the baby's bottle is a nuclear warhead. Or Reagan's not mowing a lawn or a carpet, but a tall shag of people. Men fish for money.

It's not to say that Winston is heavy handed or has a ham for a brain. Far from it. With no shortage of humor or lightness in a fundamentally grim situation, much of his work simultaneously operates on an extremely polite, soft talking, artistic level. This is how I found Winston, the person: cutting into loaded topics with dexterity, wit, and firm grip on the lamp that shines across the face of America's popular culture.

Since the advertising budgets of mega-corporations have come to far exceed most countries' gross national products, civilization, for the first time in its history, has taken on a commercial assault akin to the twenty-four hour B-52 carpet bombing of North Vietnam: non-stop turbulences, disorienting buzzbomb noise, supra-fast flashes. It creates vacuous craters in not only the landscape, but in the public's mind. Think of Winston as a bomb shelter against the assault, or better yet, the medic who picks select pieces off the pocked battlefield and glues them together how he thinks they should have been in the first place.

Todd: So, what do you do?

Winston: As *little* as possible. I try to synthesize everything that I see in contemporary culture into its real meaning and in order to do that I have to condense many images because our culture is so image based. I condense what are, to me, the high points into compositions that betray their true meaning.

Todd: Portray or betray?

Winston: Betray, because the true meaning of some of these things is really hidden in contemporary culture and I think to show what it is really saying is a betrayal from what the origins are. They want you to think that this wonderful food or soap is terrific, and if you don't buy their food or soap, you're not going to get laid or have a nice car or have a wonderful life or have 3.2 children, whereas my thing is that their soap is really just poison. It poisons the environment and it poisons you and you wind up enriching them because of giving them your money for blah, blah, blah. So, by taking things out of context, you actually can create a truer meaning for something than it had in the beginning because of advertising. All of these things are coming from old advertisements and illustrations sometimes, but mainly old advertisements from the '40s, '50s, and '60s. Their original intention was to lie to you. That's what propaganda is all about. Not that all propaganda lies, but to propagate anything just means to tell your version of it. Commercial versions of telling you anything is generally done to enrich them monetarily at your expense. I don't know why I have such an axe to grind over that, because I'm a happy participant in enriching them myself. If I had more money, I'd spend it on more crap. More plastic shit. I'm not really much of a saint when it comes to those things.

Todd: How old are you?

Winston: Do I really have to tell? Anyone who knows their arithmetic will know how old I am if I say that I was born in 1952. Right at the end of the Korean War.

Todd: Why are punk rockers familiar with your work? How would they know Winston Smith?

Winston: People know my work mainly from Dead Kennedy records and from some things in *Maximumrock'n'roll* or just other underground punk scenes during the period of the late '70s throughout the mid and late '80s. I guess even into the 1990s because there was a resurgence of the punk trip. I think when the (first) Gulf War came along, I think that actually added—I don't know if one thing had to do with the other—but there was a protest movement that built up. Instead of the frumped-out hippies who, after the Vietnam War, had turned to television and cocaine and money making, these frumped-out punks—just becoming slackers, but I think when the Gulf War came along in 1991, that a lot of people woke back up again. They figured that, "Well, this is something that a lot of half-old farts

like us had better stop." Enough of them are old enough now where they
are half-old—they were teenagers in the late '70s and now they're in their
early 30s or older and now they're mature adults in a certain sense. They
actually have the wherewithal to do something about society, although
we're all contributors and we're all steeped in what our society does, both
good and bad. And who knows, maybe it's been around long enough that
there's been a marketing aspect. I never thought punk rock could ever be
co-opted by the mainstream. It's so ugly and so tawdry and off-putting and
so repellent that I was always thinking, great, this is something that won't
be that flower-power, hippie-dippy, love bead shit and no headbands and
sandals can be sold to promote K-Mart, because you could go to some
dime stores and see all this flowery crap with all this hopeful hand-woven
stuff of the hippies being re-marketed from the late '60s and early '70s to
the mainstream. Suddenly, every product in the world was being marketed
in that direction. And I didn't think punk rock would ever do that, although
unfortunately, it actually has. The mainstream has actually embraced it,
which shows how far the mainstream has sunk.

Todd: When did you first think of, "Hey, I wanna cut out some scraps of
paper, glue them together and make something"?

Winston: The first time that occurred to me to cut out pictures and glue
them together was some time in late 1958 and I was probably about six
years old then. I recall being shrieked at by my mom because I cut up one
of her art books. It had Michelangelo and Leonardo and I cut out pictures
of the Mona Lisa and put Mickey Mouse's eyes on her. I thought it was
really clever. I think I got my behind paddled severely, so I had to cut up
things that weren't her property. Years later, when I was in high school in
the late '60s, there were no Xerox machines at the time. You couldn't go
down to the Kinko's and push a button, so I would draw pictures out of old
magazines. The fear of being punished was so strong—even when I was a
teenager, I refused to cut up anyone else's magazines. I'd draw the pictures
and then cut out the drawings and then collage those together. That had a
certain effect, being able to draw helped because I was able to reproduce,
at least to my satisfaction, what I was drawing. Although, unfortunately, it
all had the same tone. It was all black and white drawings. It wasn't color.
Also at that time, the pictures that I'm using now didn't have, for me, any
nostalgia factor because they were too recent.

Todd: Going back to the first time you cut out scraps of paper and started
gluing them together. Have you ever huffed the glue just for fun?

Winston: Yeah, it's great. It's my favorite high. [laughter] Next to angel
dust, it's my favorite drug. Actually, the glue I use is Uhu glue, and it's a
German glue and you can get it at the dime store. Unfortunately there's no
odor. No aroma. There was no high. Any high I get is...

Todd: Purely artistic. [laughter] What's the newest technology that you're really excited about?

Winston: There's a new technology for reproducing pictures of limited edition prints onto fine art or archival paper. The new technology's called Iris Prints and it's a form of reproduction that involves the artwork being scanned by computer and then computer outputted onto canvas or archival paper. It's very high quality ink and very high resolution so it's actually the closest I've ever come to using a computer in my work. People ask all of the time what computer I use to do this. I don't do this on computer. The only digital action is my digits. Razor blades and glue. Sometimes I wish I had a computer just because it might make life easier, only I simply don't have the patience to deal with computers. I think I'm too old-world for that or I'm just too old for that. You can't teach an old dog new tricks. Maybe someday—I even said that in my book—I will get hip to using computers about the time that implanted mind control computers are the standard. I will still be using some archaic Mac. In fact, the one I got—I actually own a computer that I bought about three years ago that I've turned on about five times. I don't know how to turn it on or off without help. I must say it was temporary insanity. I don't know why I bought it. It was cheap. It was a couple hundred bucks and it was a garage sale computer. My friend said, "Oh, if you'd had that computer on your desk ten years ago, it would have been the fastest computer on the planet and now it's landfill. You were over-charged." And people ask what I have on my computer and I tell them that on my computer are a pair of tennis shoes, a hat, and a can of cat food.

Todd: Have you ever attracted a fan that you wish you never had? Has there been anything non-productive?

Winston: For the most part, people who write or email me now (my girl-friend knows how to run the computer) usually have said pretty positive stuff. People have been, over the years, very supportive about my work. They also tell me how my work may have opened their eyes about something or inspired them or given them encouragement, which I think is what we're all here for. This may sound really corny, but I think we're all here to encourage one another because life is so hard that it's pretty bleak for most people in the world. We're kind of lucky where we are, but for the most part, encouraging others is really where it's at. So it's nice to know that people are encouraged by it, although I have gotten a couple of things from people over the years that are pretty zippy. Years ago I would get these giant containers from a lady named Julia in England and Biafra (ex-lead singer of the Dead Kennedys) would get them too. They were sometimes long, rambling letters like someone was reading someone's diary. "Okay, good," I'd think, "Now what does this have to do with anything?" And there would be long diatribes and there would be these boxes that

were obviously pretty expensive to send from England filled with newspapers—*The Daily Press*. I kept looking through them trying to find...
Todd: Something somehow applicable.
Winston: Is there something like a message? It was just your standard newspapers and tabloids and sometimes I'd go through them and would see a little circle that would say, "Winston and Biafra" and there'd be a little arrow pointing to a house or there'd be some cryptic thing. The woman may have unfortunately have had some certain psychological problems. Biafra actually figured that she had been in a home some place and had managed to get to the post office and was, from time to time, able to send us stuff. So that was a little bit disturbing to know that she had my address, but it was really nice that she was over in England and not here. I have a few people come up to me at shows or my expositions or at book signings who want to kind of challenge me over the artwork. "You must be some kind of commie." And I say, "The work just speaks for itself" and it turns out they were Reagan supporter types and had been listening to Rush Limbaugh and so they saw me as a convenient target who represented the other side, the antichrist or whatever. I would say that for the most part, people. If they like it, they really like it. If they don't like it, they don't mention it. I'm a non-entity to them, which is fine with me.
Todd: What's the largest cache of images that you've gotten? Have you ever scored a mother load?
Winston: Years ago, I used to buy old magazines for five or six for a quarter. I would get old war-time *Life* magazines from the '40s for fifty cents apiece and then the last couples of years because of the vintage craze—everybody's into vintage now. Everything that's ten years old is called "vintage" now. So people would say, "Oh, that's vintage so therefore this magazine that was formerly fifty cents or a dollar and a half is now five dollars." $2.50, $3.50, $4.50, $5, $10, $20, $100. I even had somebody who wanted to sell me some of their old magazines and then they said, "You need to take care of these" and I said, "I'm not going to take care of these. I'm going to cut them up." And then he wouldn't sell them to me. I should have said, "Yeah. I'm going to give them to my grandmother. I'm gonna put them in lucite. I'm gonna put 'em in a time capsule." No, sometimes I feel bad when I cut them up because I feel like, "Oh, these are things that should be preserved," but the fuckin' library of Congress has them. I don't have to preserve everything. I'm not an archive.
Todd: You're not a historian?
Winston: I really do enjoy the history factor of it a lot, but someone did point it out to me once. They said, "Well, actually you are preserving them in your own way. You're taking images that would have otherwise never seen the light of day any other way. They were cast-off, commercial images from before the war or the '50s, stuff that people had forgotten

about. That generation's past now and those products no longer exist and the whole rationale for selling them no longer exists. And so you're actually resurrecting this as a cultural icon." So that made me feel better. I bought it. [laughter] "Okay, I agree with you."

Todd: According to the artist Robert Crumb—the piece of art that he did that people almost immediately identify with him was "Keep on Trucking."

Winston: Oh, was it The Mr. Natural Guy?

Todd: Right. But it's also the bane of his existence. Is there any piece that you've done that would fit that bill? Is there anything that you're glad you did, certainly, but people identify you way too immediately with it?

Winston: I would say what people identify me with mostly is work done in concert with the Dead Kennedys. Biafra referred to me a few times in articles as the artistic conscience of the Dead Kennedys which I interpreted as meaning the artistic *guilty* conscience of the Dead Kennedys. The bad conscience. I think that, perhaps, the cross of dollars, the cross of money, is the one thing that people identify with. They identify it with, perhaps, not me, but they identify it with the band. The DK logo is also something that people make cheap t-shirts of. The cross was something I made quite some time before I knew Biafra and I made it specifically because of people making money off of religion. People can make money off of anything. Selling landfill, if they want, but to rip off money from little old ladies living off of their retirement fund and people who maybe aren't terribly deep thinkers or aren't scholars is something else. They either end up giving Jerry Falwell and Pat Robertson all this money and other people in between who are several layers down. That kind of thing is what really irked me and I grew up in Oklahoma and that was the bible belt and I'd see a lot of this stuff. I'd see people flock to these guys. Not that I think I'm much of a deep thinker or a big scholar, but, god, I just feel bad for these people who are being ripped off. To me, it has nothing to do with Jesus. It has to do with the fact that their idol, what *they* worship, is dollars, and they were doing it over his dead body. That's essentially how it breaks down.

Todd: A couple of questions about the piece *Idol*. Why did that take three years to do?

Winston: Because the first date is the date of creation. The second date is the date of publication because I had to alter it. The Secret Service came by and they said, "You really can't print it the way you're doing this."

Todd: The Secret Service? Really?

Winston: Yeah. Well, we were warned, actually. They said that this could constitute legal problems and it was their first record and Biafra figured, "Ah, let's not fuck with this. We'll fuck with it later."

Todd: I noticed that there's double eyes on the pyramid.

Winston: Yeah, you noticed that. Good. Actually, I was kind of happy that that happened. At first we were kind of bummed that we had to change it, but it gave us a chance to change it in a much more sinister way than it would have ever been if they hadn't ever intruded.

Todd: Forked tongue out of Washington. Snakes over the crucified hands.

Winston: See this part right here? That's on the dollar and to me it looked like a rattlesnake tail, so I made this as the back of a rattlesnake. I think it was a little while later that on my ranch I had to dispatch a rattlesnake that was going to kill my cat. It was about as long as my baseball bat and just about as thick, and I didn't have a gun at the time—they were locked up some place—but I had a sword. It was a renaissance fair sword that I'd carry around when I worked at the fair, a costume sword, and I stabbed the snake. I made stationery with it. I used the snakeskin and the rattle. In fact, on the day I was photocopying it, I had to go answer the phone and the shop lady went to put something in the photocopy machine and opened it up and went, "Yeahhhooww" because she saw the snake. There is a visceral thing to seeing a snake, especially when it's unexpected. So she shrieked. I sent some letters to Biafra on that stuff and unbeknownst to me, he cut them all out and put them all over his next record, *Let Them Eat Jelly Beans*. That snake became more famous in death than he ever was in life. My cat, 101, I had the snakeskin hanging on the wall for a long time, and I'd wake up in the middle of the night hearing this "prrr-prrr," thinking that I was hearing a rattler in the room and in the morning the rattle part was all gone. He had gnawed it all off. Good 'ol 101. So, yeah, I was able to change a lot of things on that cross. Like the atom bomb at the top that made the UPC.

Todd: With the 666.

Winston: Behind the INRI thing.

Todd: What's INRI?

Winston: Usually over the cross is "INRI," the abbreviation from Latin, *Iesus Nazarenus Rex Iudaeorum*. Something about, "Jesus Christ, king of the Jews" which is what the Romans put over the thing to mock him. So I replaced that with the anti-Christ symbol because money essentially, if you want to get abstract about it, money is the anti-Christ. The bible says you can't serve both god and wealth. It's mammon that's become their god, not that I'm a bible thumper, but there is in our culture we've absorbed, what becomes prominent in our culture. And in the "United States of America" I took out the letter "s" so it's the United *State* of America, and then behind the one, I made it into a German iron cross. I had a cat named 208 so I changed the serial number to read 208 there and I put it as series, *1984*. And then I put two eyes over the pyramid and it says something like New World Order over it in Latin so I just changed to read "Nuit," which I think is French for "Night." On a few record artworks, I would put my name at the bottom right-hand corner to be indiscrete. Unfortunately, by the time the record got made, it had to be cropped here and there to make it fit and then, boom, my name's gone, and it's not like I'm making a big fortune doing this anyways, so you'd like to get credit if you're not getting any money for it. By and by, I learned a lesson from Michelangelo.

Todd: Incorporating it in the middle.

Winston: Apparently, people thought when he made the *Pietà*, an incredibly beautiful statue, that they thought it had to have been made by Leonardo. "Only a master like Leonardo Da Vinci could make this." And he hated Leonardo and Leonardo hated Michelangelo. They were rivals. He was twenty years younger and it was a different generation. That was the old shit and he was the new shit. He went in the middle of the night and he carved on the sash across the Madonna's chest, so it said, "Michelangelo Buonarroti made this." Basically saying, "I made it, damn it, and nobody else. It's mine." So on some things I actually wound up putting my name in the middle which people may have thought, "Oh, this guy has an enormous ego." Well, not quite so much that, it's just because I figured that if it was in the middle, then it can't get cut out. So it's right underneath the torch, right above the hand of Lady Liberty on the *Bedtime for Democracy*.

Todd: What other jobs have you taken to keep yourself fed?

Winston: For a long, long time, I worked digging ditches. [laughter] For the last 17 years I've lived on this ranch up in northern California and I'd do carpentry for people. I'm not much of a carpenter. I can swing a hammer, but that's about it. That, and I worked at a solar power company for a while doing packing and shipping and stuff. I did lots of illustration work for local magazines and illustration work for newspapers. A few years ago, for a couple of years in a row, I was working at a photocopy place, which was great because my work is basically based on photocopies. I even told the owner, "Do you realize that by hiring me, it's like hiring an alcoholic to work in a brewery?" I was pushing that button all day long, but he was very cool and he very much liked my work and I think without his help, a lot of what you see around me wouldn't even exist because I wouldn't have had the opportunity to experiment with things. So that was actually very good. Now I'm successfully "self-unemployed." I don't know how successful that will be in the future. At the time, I'm still here and I actually do have somewhat of a roof over my head even though by this time next month or next year I could be living behind a 7-11, eating out of a dog food can. "Mighty Dog. Mighty good. Mmm." Maybe I could get a job advertising that: "Winston says: Mighty Dog is *great*."

Todd: Have you ever gotten into any trouble with the images you've used from a copyright standpoint? Have you ever been approached by that?

Winston: Knock on wood. So far, no. Most of what I use is copyright-free and it's so old that it's over with. I try to stay away from photographs of individuals—photographs of celebrities. I'm not going to use a picture of Sinatra or Coca-Cola or Disney. These guys will clobber you if you try to do that. I also take pictures out of context; pieces or "elements," is what I call them. Like here you have somebody holding a fish. Well, he was holding a flashlight originally and I put a fish in his hand so the fish came from another piece. The fish came from maybe a famous painting or something. But being taken out of the context, it no longer is associated with that painting or that product—fish food or whatever it was. If I ever get hauled into court, I guess I'll have to practice saying that again in front of the judge. [laughter] "I'm just a working stiff trying to get by, your Honor."

Todd: Name some of the bands you made up, that you said were playing at the Mabuhay Gardens.

Winston: We used to do these posters. When I first started out, I didn't know a whole lot of people in the scene in the late '70s. I knew different bands and stuff and would go to shows. It wasn't like I was associated with them in any sense so in order to do band art, I wanted to show people in bands what I would do. They would say, "Well, what kind of style do you do?" So I'd make up bullshit bands. Names of bands that didn't exist. The Clip-Ons, Lenny and the Spitwads, PTA, The Dip Shits, Anonymous Technicians: a whole series of weird, bullshit bands. The Clones, The Rejects, and one called Half Life and then Biafra reminded me that there was probably a band called Half Life in almost every major American city. Certain ones were pretty obvious names. By and by, some bands took names just like them. I'm certain I had nothing to do with it. They came upon them on their own, I'm sure. Biafra has a long list of the most repulsive combinations of names that are possible to have. They could never have been thought of by anybody else. I mean, other people could think of them, but it's not like it could be duplicated by accident. George DiCaprio (Leonardo's father), I was having lunch with him—not to drop names or anything—but he has his own long list of names that were so funny that as I took a drink of beer when he was telling us these names, I spit out my beer. It's the only time I've ever done that in reality. It was so fuckin' funny. And he was saying, "Gee, I wish there were bands with these names." I can't remember it, though. My memory fails me. It's incipient, advanced Alzheimer's. Don't do drugs, kids. Either that or do lots of them and if you do, share them with me.

Todd: What's the biggest light bulb that's gone off when you made a connection that wasn't there before—like putting a strategic bomber in a lady's arms—or was there one idea that was the catalyst for a lot of other ideas that came along that burst upon you?

Winston: That's a good question because that's happened. There were some things that I know were watermarks of evolution that changed the course of things—the concept that less is better when it comes to composition. Imagery is more effective when it is most direct visually.

Todd: Have you ever met somebody who Winston Smithed you: who used your images or ideas that you've used and done it to you?

Winston: Yeah. Actually, one time I saw a zine—this was, like, in 1979—and I saw a zine at a little punk shop somewhere in San Francisco and it was exactly my picture, only the guy was in a different position. It was the guy cut out and put into another picture and he was floating the wrong way and I thought, "Oh man, they ripped me off." But then I thought no, they couldn't. If they had cut it up, the part behind it wouldn't even be there. So it means that whoever did this had to have gotten the original stuff and did it on their own separately and decided where to put it because otherwise the figure would be gone—there'd be a hole there and it wasn't there. It was nice and clear. You saw the background as it was in its entirety. So I got in touch with this cat. His name was Keith Ulrich and I think he lived in Pasadena at the time. I have not heard from him for years and years. We corresponded. He sent me a lot of his work. He did incredible collages and he just happened to be using the same stuff I was using. The same idea occurred to him as it occurred to me only he made it a little bit trippier by making this guy floating around where I put the guy on solid ground. That was kind of cool. And then I've had people send me things or I saw pieces of my work photocopied from my books or records cut up and made into collages. The first time I saw it I thought, "Oh, they fucked up my thing," and then I had to think about it and I realized, "Oh, wait a minute, that's what *I* do." The reason I'm doing what I'm doing is to fuck up other people's things. I'm screwing up other people's hard work. And so I thought, "More power to him." That's fine. And there's this guy named Joachin; he is in a band called The Hellworms and he does really cool collages. He made an entire collage based on one of my pieces and without knowing it, used that same piece; exactly the same picture, *The Last Supper*, and put a bunch of my figures in this *Last Supper* thing and he didn't even know that that was one I used myself. That was irony on top of irony. He sent it off to me and said, "Look, I hope you don't mind my doing this. It's just kind of a thank you note for what you do." I thought it was totally cool. It was an honor to have someone make something out of what I've done because now I don't feel bad for all of the things that I've ripped off of other people. One time I met an artist who was one of the commercial artists in the '50s who made some pictures that I'd used and when I met him, he mentioned that and I went, "Oh, man, I hope you don't mind. It's strictly for laughs. I'm not getting rich off of this or nothin'," and he said, "Oh, no, I totally approve." Art is art. Even in the history of art where people see paintings and then a generation later it changes to a different style of painting, but it's because those artists would study the work of the past and then alter and change it. None of us have any original ideas. We all formulate them off of the things we have grown up with. So many of the 1950s images of housewives make them look as though they just had a nose full of cocaine and their eyes are big and they're so happy to wash that pan. Happy white guys with little bow-ties. That was the image people wanted to live up to, but I've seen some things from other countries, especially from behind the iron curtain, that I think really hit the nail on the head because they live that life. They live what we protest against.

Todd: Secretly, do you wish that Reagan was still president?

Winston: Yeah, yeah. I wish Newt was still around. I would join the Republican party just to get votes for the bastard [laughter]. We made these shirts: "Newt Hates Me." Yeah, I even told the guy I made them with, "We should go out and campaign for Newt so we can keep peddling these shirts." Actually we could re-sell the shirts by writing underneath the image of Newt, "I Voted," because the vote that took place when the Republicans lost all those seats in the mid-term vote here in October and the Republicans lost pretty much big time after they thought Monica Lewinsky was going to help them win. Monica helped them lose and Newt had resigned probably for a lot of reasons and he knew he didn't have the votes to remain the speaker. Who knows, maybe Larry Flynt has some shit on him. I told Biafra that when Reagan had completed his second term, "God, now that Reagan's no longer president, we're gonna be unemployed real soon. Now what?" Reagan was only Bush in sheep's clothing.

Todd: Reagan looked better, though.

Winston: He was a better actor. People think he was a bad actor, but he was actually a very good actor. He swindled the public and the world into thinking he was a President for a long time.

Todd: Eight years.

Winston: I call that...

Todd: Pretty damn good acting. Have you ever wished that the worlds which you created would come true and that you could live inside of them?

Winston: Oh yeah. That's why I wish I'd shown you this video tape I had. I was doing this interview for this woman from the Canadian Broadcasting Television Company and she was asking me "Why do you even *do* these silly pictures?" I pointed to a picture called *Enough Is Enough.* (It's in Winston's book, *Artcrime.* There's a platypus harnessed to a little cart, pulling a pygmy hippo down the road beside children holding bunnies and spacemen and robot dolls.)

And I said, "Well, because I *wish* that there was a world where a platypus could trundle down the road with a pygmy hippo in the back of a cart and a meteorite would be coming down and a man would be being chased by dinosaurs in the background and a clown would hold a sledge-hammer up to the meteor." But there aren't any worlds like that, so I make them up myself and I do these things to create my own little dream states and nightmare states. Although, on the same level, I'm glad that these things don't exist in reality. It would be pretty scary.

Todd: Have you ever dreamt of driving an Austin Healy into ancient Egypt and running into a snowman? (referring to the piece *Eclipse of the Gods*)

Winston: Yeah, the snowman is definitely in the wrong neighborhood and in the wrong time of year for him. [laughter] When I was a teenager I used to draw rooms where all of these divergent things would be put together because I couldn't cut them out so I would draw them in and make these surreal environments. It was during the craze of the pop art thing in the late '60s, like Roy Liechtenstein, and I kept thinking, "Well, why not? This *could* be. You could make one of these. It could be this way." If you cut them out precisely enough and assembled them closely enough, they would appear to be the way they are. My thing and my personal style is that I try to make these things look as though they were born that way. I've actually had people look at certain pictures I've done and there will be two or three subtle changes and they'll think, "Well, what did you do? So what? Big deal. There's no change here." And I'd kind of point out that, "Oh, here's a fish coming out of this guy's hat." I want to create the illusion that you should be relaxed while looking at them and then be startled by the things that you notice; the nuances that you see that are out of place and then perhaps that would surprise or shock people in a certain way.

Todd: Have you ever been accused of being a "bastard artist?" You don't create anything yourself. You don't paint anything, you don't draw anything with the collages and the montages.

Winston: Every now and then I have to paint some edges to make them match up with something else, but I try to avoid that. Even though I can draw, I definitely can't draw as well as some of the people who I rip off. I had someone tell me about ten years ago, "Winston, what you've been doing for years and years, that's all the rage now back in New York. They call it 'appropriation.'" Unfortunately that didn't help me. [laughter] It doesn't mean much to be a pioneer. I rarely have people get completely on my case over that. I guess that I change things significantly enough and make enough alterations that it does create a new work of art; a new com-position. And not all of them are works of art. They're simple composi-tions. I may like them, but they're not masterpieces in any sense of the word. It's funny, too, because you never know what people are going to hit on. Some things that I like a whole lot because they mean something to me and they're relevant to me but they don't grab anybody much. Other times,

I've had things I've liked because they were kind of interesting to make
and I liked it at that moment, but later it didn't grab me but other people
just flocked to it and said, "Oh, this has such deep meaning." And that's
okay. Even if it has no meaning to me, if it has it to them, then that's what
art's all about. It means whatever you bring to it. I have people interpret
things good and bad. Sometimes, people will look at things and go, "Oh,
that thing's about animal abuse. You're terrible." No, I'm not talking about
the abuse of animals. I'm not into that. This is strictly pygmy hippos being
taken down the road by a platypus. Marsupial abuse is probably the proper
term. You can't second guess people. You can't take guesses of what
they're going to be offended by or intrigued by so my thing is just to do
what I do. These images are in our culture that we've all grown up with or
we've all seen in one form or another or we haven't seen those images but
have seen the things that have been created through their inspiration. Not
everyone has seen certain ads that I'll use, but they'll see the things that
were made by the people who did. There's a generational difference
between it and it all contributes to the great cosmic swarm that makes up
our society and our civilization, and when people see things, they bring to
them whatever baggage they have psychologically, emotionally, or mentally. I have things that I've made because I just thought they were funny
looking and one guy would look at it and go, "Man, that reminds me of a
story I heard when I was in Australia about one of the first men on the
moon that said he saw a Russian base there and that he couldn't be quoted
in American newspapers." And I'm all, "Whoa, back off, this is a picture
of a space man holding a fish." It was called "The Fish on the Moon" or
"The Fish That Knew Too Much" and this guy's like, "Yeah, this was the
astronaut who knew too much and they had to silence him because he
claimed that he was up there and there was a Russian base. He was one of
the guys on the Apollo 16 or 15 and in the United States. Everything he
said was completely blacked out from the media and he had to go to
Australia to get it on the air." It could be bullshit or not, but the thing is is
that he had a different take on it and it had nothing to do with what was
going on when I made it. We could look at a painting by Michelangelo or
Botticelli and think, "Well, we can see clearly that Botticelli meant that
this is an allegory between good and evil but *maybe* he just made it
because he got the money up front. I can just hear the guy who commis-
sioned the artwork: "I want a naked chick over here and a babe over here,
I want another babe over there. I want a waterfall in the middle." [laugh-
ter]
Todd: And make her hair flowy.
Winston: Same thing with *The Birth of Venus*, the woman on the half
shell. She was a beauty pageant winner in Florence at the time. She was a
big star. She was apparently a very nice woman, beloved by everyone, and

she died very young. Botticelli was hired to glorify the prince's concubine. It was his girlfriend. He was married and had kids and this was his mistress. She was the cousin of Amerigo Vespucci, the Florentine navigator for whom they named America. She died at age twenty-four of consumption (tuberculosis). A lot of people died young in those days because of consumption. Naturally, she caught pneumonia. She had no clothes on... what did she expect?

Todd: Are there any nectars of creativity for you—food stuffs? Garry Larson, who wrote and drew the *Far Side* said that he just got tanked up on caffeine and whatever came out, came out.

Winston: I get tanked on Chianti and whatever comes out, comes out. Beer is my favorite drug. That's probably not a very good thing to say to people because it's obviously not good for you. Too much of a good thing can screw things up. I like coffee, but not really to work by. It doesn't really jazz me up so much. I do most of my work at night. I'm very nocturnal. I probably was born in Hong Kong because my circadian rhythm is completely the opposite of everybody else's. That's one thing Biafra and I have in common. We are up 'til three or four in the morning and don't wake up until noon or one o'clock at least. That would be early for us. I've been an insomniac all my life. When I was doing the cover for Green Day, I finished it, finally, and there was kind of a deadline for getting it done. It took me a couple of weeks to get all of the pictures together. You have to find a million pictures, go through those million and then find a few thousand and go through those few thousand and find a few hundred. You whittle those down to a couple of dozen. You cut out a hundred of them and you have a dozen or so images and you select the ones that will work, but you have to go through all of this high-grading to get to that point and that took a couple of weeks. And finally, in all of three days, I worked and worked and worked on that and at one point I just didn't go to sleep and I was up for thirty-five or thirty-six hours and then I got it finished. Then I called up Bill and Tré and said it was done and that they could come and get it and they said, "Well, bring it over to the studio downtown so we can check it out." And I go over there and I'm still zipping along 'cuz I'd been awake for thirty-eight hours by that time and I'm on a second wind but I'm really buzzin' like I'm on an acid high almost. Sleep deprivation, essentially. Everything was glowing and fuzzy. I get there and they immediately loved it. In fact, they recognized certain things. The title of that piece for *Insomniac* is actually called *God Told Me to Skin You Alive* and Bill recognized it immediately, being an old Dead Kennedys fan. It came off the first poster we made for the DK's first LP. There was a Jack T. Chick cartoon with a little arm coming out of this Armageddon cartoon about the world coming to an end. There was this little bubble coming up but you don't see anything past the paper. It says, "God Told Me to Skin You Alive!" So they were jazzed on that and at that time, the working title for their record was going to be *Tightwad Hill*, which was one of the songs on the record, and they kept saying, "Well, do whatever you want." I was like, "Do you want this? Do you want that?" "No, just do whatever you want." Which was cool because it meant that I had free reign. I had no constraints. Usually people say, "It's got to have horses or flying saucers in it. No dolphins and no chickens." So I felt pretty free to do what I wanted and when I got it done, he said, "How long does it take you to do this?" "Well, over the span of the last few weeks I sorted through ten million images to get to this point. I finished the whole composition in the last 36 hours," and he said, "How could you stay awake that long?" And I replied "It's easy for me. I'm an insomniac." And we hung out for awhile and I went back home and slept for twenty-four hours. When the record came out, they called it "Insomniac." It was probably a big coincidence because there's no song on the record called insomniac, but I wondered if they had taken it off of that experience. Maybe I deserve an extra royalty check. I'll have to talk to Tré about that. [laughter]

Todd: Have you ever walked into a store or gallery and said, "Hey, I did that. I'm Winston Smith," and they didn't believe you?

Winston: Often, I've come into places and seen things, especially the things that are out of context that I did, but they were bootlegs or the things that I know are clearly unauthorized reproductions of the work and I would say, "Oh, I made that, blah, blah, blah" and they'd go, "Oh, shit. Really? Naahh." I'd have to tell them that I wasn't going to sue them or anything but that they *were* bootlegs. It's kind of fun because I've seen my work in Rome. I saw it in London and back east in several places where they were clearly bootlegs and the guy would say, "Yeah, I'll give you this for half price" Another guy said, "Oh, then you should have one for free. Have one for your girlfriend, too. Take another one for yer mum," just so I wouldn't get uppity about it. I wasn't trying to wig on him. I was just surprised. I don't mind. Again, I can't get on anyone's case over it because I, myself, have made a career out of swiping work from other people—*real* artists. [laughter] Only one time I was in Florence   I was going back there for a visit and I was showing some friends around—in fact, it was the assistant guy from Alternative Tentacles there for the musical convention of alternative music in 1989. I happened to have a shirt they gave me in London that was a DK logo shirt and I just had it on. We'd gone to see the statue of David by Michelangelo at The Academy of Fine Arts, which is the school I went to in Florence. I wasn't a very good student, but I was there. So we walked out of the place with the statue and the woman I was traveling with. I walked down the block to the front door of the academy and I was saying, "Here is where I went to school and where I would hang out in front of the 'loggia' (the porch) everyday, waiting for the doors to open." Then we go into the courtyard and on the wall is a giant DK logo painted with a paint brush and my mouth just fell open. "Son of a bitch!" I took a picture immediately because I wanted to send it to my mom. "Mom, I'm not *in* the academy, but I'm *on* the academy. I finally made the big time!" So I'm taking a picture and this guy comes up on his Vespa and he takes his helmet off and he was talking Italian and he said, "What the fuck are you doing? Are you some kind of tourist? Fuck you, man." And I said, "No, no, no, I'm taking a picture because that emblem over there on the wall is this emblem I made." And he said, "Oh no, you just have that shirt. Blah blah blah blah blah (in Italian)... Winston Smith." And this woman who doesn't know Italian says, "How does this perfect stranger know your name?" So I said, "Well, that's me and I'm taking the picture because it's..." "Nah, that's bullshit, man, you're not even American, you're Florentine." Because I speak fluent Florentine. Florentine's the dialect of Florence. It's not like regular Italian so if you were a foreigner, you'd probably come with a broken accent and I didn't have that. I had grown up there. I had proper pronunciation. Even though it's bad Italian, it's good Florentine. It's like speaking Cockney or something. So I'm rapping away with him and you could tell he was a bit stoned. "No way, you're a local boy." I pulled out my passport and showed him. "Oh, man, you could get into a lot of trouble fucking with American passports like that." He puts his helmet back on and on his helmet there's a masking tape DK logo across the middle of it—a homemade thing. He gets on his bike and takes off and he wouldn't believe it. He probably went home and said, "Man, I ran into this joker today." It was kind of cool because I had no idea I would even be known there. When I look at records and things, even when I was a teenager, I wouldn't really study who did what and who produced this. I'd like it and appreciate it and that was about it. That's where it ends with me. I'm not much of a fan type. I've never really been a fan of any band... Except for GWAR. GWAR is my one major fan thing and also my new major fan thing is Storm and Her Dirty Mouth—the singer in San Francisco who's the hardest working girl in show business and I've been a Storm groupie forever. Other than that, I'm not really a fan of anything. [laughter]

Todd: What's the largest element that people have gone and said, "I've been looking at this piece for a while, but I didn't see (fill in the blank)?" What's the largest hidden element that people didn't see that they came around to see?

Winston: One thing is a bit of an optical illusion and it was intended that way, but I always thought it was so obvious that it couldn't be mistaken. But it shows you how, visually, people react. It's *The Spotlight*—the piece I made that is a black and white drawing of two people standing in front of a spotlight, holding a couple of bottles of beer in front of a table at a club.

Well, from a distance it looks like a skull and that took quite a while to come up with. I had to make many drawings with my glasses off by candlelight. I drew it and then would take it and put it across the room and look at it and see if it worked. Then I'd come back and draw some more. I went back and forth a dozen times before I could get that just right on.

Todd: A little bit of a departure, but what do you love most about living in America today? What advantages do you think you have over living in other places?

Winston: My work probably would not be as easily given out into the public if it were not for photocopy machines which have, of course, been around for thirty years. I think that we do have other advantages over other countries. Like it or not, we have certain freedoms that other people don't have that we take for granted here. Unfortunately, a lot of our freedoms are backed up by the U.S. Marines and we can pay a dollar and a quarter for a gallon of gas and everyone else is paying four and a half dollars. And why? Because of the U.S. Marines. We're used to flipping on the electric lights magically. It's just like science fiction. Push a button and the house heats up. Where I've been living on my ranch for years, I've got kerosene lamps and I've got to go and chop wood to make the house warm; throw it in a fire box. In the rest of the world, with the exception of America and Europe, that's how it really is. Europe is essentially the 51st American state. They don't like to think of it as that, but that's what has happened, unfortunately. We have advantages that other people don't have as far as freedom of speech. I say in *Artcrime* that it's easy for me to sit in my studio and slice up little pieces of paper, put them together and think I'm an anarchist and a big revolutionary, which is horse shit. [laughter] If I were really in a position to have to deal with that, I'm afraid that I'm so much of a coward that I'd keep my mouth shut. If I were in El Salvador or Nicaragua or from some Nazi country in central America that has death squads wandering over the countryside shooting pregnant women because they're all rebel communists. Their attitude is: if you shoot a pregnant woman, you kill *two* communists for the price of one bullet. It's easy for us to protest and make remarks about things because there are no significant repercussions. In this country, the only significant repercussions that they can hand to you are economic bars. You can get put in jail if you knock somebody off or stick up a bank, but the way of punishing people in America is to economically deprive them and make it really hard and bitter for you to deal with all of the expenses that are necessary to live in the United States by fuckin' up credit cards or your mortgage or your student loan, just making it really hard for you. A friend of mine made this observation once; he said it's all about rent. He said in the '50s and early '60s you could live in San Francisco, for example, and have a nice little apartment and maybe a part-time job or full-time job and have time and energy and money left after you took care of your expenses to maybe go out and protest things. It's like they figured, "We don't need any more of this horse shit. We've got to stop these people from being able to have this leisure time." There was a thing about making life much more difficult to deal with so that you wouldn't have time to interfere with them doing what *they* want to do. "Them" being the government, corporations, whatever. They don't want you interfering. "Get back to work. Keep your noses to the grindstone." People began thinking, "All I want is to come home from work and watch a little TV and be left the hell alone." The screws started tightening around the late '60s. I think Nixon's re-election in 1973 was the end of the "'60s era."

Todd: Have you ever sold a piece of work and then seen it for sale for a gross amount?

Winston: No. I wish. It would be a big ego boost. It would mean I could go find an attorney.

Todd: Have you ever thought about changing your name?

Winston: It's kind of too late for that. I already did that more than twenty years ago. Way more than that, actually.

Todd: What was your first name?

Winston: It's a typical Irish name. My family's Irish and Scottish. In fact, my dad, one time, looked at my book and even though he approved of my being an artist, he disapproved of some of the subject matter because he was your typical older, conservative, World War II veteran, Nixon supporter type. He looked at the book and said, "You never did tell me why you changed your name." And I said, "Look at my work, dad. Don't you think it'd be easier for me to change *my* name than for our whole family to change *their* name?" And he sort of nodded, "Yeah, I guess you're right." After that, he was thankful that I was being so considerate of the family honor.

Todd: When you were talking about Green Day, you said you had literally thousands of images. How do you organize your archives?

Winston: I don't. I tried that about ten or fifteen years ago. I tried to put all TV sets over here, all the snakes over there and all the guns, or wedding pictures. I spent a couple of months sorting through things and putting them into different piles and then I realized that I'm dyslexic. I knew I was dyslexic to begin with but I realized that my being dyslexic, that was the totally wrong way to go about it because now I've completely forgotten where these images are. They're all separate and I can't even get to them because I don't see things as words; I see things as images and if I don't see them, they don't exist to me. If they're not directly under my nose, they're not there. That's why everything in my life is so cluttered. I can't put things on computer discs and I can't put things in drawers. They all have to be out. If not, what's out of sight is out of mind. That's the story of my life. That's why I didn't graduate from high school. That's why I flunked algebra four times. I just don't have that kind of mind to sort things into different compartments. I would trade anything to be able to do that. I would love to have that kind of memory and sorting mentality. It would really help me in what I do. To find an image, I have to go through everything I've got—billions and billions of images to find it. A monkey holding a chainsaw. It's like trying to find a name in a New York City phone book when it's not in alphabetical order. It would take you years. In fact, it's a big drawback 'cause sometimes if I'm doing illustrations for people and the deadline is next week—"Can you drop everything you're doing and make a picture of an aardvark flying over the Empire State building?" So then I have to find the aardvark and I know I've got one, but I don't know where it is. I know I have the Empire State building, because I just saw it last week. Sometimes I've gone through a pile of shit and found it right at the bottom. Doing the cover for *The Sky Is Falling and I Want My Mommy* (an album with DOA and Jello Biafra) there was something I needed to have. It was a pair of cars that were crashing. I had the entire composition done in a couple of hours and I spent about four or five hours until dawn to find that piece and it was literally under my nose. I'd gone through sixteen stacks of paper. "I know it was here. Did I eat it?" [laughter] I finally found it and it worked, but it was one of those struggles that was like salmon swimming upstream. My organizational skills are nil and the fact that I can keep things together as well as I have is a miracle. Dyslexia has its limitations.

Todd: Do you ever associate what the band is releasing to what you produce? Do you listen to *Breed, Spawn, and Die* from Lard? Is there any direct correlation to that or does somebody say like what Green Day said: "Go with what you have, whatever you want to do."

Winston: Actually, for Lard, I had made that piece over one weekend. I had not done anything for a long time. I had broken up with some girlfriend of mine. Suddenly, over that weekend I had the free time and I did all this stuff. When I went and showed this lady I knew and showed her my new stuff she said, "You should break up with your girlfriends more often. You're gettin' some good stuff." In fact, she looked at that one piece with the steam shovel about to eat the lady holding the baby (the Lard cover) and said it's a real Buddhist piece. The title is *Welcome to the World* and it's like, here you're born and this is what you have to deal with. You're fed into the machine psychologically, physically, economically, everything. Even if you're a baby, you become a consumer and a producer. When Biafra saw that, he saw it as a potential cover so it was selected without my having to puzzle out anything from his work. I was off the hook. I didn't have to listen to the music. [laughter] One of my favorite things that they've done is the song "Lard." "What we need is llaarrdd." That's actually a wonderful song.

• • •

"People expect me to walk up with hypodermic needles in my arms, throwing up, and dragging crucifixes where ever I go."

—Mike Diana

FREEDOM OF SPEECH. IT DEPENDS WHERE YOU LIVE, EVEN IN AMERICA: AN INTERVIEW WITH THE COMIC BOOK ARTIST, MIKE DIANA

Mike Diana, while based out of Florida, was the only illustrator in the history of the United States to be put in jail solely based on what he drew. I won't lie to you. His comics are crude. Some of them aren't particularly well drawn. It involves no stretch of the imagination that some people might find them offensive. All of that is true. However—in my estimation at least—it's a far cry between considering a drawing offensive and enforcing a law, prohibiting the artist to draw future pictures and putting that artist in jail for what he's already drawn.

Todd: How was dancing last night?

Mike: It was nice, dancing up on the bar, doing the usual thing there.

Todd: I see that you did the cover of a 7" for Blondie (newly reformed and going under the pseudonym Adolf's Dog).

Mike: It was fun drawing it for them. It was Jeff's idea. He said, "You have to draw Iggy with six arms," and I said, "Okay."

Todd: How'd you hook up with Jeff? He's up in New York and you were down in Florida.

Mike: Well, Jeff wrote me through the mail when he heard about my case. He wanted to wish me good luck at the trial and asked for a picture in his personal zine, *TESTticle PRESSure*, so I did a drawing for the magazine and visited New York and ran into him. We've just been in contact ever since.

Todd: Is doing album covers helping? Part of what was brought up in your case was what you were doing could never be considered art—to help the authorities re-think that what you're creating has solid artistic merit?

Mike: I had already done some work for some album covers before I got in trouble and the way they are down in Florida, I think that would make it worse. They feel like I'm spreading filth or something. Only if perhaps they hang it up in the Museum of Modern Art will they think, "Well, maybe it is art." Even then they'd still have a reason to hate it.

Todd: Are you getting any more jobs, new contacts in New York?

Mike: Yeah, I've been doing drawings for the *New York Press* and different magazines that you have to be in New York to talk to or whatever and there's not too many illustration jobs down in Florida. Back there, it was mostly through the mail.

Todd: Are you for hire right now—through an agent or a second party?

Mike: I would consider it.

Todd: I've heard that you look like one of the kids in Hanson. Is that true.

Mike: [laughs] I guess because I have blonde hair. A few people have said that.

Todd: When you tell people your name and they put two and two together, are they surprised how you look? Are they expecting Leatherface from *The Texas Chainsaw Massacre* or a young Ozzy Osbourne?

Mike: Yeah, definitely. They expect me to walk up with hypodermic needles in my arms, throwing up, and dragging crucifixes wherever I go.

Todd: ...running over old ladies whenever you get the chance.

Mike: ...on the way to a crack house

Todd: ...after sticking a drill into some kid's head. Daily stuff.

Mike: I felt like running them down in Florida. There's just so many old people. They just get in the way, walking slow. I'm like "When are you going to die?!"

Todd: Well, I bet you ten-to-one that most readers don't know your full story of what went on. Why are you in New York and what happened down in Florida?

Mike: That's true. My case didn't get much major news coverage like it should have.

Todd: This is the first time in American history that the artist himself has been incarcerated. With the 2 Live Crew, the people who sold the album were jailed, not the label or the band. Is it true that you can't come in contact with minors?

Mike: Yeah. I'm supposed to stay at least ten feet away from anyone under eighteen. This condition of my probation was dropped but my probation officer told me to obey it.

Todd: What type of community service do you have to serve?

Mike: Right now I work with god's love. We deliver. [laughs]

Todd: Have they ever tried to convince you to do a series of drawings like My Little Pony or Strawberry Shortcake to purge you?

Mike: No, I wish they would. Then they would say that I'm trying to tempt children. I'm sure they'd think there was a hidden message or something in it that wasn't supposed to be and I actually thought about doing really nice kid's drawings and taking them into the court room and saying, "Look, you've cured me. I'm drawing nice things now."

Todd: What charges did they file to put you in jail for four days?

Mike: It was three charges of obscenity. I got a summons in the mail in early '93 and went to arraignment and there were a bunch of religious protesters protesting *Boiled Angel* (a comic book series) and me, telling me to repent. I plead not guilty. The Comic Book Defense fund got me a lawyer, a First Amendment lawyer, Luke Leroux, and he had been well known for defending the strip clubs and adult video stores in the area that I lived in. We went through a whole jury trial and I lost. And the judge ordered me to go to jail. That was on Thursday when I was found guilty and I was to stay in jail until Monday for sentencing. Over the weekend. They needed to make an example out of me and show me that they could put me in jail if they wanted to. So, Monday, I went back in and saw the judge. He's asked, "Did you learn anything in jail?" and I said, "I learned that I don't want to be in jail." "Is that all?" I said, "Well, I learned that what I drew was wrong," which was just a lie. I had to say something happy and they sentenced me: no contact with minors, you have to stay at least ten feet away from anyone under eighteen. That was just because of my artwork. I've had no problem with minors.

Todd: Just for the record, have you ever killed anyone?

Mike: No. Not yet, anyway. But I never would.

Todd: Ever tripped an old lady crossing the street?

Mike: No.

Todd: Ever kicked a dog?

Mike: No.

Todd: Ever steal peanut brittle from the store?

Mike: No. But once I stole a fruitcake at Christmas time as a gift for my Mom.

Todd: Ever skipped out paying your check at Denny's?

Mike: Nuh uh. But I did get a free birthday meal once and a sliver of cake.

Todd: Any parking tickets unpaid?

Mike: No.

Todd: So, you're doing pretty good on the crime side of things.

Mike: Only obscene art.

Todd: You'd think they'd spend more time tracking down true, convicted pedophiles or serial killers. How old were you when you got arrested?

Mike: I was twenty-three when it all started.

Todd: How old are you now?

Mike: Twenty-nine.

Todd: You sound really young.

Mike: Oh yeah, [in falsetto voice] Hanson.

Todd: Who came to help you out besides the Comic Book Defense Fund? The ACLU? Oprah Winfrey?

Mike: The Comic Book Defense Fund paid for the lawyer's fees and paid a bond to get me off probation until the appeal and I asked the ACLU to help me at first and I never heard back from them until I actually lost and then they were interested. By that point, the judge involved with the case said that he didn't want the ACLU to get involved then, so they screwed me. The ACLU submitted the case to the Supreme Court but the Supreme Court decided not to hear the case.

Todd: Isn't obscenity judged by community standards and it can vary from region to region, city to city? Who picks these people?

Mike: It's like a jury trial. Six-person jury. Supposedly a jury of my peers and they all said that there should be limits on art. It started out with thirty people during jury selection and only six people get through. And it ends up being like the worst jury you can get. There were two people in the jury (selection); one guy, about eighteen or nineteen, and there was a woman who, during jury selection, said that there should not be limits on art, and they said things that made me know that they would be decent jury members. Of course they didn't get through. The prosecution struck that off.

Todd: Is it true that Baggish (the main prosecutor) had evidence on his desk for two years before they decided to arrest you?

Mike: Pretty much what happened was an undercover officer bought the *Boiled Angel*s from me through the mail.

Todd: From Largo, right?

Mike: Yeah, and they had it on file at the state attorney's office from 1991 'til '93 and I think Stewart Baggish just happened to come across them and found them maybe on accident. And up to that point, I guess nobody wanted to prosecute the case or something.

Todd: Was it an election year?

Mike: [laughs] Exactly.

Todd: How did the appeals process go? Didn't the state of Florida spend $50,000 on your case?

Mike: Yeah, I lost everything now. I'm just going through my probation and hoping one day I'll get through it so I'll be free.

Todd: How long is your probation for?

Mike: Two years. Initially, it was three years but during the appeals, my lawyer was able to get one of the charges dropped—the charge of advertising.

Todd: I remember it being in *Factsheet Five* and *Answer Me!* What are the other terms of your probation? Is there anything that strikes you as odd?

Mike: I had to take my journalism ethics class.

Todd: Did you hire a stunt double for it?

Mike: No, I had to do it.

Todd: Did you have to get a passing grade on it?

Mike: It was a credit class. I took that at NYU. It was a six-week course and it was a pretty good class. My teacher works at the *Daily News* building so on the last day of class, we all got a tour of the building and how it works. The only bad thing was it cost three hundred dollars. I've been paying my fine off. I have to pay over three thousand dollars in fines. They ordered me not to draw anything that might be obscene, even for my own use.

Todd: Is that according to Florida law?

Mike: Yeah. When I was on probation in Florida, the police were allowed to search my home without a warrant at any time.

Todd: Did they?

Mike: They never actually showed up, though.

Todd: Are you under a different probationary system now, so you can be in New York, or is this a touchy subject?

Mike: The state of Florida probation gave me permission to live here. I send stuff in the mail to them.

Todd: Off of one of the *Boiled Angel*s, didn't you somehow get linked to the Gainesville student murders?

Mike: Oh yeah.

Todd: What was their thinking there?

Mike: That was *Boiled Angel* six. I was coming home with my mom to our house from Christmas shopping for my grandmother and two detectives were there. They had a brief case with a copy of number six in it and started showing it to my mom and my mom was like, "I thought you quit drawing that stuff." And they're showing it to her. The introduction had a little rant about how I hate the police and stuff, how they're pigs and all this. One of the detectives starts reading that out loud to my mom and they were trying to get me in trouble with my mom and make her upset. They told me I was a suspect in the murders just because of my artwork and later I read an article in the newspaper that said they had over 10,000 suspects. They were trying to get everyone to give blood samples. People wouldn't give them unless there was a court order.

Todd: Do you think that you're going to stay in New York or just stay out of Florida?

Mike: I'm going to try to stay in New York. If I ever get through my probation—I felt like I had to actually escape Florida. I was feeling like I had to get out of there by early June and decided to do it. I was talking to Kembra who lives in New York, who's in the band The Voluptuous Horror of Karen Black. She said I could live with her for awhile until I got on my feet. If it wasn't for her helping me out, I don't know what I would have done. I took a bunch of stuff and drove up to New York and right after I arrived in New York, I found out that I'd lost my appeal and the news cameras were looking for me where I was working, at my Dad's shop. I had already left, luckily.

Todd: What kind of jobs did you have at the time you were drawing *Boiled Angel*?

Mike: I was working for my Dad's convenience store, selling beer and cigarettes. Customers gave me lots of inspiration. Also, I worked as a janitor for an old school building for three years.

Todd: Working in the service industry will give you front row seats to the worst in human behavior. Did they do a psychiatric evaluation of you?

Mike: Oh yeah.

Todd: Did you ever look at a Rorschach test and go, "Hey, that's a good idea for a drawing"?

Mike: Uh huh. I did that in Florida. They tried to screw me there 'cause I went to see the psychiatrist and they told me they charge a hundred dollars and hour. I did an hour of a monotonous test where you mark A, B, or C and true and false. They keep repeating the same questions over and over. Questions like, "Do you hear voices?" and, "Do you think people are after you?" and I was like, "Yeah." And I did the ink blot test. And then when I was with her, the psychiatrist woman, she starts flipping through the *Boiled Angel* pages one by one. She's like, "Did you draw this drawing?" and it was drawn by someone else and had someone else's name on it, and I'm like, "No, I drew the ones that have my name on the bottom." It seemed like she didn't spend any time looking at the books and when I was on my way to go, she's like, "It's time to pay the bill." And I didn't have any money on me but I figured it would be like two hundred dollars because I'd been there for two hours. She's like, "It'll be twelve hundred dollars."

Todd: Twelve hundred dollars?

Mike: She said she spent ten hours reviewing the *Boiled Angel*s—a thousand dollars there. She asked, "Will that be cash or check?" and I said, "It'll be IOU." She said, "Well, I can't do the evaluation until you pay and it's going to screw up your probation." It just seemed like she was using the fact that I was ordered to do it, to get some more money out of me. She actually lowered the price to five hundred dollars and I was like, nah. When I moved to New York, I still needed to get that evaluation so I found a psychiatrist to talk to me for ten minutes, who wrote me a note and it only cost one hundred dollars. I was getting screwed left and right in Florida.

Todd: Does it seems arbitrary to you that you're the only person in the history of the United States who's seen prison time for drawing? I know you're not drawing daisies but there are definitely other artists out there, right now, who are hitting the same buttons.

Mike: I think so. I was probably in the worst place to be doing it. My parents would say, "You're going to get in trouble some day," and my Dad would look over my shoulder and look at my art and say, "You're going to get arrested for pornography," and I was just like, "It's just a drawing, a comic." I never believed in my wildest dreams that I would be charged and all that would happen and then when it happened, I was like, you fucking bastard.

Todd: Have your parents been supportive of you?

Mike: Yeah. They are now. At first, they were very afraid and nervous, just as much as I was because they would see the news reports that would say that I was once a suspect in the Gainesville student murders. They showed footage of the Gainesville student murders when they were talking about my art. It looked very bad. You know, people would come up to me, "Whoa, you killed a bunch of people?" I'd be sitting in my Dad's convenience store and they'd be all, "You got away with it, fuck yeah." I was like, "You think if I killed someone, I'd be sitting here selling you cigarettes?"

Todd: Like "can you sign my carton of Luckys?"

Mike: Exactly. At one point, I was actually selling my books there, at my Dad's store.

Todd: How did that go?

Mike: He didn't like that. I got a few copies out. People would take it over to the bar and they'd like it.

Todd: How's the *Worst of Boiled Angel* series going, put out by Michael Hunt Publications?

Mike: Very good. The way it came out, it reminds me of one of those cheap fun pads.

Todd: Yeah, the stuff where you try to figure out a puzzle or something.

Mike: I think it would be good for kids, almost, so they can color them up and stuff. Kids, if they were really young, would probably think it was a pretty drawing. They wouldn't understand what it was.

Todd: So what are you working on now? Isn't *Boiled Angel* a complete set?

Mike: I dunno what I'm going to do with it yet. I'm just waiting to see if I get off of probation and maybe I can do a new issue one of these days. Or perhaps a collection of comics about the trial. I've done a few. One of these days, I'll do a comic about everything, going more in-depth. I just lived through it recently and I'm not ready yet to spend hours and hours drawing it out.

Todd: With the possibility of it getting confiscated.

Mike: They would do it, too.

Todd: Are you still doing *Superfly*, too?

Mike: Yeah, but that's pretty much been done. Number one and two were pretty much done before I got in trouble and that's why we're selling them, because after I was ruled not to draw, I hadn't really published anything on my own or let anyone else publish stuff just because I was afraid of getting in trouble. But as soon I get off probation, I think I'll feel better and I've also been doing little acrylic paintings and color stuff.

Todd: Do you have any illustrators that you really admire?

Mike: I've always liked some of the old EC (Entertaining Comics) artists from the horror comics and science fiction ones. Spain Rodriguez—an underground artist—he was one of the ones who did Zap Comics. I used to collect some of the more underground comics. When I was sixteen, I would go to the flea market and try and get comic books for my collections. I like looking at all of those weird drawings and crazy things. That was part of my influence. Also Greg Irons.

Todd: Did you ever get into Jack T. Chick, who does all those itty-bitty religious pamphlets like *The Scam*?

Mike: Oh yeah. I've always liked them. I remember seeing those when I was really young too, back in the '70s.

Todd: Have you ever gotten a chance to see Ralph Steadman? He's mostly known for illustrating *Fear and Loathing in Las Vegas*, but he also illustrates and writes kids books, books on whiskey, and did a book on Sigmund Freud.

Mike: Definitely.

Todd: What's your favorite thing to do? If you were left to your own devices and you continued to do one thing, and you could live off of that, what would it be?

Mike: Probably just drawing. Drawing nasty pictures. [laughs]

Todd: Not to sound like a psychiatrist, but why nasty pictures? Why isn't it My Little Pony but the subject matter that you cover?

Mike: Well, I look around, and there's so many nice drawings everywhere I look, and I think to myself, I don't see enough gross drawings, enough stuff to make a balance between the really sickening sweet and cute drawings and art and stuff and the more—of what they think—obscene drawings. And I just like to push the limits of free expression or go over the boundaries, in a way, because I thought I was allowed to do that, that I was free to, protected by the Constitution and everything. Now that I've found out that that's not true, it kind of changes things but I still feel like I've always felt like. I don't feel like I've held myself back yet.

Todd: Do you feel that the freedom of speech has turned, in many ways, into the freedom of possible imprisonment?

Mike: It seems like it in lots of ways and I'm sure that it's going to get worse, but piss on 'em. That's what my grandmother taught me. She said, "Piss on 'em, Mikey."

Todd: Have you had any surprising supporters come out of the woodwork?

Mike: Every now and then. Gary Groth's (editor/publisher of *The Comics Journal,* co-founder of Fantagraphics Books) parents came to my trial. They said, "Gary sent us down to check out how things were doing." Good old Chuck Sheppard who does *News of the Weird*. He lives in St.

Petersburg. I met up with him and did a few interviews back when I got in trouble and everything came together. Just people I've met because of the situation who I probably would have never met. A lot of people on the street would recognize me and go, "Good luck." An old lady walked up to me once, "You're that guy that's on the news." I thought she was going to sock me. She reached in her purse. I thought she was pulling out a gun, and I'm like, oh no. She pulled out a little autograph book. "I think you're wonderful." I signed her book for her. There's some good stuff like that but awful lots of religious nuts were after me, trying to hand me pamphlets and telling me to repent and that I'm evil and possessed by Satan. Going on the different talk shows was crazy, too. Everyone's screaming at you and no one in the audience seems to know what's going on.

Todd: Is this whole thing weighing you down? Do you want to give up on it or do you want to follow this through?

Mike: I'll keep drawing and see how the probation goes. Hopefully, I can get through it some day. Otherwise, I'll be a fugitive for the rest of my life.

Todd: What do you do to alleviate the heaviness—any things that help you escape?

Mike: Not really. It's always on my mind one way or another. I guess I'm looking forward to the time when I'll be off of probation, when I don't have to worry about coming up with money for the fine and all that other stuff—worrying that my probation is violated and they'll tell me to go back to Florida.

Todd: Is there the possibility of serving more jail time?

Mike: Yeah, it's always possible. Especially if I don't get through my probation, they'll put out a warrant for my arrest in Florida and if I ever step foot in the state, they'll arrest me and who knows how long I'll be in jail. I'll be sitting in there, not allowed to have any pencils or papers. When I was in jail the first time, I wanted to keep a journal about each night in jail and they gave special instructions for me not to have pencils or paper.

Todd: Have you learned any details that shouldn't be overlooked when you're publishing something in the United States that could possibly be construed as obscene?

Mike: Probably not. The only thing I would have been more careful about would be sending them to the police [chuckles]. They were using a fake name and they wrote me a letter saying they saw my magazine in Ft. Lauderdale and they'd just moved to Largo. And that was the first person in Largo who ever knew about my book. I thought it was kinda strange or something. I sent my phone number and said, why don't we just meet, get together, and I'll sell you the book in person. He wrote that, "Oh, we're too busy with work," and, "I tried to call your number and there was no answer." I should have been more suspicious than I was but I never dreamed what was going on really was.

Todd: How many *Boiled Angel*s got sold through you?

Mike: About three hundred of each issue. Very limited and mostly I'd print them per the amount of subscribers that I had. I was very cautious about having new people get it. Most of my subscribers had gotten past issues and I knew they knew what to expect and not to worry about anyone getting too freaked out. But, of course, that didn't help me. [chuckles]

Todd: How much are you looking at in total fines right now?

Mike: Around $3,000 at least and I've already spent over $2,000.

Todd: Does it suck being a martyr? Do you want to be something else?

Mike: No. I don't mind. I just feel bad that the Supreme Court didn't overturn the conviction and it means that in Florida and other states, there can be a prosecutor somewhere prosecuting someone else for artwork or writing obscenity and they can always bring up my case as a successful prosecution. I'm just sad and hurt that I didn't get vindicated. That's probably the worst part. The only part I would change is that I wish that I could win at the end and sue the state of Florida for violating my Constitutional rights, but of course, that'll never happen.

Todd: The good thing that, I hope, is coming out of this, is that it's not just a theory any more: in the United States, you can be forced not to do something that doesn't have a direct link to criminal activity, and more people are seeing this.

Mike: I think that it's also good that it woke some people up to what's really going on and what can really happen with those close-minded types of judges and prosecutors.

Todd: Any last thing to say?

Mike: People should draw whatever they want and I don't think people should feel pressured to tone anything down as far as art work and writing for fear of being prosecuted. If they have to fight, to fight it all the way, try to win. Fight the bastards!

Todd: There's a need for balance. All those pieces of pastel art hanging up in hotels across America have to be balanced out somehow.

Mike: Who knows, two thousand years from now, maybe they'll have one of my drawings on a flag.

•   •   •

THE GAIN

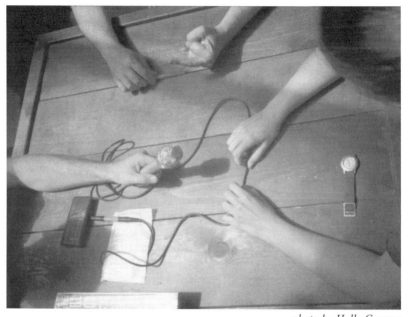

photo by Holly Connor

"The best punk has always been done by really dumb shits."
−Tim Yohannan

BAD TASTE IS IN THE MAJORITY:
AN INTERVIEW WITH TIM YOHANNAN AND JEN ANGEL OF MAXIMUMROCK'N'ROLL

Maximumrock'n'roll proved that one man, without substantial financial backing, yet armed with an insatiable dedication, could change the world. Tim Yohannan, arguably, has had the deepest effect on DIY punk rock since its inception. Although most of the efforts he was involved with were formed by committee—*Maximumrock'n'roll*, The 924 Gilman Street Project (a live music venue), and the record collective Epicenter—he was a major, guiding force not only in San Francisco, but the entire world. His plan of operation was as simple in theory as it was hard to pull off in real life. It was this: stay true to your original principles. Tim had a strong vision and the backbone to keep a strict monthly release schedule and a tight core of dedicated writers. He kept a massive, complicated machine moving for the better part of twenty years. His lasting legacy went beyond the most coveted punk record collection in the entire world and beyond helping compile some of the most influential international hardcore compilation records of all time. For better or for worse, he helped settle the bedrock and ballast of what punk rock itself is today.

Tim's policies were enormously controversial because he was one in a small handful of critics in the world who people take for gospel concerning what is or isn't punk or hardcore. No small feat, which bestowed *MRR* considerable power and influence far and wide. When I was younger, two of the three magazines I could count on getting in the mail in the gut of a small town were *MRR* and *Flipside*. I really didn't see a competition between the two but rather saw them as complementary views to similar music.

Not that I agreed with Tim down the line, but I afford you this one note of caution: if you don't agree with *MRR*'s policies on covering music, remember this, this is punk rock. Nothing's stopping you from making your own zine, soliciting album reviews from different publications, or picking up one of the hundreds of punk zines circulating the U.S. at this very second. Many people had gripes with Tim —often disagreeing with him on either his politics or his definition of what would be listened to at *MRR*. Yet, he was such a deep believer in punk ethics. It was hard to deny him respect. He built so much with his own hands from the ground up. How many of us can say that?

Several months after this interview, on April 3, 1998, Tim died of Non-Hodgkin's lymphoma. My mother, also, was diagnosed of the exact same disease. Before the interview, we talked a little about cancer treatments and how far along his cancer was before his was detected. My mother had found out about her condition two weeks before Tim and started treatment immediately. My mother almost died but had a miraculous recovery. It's such a fine line. Petty differences melt into nothing when faced with death.

At the time of this interview, one of his last, seeing the mortality of his own situation, Tim had picked a successor to keep *MRR* on the right course, Jen Angel, the creator of *Fucktooth* fanzine. After a tumultuous time following Tim's death, Jen went on to help form another magazine, *Clamor*.

MRR continues on to this day.

Todd: Tim, what's your day job?
Tim: I do shipping and receiving for UC Berkeley.
Todd: Jen, what's your day job?
Jen: I work at Punks For Presses.
Todd: Oh, I talked to you yesterday. You're the same Jen. I did not know that.
[everyone laughs at Todd]
Jen: I was gonna ask you if you knew the answer.
Todd: What's your occupation then?
Tim: I never thought of it like that. That pays my bills and keeps me grounded and this is my hobby or fancy or whatever.
Todd: What is this? Say you're going to give a resume. What would your job description be?
Tim: Coordinator.
Todd: And Jen, what would your job description be?
Jen: Tim's is tyrant.
Todd: Oh, that's right. I thought it was dictator.
Jen: Bad cop, good cop. I guess it would be coordinator, too.
Todd: How do you delineate between what's punk and what's not punk? In early issues you review The Jesus and Mary Chain. Would you do that now?
Tim: Stuff that sounds like their very earliest stuff, yes.
Todd: Why do you guys review surf music and not synth-pop?
Tim: Actually, we don't review surf anymore. We did about two or three years ago when it was sort of surf and garage and everything was starting to perk up again. But then, about a year and a half ago, I decided that most of the surf stuff—if it was just instrumental stuff, the bulk of it was actual-

ly not what I would call maximum rock'n'roll. Most of it is pretty laid back.

Todd: Medium.

Tim: Not even.

Todd: Background rock'n'roll.

Tim: Right. Every now and then there will be a record that will come out that we'll say has an instrumental track and a vocal track and if that's more on the rock and roll side, we'll review it.

Todd: Jen, what do you think was your deciding factor on coming out to *Maximumrock'n'roll* from Ohio?

Jen: It's just a really big thing and I've been doing zines for a really long time and *Maximum* is the biggest zine there is. And if I want to keep doing zines then *Maximum* is pretty much the way to go.

Todd: How many issues do you work ahead of time?

Tim: Four or five.

Todd: Everything—layout wise, ad space wise and all that stuff?

Jen: Yeah. Well, ad space gets reserved about a month in advance. Completely reserved.

Tim: I would say probably sixty to seventy percent of the ads are automatic and then the rest get filled in as we have space available. We have a master layout chart in the computer for each issue and when one gets all blocked in terms of content then we'll start the next one. The first thing to go are the interviews. Then the articles and stuff like that. Now that Jen is here, we're hopefully gonna have more articles.

Jen: Well, we have a special issue and then two articles lined up. So we're workin' on 'em. We have to plan so far in advance to make space for a special issue and articles so they don't happen for awhile.

Tim: When it gets to the point where we're backed up six months, then we've got problems. An interview with a band gets done, it takes a month or two before it gets sent to us, four or five months before it comes out, band's broken up.

Todd: We run into the exact same problems. Where did you get the title *Maximumrock'n'roll*?

Tim: It was when punk started in '75, '76. The Who called what they were doing in '64, or whatever, Maximum R&B, where they were taking R&B and updating it and to me that's what punk was doing to rock'n'roll. It was updating it, so that's why I called it *Maximumrock'n'roll*.

Todd: So, you like The Who?

Tim: Their earliest stuff.

Todd: Is there any popular band that you like their later stuff?

Tim: Huh! That's a very good question.

Todd: Do you mind talking about your cancer treatment at all?

Tim: No, I don't mind.

Todd: 'Cause I've heard it's lung cancer, pituitary cancer, skin graph cancer. I don't even know what a pituitary is. What kind of cancer is it?

Tim: It's lymphoma. Non-Hodgkin's lymphoma.

Todd: Lymph? [Points to the lymph nodes in his neck].

Tim: Yeah, it turns out you have lymph glands all over the fuckin' place but mainly, in my case, the ones that are affected are in the throat area, the armpit area, the groin area and the abdomen area.

Todd: Is it treated or in remission?

Tim: This kind of lymphoma doesn't usually go into remission. They can knock it down for a couple of years at best and then it's back. They tried three different types of chemo and it didn't really work. Then they gave me some kind of experimental treatment recently and in another month, or a little more than that, I'll know whether that has some effect. Now whether it's gonna have a big effect or not; I don't know yet.

Todd: How would you describe chemo in non-medical terms?

Tim: They shoot you up with poison and it kills all the fast growing cells. That's why your hair falls out. That's a fast growing cell. Your nails turn black. Those are fast growing cells. Taste buds. Things like that go. So, it's pretty indiscriminant. It's like the modern day equivalent of leeches.

Todd: What's the new treatment that they gave you?

Tim: It's something called a mono-clonal antibody which I guess apparently knows how to just find your cancer cells and attach themselves to them and then damages the cells and then that prevents those cells from duplicating. It doesn't shrink things right away but down the road, when those cells don't duplicate, they will disappear and die. And then they also combine that with radiation. The humorous—well, it's humorous now—part of that was that I had to stay in a lead lined room for six days.

Jen: And just a reminder—Tim doesn't read.

Tim: I was going nuts. And then they would come in with a Geiger counter and measure me every day until my level got down to a point where they could let me go. I wanted to bail after about four days and they told me that they'd report me to the Nuclear Regulatory Commission if I left. But anyway, it looks like there's some effectiveness so far to this treatment. The nice thing about this is that there are no side effects other than that you may get leukemia. But other than that there are no side effects.

And an answer to your band question, I cannot think of a band who I think... of modern day bands... none. I can't think of any. I think the last band that put out a surprising amount of good records before they put out a surprising amount of really bad records was The Rolling Stones. Up to the point where Brian Jones died, I think all of that stuff is still amazingly great and then after that they just sucked. I really think that in most bands, their first record is best because that probably represents years, well, used to represent years, of work. Now it represents even less practice and that's why I think those are usually the hottest thing. After that they then felt sort of like, "Oh, we have to get records out all of the time" and the excitement drops and the quality drops.

Todd: Jen, what are your three favorite books because Tim doesn't read?

Jen: It's kind of hard 'cause...

Todd: Just pound 'em out.

Jen: Well, I don't know. There's a lot to choose from. One of my favorite political books is a collection of essays called *Declarations of Independence* by Howard Zinn. My favorite fiction book is a fantasy, called *The Wizard of Earthsea* (by Ursula K. LeGuin), which is wizards and dragons kind of stuff, the stuff I read when I was little and is still one of my favorite series. I can't think of a third one. I read a lot of stuff but tend to get bored halfway through the book.

Todd: What's the biggest difference from initial vision of *Maximumrock'n'roll* to the vision you have for it today? I mean, it's been around since 1982.

Tim: '77 actually. That's when we started the radio show and that's when we came up with the name Maximum Rock'n'Roll. How has the vision changed? Probably then I had more hope that, counter-culturally, the world could be affected better. Another is that it could be something that could have positive impact on consciousness. Now I don't necessarily believe that. I think I have more of the belief that it's a refuge for alienated people to sort of establish something of their own. I don't really hold out hopes that it would be a big vehicle for societal change.

Todd: What do you think took its teeth out?

Tim: I would say that maybe over the last ten or fifteen years, the way capitalism has developed in terms of conglomeration of power and wealth more and more in the hands of a few people and the way the media has affected how people think. What people think. I think that's part of the technique, to just bombard people with so much bullshit information and so much bullshit that they can't see the forest for the trees. I think it's been highly effective. And I also think that with the defeat of any alternative, in this case communism, this is the reign of capitalism now—until it destroys the world or destroys itself or whatever it's gonna do. So, I think that has been the change I have seen in the last twenty years. I don't think that there's an effective resistance on a large scale that can be mounted against the power that they have. It's more a matter of them self-destructing and if there is going to be anything left for anybody else after that. If there is an after that.

Todd: [Silence] Well, that kind of depresses me. [Laughter]

Tim: Which is not to say that you shouldn't fight. In other words, I don't feel depressed by that. People should resist any way they can. They should try and cooperate any way they can and they should try to create environments where they can maintain some kind of sanity and they should try to have some fun. If you're stuck on this plane, you do what you can do, otherwise you just become a complete cynical fuckhead, which is a victory for them. So, if you have any self respect you have to resist. So, to me, that's not depressing. It's sort of like that's how it works and maybe in a way this is more honest, ya know?

Todd: What was you initial idea of becoming part of *Maximumrock'n'roll*? How long have you been here for?

Jen: Since April.

Todd: Has anything changed? Has your initial thought when you got in your car in Ohio, from the time you got here, to now, changed? Had anything changed when you met Tim and you walked in here? Was it like, "Oh, I can't do that" or, "Oh, good"?

Jen: Well, some things have changed. Now I know why there aren't more articles. I've been here for how long and there hasn't been an article yet that I've worked on. You can ask people so many times or people are flaky and people don't commit. So that's why I realized that there aren't that many good interviews. I know that it's me working on it a lot more than Tim does and we still don't have a lot to show for it. That frustrates me a lot because we can't do this by ourselves. So that's the big thing that has changed and now I understand more why *Maximum* doesn't live up to some people's expectations or whatever.

Todd: Have you found another person to help Jen out yet?

Jen: No. We've considered a lot of people but we're still looking.

Todd: In the job description for the vacancy, it states, "You don't get paid." How can somebody work like sixty hours a week, or how many hours you're asking them to work, and not get paid?

Jen: I don't get paid. Tim doesn't get paid.

Tim: In other words, there's some re... What's the re word?

Todd: Remuneration.

Tim: Thank you. You won't pay rent, but you have to live here for twenty-four hours a day, essentially.

Jen: I don't really think it's that bad. I think there are definite times when, say a review deadline or whatever, that it is a lot of work but it's really kind of off and on. You answer the phone and deal with that whenever someone ever calls you, but it's not like I have to be here eight hours a day. You have to work with the deadlines but it's not like it's sixty hours I put in every week. It's like the week after the issue comes out where there's not much to do and you do a lot of the other work that isn't related to the magazine.

Todd: How many people work here on a regular basis?

Tim: On a monthly basis, there's about a hundred all together who contribute in any way, shape, or form. Maybe about seventy of those live in the area and they all have keys and they come in and do typing or reviewing or layout or whatever it is they do. Compared to how we did the mag, let's say about three years ago, it's a lot more decentralized. After I got sick, a lot of my job duties got distributed to people. In other words, I used to go pick up the mail every day, but now different people do it every different day. They go to the PO Box, pick up stuff, come over here and do it. Someone else comes over and types in stuff that day. Someone is in charge of the letters to the editor section, somebody's in charge of the scene report. It's a lot more decentralized. Our job is to make sure that all of these things interconnect and, "Are they gonna do what they say they're gonna do?"

Jen: What we do is call people and remind them of their deadlines.

Todd: Any problems with matters of theft or trust? Do you have a lengthy or large selection process for somebody to get a key?

Tim: Considering how many people over the years have had keys, the amount of either theft or whatever is really minuscule. We're not that discriminant.

Jen: When we select a reviewer, we select them on the basis of their knowledge or whatever about music and whether or not we give them a key right away is, "Okay, how do we feel about them when we meet them?" "Do they seem shady? Do they seem really cool?" It's basically the first impression. I can only think of one or two cases where I delayed giving keys to somebody for any given period of time. In most cases I'll give keys right off the bat.

Todd: All right, true or false: Reverend Nørb has three testicles and his drummer has one thus they can still have the title of their album *8 Testicled Pogo Machine*?

Tim: Well, I haven't inspected.

Todd: Because that guy had a lot of energy and I'm trying to trace it to something.

Tim: That's true. What can you say about somebody that when you meet 'em and you're shaking hands with him, he's pogoing?

Todd: Exactly.

Tim: What does that say?

Todd: Do you have a lot of hair on your toes?

Tim: No, I'm not Armenian.

Todd: Did you give the band Head a hundred dollars and say, "Keep on doing what you're doing 'cause we like it?"

Tim: [laughs] Well, have you heard their new album?

Todd: No, I have not.

Tim: Then you would know the answer is yes.

Todd: All right Jen, what are some things that make you blind with rage? What are your buttons?

Jen: Last night I went to this show where the promoter didn't really promote it. When we got there, there were like five people which means he didn't publicize it very much. He didn't collect money at the door. He promised the band gas money and didn't give it to them. All of that is just so irresponsible and it makes me very angry. But I can't do much about it. It makes me so mad. Tim always makes fun of me being a very even keel and not an angry person.

Todd: That's a weird thing to be made fun of.

Jen: That's probably a question you would better ask Tim because he's the one who has the reputation of flying off the handle. I think that one thing for him is honesty. When you know that someone deliberately lies. I think that's a big one.

Tim: People who know better using the term "fag." I blew up at this friend of mine the other day for indiscriminant use of that term. It was literally that the fuse went and within twenty seconds I was giving the finger and telling him what a fuckhead he was and stuff. And then after I got it out of my system we worked it out. Actually, I think it's good to blow your top sometimes. I think it cleans the pores. What else makes me really pissed off? Yeah, I would say people lying. That bothers me a lot. And people just being fucking lazy. The path of least resistance, which then includes lying, is just so unnecessary and so hurtful and that'll make me get mad sometimes.

Jen: Something that's essential for me is don't commit to a project if you're not going to do it. If you don't want to do it, that's fine, as long as you tell me and then I can deal with it or find someone else to do it or whatever. If you wait until the very last moment to tell me that you're not going to do it, that's obviously the wrong time to do it.

Todd: Have you ever had a voodoo doll?

Jen: No.

Todd: A person's face on a dartboard?

Jen: No.

Tim: I think I've been on the receiving end of that.

Todd: Maybe you can clarify something for me. I have no idea how big of an audience Head has but I assume that there is a lot of positive press about that band. Then you have a band like Agnostic Front who you've butted heads with and gets written up pretty poorly but there's a huge amount of people who really like them. How do you make up that discrepancy? Can you trace any reason why if this band gets no press or bad press all of the time and they still sell out a lot of shows?

Tim: Well, bad taste is in the majority, right? So you can account for things like that. Recently, we were taken to task by Mordam because of a bunch of articles we had written attacking Lookout. The assumption that some people there were working on was that we had hurt Lookout's sales. My feeling has been that in the past whenever we have attacked somebody their sales go up and so I don't agree with that theory. But you can give great press to a band like Head or whatever that will always remain a little cult band of geeks and their fans are going to be geeks and that's how it's gonna work. Or you can attack some bands and that will help them. Any publicity is good publicity.

Todd: I feel the same about The Fixtures. I wish more than four people would show up to see The Fixtures.

Tim: Jen, do you have any thoughts on that?

Jen: Just that it's controversy. That's better press than good press. It's like the band Race Traitor from Chicago...

Todd: What was that catchy tagline? In Your Face or... Simple Disgrace?

Jen: Guilty Disgrace.

Tim: Any bad puns on the cover are mine.

Jen: There's been very little good press about them, but people talk about them a lot and that's because of controversy and people saying bad things about them. I definitely see that controversy is better press than saying good things about them.

Todd: What's the importance of a scene? When you were in high school, where a lot of our readers—and I assume a lot of your readers are in between the ages of fourteen and twenty-one—when they are in high school they have a scene of their own that's set up by the high school. Either you're in football or drama or your anti-football and anti-drama and you're in a group by yourself. Do you think that the scene is kind of like a middle ground before going into something else or do you think the scene is important for itself? Do these people need to act collectively or do these people need to operate independently? I can give you some examples like when Pushead used to work for you guys and write for you guys and now he's doing Metallica t-shirts. Is that a good thing or does that mean you're very, very angry or do you think that he should have stayed in the enclave?

Jen: I definitely think that in terms of activism that a lot of people will be politicized by punk rock and then will move on and do something else totally unrelated to punk. I don't think that's betrayal. I just get frustrated because I wish that they would help out the scene that helped them out and that got them to that point. I think a lot of people have criticisms about the scene which I agree with but if everyone leaves the scene because they're critical about it then the scene doesn't get any better. There aren't a lot of women and there's sexism that's not going to get any better and not going to change if all of the activist people who want to change it go out to do politics or to do their own thing. So, I do get mad when people leave. Plus, it's kind of annoying when there's someone who you've looked up to for a real long time or you respected what they do and—not necessarily did they sell out—but those things aren't important anymore to them. They don't have the same values and they move on and do something else. That makes me disappointed.

Tim: People obviously get involved with, in this case the punk scene, for different reasons. Some people get involved because they need a sense of community. A lot of people I think, actually. They're very alienated people, or at least in the past that was the case. So, they try to build a community that they can relate to. If it turns out that they can't relate to it and it's not supportive enough then they seem to go and find some other kind of community. An example: it would be some people looking for god and they get in the punk scene. They don't find the fulfillment, so they get into some sect or become religious or whatever. Some people, when they don't find the satisfaction, they may revert back to the values that they were brought up in and they would become business people or whatever the fuck. For some people this is home and that's all they've got and so they will stay with it and work with it over years and years and years. So, it depends on why people get involved and what they are looking for. I do think that there are a lot of people who benefit, and have benefited, from this stage of involvement. I do think that it would be nice if they, in turn, would—they have learned a lot—and then let's say they go on and they're specializing in this or that, that they would share that on some level with this community and with the younger people coming into it. There'd be some sort of responsibility like that and perpetuation. But that doesn't happen that often.

Todd: Can you name a couple of people who have remained faithful? You've run Fat Wreck Chords stuff in your magazine. They're pretty high profile but every time I've had association with them they've been very helpful and they seem to have very reasonably priced stuff. Their videocassettes are ten dollars.

Tim: Do you want me to say something nice about Fat Mike? Actually, I don't have anything against Fat Mike. In some ways, for a bigger label, they've stuck more to certain principles than other labels have. There's a lot of people in their thirties, forties and even fifties who still view themselves as punk and are still working in this community. Not that many, but enough. But there are a lot of people who have gone on and gotten rich or have become professors or they have a lot of information. They could write some great fucking articles when we're talking about articles that would maybe effect a lot of younger people. I wish those people would think of that and get in touch and say, "Hey, we want to do this!"

Todd: Have you solicited anybody?

Tim: Oh, every now and then I'll hear of somebody who comes out of the blue. It depends on what they are doing nowadays. In some cases I wouldn't want to touch them with a ten-foot pole. Slur on the band. And then there are other people who, I think on some level, their heart is still more or less in the right place and I might occasionally ask someone like that. But I don't want to be beholding to them. I just wish that there was more initiative coming from people in that position.

Todd: What happened to the Maximumrock'n'roll radio show? Why did it end?

Tim: The last ten years this one person, Radley Hirsch, had been doing all of the tape duplicating in real time for all of the tapes that we sent out, did all the mailings, all the billings. He burned out after a decade. It wasn't going to be easy, if at all possible, to find somebody who could do that.

Jen: Especially emotionally.

Tim: And who would be really responsible? If I thought that it was really, really important that this show stay alive I would have fought harder to find someone. But I don't think it is. I think that a lot of the college stations that take the show have DJ's that have access to a lot of stuff. Nowadays, whatever your specialized interests are in punk, you can find a mailorder that has the stuff.

Todd: It's getting more reliable, too.

Tim: Right. To me, it wasn't a crucial thing and I don't think the radio show's been crucial for the last seven years. It's a fun thing to do but I think that when it was live and we were doing it from KPFA—which was a 59,000 watt station and it was also relayed up and down the valley—then it mattered because then we could get a lot of music and a lot of ideas to a lot of people outside of San Francisco, Berkeley, Oakland. It was reaching kids in Fresno, all the way down to Bakersfield, and all the way up to Redding. That mattered to me. This was more of a lark. It wasn't crucial.

Todd: How do you feel about contributors who are double dipping? Ted Rall is a staff writer for *P.O.V.* magazine and he has his own radio show. He's also a contributor for you guys. How do you feel about that?

Tim: If they do it for free then that's fine. The only thing that bothers me is when people send the exact same article or interview to us and to you and to *Rolling Stone* and *Spin*. That's happened where the identical thing has been sent to *Flipside* and *Maximum*.

Jen: Or people call and say, "I have this interview." Like someone called and wanted to give us this interview with Greil Marcus. I was like, "Okay, maybe that would be an interesting thing but we're not going to pay you for that!" We don't pay people. If that's the reason they're interested in giving that to us then we're not interested.

Todd: Yeah, this guy wrote, saying he was a punk rocker from West Virginia. I said, "Okay, you can do some reviews for us." He was like, "Well send me stuff." I'm like, "You don't have anything? How do you know about punk rock? Just show me a couple examples and we'll see what happens." He was like, "I can't do that."

Jen: We actually have a zine reviewer who's thirteen and he does really good. It hasn't gotten to the point where he thinks all zines suck. He actually reads all of them and does a really good job.

Todd: On every piece of vinyl in the music library, all four edges of the record jackets are secured with thick, green tape. Why?

Tim: Purely arbitrary. I went to Mexico in the summer if 1966 and there was this really great band that I hung out with in Mexico City that summer, this R&B band, and the main guy in the band, Javier Batiz, put tape on the edges of his records. He had this really cool R&B collection. It looked really cool and I said I was going to do that and at that point I had forty records or something. Had I known, I never would have started.

Todd: Is it hard finding green tape?

Tim: Well, the green tape company went out of business and panic struck. But due to the wonders of capitalism, another company filled the gap.

Todd: Any discrepancies in the tapes?

Tim: Yes, there are actually shading and texture differences.

Jen: But there are good things like now if you see a record with green tape on it you know where it came from.

Todd: Or a stunning duplicate thereof. Where do you draw the line between revolutionary culture and radical fetishism?

Tim: I don't have any idea of what you are talking about but if we're talking about the '60s counter culture, it was radical and meaningful to people up to the point where they got rid of the draft. As soon as they got rid of the draft and people's asses weren't on the line anymore, the radicalism faded and became more of a form. So, to me, that's what, in looking at the punk counter culture, there is a period, especially obvious in the early founding stages, where it's radical. I think it's radical to have networks outside of corporate or governmental control. That's radical and that's not just the early stages, that develops, and that's cool. But this society is really excellent at co-opting. Most people are going to be co-opted and if you look at most people, even the people who are most vocal and charged up at one point, five years from now, where are they gonna be? Unfortunately, most of them won't be here. There will be a few who will, but most won't be. At least that's been the historical pattern. But I don't want to spend my time trying to figure out who is genuinely radical and who isn't. It's like, well, you can try to create what you want to create. You try to resist what you can resist. You try to point out historical patterns so that maybe people can avoid some of the downfalls of previous counter cultures.

   Let's say some of my beef is with Jello (Biafra, owner of Alternative
Tentacles Records, ex-lead singer of the Dead Kennedys) or other people
like that are all about trying to show patterns of how people change, how
values get co-opted, how one goes from radical to liberal and what that
means, if not so much to attack the individual but to show... In fact, at that
Mordam (Distribution) meeting someone said, "Why do you spend so
much time nit-picking about these little things when there are these big
issues?" Well, to me these little nit-picky things... It's very easy to espouse
rhetoric about the corporations or this or that and you need to, but, sometimes you have to show what's right in front of you and how those things
change. How those people change. How their values change. And I think
those are very valuable lessons in terms of trying to keep something alive
and radical.

Todd: Jen, for you right now, what is the most difficult thing about working for this magazine?

Jen: Tim. No, that's not really true. I'm definitely getting used to it. It's a
big thing. We had our little...

Todd: Cap off the toothpaste kind of thing?

Jen: Yeah. There are a lot of difficult things. Certainly, getting people to
write. We're already dealing with people who have already written off the
magazine who I think could make good contributions, who are interested.
That's very difficult. Sometimes with people making assumptions about
what I do here or why I'm here.

Todd: What is the number one thing that people wrongly assume about
your position here?

Jen: I think a lot of people don't know exactly what I do. Sometimes people call up on the phone and won't talk to me and want to talk to Tim and
it's like, "You can talk to me. It's okay." We haven't really had a problem
with people deferring to Tim because once people know that I can pretty
much do exactly what he does, except for history stuff. He does all the
music stuff. I can do whatever else and once they know that then it's fine.
The thing that bothers me the most is people who think that my whole
entire life is the magazine, which it's not. I don't want it to be, but a definite major portion of it is. That's the biggest thing that bothers me.

Todd: What's the biggest misconception people have about Tim
Yohannan?

Jen: That you're tall!

Tim: [Laughter] It used to be.

Jen: The other one is how old you are. So many people are like, "Oh my
god, he has white hair!" Most people don't know that. They think it's really crazy.

Tim: Right.

Todd: So how old are you?

Tim: Fifty-two.

Todd: What's the biggest misconception people have about you?

Tim: I think that in print I come off as very rigid and dogmatic and just dry and political. I think that I actually have a pretty good sense of humor but it doesn't come across in print and so that's the misconception. I've been stereotyped by certain people as this or that and unless people meet me first-hand they aren't gonna really know, but that's how it goes. I accept that and also I think that if you're going to put yourself in a public position and if your gonna be pretty opinionated, a lot of people are gonna get a weird idea about you and that's the price.

Todd: Do you regret not having listened to anything because it was on a major label?

Tim: No. I do listen to stuff that's on majors and I will buy stuff for the collection that's on majors. I just don't want the magazine to be a vehicle of support for that. So that's my feeling although there's very precious little I can find to buy on a major that is worth buying.

Todd: *Maximumrock'n'roll*, the zine, started in 1982. What music could you have covered with your current policy, because the big ones that I can think of right off the bat are gone: The Clash, The Sex Pistols, Elvis Costello and even the Go Go's.

Tim: The bulk of the seventies punk bands were on majors and at that time being on a do-it-yourself thing was not part of the consciousness. Some people put out their own records and their own labels but it wasn't a big anti-corporate kind of thing to do. I was just sort of like, "Uh, let's put out a record."

Todd: "Maybe we'll get picked up."

Tim: Right. There wasn't a consciousness about it and that evolved as punk evolved. As the first wave of punk sold out, for want of a better word, and diluted itself and went to majors, it became a piece of shit. As the early hardcore thing started emerging as a reaction to that, then it started becoming part of consciousness which is, well, maybe, "If you do that, you're gonna suck."

Todd: Would *Maximumrock'n'roll*'s focus just follow that large trend of what *Slash* did? When The Clash's *Give 'Em Enough Rope* came out, *Slash* ran a full page ad—their pages were huge—and they exclaimed how wonderful that album was. Do you think *Maximumrock'n'roll* would have done similar things like review major label stuff?

Tim: We did definitely review major label releases in the early years of the magazine. I think only as it became more of a conscience issue that the network that was being established was an alternative to what the corporations were supplying and that it was something that they would attempt to co-op at some point. That's when it sort of became an issue or a cause to defend or fight or whatever.

Todd: Have things been repaired between you and Ben Weasel? In the last Riverdales CD's liner notes, they wrote, "Tim Yo, right on!"

Tim: We're friends. There was only a brief period when he was really upset that I'd asked him to leave, but after a while I read something that said, "Geez, I don't know what took him so long to kick me out." Our friendship has withstood that, as with Jeff Bale (who helped start *Hit List*). We're still buddies and I think that's kinda cool that you can go through that with some people and still have a friendship. I can get really pissed off at somebody as long as they will stand and take it and then they dish it out themselves and, to me, I respect that.

Todd: Is there a band you have sought out that you've never been able to interview? Say they broke up or all died in an airplane crash.

Tim: Some bands have been a pain in the ass to try to get. Like Propaghandi. We tried many times to get an interview arranged with them.

Jen: Wasn't there some band you printed—you called them and then printed them saying they weren't going to...

Tim: That was essentially it. "Hey, you wanna do an interview?" "Uh gee, I don't know." "Okay."

Todd: I've realized that not many bands have been interviewed twice. Can you name a couple?

Jen: We can't do it.

Todd: Have you ever slipped up?

Tim: If after five years or something like that and a band is still around and the first interview was some little piece of shit then I think it's time to do another one if they have anything to say.

Jen: If they've lasted that long, if they have anything to say, or if it's changed significantly in any way.

Tim: Most never had anything to say to begin with and still don't later on. It seems to be a criteria for being a great band. That's my perspective. The best punk has always been done by really dumb shits.

Jen: Which is why we don't mind printing interviews with people who have nothing to say.

Todd: How many pieces of music—CDs, vinyl, or cassettes—do you receive a month?

Jen: Tim doesn't listen to CDs at all. He doesn't like them. The first time I came to visit there wasn't a CD player in the house except for the CD Rom. He doesn't listen to CDs. This guy, Ray, does it. He does basically what Tim does with the vinyl. We probably get thirty or more. No, more than that.

Tim: I don't know how many come in per day but I do know that the rejection rate on CDs is actually higher than it is on vinyl. It must be amazing what's going through some peoples' heads when they're sending all the stuff in.

Jen: We get some stuff from bands that are severely metal. Pure metal. We're like, "Why are you sending this to us?" It's not even close. I remember once we got a Willie Nelson CD.

Todd: Do you feel that you are viewed as the delineator between punk rock and not punk rock?

Tim: Yes.

Todd: Why do you think that is?

Tim: Because I do that.

Todd: What's your delineation?

Jen: He strongly believes in what he says is correct or he wouldn't have said it. For me, coming from scenes outside of Tim's scene, I think there are a lot of kids who follow him but I think there are a lot of people who know he's just opinionated. If Tim says their favorite band isn't punk anymore, they kind of realize that that's just Tim's opinion and it's not set in stone.

Tim: I think there's people who will either take my word as the word of god or conversely hate me 'cause they think I'm pronouncing the word of god.

Todd: What's your distribution level?

Tim: I think currently it's 14,000.

Todd: It comes out every month?

Tim: Yeah.

Jen: What about *Flipside*? How often does that come out?

Todd: Well, let's put it this way. You know how you say that you'll have a hundred people come in and help you? There's two at *Flipside*. There's about fifty people who write and take pictures and help with material, but two who put all the pieces together.

Tim: Aye, yeh, yeh, bonkers!

Todd: Do you guys think that you have any direct competition?

Tim: I think there's a lot of different zines that all have different and interesting approaches. At even the height when *Flipside* and *Maximum* were... there was some tension there at different points, but, to me, it was never really competition. *Flipside* definitely had an LA perspective and a more laid back approach and *Maximum* was San Francisco and more political and I think now you have a lot of regular zines that come out that all have their own perspective and the types of stuff they like more. I don't see that much duplication as there's overlapping. I think, zine wise, things are very healthy.

Jen: I agree. People go to zines for different things. There isn't another zine that people go to for the exact same thing that they go to *Maximum* for so that's why I don't think there's a lot of competition.

Todd: I feel the same way. I like to read around eight or nine zines every month. My personal favorites. It's like a good friend. You like to go back and see what they have to say... What are your feelings about dealing with people who you know, right off the bat, don't share your value systems? I was thinking of the problem *Maximum* had with the AntiSeen using a confederate flag. How do you get beyond that or is that a breakdown of discourse?

Jen: It depends if you let it get down to that.

Tim: Right, it depends whether you let it get beyond that.

Jen: I think it really depends on how much because sometimes there's bands or whatever that I might get beyond that, but I might tell them right away that I don't agree with what they do. Bands that are pro-life or whatever. I'm gonna tell them right away that I don't agree with that and if you still want to talk to me then that's fine. They need to know right away.

Todd: Do you guys review AntiSeen stuff?

Tim: Yep, and we'll review racist bands. I won't take ads from them if they're straight up racists.

Todd: Will you take classified from them?

Jen: It's hard to get it all. We want to do that. If we get a band that's completely sexist, you want to review it so that people know that.

Tim: And you know, if one of the numbers in the PO Box gets transposed, then...

Todd: What precipitated the title of tyrant? Before I remember it was "Benevolent protective order of Tim," then "Tim with attitude," then "Tim with thick boots," and then it became "Tyrant Tim."

Tim: I took the gloves off. I figured that if everyone thinks that's what I'm about then I decided to sort of make fun of that. It was actually Timojhen Mark who got me cards made, little business cards that said, "Tim the Tyrant." So I just reproduced that for the little header.

Todd: Nice. That's the one with the rolling pin?

Tim: No, that's my regular one: "Yo Mama." There is one, "Tim the Tyrant" that occasionally gets used.

Todd: Why has the look of *Maximum* stayed relatively the same?

Tim: Because we suck.

Todd: You guys definitely have a lot more technology than *Flipside* does, but you know, Al likes that glossy cover. Is there a definite conscious decision to forego...

Jen: Well, there's the newsprint for life rule.

Todd: So you want to stain people's hands for the rest of your lives?

Tim: Absolutely. You can tell if they've read the magazine if they have black stuff all over their foreheads and all over their clothes.

Todd: The possibility of you dying is here. What's your largest fear of what will go wrong with the magazine?

Jen: Turning it into an emo zine!

Tim: That is exactly true. I think that, on one hand, I would like to see a perpetuation of the musical discriminatory policy that we have. It's ironic that the person who's actually—I've been assigning all vinyl up to this point but beginning next month somebody else is going to start doing that.

Jen: He writes the emo column. It's luring Tim into a sense of security.

Tim: That's right. There's certain parameters that we've set and a certain attitude that we've created around that policy and I think it's part of *Maximum*'s persona, so I would like to see that continue but it's something that can't be guaranteed.

Jen: When we're looking for the second zine coordinator and third zine coordinator it's like you need to agree with the music policy. It's not like you can think that you're gonna come and change things to what you want. *Maximum* has a set policy and you need to understand that before you can consider coming to the magazine.

Tim: Jen actually disagrees. She wrote her last column on how she disagrees with that policy.

Jen: Yes, I disagree with it but that doesn't mean that I can't uphold it or that I don't recognize the function that it serves or I wouldn't be here. I don't dislike emo.

Todd: Have you ever been married to anything besides punk rock?

Tim: Rock and roll.

Todd: Have you been married?

Tim: No, thank you. I think that is the worst institution. That as a manifestation of relationships which I think is actually evil. They bring out the worst in people.

Holly: He's not bitter though.

Tim: No, I'm not bitter. I'm not at all bitter. I think love is great but I just think that relationships bring out the worst in people. They exasperate weaknesses and dependencies and co-dependencies and to put your official stamp of approval with marriage on top of that is too much for me.

Todd: Was there one band or a defining time for both of you when you knew you wanted to cover this type of music—that you wanted this to be the rest of your life, whether it is or not.

Tim: You mean as a progenitor of a certain style of music? Is that what you're talking about?

Todd: Yeah, when you realize that you wanted to be a part of that. Was there a band, a piece of music, or a time frame?

Tim: I could go back to 1955! The first time I heard rock and roll was probably about '54 or '55 on the radio and that just completely blew me away and changed my life. It's that simple.

Todd: What do you think was the first band that was a threat to your well being; that you saw where you thought they were going to just burn themselves down, burn the club down or kill you?

Tim: MC5 was the first time I felt that at a show where I felt like the whole fuckin' building was going to collapse and everyone was gonna die.

Jen: I don't think this was a very fair question because once we went out to dinner with Tim, and remember, Mark was there and Martin and they were like, "What's the best show you ever saw?" And they were all like, "Devo in '79!" Hey, I was four years old, so I don't think that was a very fair question.

Todd: What do you consider most militant in your personality?

Tim: My desire to have all of the rich people in the world lined up and shot or be made to become high school janitors.

Jen: I think that Tim would argue that there's not very much that is militant about me.

Tim: She's militant about her email.

Jen: No, the phone.

Tim: Yes, does have a phone sewn into her body somewhere.

Todd: How much TV do you watch a week?

Jen: Including baseball games?

Todd: Baseball games are TV.

Tim: Well, other than baseball games, which are mostly on radio here but some are on TV, I probably watch two hours late at night when I go to bed.

Todd: Any favorite TV shows?

Tim: No.

Jen: The Japanese cooking show.

Tim: Oh yeah, the Japanese cooking show (*The Iron Chef*)! They have a competition between cooks and they have a panel that's talking and all excited about what they're doing. It's totally insane.

Jen: I probably watch two hours total. I watch *The Simpsons* and *The X Files* on Sunday. Those are the only things I watch regularly.

Todd: What character do you mostly associate with in *The Simpsons*?

Jen: Lisa. That's pretty obvious.

Todd: What is currently on your answering machine if you have a personal answering machine?

Jen: We don't have an answering machine. It'd probably just say, "Hi, this is *Maximum*, leave a message if you have to."

Todd: If you call up information, why isn't *Maximumrock'n'roll* listed?

Jen: Because it's not in the phone book.

Todd: *Flipside* never declared being a business. Do you think there is anyone who is justifiably rich off of punk rock who exists right now and they worked really hard and they're still contributing back to the scene?

Jen: That kind of says that being rich can be justifiable in a way. Does that make sense?

Todd: Okay, who is rich that you do not want to shoot who is living off of punk rock?

Jen: Tim.

Tim: I basically have a problem with people making hundreds of thousands if not millions off of punk rock. I think there's something so basically apparent about that concept that it has nothing to do with punk rock.

Jen: Plus we're saying that we think there's something wrong with rich people. There's nothing punk rock that says that's okay. The rich person is a rich person whether they're into punk rock or not.

Tim: To me, punk rock is about being rebellious, about being a jerk, about you can't help yourself about a lot of alienating and alienated qualities. To me, it's not about business and it's not about commodity and units and things like that.

Todd: If you could line up one band and shoot them which one would it be?

Tim: I don't think there's anybody I feel that strongly about in terms of a band per say. Like I said, they should just be janitors. Anyone we would mention would get all sorts of attention for that.

Todd: There seems to be a lot of people, this is a Jello question now, who not only disagree with *Maximumrock'n'roll* but go out of their way to make sure that they are mad at *Maximumrock'n'roll*, who are disenfranchised with *Maximumrock'n'roll*. Why is that?

Tim: Those people who I have attacked in terms of their value system, how they're making their money, what they're doing with their money, have been the ones who attack back the loudest and strongest. I understand why they do that 'cause I definitely hit them in a place where they don't want to be hit. With some people, it's just out of genuine disagreement over issues and I think that's fair.

Todd: If nothing else, *Maximumrock'n'roll*—in the world of zinedom—it's very well known and also known for being attacked or attacking. There's a definite combativeness.

Tim: With *Maximum*, we've always been opinionated and political.

Jen: It's not like *Maximum* attacks people for no reason. There's always a reason.

Tim: To me, it's fine that people love us or hate us or whatever. I'd much rather have people with strong opinions in general rather than no opinion.

Todd: Does operating *Maximum* make you feel defensive about things? Do you think you have a more defined idea of what you like? A lot of people are either attacking you or praising you.

Jen: I feel like I have to defend Tim a lot. People will be like, "Why isn't this record reviewed?" Friends of mine who are like, "Why didn't you review our record?" and I'm like, "Well, you'll have to talk to Tim about that." People either want me to defend him or want me to say, "Oh, I think it should be reviewed." You were talking earlier about what misconceptions people have about me being here and one of them is that I'm going to change the zine policy, which I'm not going to. I pretty much can't, you know? Like I said before, *Maximum* doesn't pick fights. We do it for a reason. Tim?

Tim: Well, I'm used to it by now. I think maybe the first few times I felt misinterpreted, I reacted defensively and I'm sure that's happened in the past. Now it's sort of waiting for it and, "Why haven't they reacted yet?" That kind of thing. Now it's part of the whole chemistry of doing things. It's like, "Okay, that will happen. Is there a way not to get caught up in hysteria and deal with it as reasonably as possible?"

Todd: Have you ever been in a riot?

Tim: Yes.

Todd: Which one?

Tim: A lot.

Todd: Ever broken car windows?

Tim: Yes.

Todd: Hit someone in the kneecaps with a tire iron?

Tim: No.

Todd: Hit another person?

Tim: Yes.

Todd: Intentionally?

Tim: Yes.

Todd: Was he or she uniformed?

Tim: Yes.

Todd: Did they fall down?

Tim: Sometimes.

Todd: Did they bleed?

Tim: I didn't stick around.

Todd: Did you get caught?

Tim: No, amazingly.

Todd: How many incidences?

Tim: Well, I can think of at least three where grievous bodily harm was done.

Todd: Ever been hit by a rubber bullet?

Tim: No.

Todd: Tear gassed?

Tim: Yes.

Todd: Have you ever told anyone to take a bath? To come back and talk to you later but take a bath now?

Jen: There have been many people we should have said that to. No, I've never said it to anyone. That's just something you deal with.

Tim: No, there is, I just can't remember who. There's was an incident where I actually told him to do that. I think it was you, Jen.

Todd: If you could plant a bomb under any one edifice and be 100% sure that no one would die, what building would it be and why?

Tim: Well, in the past I would have probably said the Pentagon but maybe now if there were some giant media center of some kind where everything is was conglomerated…

Jen: For me, it would be a cross between that and some branch of the government.

Todd: Have you ever saved up a huge buttload of UPCs to get a prize?

Tim: No.

Todd: Never got a secret decoder ring?

Jen: Nope.

Tim: Well, when I was a kid yeah.

Todd: What did you get?

Tim: A little frog man where you put baking soda in the back. I got some dinosaurs too. When I opened the box some of them were missing so I chased the mailman down the street and asked him if he had any dinosaurs in his thingy.

Todd: Did he?

Tim: It turned out he did!

Todd: Do you see yourself as a role model, as somebody to aspire to?

Tim: I'm not shy from asserting and I think that if you're going to assert you have a certain responsibility and I do think on some level that leadership is leading by example. I totally believe in working hard and being responsible with the work I do and the commitments that I make. Also, in the age factor in my case, I think that it's good for younger people to see that rebellion doesn't just have to be a stage that you go through when you're young and so in that sense I don't at all mind being a role model. I think that is good and wish I had seen that when I was a kid. So, in those ways I have no problem with that. It's not a matter of ego. It's a matter of responsibility. And the records. I'm in it for the records. Which is partially true. [laughs]

Todd: Do you have a comfortable lifestyle? Are you comfortable with how everything is set up? Did it reach what you thought it would?

Tim: Yeah. I'm pretty much an organization person and that's why I've started things like Gilman and Epicenter. I like providing a vehicle for things to be organized and accomplished. As you can see, things here are very organized.

If I wasn't constantly derided by everybody, you could say there's a cult-like atmosphere going on here, but since I'm on the receiving end of much abuse here, we can't say that. In other words, between my part time job and the amount of time I'm able to put into this, I'm proud of the fact that it's lasted this long. It's weird. When I found out I had cancer, it was sort of like, "Am I going to change now?" People will say, "Don't you want to go travel?" And I was like, "No, I want to work on the magazine." This is what I really want. This is what I really want to do and nothing has changed in terms of that lifestyle. In terms of life savings, I have two thousand dollars or something like that. This is what I want to do and that was neat to find out.

Jen: You should ask him when the last time he's been out of California was.

Tim: 1975.

Todd: Wow. Where did you go?

Tim: I drove cross-country.

Todd: Do you have a car?

Tim: Now, yes.

Todd: Why don't you drive outside of the state every once in a while?

Tim: In the past, I spent a lot of time in Mexico and I lived in Europe when I was a kid. I just don't have that wanderlust. Ever since I hit thirty, what I've wanted to do was organize. That's what I wanted to do. I don't have that in me. I just want to build things. That's what I want to do. That's where my joy comes from.

Todd: Do you have any other hobbies other than this? Is there anything that will release steam that the magazine can't do?

Tim: I love baseball.

Jen: Miniature golf.

Tim: And there are other aspects of personal life which—at this point— are on hold with me. It's hard to have a personal life when you're living in a live/work situation and, once I got sick, I couldn't have a personal life because my life is in limbo, essentially. But there are obviously needs there that could not be met by doing the magazine. I will say that a lot of my needs are about communication and the magazine and the radio show has served me personally and selfishly very well and I think that in some ways that has made me less needy in certain other personal ways. I want intimacy with other humans but when a lot of your communication needs are already being met, maybe you don't need them so much in a relationship.

Todd: It gets converted somehow.

Tim: Yeah, or met.

Todd: What did the young Tim want to do when he grew up? Tim at five.

Tim: I wanted to be an archeologist.

Jen: When I was first in high school I wanted to play in an orchestra and that's why I went to college. But that's the kind of thing where you'd have to give up everything just to do that, which I wasn't willing to do. That's why I'm not doing it anymore.

Tim: Tell him what you played.

Jen: I played the bassoon. Nobody would let me in their punk band.
Todd: Do you have any socialist or communist affiliations anymore?
Tim: Yeah. I've never been a member of a party or anything but my belief system is still very much expropriating the rich and giving to the poor. As long as there's these disparities between not only the power the minority has but the... Most people born into this world will never have the chance to realize their potential. As long as that is the basic setup, I'm gonna be a communist. So that's my M.O. I've never felt comfortable with any particular group. I do also have some anarchist tendencies and that's why with *Maximum* you couldn't really tell if I was straight-out communist unless I say I'm a straight-out communist. Most of the political writings in *Maximum* tend to be anarchist, anti-stateist and that's not my particular outlook but I do feel like progressive-minded people should have more in common than not, so they should be able to work together. That's my attitude.
Todd: Do you know of any essential anarchist writings?
Tim: I don't read.
Todd: Or videotapes?
Tim: That would be Jen's area.
Jen: I do a lot of reading and stuff but I wouldn't say that there's one essential thing because anarchism, like anything else, is so varied. There's so much within anarchism that it really depends on what you need from it.
Todd: Well, just an overview of anarchy. Like anarchy 101.
Jen: Well, there's a lot of semi-good introductory books. There's *Anarchy in Action* by Colin Ward and *The Pros and Cons of Anarchy*. There's a bunch of pamphlets. There's also Daniel Guerin, who has a book called *Anarchism,* and it's pretty good overview of, "Some anarchists believe this and some anarchists believe that." It's definitely good to start with something introductory and then that can lead you to things that are more specific. When you talk about anarchists at the turn of the century, they didn't all agree. There's not one type that's good or one essential thing.
Todd: What is your comfort food?
Tim: Every Friday night at this place called the U.S. Restaurant up in North Beach—it's an Italian joint despite the name—they have the best fried calamari. You can get combos with their other specials. I get that and rabbit with pesto. Fuckin' great. At this place, the waitresses don't write down your order, they remember it all. Hours later, you can go up to the front and the waitresses remember exactly what you had. It's very old school.
Jen: And the one time I went with Tim, as soon as we walked in, the waitress told him that if he wanted lamb chops there was only one lamb chop. I was like, "How often do you come here, Tim?" She knew what he was going to order.

Todd: Jen, your comfort food?

Jen: I don't know if I really have one. There's certainly things my mom made. Actually, there is one thing. Pasta soup that my roommate, Heather, made for me. It's good. Good, good, good.

Todd: What band has been on your A list for the longest time? It doesn't have to be currently on it but the longest block of time that they were on the good list.

Tim: We're just talking post '77 punk bands?

Todd: Any band.

Jen: Or are you talking about what record did you listen to for the longest or what band? A band for me would be Minor Threat. They've withstood the test of time but I don't listen to their record everyday and I don't listen to it that often anymore but I really like and respect them.

Tim: One album by one band that I would say has stood the test of time for me and that's Cock Sparrer and god, what is... *Troops to...*

Jen: He can't even remember the name.

Tim: I can't remember the name of the album but it's got this song called "Where Are They Now?" The whole album (*Shock Troops*) is heartfelt, I guess.

Todd: Who is the person that you most admire?

Tim: Different people for different things.

Jen: Someone asked him that question and he said Jack Kevorkian.

Tim: Right.

Todd: I like Jack Kevorkian. You kind of look like him.

Tim: I keep telling you I'm not Armenian!

Todd: He actually has an album out, too.

Jen: You mean Jack Kevorkian and the Suicide Machines?

Todd: No, no. It's called Jack Kevorkian and the Morpheus Quintet, I think. Seriously, it's Jack Kevorkian.

Tim: Yeah, he plays jazz or something.

Todd: Would you review Jack Kevorkian?

Tim: No. He is feisty as fuck though. He's great. He does not give a fuck whatsoever. They can jail his ass or whatever.

Todd: He's got one savvy lawyer, too… What's the largest perk you get working for *Maximum*?

Jen: Hanging out with Tim!

Tim: I know what my answer would be.

Jen: Go ahead.

Tim: Records!

Jen: Mine would definitely be the people I get to meet. People who write in or people I would otherwise never have the chance to meet.

• • •

"We do everything we can to get by, and sometimes it's scraping the bottom of the barrel, but man, I'm fucking happy."

–Chuck

IT'S NOT ABOUT LIVING UNDER COMMAND: AN INTERVIEW WITH HOT WATER MUSIC

Gainesville Florida's Hot Water Music was one of the first bands that made me seriously reconsider what I wanted to get out of listening to music. They were also one of the first bands that I saw with my own eyes who were stretching musical boundaries without abandoning a strong sense of tradition. It was also obvious to me that they hadn't lost that hard glint of defiance while entering new territory. The first time I saw them, I didn't even know they were playing. I'd gone to see Discount in a DIY record store as big as a studio apartment. When they plugged in, everything they had invested into the band, literally, came pouring out. Their shirts were off after a couple of songs, and while they bashed their instruments and charged about, they were careful not to knock over the t-shirt and LP racks. Such finely tuned and positively charged aggression. When they were done playing, it looked like they'd stepped out of a river. They laid everything out in that tiny linoleum corner for no more than thirty people.

Controlled burn fires. The forest service sets them at the perimeter of where an out-of-control fire is heading. The expertly placed and timed ridges of smaller fires contain the larger one, scorching the earth in the right direction to limit total destruction, sacrificing the small distance in hope to extinguish possible annihilation. A calculated risk, dangerous nonetheless. Hot Water Music is a controlled burn fire. They've got the agony, the rage, the pounding, and the tools to clear-cut their bit of resistance—and it's in the right direction. Too often, bands set their fires wrong. Some set the flames under themselves, burning out too quickly. Some place them directly under their audience and the show erupts into unmitigated violence. Without compromising the friction of great rock'n'roll that emits showers of sparks on the audience, Hot Water Music set their fire so it battles and maintains a circle around them. They took positive hardcore's interpersonal pyrotechnics, injected that into the smart sonic charge of Fugazi, overlaid it with the gruffness of England's Leatherface, and emerged with a style of music that's patently their own. Fire, pure and simple.

Chuck Ragan: vocals, guitar
Chris Wollard: vocals, guitar
George Rebelo: drums
Jason Black: bass

Todd: Have you guys ever been sued or asked to cease and desist by Black Sparrow Press? (Bukowski's publisher. Bukowski wrote a book titled *Hot Water Music*.)

Jason: No, really. No contact from them at all—and as far as I know, none of the other bands have either, which is something we were wondering about when the other cease and desist thing went through. We were like, "How do you say anything without being from Black Sparrow?" They've never even gotten close to talking to us. (Another band has claimed the name Hot Water Music.)

Todd: I was under the impression there had been a talk because on *Forever and Counting*, you call yourself The Hot Water Music Band. I didn't know if that was a concession.

Chuck: That was more or less just a safe call just in case we had any more trouble with whoever actually got a copyright on the name Hot Water Music.

Jason: Doghouse's (Hot Water Music's label at the time) lawyer was really sketchy about putting it out. And he's like, "We can wait a while and find out—because we're having a really hard time tracking it down. The copyright's registered to someone in New York and it's not the band there and we could not get ahold of the person who had it. We had a phone number for him and everything. It was totally not the right address or anything. He was like, "I don't want to put it out without changing it." We agreed to just do that because we were going to have to wait two or three more months for it to come out.

Chuck: It was either delay the record or throw caution into the wind.

Jason: I would imagine at this point in time, with as many records as we've put out up to now, and doing well and everything, I think we're basically in the free and clear—not to curse us.

Todd: Do many people get the Bukowski reference?

George: Not many, but we do get asked about it every once in awhile.

Todd: Why that name and not Chuck's Gopher Squad? Is it thematically important?

Chuck: Not necessarily. It's not like we represent the book or even Bukowski. At the time, we were all fans, Chris was reading it, and we had gone through name after name after name and nothing ever stuck and we weren't happy with anything and we just settled on it.

George: We needed the name for a flyer. We had a show but we had no name and Chris was looking through the book and he was looking at the titles of the short stories and me and him were discussing it.

Chris: We went through a lot of books. Hunter S. Thompson. Everything I could find.

George: He was looking through that particular book at the time and we needed it the next day.

Chris: I was looking at it on the inside and he saw the front cover and he's like, "How about Hot Water Music?"

George: He just stopped. "I can live with that."

Todd: So you were potentially close to becoming The Roominghouse Madrigals.

All: Totally.

Todd: Why do people call you The Florida Weird Beards?

All: We've never heard that.

Todd: I guess it's a West Coast thing. About five people who don't know one another call you guys that.

Chris: The Tiltwheel guys were saying that. I couldn't quite figure that one out.

Todd: Do your shoes wear out before you throw them out, and what's the longest wearing pair of shoes?

Jason: I throw mine out before they wear out.

Chris: There you go. [A heavily duct-taped black Chuck Taylor Converse is pulled up over the seat.]

Todd: What's the longest wearing pair of shoes you've ever had?

Chris: Here you go. [Chucks again.]

George: About a year, maybe.

Chuck: Wear 'em until they practically fall off.

Jason: I save the ones. I don't really throw them out. I just switch on to a new pair.

Todd: What's the best or worst bribe you've received for playing a specific song? Has anybody given you monetary persuasion or favors of a physical nature?

Jason: Have we ever had a bribe before?

Chuck: Not that I know of.

Jason: Not that we've taken, anyway. If we're not going to play it, we're not going to play it.

George: Someone offered us a dollar to play "Incisions" the other day but it didn't happen. Then he upped it to $3.50 and it still didn't happen.

Jason: That's going to have to get much closer to fifty on the dollar amount.

Chris: There's a lot of songs that we can't play any more, so it's just not going to work for us.

Todd: Would you take a bribe if you were going to play a song anyway?

Chuck: No. [laughter]

Chris: Make it five bucks and I'll play it.

Todd: By sheer hourage—I'm not necessarily talking about you favorite album of all time—what album have you listened to the most in your life?

Chris: I go way back to before I can remember it with Lynyrd Skynyrd's *Second Helping*.

Chuck: Probably either *Chronicles*, Credence Clearwater Revival or *Mush*, Leatherface.

Jason: *Start Today*, Gorilla Biscuits. I still can't stop listening to that.

George: Iron Maiden, *Peace of Mind*. When I was nine, I listened to it constantly.

Todd: Has a complete stranger come up to you and provided you with insight that people who know you really well haven't been able to give you?

Chris: Oh yeah. That's one of the really cool things about tour. I'm sure everybody in this band has left for tour and left with a problem and known that they're going to have it figured out by the time they got back and a lot of times that was just a matter of talking to somebody who seems really on the level and you just get in a conversation. For me, that happens a lot because that's totally unjaded advice. I think that's great.

George: I don't need help. I figure out my own shit. [laughter]

Todd: What's the stupidest cut down you've ever heard?

Chuck: I think, "I farted in your personal space."

Todd: If you could line up your broken drum sticks, guitar, or bass strings, how far would that stretch?

Chuck: We wouldn't have to fly to Japan. We could probably build a boat.

Chris: Since when? C'mon. You have to give us a time frame.

Todd: How about we give it a week and I'll do the multiplication.

Chris: Does it have to be broken strings? I restring all the time.

Jason: Go back to when you didn't use to.

Chuck: Two or three every night.

Chris: Remember that one show at The Hardback where I told everybody that I wasn't going to restring until we couldn't play anymore and I ended up with two strings that show?

Jason: I've ended up with two or three strings before.

Chris: And that was one show.

George: I've gone through five sticks a night sometimes. Sometimes it's one or two, sometimes it's none.

Todd: So how many shows do you do a year, on average?

Chuck: Last year, we toured close to ten months.

Jason: If you added up all the days we were on tour and divided by thirty, it would not come out to ten.

Chuck: I think we toured eight, eight and a half months, because we took two months off to write songs and it was going to be ten months but we canceled that last one.

Jason: I would say that an average year is a 150 to 200.

Chris: 150 to 200. Definitely more than 200.

Jason: We're trying to slow it down a little bit.

Todd: How long have you guys been a band?

Jason: It'll be five years in October.
Todd: Why did you guys almost break up? Because when I talked with Tim from Avail, he was bummed.
Chris: No, we did break up.
Todd: When I talked to him, you were on the cusp of that.
Jason: We definitely broke up.
Chris: We didn't talk to each other for three months. I locked my guitar in the closet for three months.
Chuck: We just saw our friendships falling apart so we just broke.
George: Just from being in the band too much.
Jason: Too much touring and no time for personal lives.
Chris: I think that that's really a big part of it because we all pretty much quit our personal lives and when you're in a band that's trying to tour for ten months—even though we didn't quite make it—I know that I quit thinking of myself as a person and was only in this band. We all just started arguing and hating each other and it got really, really bad.
Jason: A lot of it was making the band the be-all, end-all of our lives. Now we've got it down to two U.S. tours between now and the end of the year.
Todd: So, do you feel stronger as a band?
George: It was the best thing that ever happened to us.
Chuck: We wouldn't be playing now.
Chris: That was the thing. We decided to break up because we were singing songs about brotherhood and working together with each other and other people and we were miserable and it just didn't feel right anymore so we broke up and were like, "We'll see each other at the end of the summer when we have to play this last show and we'll just deal with it then. We went out to shoot pool to talk about it and we all missed playing with each other and we all had three months to be our own people and figure our lives out. It just so happened that we all came back together and it worked.
Jason: A lot of that is making it easier for us now, too. As long as we keep working like the band, we make enough money that we don't have to get a job every single time we come home. If we take a long time off, there's a good chance we'll wind up working again, but usually, if we're not on tour, we're not going to work every day. We can actually have a personal life and do things that most people do when they get home from work at night. For me, it's made it a lot easier that I know I'm going to home for two weeks and I'm just going to be home.
George: It's really unstable every time you go on tour and you don't know if you'll have a job when you get back or if you have enough money to pay rent.
Jason: When you get back and have five dollars in the bank.
Chuck: Going to your boss and begging him...

Jason: For the fifth time...

Chuck: That sucks.

Chris: It's totally stressful. The whole time you're on tour, you don't know if you're going to get your job back and also you don't know if you're going to make any money on tour, so you're coming home to your girlfriend: "I don't know if I can pay my fucking rent."

Jason: "Hey, I have to go to work tomorrow. Sorry I haven't seen you in six weeks."

Chris: It's been a lot easier now. We've grown as individuals and grown as a band and we're having a lot more fun and trying to take it easy now.

Todd: Can you give me an inherent paradox in the music scene you're in?

Jason: I think there's towns—Gainesville's an example—and some experiences we've had in San Diego, there are specific towns, to an extent, that only support their own, which I think is self-defeating to the whole thing. That was the cool thing about punk rock when it started. Anybody could go on tour and play and kids would go because it was a punk rock band. Now, we're definitely inundated with a lot of poor quality bands, as opposed to back then, so I can understand that. At the same time, I think people—I don't go to shows that much just because I do this all year, unless it's somebody I really want to see. But as far as people who complain about how punk rock, I don't complain about it, how it's going. I know I'm part of the problem as far as that goes—but I think that's definitely something for the broad spectrum of it. People are too narrow-minded about what they're going to support in punk rock.

Chris: Also, there's definitely a faction of our scene that spends a lot of time bitching about the scene and the community, blah, blah, blah, and then we're at the show, with them together, and all they do is point fingers at people.

Chuck: Rather than change and do something about it.

Chris: I know a lot of people like that and you see that everywhere, you really do. People love to point fingers. You've got kids with mohawks pointing fingers at the people who have the Romulan haircuts, the skinheads are pointing at everybody—but everybody's bitching about the scene. Everybody wants to point fingers because the other people aren't supporting the scene. It just doesn't make any sense.

Todd: Do people ever get pissed off at you for jumping around too much—like club owners who were expecting, say, a mellow emo show? I mean, you're well behaved, you're just moving around a lot.

Jason: The microphone into the crowd doesn't make the club owners happy. But we've solved that problem. One of our roadies started duct taping them to the stands because we've had them get lost before and it's a $100 down the drain for every microphone that goes.

Chuck: We had to pay for a mic not too long ago.

Jason: The Ditch. We're friends with the guy that owns it, a club in Gainesville.

George: One time, Chuck knocked over the entire PA. He kind of tripped over his feet.

Chuck: It was in The Flood Zone in Richmond.

Todd: How did you guys come around to playing as aggressively as you play? It seems like the bolts are snapping off a machine. It looks like you're stepping on land mines.

Chuck: That's just what happened.

Jason: It's been that way since the first show we played.

Chuck: Ever since the first practice.

George: I think that any bands any of the four of us have been in, we've always done that.

Jason: I've always jumped around like a jackass.

George: I've always just gone off. I know Chuck has and I know Chris has. It just happened that the four of us got together.

Todd: Have you ever had a hard time getting down from the aggression of the show?

Chris: Usually, after a show, I can't even talk a lot of times. I get complete heat spells.

Chuck: Usually, it seems like we have our minds set—that's our time, that's our space, that's our outlet to release, so we do everything we can to get it all out at the time. By the end, you're fucking spent.

Chris: A lot of times, I'm just puking in the back yard or wherever we're playing, and it's not because I'm drunk. Sometimes you're just so worked up. All of a sudden it's over and your body can't even handle that. You're just sitting there, and some times it's really hard to wind down.

Todd: How do you guys know so many painters to do your album art?

Chuck: In Sarasota, the Ringling Art School.

Chris: We've only used one guy so far.

Todd: One guy? Really? He's talented.

Chuck: Scott Sinclair.

Todd: He's got a lot of different styles.

Chris: Ringling Art School is where we lived. It's huge.

Chuck: Our first tour was with his band.

Todd: What's his band?

Chuck: It was called Vent.

George: He's not in the band anymore.

Chris: But the singer in that band is the guy who did the Snapcase artwork.

Jason: We're kind of spoiled. We know a lot of amazing artists. They all happen to be in the same town we're in and happen to like hardcore, and we just started hanging out with them.

Todd: At the level that you guys carry off your music, I suspect there has to be a true passion for it. And I also think that for a lot of people, there's a precipitative moment in their life that helps them direct and focus their energies on what they want to do. I'm not asking for you to cry, but what crisis or epiphany steered you to the music you're playing now?

Chuck: My grandfather. Even nowadays, my parents agree with what I'm doing. My dad's a pro golfer and my mom's an evangelistic ventriloquist.

Todd: What type of ventriloquist dummy?

Chuck: As far as the Christian scene, she's world renowned. Geraldine Ragan—Geraldine and Rickie is her stage name or whatever you want to call it. Anyway, in a sense, I'm doing exactly what my father and my mother have done. My mom still tours. My dad has been all over the world playing golf. He's done tours as well. Neither of them supported me. They've always backed me up but they've never been down with what I'm doing.

Jason: They don't understand hardcore.

Chuck: Yeah, they have no idea. They don't think of it as a community. They don't think about bonds—or family.

Jason: They think what the outside world thinks of.

George: Skinheads and fights and all sorts of things.

Chuck: My grandfather, years ago, I never even knew he played guitar, and I was sitting down for him, and he started playing a little bit, and I was blown a way, and he told me, "You like to play that thing?" I told him that I loved it. And he told me, "Never put it down." And he told me that I was fool if I ever put it down if I loved it and I never have since.

George: I just see my family busting their ass twenty-four hours a day and doing something they're not too happy with just to put food on the table.

Jason: I just happen to be good at it. I played string bass in orchestra in seventh grade, figured out there was an electric bass, and bought one. I was good at it so I just started doing it and it was fun. I was always doing art before that and I stopped doing art soon as I started playing.

George: I liked Animal a whole lot when I was a kid.

Jason: My dad's a science teacher and he loves science, but now he hates it because he's a science teacher. If I'm going to do music at all, I'm going to do it in a band where I'm writing everything, where it's our own music. I'm not going to be a studio musician. I don't think I'll necessarily do music my whole life, but I'll always be playing.

George: It's a hell of a lot more fun than anything else.

Chris: I can't remember not playing. My dad, like I said, liked Lynyrd Skynyrd. He used to sit me down in front of the player, when I was one, put headphones on me, and he told me I'd sit there for album after album and just listen and smile and love it. Before I got a guitar, we lived on this lake in Michigan, and my dad had a friend who was playing square-necked

Dobro on the side of the tree. He was taking a work break from my dad's shop, and I just sat there and listened to him. I couldn't believe it. He was terrible, terrible, but it's a Dobro—it was vibrating through everything. Middle of nowhere on this lake. Right after that, they bought me an acoustic. I was eight when I got my first actual, real guitar. I don't remember not having a guitar, even if it was just a toy guitar. Actually, my parents told me they bought me a plastic toy guitar and I guess I'd seen it on TV and it was Christmas morning, and the second I unwrapped it, I pulled it over my head and smashed it on the ground because that's what I thought you were supposed to do. I didn't even get a chance to strum it.

George: My parents bought me a toy drum set on a Christmas. I was five or six, hit it about three times, and broke the whole thing, and that was the last time I got a drum set until I was thirteen.

Todd: No disrespect—why is Leatherface opening for you on this tour?

George: That is a very uncomfortable thing for us, too. We don't want it to be that way.

Jason: The main reason that we pretty much came up with that, as weird as that is, the reality is a lot of the shows, the majority of the kids are going to be there to see us.

Chris: Well, they've never been here before. Yesterday was their first show ever in the United States.

George: We would rather us play last, and if people leave, they leave, but for Leatherface to come over here, if we play before them, and half the crowd leaves, that sucks for them. I'm not saying that they will.

Chris: We all know—you included—we're all big Leatherface fans. I can barely find anybody who has a record that I know that I can tape.

Todd: Right. How many people have *Fill Your Boots*?

Chuck: Not a lot of people have that stuff at all. Most of the people who we've talked to and told them who we're touring with, they say, "Who?" To us, that's absurd.

Chris: And on the other hand, there's a bunch of people asking "Why in the fuck are they opening up for you guys?"

George: And I totally understand why they're saying that, but we want them to have the best possible shows.

Chuck: We feel like shit enough as it is.

Jason: I think they'd be totally fine by themselves in places like LA, Chicago, New York, but all the little places on a five-week national tour, where we can still pull three or four hundred kids out who don't know who the hell they are because the kids are fifteen years old.

Chris: We can barely even do a show in Boise, Idaho.

Jason: I just think it's going to work out best for everybody this way. That way, if anybody's going to take it in the ass, it's us.

Todd: Can you identify one another by their smell? Describe wistfully, like you were talking about wine bouquets.

Jason: I wish one of us smelled like wine.

George: Bad, old wine. Jason never really smells.

Todd: So he just glistens, is that what you're telling me?

Jason: I get dirty but I wear cologne so it covers it up. Chuck smells like there's something wrong with him in the nether regions.

George: Not all the time.

Chris: A lot, though. Chuck has the worst farts I've ever smelled in my life.

George: If there's six people in the van and somebody farts, you know if it's him. If it's anybody else, it's "Who did that?"

Chris: And it happens enough that we can describe his smell by his farts.

Chuck: I drink a bunch of juice.

George: Wollard (Chris), bad armpits every once in awhile, feet.

Chris: Ohh, I wear Chuck Taylors. I have Chuck foot.

Chris: George, he just gets weird aromas.

Chuck: He's got serious fucking morning breath that has an eight-foot span.

Chris: It's not just that.

Chuck: He smells like cereal some times.

Chris: Cap'n Crunch.

Jason: George, every bathroom that you've ever had, smells like a thirty-five or forty year old dad's bathroom.

George: I'm a hairy dude. I use aftershave.

Todd: How would you say your songwriting's improved?

Chris: Here's the thing: *Finding the Rhythms* was a lot of individuals coming with songs that were done. Now, with *No Division* and the Leatherface split, for the last few years, I can come to practice—anybody could come to practice—and have written the most amazing song ever, but there's no way in the world it's going to get played out like that. Everybody has such an active part in the songwriting and everything gets screwed with and that's how we've developed what we do.

Jason: We all try to put our own thing into it.

Jason: The record that's coming out in September of '99, is the first record that I think all four of us have been one hundred percent excited about. I think we finally figured out something that worked for us really well. It's a little different than everything else. It's more fun. It's catchier. The songs are put together a lot better. There's a clinker on every record we put out, but there's no clinker on the new record, for us anyway. I'm sure there'll be a clinker for someone.

Todd: What's the largest thing that you've given up to be where you are right now? Was it a gamble?

Jason: Getting a job after college.

Chuck: Ice hockey scholarship.

George: Ever since I was five I wanted to play music. It's not really a gamble for me. It's what I've always wanted to do. It's something that if I stick with the path that I'm going, it only leads to good. Regardless of how much money I ever make, I know that my being will be happy.

Chuck: I had no idea I'd be doing exactly this. I've been playing music since I was twelve. Everything else has been completely secondary. Like hockey. I could have played well and gotten really good but I just liked to play for the hell of it. I didn't want to go to school for it.

Jason: I figure I can always get a job. I've got my degree so if I get tired of this, my degree's still good... maybe a little peace of mind. It gets to you after a while—being on the road.

Chuck: It definitely takes its toll.

Jason: More so the older I get and now that I'm actually happy in a relationship, it takes more of a toll, too. At the same time, I'm really glad—no matter how much longer it lasts—that I've been able to do it because we've been to Europe once. We're going back. We're going to Japan. We've been all over the States. And that's been playing. Now I actually get to pay my rent when I go home to go see all this stuff. I wouldn't trade it for anything.

George: I can't hold a relationship. I'm just a weirdo like that, I guess. That's kind of a bummer to me.

Jason: That could have something to do with us touring all the time.

George: That has everything to do with it but, like I said, I play music so I'm going to stick that way. Somewhere down the road it's going to work.

Todd: Which have you had more of: broken hearts or broken bones?

George: Broken heart, definitely. Only broke my arm once.

Jason: [pointing to Chuck] This guy's had more broken bones, I can guarantee that.

Chuck: Where's a piece of wood? I've never broken a bone.

Jason: Really?

Chuck: Find me a piece of wood. [He finds it and taps it.]

Todd: When's the last time you were in abject fear?

Chuck: I thought I broke my hand last month. That was pretty scary.

Jason: Leaving for this tour. We haven't done a tour since we broke up. We did nine shows in December.

Chuck: We've never done a tour this long and made it.

Jason: And it's not that long. It's only about five weeks. That, and it's a combination of leaving everything else behind at home.

Todd: Is there a question in the back of your mind that you wished an interviewer asked but never has?

Jason: Nobody ever talks to us in interviews about sellout issues or anything like that, which I'm kind of surprised about. We've always been driving around in a nice van, and we have nice equipment and people know that we don't work, and nobody gives us a lot of grief about that.
George: Now we will. Thank you. It's because we'll bust their ass. We work hard for everything we have.
Jason: People are jumping on Avail left and right for being on Fat now.
Chuck: Fuck that.
Jason: If that's what Avail wants to do, go for it.
Chris: I'm sure it's really hard to be someone interviewing and have anything but questions about the band, but I would more interested on every level, if it was more questions about the people in the band and their personal lives. Personally, I don't give a fuck about all this band stuff. A lot of questions people ask center around, "When did the band get together?" A lot of it you do need to know to give a representation of the band, but I would rather read an interview where, if you're going to take the time, to go into it and learn about those people. That's a lot of stuff that I love reading about musicians—like sitting down and reading about Bruce Springsteen or Lynyrd Skynyrd and about what was going on during this album, what inspired all this stuff. Something had to get this guy to write all these songs. And it's not just the fact that he wants to play guitar. There's a lot going on. I don't think that people think of band members as individuals and I told you earlier that I don't like doing interviews. I really don't and that's why; because I don't like thinking of people in bands as someone in a band. I want to know them as a person.
Jason: There's plenty of people in bands who I like, like two out of the four people, and I think that the other two are assholes or something. It is pretty bad when people group bands as a whole.
George: But for the same time, for an interviewer, you don't know who you're going to step on. A personal issue is a personal issue.
Chris: But I also think that if it's something—that is what an interview is—you're trying to get personal with somebody.
Jason: If you present the question right, with "Listen, if this bothers you, don't answer it..."
George: I understand that's why people don't really get into it because they don't want to offend anybody.
Chris: I think that's what crosses the line. The best interviews—not even the ones I've enjoyed the most—but the best ones that I thought were really great, were the ones where I kind of felt uncomfortable.
George: I agree with you. I don't really have any bones in my closet that I'm not willing to talk about.
Chris: Some of my favorites that I've read—I want to know this person because these are the people who are writing...

Chuck: The people behind the music.

Todd: What's the last thing that made you feel radiant?

Jason: The fact that we can get Leatherface over here and go on tour with us and we can now go on tour and call the shots as far as the shows go, making sure they're all ages, getting the bands that we want to play, that type of stuff. Everything we've been able to do with the band lately has been good because it's finally come over to our terms where we run the show as close as possible to the way we want.

Chris: This last year for me has been just tremendous. I've never been anybody that's ever felt radiant. I've never really been happy until this last year.

Chuck: Same here.

Jason: Me too.

Chris: When I brought my son up to my house with my fiancée, I just had the best feeling. My son was there. My fiancée was there and they love each other so much, and I actually felt complete because I'm doing all this shit. I've got a beautiful son and this beautiful woman and they're right here with me and they love me and I just kind of sat back and I was just like, "This is too cool." My dog was running around, super stoked. And what am I doing with my life? I'm not this rich man but I'm doing what I want to do. I'm playing my guitar and I have this amazing life and it just blows my mind because I never, ever thought it would ever be this good. It just kills me.

Chuck: I sit back and look what I've been through. Last January, the beginning of the year, I got married. I've had turning points here and there and the last major turning point that I've had that's really changed my life was the beginning of this band. That happened. Then I met my future wife. Then we just got married in January and since then everything's been just going up and up and up. Like he was saying, we're not sitting back at home living like kings; we still struggle. We do everything we can to get by, and sometimes it's scraping the bottom of the barrel, but man, I'm fucking happy. I could not ask for anything more.

Jason: This is the first time in my whole life that I've been happy with, for lack of a better terminology, both my "professional" and personal life. I don't have any complaints that aren't going to go away. Anything I've got to complain about is going to be there for the rest of my life.

• • •

"*I remember these clowns doing cannon balls into the pool and shit like that. 'Wooh! Check me out! Wooh!' Clown style. This is the shit I lived through every weekend as a kid.*"

–Davey

BAD LUCK, BAD BOOZE, AND BAD TIMING: AN INTERVIEW WITH TILTWHEEL

San Diego's Tiltwheel (a.k.a. Shitwheel or Asswheel) can drink most people blind. They're a band that I gradually got into, bit by bit. Now, I'm a full-blown fan and they're the band I've seen the most in my life. One of the first times I hung out with them was when they were recording *Hair Brained Scheme Addicts* several years back. I barely knew their old songs, knew them even less, but was struck at how down-to-earth they were. Pretty simply, they're three unpretentious, self-effacing guys who play their guts out. They aren't flashy. They aren't relying on easy hooks.

Triumphant and proud, they've been the worst bowlers at the DIY Bowling Tournament three years running. By far.

Their eight-year history involves brushes with clown school, a stint as a mall Santa Claus, go-go dancers, broken cotter pins, and siphoned gas. They've ebayed gay porn for their van's catalytic converter. They've played barns with elks' heads and disco balls. A happy, dancing pill is their calling card.

The band, at first, sounds like they're playing very happy music. The tones are bright, the songs are swelling and powerful. But there are voracious, rusted, chained monsters lurking underneath. It's a very sneaky dynamic. Take the broken whiskey bottle gruffness and the muted guitar explosion of Leatherface, the duct tape barely holding it together-ness of living in the belly outside of San Diego, the so-tender-it-kills lyricism of Frankie Stubbs, and spray it with extra shots of sunshine and desperation.

Davey's the constant. He's charming, tells a great story, and is cutthroat honest with himself. The fact that he's got a large, sad heart makes itself evident when he plays guitar. There seems to be a direct line from his aorta to the amplifier. How he plays can't be replicated in a lab because it sounds like his life depends on it, and you can't fake that type of soaring and sorrow. And in no small way, and without making this too important, his life does depend on music. Playing it, listening to it, being a fan of it.

What follows is one of the most personal interviews I've ever done. It's about a guy who won't let a band die, what he's actively doing about it, and who doesn't know if every hit upon the musical anvil will break him apart or if it'll really make him stronger.

This interview took place in Tiltwheel's tour van in Dubuque, Iowa. I was tagging along on part of their tour from the East Coast to the Midwest.

For clarification, there are several versions of Tiltwheel. They often tour with different bassists and drummers. For this interview, there's Davey—lead singer and guitarist, and he talks about Mark—drummer, and Kris—bassist.

Todd: What's the Tiltwheel curse?

Davey: The curse. We don't know where the curse came from. The curse is elusive. The reasoning behind it—I have no idea, but that's what a curse is all about. The curse first started the first time we ever thought of going out of town. It was right after recorded "Volume," maybe '94. I have no idea. Aaron Reagan's mom had a station wagon. We were going to do some shows in Arizona and, I think, in New Mexico. And the curse came about because it's got satanic overtones. We booked three or four shows. I had never been in a band that had toured before or anything like that. You read about it in punk magazines about bands that tour. You're like, "Yeah. Fuck yeah. We're in a band. We're gonna tour." Aaron says, "I can't go." And this was two or three in the afternoon and we were supposed to leave at five. And we're like, "Why?" He's like, "Well, I'm supposed to go out to dinner with my girlfriend and I've got tickets to Cannibal Corpse on Saturday." So, I think that's the satanic overtones. When you've got a curse, satan pokes his head in. Maybe that's where it started. I don't know. We had gone to Arizona and back once. When the band started, Bob was a Christian. Full on. He was friends with Gator.

Todd: The Gator?

Davey: Gator the fuckin' murderer, who'd turned Christian before he chopped his girlfriend's friend to bits. I remember driving in that station wagon to Arizona for some skate demo. It was the opening of a skatepark benefit type thing. We were listening to Crucified—name a band—By The Cross, or some shit like that and I think there was this, maybe the word is dichotomy. Our drummer wants us to listen to Jesus rock. Our bass player wanted to see Cannibal Corpse. Well, obviously Cannibal Corpse won. I think that's the basic foundation of the curse.

The next instance of the curse—I booked a tour. It was a week, maybe two weeks long. We'd talked Liquid Meat (Tiltwheel's then record company) into buying this van off this guy. He worked at a pizza place, Sorrentino's in Escondido. $500. Fuck yeah. Good deal for a '69 Econoline. We bought his van. We're loading up the fucking van in the driveway. It's loaded, ready to go. Aaron's standing there with his bag. And some cunt in his Mercedes—he's probably the only other person in the entire history of the world who wanted to go up this same alleyway. "All right, he wants to get in. He's fuckin' honking at us. He's being a twat." So I crank it into reverse and all of a sudden, the van starts rolling, with it in gear, in reverse. What ended up happening is a cotter pin snapped. Tour's cancelled. Forget about it.

Todd: So, what about the guy in the Mercedes? Was he just being a dick?

Davey: Well, no. I was parked. The emergency brake was on. And he had to get through even though there's a thousand parking places, but there's people in the world who are too good to park on the street, even for a second, and he has to park in his little spot. There's shit everywhere, there's people loading out. He ruins our fucking night.

Todd: How important are UFO sightings in the formation of Tiltwheel?

Davey: Not really that important, but I always search for them. I've had one UFO encounter that I'll admit to. That's real. Completely real. Bob had this girlfriend named Jessica. Really nice girl. She was a young girl. She comes to my house one afternoon; she's like, "Let's go to the desert." So we go out to the desert—here's a great, convoluted story again. We got to the desert and go get a five-gallon bottle of Rhine wine, which always makes a good party. I'm cracking these jokes. You know when you'll have a song stuck in your head? Well, that night the song just happened to be "Little Green Men" by Haunted Garage. So, we're driving through the Anzo Barrego desert and I'm singing "little green men, little green men, little green men." I was looking out the fucking window going, "Wouldn't it be rad if we saw some aliens or something right now? I heard there's alien sightings." She's freaking the fuck out. We go to this spot. It's an unincorporated area of San Diego—it's between San Diego and Riverside Counties, about a five mile stretch where there's no police allowed, no wildlife preserves, and I know because of that you can get completely fucking mangled. We've had two or three day little parties, kegs of beer. We get out of the car. All of a sudden I see this—it's a triangular type of object and it's not too high off the ground. It's low enough where we can see the shadow on the ground, flying over. The moon's full. Didn't make a sound. It had six or seven red lights encircling the thing and it just kind of like cruised past us at a convex angle—when you're outside of the circle— and it fucked off. The Anzo Barrego desert is a fucking desert. There's absolutely nothing. And there's one highway that goes through it that goes to Riverside. So, I'm standing out of the car, going, "Fuck yeah! Woo!" She's freaking out. She's got her hands on her face. I started cracking this joke, "That's a UFO. We fuckin' saw one." Kinda joking, then all of a sudden, we hear this car [makes a brake screech noise] stop really fast. In the distance you could hear, "What is that? What is that?" And I yell, "Did you see that?" And all I hear is car doors close and they fuckin' take off. As far as I'm concerned, that's a UFO because we weren't the only ones affected by it. Does that have any effect on Tiltwheel? No. But it's a great fucking story when you're drunk in Iowa. Were we probed that night? No.

Todd: So, you were a clown.

Davey: [dejected] Yeah.

Todd: What was your clown name?

Davey: Birdseed.

Todd: Were you admitted to Barnum and Bailey clown school?

Davey: Yes I was. San Diego State University runs a clown school and my parents went to it. I remember them coming in one night—I'm watching

TV with my sister or something, and they're like, "Kids, we're going to be clowns." They didn't want us to have baby sitters or something. My dad's a great guy. "I'm a clown, I'm going to make my son and daughter be a clown. Draw what clown face you want." I was really young. Probably seven, tops. My sister was six. Fast forward. We used to do mall openings, birthday parties, parades—fucking parades—all the time. Dress up as a clown, walk down a fucking street, go home. But, but, that movie, *Shakes the Clown*, true fucking story, right?

Right now, what we're doing; we played this punk rock show and we go to somebody's house and we drink. Right? Okay, clowns do that too. Clowns don't remove their fucking makeup. So, we'd have these parties and once in a while they'd be at our house. I remember this one pool party in Poway, California. I remember these clowns doing cannon balls into the pool and shit like that. "Wooh! Check me out! Wooh!" Clown style. This is the shit I lived through every weekend as a kid. We'd have these fucking parties at my house. Most of the fucking parades were on Saturday, so Sunday mornings I'd wake up to watch cartoons and there's not many cartoons, but you've got to get in on the good ones. Dude, this fucking clown's in my fucking seat, passed out, where I wanted to watch cartoons. So, I've got some pictures of passed-out clowns with beers in their hands at my house.

Daisy the clown, he was an all right guy. For a clown, he was pretty fucking cool. Then I got into the whole band thing and all that shit. I didn't want to be a clown. You're a youngster. There's girls. There's tits and there's cocks. So, you don't want to be a clown because chicks don't dig fucking clowns, right? But I'm eighteen. My dad, every year Ringling comes to town; we're front row. "Hey, Frosty, Lou Jacobs, Gable Williams," who passed away a couple weeks ago, bless his heart—and they all knew us. So, anyway, my dad's all, "So why don't you come to the auditions with us?" I was, "All right. I've got nothing else to do." Go to the auditions. At the Ringling auditions, they get a group of three people lined up and you walk an imaginary tightrope across a circus ring. And then they make you walk around the circus ring. What they really want— they just tell you, "Do this." And they want to see what you do besides that, how you elaborate on it. I walk across [makes very strange noise].
Todd: An orangutan?
Davey: Like an alien monkey... or an orangutan. You're right. Next thing I know, these clowns pull me aside, totally grilling me and shit. "We liked what you did. Fill out this application." And they always ask this. They ask, "Do you have family? Do you have kids? Do you have a girlfriend?" My dad was accepted a couple years before that but they denied him because we were young. In Ringling Brothers, you go on the road for at least four years. There's two units in Ringling Brothers. Red unit and blue

unit. Each unit goes on tour—one year you're in the U.S., one year, you're in Europe. They switch off each year. And they were, "What do you have here that's anchoring you to San Diego?" I said, "Well, I play in a band." And they're like, "Do you like your band?" "Yeah. Punk rock. I really like playing music." I pretty much decided right then that by the time I was thirty that if I wasn't happy or if I wasn't playing music, that I'd fucking join the circus. Seriously, the day I turned thirty I thought about it. I remember—I was actually taking a shit at the time—you've seen my bathroom. I've got that fucking mirror. You can do a lot of thinking when you're staring at yourself taking a shit. [speaking to himself] "So, what's the deal? Do I sell the guitar and join the fucking circus or what?" I decided thirty-five would be a better age to decide.

Todd: Did you ever get nailed because you were a clown? Are there such things as clown groupies?

Davey: From what I understand, there are clown groupies. And from what I understand, they're not showgirls. I guess they're not allowed to commingle. No. Never got nailed because I was a clown. No. Never got nailed because I was in a band. Never got nailed for nothing.

Todd: Have you ever been in a long, serious relationship?

Davey: One that I count, yeah. [joking, well, half joking] It's called Tiltwheel.

Todd: What's the worst job you've had to take—or the one you're most embarrassed about—to keep the band together?

Davey: Never been embarrassed about a job, ever.

Todd: So, how was being Santa at the mall?

Davey: I liked it. What the fuck? Pyle [who provided the question, and was outside the van], I hate you. I liked being fucking Santa Claus, right? That's good. You make a fucking hundred bucks. You walk around for three hours and give candy to kids. It's all right.

Todd: How many times did you do it?

Davey: I did it just the one time. I try every year to do it. It's hot in that fucking suit.

Todd: Did you have to shave the goatee?

Davey: No. It's a really elaborate suit. My dad saw the suit and he flipped. "I want that fucking suit." My dad is a staunch Catholic. He was a brother when he met my mom. He was becoming a priest. This guy is a straight-up, by-the-book Bible man, but he believes in previous lives. He believes in his previous life that he was the Santa Claus. My dad dresses up in his Santa Claus suit more times a year than anybody should. I got a great picture of him with a Bloody Mary in his hand, dressed in his Santa suit. Look, I'm thirty-two years old, I'm sitting in a fucking van, drinking wine in Dubuque, Iowa. I should have grandkids for him. He's fucking proud that I was Santa Claus at the mall. Good for him, you know?

Todd: So what was the number one request you got from kids?

Davey: Pokemon and trains. Gotta lot of trains.

Todd: Did you ever get nailed from being Santa Claus?

Davey: No. But I tried to nail an elf.

Todd: How'd that go?

Davey: She didn't want any part of it... I never got nailed because I was Santa Claus. I want to. I would love to look at a girl's tits and say, "Ho, ho, ho! Rudolph."

Todd: What, specifically, are you trying to do to keep Tiltwheel full time?

Davey: Sitting in a van in Dubuque, Iowa.

Todd: There have to be conditions, concessions.

Davey: I live with my parents. I'm thirty-two years old. I work for forty dollars a night doing sound. I wake up and do what I call "band shit." Emails. Playing guitar. Writing songs. I've started a few labels. Basically, I sit at home and wish I was on tour. Then we practice. Then I go, "Hey, let's go on tour." That's all I think about because I can't fucking do anything else.

Todd: What number tour is this?

Davey: Four. I consider the first one—a trip out to Provo and back. But that was the tour. Five—because we've been to Fort Collins twice.

Todd: Are you scared of what the band could become?

Davey: No, I'm scared of what the band can't become. Laziness. Comfortability at home. I call it flypaper. Streets are covered with flypaper. It's a lot easier to stay in your own little prison then to go out and experience the world.

Todd: Are you personally scared—beyond comfort?

Davey: I'm scared of what's going to happen when, to quote RKL, I break the camel's back. I'm scared of what's going to happen but I'm really not scared because for a long time I've had this vision in my head of sitting on a street corner on Fifth and Broadway, downtown Escondido, or B Street where the drunk tank is, where all these bums sit and that's what I see as my future. Everybody sees their future in a different way. Literally, I look like Charles Manson. I'm wearing olive drab. I could probably point out the dirt marks on the jacket. I'd just be drunk all the time and hopefully—hopefully—having a guitar.

Todd: Do you feel guilty that there are bands that you admire, such as the Urchin, who are opening for you?

Davey: No. What I worry about is having some convoluted hair-brained scheme to tell a band that I love—and chances are that I may be the one of the fifteen or twenty people in the U.S. who feels that way about this band—and to bring them over and have them spend all of their money and lose their jobs. It just breaks my heart.

Todd: Is it breaking your heart right now?

Davey: Oh, completely. I've been a wreck for a couple days over this shit. Especially last night. There was forty people or so watching us play. Those people were all watching Toys That Kill and The Arrivals. It was really hot and I was completely mangled so I didn't get to see The Urchin (from Japan) too much. I caught about five songs, but it was us, the people in the van, who were watching. That's a heartbreaker. Punks in the U.S. are a bunch of snobs. It's fucked up. This is the one thing. If you're a punk, music should be the only thing that makes you happy in life and to not pay attention to a band for any other reason than you're totally burned out or tired, it's just wrong. It's snobbery. And then I get depressed when we show up in a town with six fucking dollars between us and a band we spent $3,000 getting over here, who worked their fucking jobs just for the opportunity to not to work those jobs. To get that one bit of happiness in your life. You know what I mean? The one little shining moment. You're like this old man sitting on a porch, or a bum on Fifth and Broadway, just talking about what you did in your life.

Todd: Do you think your humility gets the best of you?

Davey: Oh, totally.

Todd: Do you think it's counterproductive?

Davey: Yeah, but it's really hard because it's not convoluted in any way because I've thought about it. But, yeah, it does get the best of me. The worst part is that it gets the best of other people. Kris (the touring bass player), I've seen him sad for a couple days. It's breaking my heart. I don't want to see people sad. I want to see them happy. Yeah. You're totally right. Humility is a fucking painkiller that will destroy you.

Todd: Does San Diego have anything to offer you after all of these years?

Davey: [laughing] Fucking beer and pussy. No. San Diego has nothing to offer to anybody. That's not a valid question.

Todd: It's a totally fucking valid question. Why San Diego?

Davey: Because my parents fucking moved there when I was a kid.

Todd: So you're going to use that leash as your excuse for saying that it's not worth anything?

Davey: No. No, but that's why I'm there.

Todd: Why don't you move to somewhere like Gainesville? The rent is virtually nonexistent compared to a place like San Diego.

Davey: I would love to move to Gainesville. I even liked Erie, Pennsylvania. That guy bought a two-story house for $160 a month. Erie's a place where guys can talk themselves out of drunk driving tickets. It's a great place.

Todd: Where does your hope come from, Davey? You smile when you play and really love people like Jimmy the Truth (ex-Panthro U.K. United 13, ex-Super Chinchilla Rescue Mission), and there is hope out there in bands like The Thumbs and there is good music out there. With

The Arrivals, and you said this with At The Drive-In—they were so good that you wanted to quit. Is that facetious or is that actually hope?
Davey: That's true.
Todd: Then where's your hope coming from? You can't say that the thing that destroys you completely is giving you hope.
Davey: But they give me hope.
Todd: You can't have hope and annihilation in the same sentence.
Davey: Yes you can. [stomping his foot]
Todd: How?
Davey: Yes you can. You can't explain it. [yelling] Take The Arrivals, because they're the most recent addition to the fucking two-man list. Chinchilla? They don't want to make me want to quit. They just give me hope for continuing on. Isn't that weird? I don't feel challenged. Doesn't that suck? I'm a fan of music. I like music. The only thing that's ever made me happy in my life is stinking music. Beer and pussy. That shit's great.

[flustercd] When you're at home, Todd, and you're sitting in your fucking house and you're completely just washed up. You're to the point if you had a gun—I don't for a reason—and knives and poison and heroin, or whatever and you don't want to wake up tomorrow and you put in a stinking fucking band that nobody's ever heard of. Sometimes it takes two seconds. Sometimes it takes a minute and a half. It's like your fucking window of opportunity to make you forget about everything. The next thing you know, at three in the morning, the fucking world around me is asleep. Miserable fucking cunts because they have to wake up in two hours, and I'm fucking dancing in my house to a band I love and they make me forget that I didn't want to wake up tomorrow and that's what it's all about. If that makes any sense.
Todd: Would you say that people like Mark and Kris add to that hope?
Davey: From a selfish standpoint, it felt great, but that's a selfish feeling because the feeling doesn't include Mark and Kris. Did we meld together the first fucking time we played that last note? I wanted to move to Denton (where Kris and Mark live around). Is that selfish because I want to move to Denton and find the fucking people I've been searching for in San Diego my entire life? You know what I mean? I said "I" three times in the last sentence. I don't know how to react to a question like that.
Todd: How do you feel about being the...
Davey: It's shit. I hate it.
Todd: ..the main...
Davey: It's shit. I hate it.
Todd: The Tiltwheel guy.
Todd: What's the furthest you've traveled for a canceled show?

Davey: What seems likes the furthest? With Everready (whom Davey plays bass for on occasion), we were supposed to play Rockford, Illinois. I remember we had forty cents to our name and we hit a dollar toll and she let us through. We gave her all of our money and we had some show at a skatepark in Rockford and we went there. I had this white van. The fuel gauge didn't work on it. I kept a five-gallon gas tank in the back. And we ran out of gas in the last tollbooth to Rockford, so we're sitting in the middle of the freeway gassing the thing up. So we fucked off to Rockford, ran out of gas at the skatepark in the driveway as we rolled up. When we get there, we say, "We're Everready." They're like, "Who? We cancelled the show." We'd talked to them at ten o'clock that morning and the show was still going on. We get there at four or five. Over with. There was a bunch of cars from the kids who were skating, and we siphoned gas out of their cars so we could get out of there. They were all skating. We grabbed another gas can, just in case we needed that extra edge to get us to a gas station. No money in our pockets, three thousand miles from home. We made it from the gas station to a Taco Bell in a parking lot of a Safeway that had a Western Union and Brian Everready called Hopeless Records—our label guy, Cool Guy Records—wouldn't answer the phone. "Louis, can you loan us some money? Seventy-five to get us to the next show?" I called my mom. She said, "I'll give you $180. That's what I've got." She wired money and Louis wired money and we ended up having two hundred dollars, which was more than we started the whole tour with. We were starving. We go to Taco Bell and all order our one bean burrito. A dollar eighty for the three of us. We meet this girl. She had a Cure patch on her purse or jacket. We start talking to her. We learned that she was a go-go dancer. I guess Rockford doesn't have titty bars, but they have go-go bars.
Todd: Pasties.
Davey: And push-up bras... She was willing to put us up. She brought us to this bar and got us drunk for free. The only thing we weren't allowed to do was sit in front of the stage, even though we were the only people in there. And they were doing the full-on strip show. There's a law that if you sit in front of the stage, you have to tip. So we sat at the bar and she danced, and we thought, "This is cool." We ended up having a show after that... That was the furthest we ever had to go.
Todd: Looking at the fact that so much of Tiltwheel's releases are relatively hard to get, why don't you start putting out your own stuff?
Davey: Don't have the time. It sounds like I'm being an asshole, but there's three people in the band and for some reason I'm the only person who does anything besides practice and play shows. That's why. I've started labels. I just don't have the time. You know how it is. If I had the ability and the smarts and the conviction to be self-sufficient, I would be, but it

won't work out that way. I would love that to happen. If there were twen-ty-six hours in a day, it'd be no problem. I don't know if it's apathy or what, but it sure is frustrating. Part of that, too, is why we only have two records in seven years.

Todd: Speaking about songs, with "It's Amazing the Things You Find in Your Pocket After a Bender," give me some pertinent lines in that and then give me the gist of the song.

Davey: Okay. You go into a bar and you just want to get mangled. I do this. I always tell the bartender straight off, "Here's the deal. I'm fucking depressed. I'm pissed off. Something's going to break." I always tell them, "Here's the deal. I don't have a lot of money. I want to shoot somebody or myself. This is the way it goes. Do you mind if you put up with me tonight?" I'll warn bartenders of what might happen. If I remember cor-rectly, that song was written at The Bombay in Chicago.

Todd: Give me three or four lines.

Davey: "Don't mind the broken glass/ 'cause this too shall pass/ and won't look back/ Don't mind the broken jaw or the broken hearts or the dreams that we left shattered/ I'm going tits up/ I'm all mixed up/ everything's falling apart/ If I pass out or even cash out/ tomorrow might not be so hard."

Todd: What ever happened to crossing musical platforms and making a pop, country, and punk record as a triple release?

Davey: As I was saying before, I don't have any options. What's to do after I completely snap and give up on being the person I am now? That's bound to happen whether you push a pencil or play music. There's a point where everybody snaps, so I was thinking to supplement punk rock—I like a lot of country music and I don't really see a difference between country music, blues, and punk rock. I think punk rock is blues. It's the natural progression from blues, from sitting on a porch, trouble on your mind and you're a long ways away from home, that's what blues is all about. To me, that's punk rock. So, that's country music, too. Real country music. Not that Alan Jackson fuckin' stuff. Hank Williams Sr., Jimmy Rodgers.

Todd: So how does this fit into the cross platform?

Davey: Well, my friend Bob, Evil Bob Thomson, was saying that he knows some people in Nashville who buy songs and you write a song and somebody buys it. There's a movie called, *The Thing Called Love*. It's got River Phoenix and Samantha Matthis in it. They're a bunch of songwriters and they're trying to get somebody to buy their song. One guy in the movie, Trisha Yearwood buys his song and he knows he's going to be rich because of it. I've always thought that the worst times in your life, for some reason, country music is all about your woman left you, you're sit-ting at a bar, truck broke down. I always thought I could write a song—a punk rock song, or a Shitwheel song—like that then translate it to country

music and see if somebody would buy it and out of that you can make a lot
of money. Dwight Yoakam, who I fuckin' love to death, has on his first
record, [singing] "I don't mind if I fall off a barstool." Perfect fucking
song. That song could be a Tiltwheel song because that's what it's about.
Kind of as an experiment to see how far it could possibly go.

I'm a humble guy. One of these days I'd like to go, "I wrote that stupid, stupid song and other people are singing it." But they're not punks
'cause I have too much respect for punks. But people in cowboy hats and
brand new Justin boots and all that bullshit will be singing it. I can't fucking stand country music in its current state. What I would like to do is take
the money from a song like that and supplement punk rock with it. Maybe
start our own label. Get our own distribution. Fund a zine. God forbid if
some stupid country song I wrote made a couple million dollars, I could
buy a fucking building and house homeless kids and, "Here's the deal.
Here's your house. You fucking run it. You're self-sufficient. If you're a
fuckoff or a drug addict, you can't live here." Completely live outside of
the system but funded by the system at the same time. It'd be fucking
amazing. I think it'd be great.

Todd: How important is beer to Tiltwheel?
Davey: More important than reality, I guess.
Todd: Will Davey ever be content?
Davey: Yeah.
Todd: How?
Davey: When somebody else takes the reigns.
Todd: Yeah? No.
Davey: When I don't have to worry about making other people happy.
When I don't have to worry about watching out for my friends. When the
people around me are actually safe. Literally, when we're an army. When
we're a threat. The day when the people I fucking deal with walk down the
street and make the businessman and the congressman, they make their
lives a complete hell. Right? I know this sounds like complete babbling.
Instead of, "What are we doing? Where are we going? What are we here
for?" When you get out of the van and say, "Let's ruin this town's life.
Let's give them something to talk about." That's when it'll be a success.
As far as I'm concerned, playing music is an excuse to go out and create
mischief. To ruin people's lives that need their lives ruined. That's when
Shitwheel will be a success. If we could blow the earth up without hurting
anybody, it'd be fucking great. That's what I think.
Todd: Are you scared of success, though?
Davey: No. We're in a world, if you're successful, automatically, you're
the enemy. Tonight, tonight, I thought we played all right.

• • •

photo by Dan Monick

If you feel passionate for something - and that passion is real - it shouldn't prematurely age you. It should keep you young, even if your body's feeling old and crookedy.

IT WILL BE A SORRY DAY WHEN WE NO LONGER DO SOMETHING FOR THE HELL OF IT: AGING PUNKS VS. THE LAND SPEED RECORD

The Therapy of Long, Satisfying Grinds

Thanks in large part to Mike Beer City and Donofthedead, I got back into skating a little over a year and a half ago. Two consecutive broken ankles and a nasty concussion six years prior, I gave my skateboard away and thought I'd given it up forever. Donofthedead wanted to someone to skate with. For years, I'd been talking over the phone to Mike, who owns a record and skate label, and he set me up with the perfect deck.

I'm no trickster. Hell, I'm lucky to stay on my wide board with big wheels without cracking my skull. I dusted off and completed an entire pad set: wrist guards, helmet, the whole nine yards. Broken bones are no fun. Let me state that I'm fully uncoordinated. I stick an arm of my glasses into an eyeball at least once a week when I put on my glasses. I walk directly into door jams of open doorways. By a good six inches. I trip up stairs. Even with a helmet on, I've taken falls in the last year that I walked away from bleeding from the head.

Then after six months of skating, something happened. I learned I was okay in abandoned, graffiti'd pools, public skate bowls, and schools that aren't a bust. (Say what you will about the lameness of public skateparks, I'm tired of getting arrested and ticketed for trespassing and willful destruction of public property.) The technical term for what I like to skate is transitions—smooth variances of horizontal to vertical. My wheels stay on the ground. I've learned carving frontside and backside and have been known to do the occasional grind, the occasional unintentional sack tap, and frontside disaster. I'm toying around with vert. I'm no pool monkey by any stretch, but I can hold my own. Most importantly, I'm having a bunch of cheap fun and getting away from the glowing lasso of the computer. As a residual effect, I'm actually getting back into shape and am currently saying hello to some long forgotten muscles.

Recently, I was at a park in Las Vegas. It's a clover—four bowls all connected in the middle. It's pretty rad. Another good thing about bowls is that, for some reason, kids don't like them so much. I've got nothing against the kids, but it's nice to be in a crowded park and have a virtually empty bowl and an open session while the street part of the park is full of collisions. A misconception I've encountered is that most kid skaters are pricks. Sure, there are those whose fearlessness is only matched by their lack of respect, but most of them are pretty nice if you talk to them like human beings and not like turds. I almost always end up talking to some young ripper who's ten times better than me asking why my board is so thick or my wheels are so big. (My answers are always, "Dude, I'm a squirrelly motherfucker. I need all the wood under my feet I can get. I can't ride popsicle sticks. Big wheels stick better.")

A twelve-year-old at the park was amazing. He could launch over a transition, fly ten feet, land on his tail, slap it silly, slide it for two more feet on the coping (the rail part of the transition), and continue without breaking stride. To him, it was nothing. To me, it's something I'll never be able to do. I'm perfectly fine with that. He went on to ollie over fifty-gallon trashcans like it was the most natural thing in the world for a twelve-year-old to do. One of the greatest things about skateboarding is that there are no coaches and no skate dads whacking referees unconscious. The kids can be competitive, but that's not the overriding sense of why they're snaking though concrete parks over and over again, day in and day out, all over the world. It's a real and true phenomenon that doesn't need sponsorship to exist. Just like punk rock.

When I was getting a drink of water, a dad walked up and talked to me. He wanted to know where his razor scooter riding five-year-old kid could get skateboard lessons and where a good place to get a board would be. I talked to him like an adult—I didn't swear as much. I made an effort to be nice and somewhat formal. I told him he should just buy the kid a board and have him ride it a bunch. The more I talked to the man, the more I realized that he and I were the same age. It was sorta strange. He was very tidy. Very suburban. Very respectful. He wore cologne. He asked me about the economy in Los Angeles. Maybe because I was doing my best to carve the bowl like a turkey (it was Thanksgiving) in tattered pants and shirt dirtied from mopping up the bottom of the bowl from falling a couple of times, and that drops of sweat were falling on my grip tape as I talked to him, was why I felt younger—much younger—than he.

The older I get, the more I'm convinced that age has less to do with the passage of time and more with how you approach the time you're given. You defeat it or you let it defeat you. Which side do you want to be on? Participating or watching?

Fuck *Logan's Run*[1]

"We'll carry the torch you fucking dropped. I'm getting old but that's no
reason to stop."
–Kid Dynamite

"Cokes and Snickers is all I need. Health sucks, health sucks."
–Jodie Foster's Army

For some reason that's quite beyond me, there's an overriding sense in
punk rock (and folks in general, but the terminology's a tad different) that
being "old school" tends to start after hitting nineteen and the condition
gets progressively worse from there. Hardened cynicism by twenty-one,
jaded by twenty-three, and complete disenfranchisement by twenty-five. I
don't quite understand this. Why look forward to and relish the fact that
you become an insufferable prick, or a hipster, or a cool piece of work,
closed off to the world in an attempt to retain something that happened in
the past? Why affect a stance when there's living to be done? I can make
some suppositions, and they sound really dumb when I write them out, but
here goes. Possible excuses: 1) "I'm so burned out because I listened to the
same records over and over again and there have been no new good ones
for the past ten years. Everything new sucks." 2) "I tried to change the
world for a couple years and it shit down my throat. You can't change anything. What's really wrong, anyway? You're naïve for trying." 3)
Someone, somewhere said that being a thoughtless, avaricious prick was
as cool as a leather jacket, and a whole subculture believed them, tattooed
it on their hearts, and thousands followed suit.

To be sure, thankfully, there are many exceptions to the old, almost-
dead, almost-certainly-an-asshole equation, but I just want to strangle people who have turned thirty and talk like they're one year away from cash-
ing in on Social Security. As I write this, I'm twenty-nine. I, very slowly,
heard my first dose of punk rock when I was thirteen. I lived in a town of
10,000. I had no idea—beyond the music on the tape—about punk rock.
To me, it was as distant as Lithuania or Molly Ringwald's[2] panties. I taped
JFA's *Blatant Localism* 7" three times over one side of my brother's Pink
Floyd cassette. On the other side was Black Flag's *Damaged*, two and a bit
times. I listened to that tape over and over again. It's all I had, punk rock
wise (it was also four years after the albums had been released, but I had

---

1. *Logan's Run* was both a TV show and a movie, and the premise was that when
you hit thirty, you were killed.
2. Molly Ringwald was my teenage fantasy. Slightly off-kilter. She hasn't aged that
well, but when I was thirteen, yeowch. None hotter.

no way of knowing). It was so much better than the *Pac Man Fever* LP I'd
purchased months prior or Marty Robbins, who my dad fancied on the
reel-to-reel. Good memories. I remember blasting my tape out in the
garage, riding my hot pink Variflex skateboard back and forth, almost
breaking my skull trying to hop over a piece of two-by-four. Years later, I
bought the original JFA 7" and Black Flag LP and I pop them in occasionally. It's still pretty great music.

Here's where the waxing nostalgic ends. Dead bands are dead.
They're finite. Their trajectory has been mapped and charted and noticed,
like the space shuttle that blew up. The notes have been put to magnetic
tape. No matter how grandiose a literary load is shot in, say, Black Flag's
face, remember this: Black Flag, and many influential bands like them,
will never, ever record another piece of original music. All bands are small
pieces to a huge puzzle that's very far from being finished. It'll never be
finished.

Also, don't take this as a slag on Black Flag (if you don't own
Damaged, I still highly suggest you track a copy down), but it's way too
easy to have the past capture you, box you up, and suck you down into the
ground. It's hard to hear new music when you're already buried, when
your ears have already died. Like the Flag? Why not go pick up some Out
Cold? Reagan SS? Crispus Attucks? Amdi Petersens Arme? DS 13?
Guyana Punch Line? All snazzy, current melody beatings that hiss musical
blood from Black Flag's severed veins, yet have leaked in their own sound
and explored new and exciting possibilities.

So, I ask again. Why look at getting old as a bad thing? Why lament
it? Why fear it? To be sure, I'm not looking forward to wearing adult diapers, shitting myself, forgetting my own name, driving slowly in the median of the road and hitting a bunch of landscape shrubs, and eating pureed
corn dogs through a trachea tube, but that's a long way off. Why act that
twenty is fifty and thirty is eighty? What the fuck are we? Some new breed
of quick-aging dogs? The more I've been in a truly do-it-yourself culture,
after I mastered a modicum of social skills, I realized that I was very far
from being alone. I'm not saying we're all laughing all the way to the bank
by hoodwinking the youth of today. You learn the schematics. You learn
whom to listen to and whom not to. One of the coolest parts of being part
of a real community that shifts and wanes is that you can make real long-
term, like-minded friends. You put calluses on your hands while carrying
out your own theories on how you'd like your own, small universe to operate. It's a very real thing.

If you really have seen it all, and better, why stay around? Why not go
do something new that tickles your soft and tenders instead of complaining
from the sidelines or going to shows as frequently as the Pope and saying
how the new generation's not only got it all wrong, but will never get it

right? Being older, you should be smarter, wiser, be able to help out others
a little better, have your shit wired a bit tighter.

Fuck "back in the day." History's fine. It's worth listening to, but if it
doesn't enrich what you're doing now, become a mortician, because all
you'll be doing is putting makeup on a corpse while the rest of the seekers
enjoy a new form of music spawned from punk, but way too big and too
new and too diverse to be given a name that will stick. To be sure, there
were fantastic bands in the past—*arguably* the best bands that ever were—
but if we don't challenge that, if we don't even try to come up with something new or relevant or our own, what's the point? Cynics dictate that
we're all doomed to be musical Bob Rosses[3], remanufacturing automatic
landscapes. Cynics can eat my ass.

What's the point of giving up so completely to an age before your life
is less than half over? What's the power in saying that you're "so old" and
not have it be a form of empowerment? I don't get it. At all. I know I've
got a couple nuts and screws sheared in my head. Seven concussions have
added up. Maybe I've got it all backwards. I loathed a lot of my youth. It
was confusing. I got along, but I couldn't seem to control myself too well,
had a tendency to punch and hate things before I understood them, was
self-conscious and had long spates of self-loathing. In short, I was mixed-
up but had a great family. I often couldn't separate enemies from friends,
couldn't say the right things, and had a hard time talking to people I didn't
know.

Maybe I'm not even close to being jaded because nine tenths of my
heroes are writers and inventors. I read tons. Always have. Writers, generally, get better the older they get. Very few writers are worth a shit before
forty. Inventors, I've always admired. By their very definition, they create
something entirely new, something that had never existed before and could
quite possibly change the world. How rad is that? Isn't that part of what
punk's ideology is about? Changing the world. If even for a second. If
even for a small group of people.

I don't want to sound cheesy like the greeter at Wal Mart, but I'm so
very excited that we are where we are. Music, in general, is in a great,
great place right now. Punk rock's got it all—twenty-five years of tradition, a solid following, a good cadre of reputable labels and stores, and is
existing in an almost complete national media blackout. That's fantastic.
Who wants to read first about a band in *Time* or *Entertainment Weekly*?
Let them dictate those who are single-handedly retrieving and resuscitating
punk rock from The Velvet Underground. It's a different world. They can
have it. Let them continue raping themselves.

---

3. Bob Ross is an afro'd, linseed oil-huffing white guy who paints landscapes by
pure technique. He whispers to his canvasses and sells hundreds of thousands of
painting kits and millions of dollars of painting supplies yearly.

Let's Put Salt in Their Wounds and Make 'Em Scream
"Everyone likes to think that they're unique. This is my way of proving it. It will be a sorry day when we no longer do something for the hell of it."
–Art Arfons

Although I realize it's a bit odd to reinforce a musical fandom point with a jet car driver, that's exactly what I'm going to do. My point is simple. Find what you like to do and are very good at. And do it. Do it beyond your current, quite often shitty, circumstances. Do it for a long time. See it through. Work at it until it's yours. Keep trying. Don't let finances or age get the better of you. Accept small defeats, but only accept a larger victory.

Think of it in this light: Art Eugene Arfons is (he's still alive) a guy who went completely against the grain, had a vision, pulled it through. Even if you aren't privy to his worlds of land speed records and tractor pulls, you directly benefited from the inventions he developed if you were in a car today.

First, a small dose of history on the land speed record. The concept was born in Europe, a little over a hundred years ago. The French Automobile Club was formed in 1895. Three years later, one of its founders, Count de Chasseloup-Laubat, carved his name into history with the first ever run for the record. He drove his electric-powered car through the flying mile at an unheard of 39.24 miles an hour. His claim to the land speed record incensed Carmile Jenatzy, a Belgian inventor, who knew he could build an electric car much faster. His entry into the annals of speed was a bullet-shaped automobile named *Jamais Contente*—Never Satisfied. These two men battled for several years. In May 1899, Jenatzy shattered Laubat's record and clocked an impressive 65.79 miles per hour. The speed record slowly crept up, using all means of propulsion from steam to gas to self-igniting rockets, to quite literally hooking a sidewinder missile to some wheels. But I'm getting a little ahead of myself.

The year was 1952. Art Arfons was an Ohio farmer who, by happenstance, saw some drag racing and was instantly hooked. He worked at his family's feedmill. He was just a regular guy with an innate understanding of engines and mechanical substructures. He could fix a tractor like a surgeon and twist and weld metal as easily as a confectioner makes fudge. He was do-it-yourself personified. Mammothly resourceful. His first dragster wasn't that impressive. Actually, it had a tendency to blow up and only had two gears, but it was significant because it was slathered in green tractor paint and the crowd called it The Green Monster. The name stuck. All of Arfons' machines were monsters. They were wonderfully ugly, utilitarian machines. All thrust. Very little aerodynamics. They were built for one purpose: speed. Most every car Art made since then—with a couple exceptions—were called Green Monster with a higher number. The second year into drag racing, in '53, making fifty dollars a week, building a house, and raising a family, Art built a second car from parts of airplanes, army tanks, and cars (he always had a huge junkyard). The car, Green Monster Two was powered by an Allison V-12 engine from a P-51 WWII fighter plane. Art's junk car clocked in at ten miles less than the then current world record.

Arfons quickly became so good at making jet-powered drag racers that he set the top speed in three consecutive National Hot Rod Association meets and whooped ass so soundly that the association out-lawed aircraft engines forever. They realized that Art had made such a fast car. They couldn't beat it, so they banned it.

Undaunted, Arfons set his sights on the land speed record. The only blueprints for the Green Monster were in his head. Arfons built the jet car in his own garage. His first speed attempt was in 1960 with a car named Anteater. It was Allison-powered, also, and had a respectable showing, but it fell far short of the land speed record of the time. Art's plan was simple. Get a more powerful engine. So, as simply as I go to Goodwill to find a good pair of pants, Art went on a quest. Every junkyard he went to, he'd tell them if they ever got a J-79 engine[4], in any condition, to give him a call, and he'd leave his business card. He knew the J-79 was still classi-fied, but he also knew that sometimes a person could luck into an engine they're not supposed to have because the military was junking them with-out knowing it. He got a call from a Floridian scrap-only yard. The propri-etor had a damaged J-79, taken out of commission for foreign object dam-age. Something—most likely a bird—had run through the engine. The junk guy wasn't too sure how he got the engine. He'd bid on a bin of stuff and it was in the middle of it. Arfons paid the man six hundred dollars and took it home.

Arfons next called General Electric, who made the engine, and requested a repair manual. GE was incredulous. First off, they told him he didn't have the engine. He did. He convinced them. Then they threatened him and told him he couldn't have the engine. Arfons didn't budge. Two days later, an airforce colonel from Washington showed up, saw that Arfons wasn't bluffing, that he did indeed have the engine, and said, "That's a classified engine and you can't legally own it." As with any pur-chase under dispute, Arfons showed the man his receipt. The colonel

4. The J-79 is a very successful engine design. It's been used in the F-104 Starfighter, the B-58 Hustler, the F-4 Phantom, and A-5 military planes. Although they were first made in 1956, they're still currently being manufactured at a cost of $145,000. In full burner, the engine consumes approximately 10 gallons of JP4 avi-ation fuel per second. During this time it inhales enough air to fill a 10,000 square foot building.

stomped out. For reasons unknown, but very fortuitous, it was the last visit Arfons had from the military. He went to work on the engine, almost by complete intuition and without an instruction manual, stripped it, fixed it, and reassembled it.

By no means a wealthy man, Art had no logical reason to spend all of that time and money. It was his calling. He hung the engine up in his shop and proceeded to build yet another Green Monster chassis around it. It took a year to build and approximately 5,000 man hours (there's no time-card to punch when you hire yourself). He worked seven days a week on it. To make a chassis to withstand such incredible amounts of heat and stress, the parts needed for The Green Monster weren't about to be picked up at Pep Boys. He would have to make his own. Arfons, after looking at an intricate metal-forming machine that sold for $10,000, and getting his hands on the blueprints of the machine, built one himself for thirty-six dollars. It performed the identical tasks. Money may buy almost anything, but creativity and skill can most often make dreams cost-effective.

Just to give you an idea of how powerful the engine was after it was fixed, Arfons would have to chain the Green Monster down between two trees when he turned her on with full afterburner. The engine shrieked, windows rattled. The first time he fired the engine, there were initially a whole bunch of spectators standing around. The engine ran very fast up to idle. Everybody started running. They ran across the road and up the hill. They thought it was going to explode. Arfons knew better. He stood still, stared at his engine, and soaked in her sights, sounds, and smells. Just from the sound of the rocket firing, from the color of its flame, and from her vibrations, he knew he had an honest-to-goodness chance at the land speed record. And, at the time, the Green Monster hadn't rolled a foot by its own power.

After seeing the insane amount of thrust firsthand, Arfons verified what he'd guessed all along. Traditional automotive wheel brakes would melt if engaged at full speed. He needed to find another way to slow the car down until brakes could be used. Almost simultaneously, the government spent $1,000 at the time to build, test, and develop an ejection system capable of parachuting astronauts safely back to earth. Arfons, faced with the exact same eventuality, except for cars, paid three dollars for a sawed-off gun, which he fired to eject his chutes. In doing so, he became the father and developer of the braking parachute for rocket-propelled cars that's used to this day. It performed exactly like the government's.

Art was many things, but he wasn't a guy with a death wish. He knew what he was doing was inherently dangerous, but he went out of his way to make his rides as safe as possible. He made huge developments in the advancements of crush zones and roll cages in cars. Testament to this, he is only man to have survived a 600 mile-an-hour crash on land. He told the emergency crew if he were to crash to look for a capsule of steel tubes, which was the driver's compartment and made to break away from the engine. When the crew got to the crash site, "Humpy" Wheeler went straight to the mass of tubes, looked inside, saw, and then removed Art. Arfons was put in a plane, tended by doctors in flight, and they found that he miraculously suffered no broken bones, just facial cuts, abrasions, and a mild concussion. Arfons was incredibly lucky, too. His helmet had delaminated—many of the layers of its fiberglass construction had separated—exposing his head, and yet he was fine. He left the hospital the next day no worse for wear.

With the J-79 engine fully harnessed and most of the structural bugs ironed out, Art Arfons set three land speed records between 1964-1965, of 434, 536, and 576 miles per hour in his $10,000, brutish, crude-looking car. (To put this in perspective, Indy 500 racecars go scarcely two hundred miles an hour.) His two biggest competitors at the time were Craig Breedlove and Donald Campbell. It cost more than four million dollars to build Donald Campbell's Bluebird and $250,000 for Breedlove's Spirit of America. Breedlove finally beat Arfons by taking the land speed record over 600 miles per hour. It has since changed hands many times. The current record is supersonic. Andy Green pushed his car, Thrust SSC, to 763 miles an hour (a tad over the speed of sound) in 1997. Arfons has yet to regain the title, but you can't blame the guy for not trying. In July 1989, Arfons, aged sixty-four, went airborne at 350 miles per hour in another land speed attempt. He failed again in 1990 and 1991.

Here's the part that's truly amazing. He's not making cars for fame (I bet you've never heard of him), money (he's not a rich man), nor the usual trappings, and when he finally realized that he was putting himself in too much risk and didn't want to burden his family with his death, he didn't give up on vehicles altogether. Although he had begun tinkering around with it for years, Art Arfons, then seventy-one, turned all of his energies and mechanical creativity away from the land speed record and entered the sport of tractor pulls (where a tractor has a set weight to pull through, usually, a length of mud). Unhappy with the powerplants the vehicles in the sport traditionally used, he entered the "modified" class. Along with his daughter Dusty, they quickly became the most feared team in the sport within three years by hooking up a single turbine helicopter engine to a tractor. The man's a visionary.

Here's an inventor, who one year before collecting Social Security, crashed a car at 350 miles an hour, was bummed that his car was annihilated—yet planned his next one, and punks at thirty are complaining like Geritol-popping convalescents, acting like the world's worth is redeemed solely by collecting old records and complaining about things. Don't you see something wrong with that? Here's a guy who did it on his own. He broke barriers. He smashed stereotypes. He didn't have a template to follow. He didn't have the support of zines, of the radio, of the corporate media. He didn't have a lot of outside sponsorship. And he full-on took the unforgiving world on his terms.

Let's take this full circle for a second. If you feel passionate for something—and that passion is real—it shouldn't prematurely age you. It should keep you young, even if your body's feeling old and crookedy. If it's not skateboarding, if it's not loud and searing music, if it's not hooking a helicopter engine into a tractor and towing something through the mud at high speeds, or going supersonic on wheels, it's up to you to find it, keep it, and make it feel like you're alive for a long, long time.

For Art Arfons, it was just him and his cars. For me, it's music, it's punk rock, it's being in the middle of all the noise, having fun, struggling, and answering a calling that most people wouldn't even begin to understand.

•   •   •

AT THE DRIVE-IN

I'll lay it on the line. You're not going to be cooler for doing an interview, there's a 99.99% chance you won't get laid because of it, and if you're dealing with punk rock, believe it or not, a zine isn't going to sell astronomically better or worse if a specific band is in its pages or not.

ON INTERVIEWING:
FROM BEER DRINKING GOATS TO POPES

I started interviewing bands in 1996. Before that, I pretty much stayed in the background of punk rock. I bought used cassettes, went to shows, hung out with like-minded individuals, did some writing, but never got the urge to put a cassette recorder up to someone's mouth and ask them questions. After I'd been at *Flipside* for a bit, I wanted to conduct some myself. What the hell, I figured. (Although I neither regret nor am ashamed of any interview I've done, there are some I wouldn't do now that I had done in the beginning.)

I had obstacles to overcome. I was, and still am to a lesser degree, very shy. I'm not one to pry too much into someone's very personal life and I really don't like my picture taken, so it's kind of strange that I took a fancy to both trying to get folks to speak candidly and then taking pictures of them, most often when they're jumping around. My first sortie of interviews were okay. I learned some valuable lessons. Here are some of them.

The first lesson: Don't let anyone talk you into an interview. If you don't come up with the idea yourself, like, "Damn, that band's awesome. I'd like to talk to them," or "I just shit myself (in a good way) and that song made me do it," it's best not to do an interview. No matter how hot or personally charismatic someone in the band is.

In the music industry, there are these people called publicists. Their job is to call you up when you're making lunch or doing laundry and try to convince you that you'd be a fool not to interview Band Fabulous. I'll go so far as to say that there are some publicists I very much admire and those are the ones who provide tour schedules and keep the pressure low. I'm a grown man. If a band's in my top twenty at the time and I've got time open to interview them, chances are it's a go and I'll schedule them in.

Most publicists, unfortunately, sound like they're selling your own car back to you. They're slippery. When I was starting out, I got talked into interviewing The Toasters. They were my first. It wasn't bad at all. Buck, who I talked to, was extremely nice. I was nervous, but after it was all said and done, it was all right. About three months later, a simple revelation hit me. "Man, The Toasters are pretty good, but are they my favorite band? Are they even close?" I came up with the answer to both. No. Life is short. I'm going to start aiming for my favorite bands.

Here's the second lesson: Never let a publicist talk you into an interview. I know it's the same advice as the first lesson, but it bears repeating. First off, don't fall for the "this is a chance of a lifetime" line. If a band really is as good as Band Fabulous is touted to be, it doesn't matter when their new record is coming out. Their music shouldn't be more perishable than a bag of potato chips.

Don't fall for the "you're a (insert nice word for dumbass) if you don't cover this band" line. I'm sorry, but I don't give a rat's butt how "deserving" a band is, how (fill in the blank with the name of the zine you're working for and make it an adjective) the band is supposed to be. Just because a band has been around for a long time, it becomes "your job" to cover an "influential artist"? Would I interview Rush just because they've been around for so long and Neil Peart has a big drum set? My hand's not up. It's just a fact that there are some bands I don't dig. For years, specific artists and their management would ask every couple months for an interview. I continued to respectfully decline.

I'm now comfortable with the word no. Here is the number one thing to think about when you're being asked to do an interview that most publicists don't consider: transcription. As much as I wish it were true, just by yelling at the computer, words don't magically appear on the screen. Transcription isn't terribly fun. It takes a long time to do correctly. So, when you think about interviewing that band or person who you're not really jazzed about, think about listening to them repeat the same words over and over and over again as you try to decipher the drunk talk and filter out the bar buzz in an attempt to make coherent sentences. Not a good time. For a good-length interview in a quiet room, it involves, on average, six to eight hours of transcription. If you're wincing at the beginning of the interview, you'll probably be hammering nails into your skin by the end of it.

Don't let the publicist fluff you. I'll lay it on the line. You're not going to be cooler for doing an interview, there's a 99.99% chance you won't get laid because of it, and if you're dealing with punk rock, believe it or not, a zine isn't going to sell astronomically better or worse if a specific band is in its pages or not. Most readers are concerned with the overall direction of the zine, not just one band. Lastly, if you're fixing on doing interviews at the punk rock level, very few places pay and it's definitely not enough to make a living off of. I haven't gotten paid a single penny for any interview that's run in *Flipside* or *Razorcake*. It's a labor of love.

As an aside, I started interviewing prior to the proliferation of the email interview and the boom and bust of the first wave of websites "looking for content." I don't want to poo-poo the entire enterprise of email interviews, but I never think they turn out as well. There are fanzines in Australia that want to talk to their favorite bands who will probably never be near Melbourne and don't want to rack up an astronomical phone bill. That makes sense. What doesn't make sense is email interviews that take place between people in the same part of the world. The problem I find with email interviews is that the interviewees have too long to think about the answers. There's very rarely large, unexpected tangents or surprising off-the-cuff remarks. Follow-up questions are either non-existent or completely forced. Band members can't automatically play off each other. Also, with rare exception, I think that people being interviewed in a live setting enjoy the fact that they don't have to type their responses into a glowing box. They're musicians, not necessarily writers and not necessarily even good typists.

I can undoubtedly say that my favorite interviews were all live. Body language speaks volumes yet doesn't register on tape. As opposed to a phoner, you can get a real person vibe, plus you can get the occasional free drink. You also see how bands deal with touring, how they react to other people, if they're thoughtful and not just quiet. Plus, a big part of this, for me, is to directly interact with people who I admire, to see them play live, share some stories, and to take pictures of them. It's about real connections not just digitized voices or symbols translated through machines. By doing this, over the years, I've become good friends with loads of bands. I doubt that would have happened if I'd just previously talked to them on the phone or shot them an email.

Okay, now that's out of the way. You have a band in mind that you want to interview live. You're stoked on them. They're coming through town. What do you do?

This part is important. Never ask any of the following questions. These are interview killers: "What are your influences?" "What instruments do you play?" "Who's in the band?" "How long have you been around?" "How's this tour going?" "Tell me a crazy tour story." All of these questions suck.

If the band has any sort of history, you can find all this stuff on the internet or by reading zines. You can cover all of this info, perfunctorily, in the introduction. You don't need Bob to say, "I'm Bob and I play the drums." It's not such great reading. I also think it's a bad idea to have an interview that is extremely perishable. It's not important that Band Fabulous went through Dubuque in 1998. What's important is if they met Sammy the Beer Drinking Goat. The time isn't that important. The story will last longer than, "Yeah, Dubuque was okay. Lots of corn."

Since "Tell me a crazy tour story" gets asked by almost every hack, most bands will either repeat the same story they've told a thousand times or come up blank. If you know part of a story, or have heard something, use a lead in, like "I heard that Sammy died from eating the beer cans after drinking the beer. Is that true?"

This is all leading up to a point I can't stress enough. Research. Research. Research. The longer you do interviewers, the easier this becomes. I always do a thorough internet search. How did I know that the stepfather of the manager of the Germs invented the Philly Cheesesteak? By reading page after page about Nicole Panter. It's amazing what's on the internet. All you have to do is set aside some time and do some digging. Not only can you look up the band name, you can find out what the band's member's names are and search for them. You can look up interesting facts about their particular scene, read message boards, find places of interest near their homes (like museums of questionable technology or gigantic balls of twine), and get a much more rounded picture of what may shape the band, long before asking them a single question. I like being thorough.

The third piece of advice seems like a no-brainer. Read the band's lyrics. Listen carefully to their songs. See who they give nods to in their thank you list. You may have mutual friends. This is especially helpful if the band is new, doesn't have a history, and you've never read an interview with them. Make it clear in your mind what they're going for and what you'd like answered yourself. If the band's politically correct, it's probably not a good idea to talk about hookers and blow. If a band's straight edge, it's best not to talk about the beer you just shotgunned in the car to the show. Make note of any lyrics that pique your interest. For example, Dillinger Four has the line: "Nelson Algren said to me 'Celebrate the ugly things.'" Not only did I find out about a great author and start reading him, but I tied the author's work into the band's and formulated questions off of that. If you're curious about them as people and artists—which is essentially the main reason to interview a band instead of just listening to their music—more than just several questions should pop up.

Thorough research also helps prevent you from conducting the exact same interview the band's been through countless times. I often read existing interviews of bands I'm interested in like they're real conversations that I'm a part of. There's often information or asides that are never followed up or challenged by the interviewer. Old interviews also contain questions that I can re-phrase to get a slightly different answer or begin a new line of questioning with.

Also, sometimes questions just pop into my mind for no reason at all beyond listening to a band's music. I write those down. Those come in handy.

Research takes time. With very few notable exceptions, I treat the interview I'm doing as the only one I'll do, ever, with a particular band. I want to make an impact not only with the band, but also with the readers, and most selfishly, myself. I want to know what makes people tick. What shapes them to make the music they do? I'm not talking about the equipment they use. I'm talking about what makes them human beings—how they were raised, what they think about the world, what struggles they've had to overcome. Yes, the catalyst is often music, but to get the to the point where a band has recorded notes onto a piece of magnetic tape or played live, they usually had to go through a lot of trials and tribulations. That's what interests me. The humanity, the debauchery, the insanity, the cognition, and the struggle behind it all.

With the exception of one or two interviews, all the people I've interviewed over the years became more engaged in the conversation when they realized I had more than just a passing knowledge of them. This has led to long conversations on topics that truly inspired and surprised me, from the Civil War to a skater who had been convicted of killing his girlfriend's friend, to Pope Pious XI blessing Mussolini's invasion of Ethiopia.

Many people think that Nardwuar the Human Serviette is solely a nutcase in his interviews—like when he asked Tommy Lee of Motley Crew if he used his wang to honk the horn of a rented boat. What I've learned is that Nardwuar's secret weapon is lots of information. While Nardwuar is definitely animated, his research is truly impressive and his interviews are some of my favorites to read because nine times out of ten, the most random-sounding question is actually relevant and tied in somehow. I think that's awesome.

Over the years, I've also become very anal about when and where the interview takes place. Again, it boils down to transcription. Ideally, it's a great idea to write down what's actually said. Anything that gets in the way of this basic equation is your enemy. Restaurants are rarely quiet. Alleys work pretty well, so do vans. Dressing rooms can work if they're far enough removed from other bands playing or sound checking. If possible, catch the band before they play. After a show, they're usually winded, scattered and looking for beverages, chatting with friends who came to see the show, and it's harder to corral them. You can't always control what's going to happen, but it doesn't hurt to make the suggestion early that you'd prefer to get the interview going. Also, if I don't interview a band right off the bat, I find myself holding my tongue. I don't want to breech any of my questions then have to repeat them during the interview and have them seem repetitive.

Over time and with more interviews, connections will be made. A band that I interviewed a couple years back often tours with bands I'm currently interested in. I can then email my friends or acquaintances and ask if they know anything particular about the people that I'm planning on interviewing. It doesn't have to be dirt, but something interesting and makes a good story, like they dressed up as a leprechaun during Halloween or they get mistaken for the lead singer of Dokken.

As an aside—and I know this goes against the unwritten creed of "music journalism" and "entertainment news"—I rarely dig for damaging dirt or force unsubstantiated gossip. I understand my purpose for running a magazine is a little bit different than most. I'm looking to build a community instead of biting someone in the ass for the hopes to sell more magazines by getting a "scoop." When the tape recorder's off, I'm no longer Todd the Reporter. I'm just a regular dude hanging out with people I enjoy or would like to know better. Doing this, I've become friends with a lot of the bands, partially because they know I'm discrete. What they tell me in confidence isn't going to show up in print in our pages. It also helps that I'm a terribly private person. I know the importance between private and public knowledge.

How do you know an interview's successful? That's tough. Some interviews that I didn't think went so well were actually fantastic when transcribed. Some interviews that were super fun to do didn't translate too well onto paper. That's where the voodoo is involved. However, one of the most gratifying things to me is when a band member looks at another and goes, "I didn't know that about you." If a band member says, "Wow. That's a great question," give yourself a pat on the back.

Okay, it's all on tape. First round through, I type exactly what someone says. As a writer, I always learn a thing or two about how people really speak, how phrases are put together, and speech patterns that I didn't realize when I was talking to someone. It holds a small bit of perverse fun for me. When I'm finished transcribing, I'll look the entire interview over. There's no reason to print, "Uhhh…. He… No. Yeah. Uhhh…." verbatim. Sometimes people take time to warm up to talking or getting to a point. I also trim the fat, remove redundancies (like if someone says fuck or fuckin' every time they pause), and tighten up the interview as much as I can before committing it to print. Although grammar's a bit looser in interviews, a little editorializing goes a long way. I want to retain how someone actually speaks, but if it's unclear, and proper comma placement or a rearranged sentence can clarify meaning, I'm not opposed to small changes as long as I'm not putting new words in someone's mouth.

There's no doubt about it; done right, interviews are a lot of work, but it's not over quite yet. The final step, after it's all written and printed, I make it a point to send some copies of the magazine with their interview to the band. It's a small gesture that means a lot. Not only does it keep the band in the loop, it underscores that in an underground which many are trying to keep alive, it's not just about units or products, street teams, or marketing strategies. It's about handshake deals and "hell yeahs." It's about saying thanks. It's about sharing ideas, treating people foremost like human beings, and giving a little back to the folks who make life more worth living.

•   •   •

THE EPOXIES

ALSO AVAILABLE FROM GORSKY PRESS

DRINKS FOR THE LITTLE GUY by Sean Carswell   **$10 ppd.***
paperback — 279 pgs.
"The best book about a carpenter since the Bible."
   —Flipside Magazine

DEAR MR. MACKIN... by Rev. Richard J. Mackin   **$10 ppd.**
paperback — 200 pgs.
"Richard is on to something here, something big... If you are not hip to Mackin, you are missing out...: Mackin is a witty genius."
   —Factsheet 5 (editor's choice)

GLUE AND INK REBELLION by Sean Carswell   **$10 ppd.**
paperback — 130 pgs.
"Sean Carswell is a wonderful story teller. Reading his stuff makes you laugh, and makes you think."
   —Howard Zinn, author of A People's History of the United States

THE UNDERCARDS by James Jay   **$8 ppd.**
paperback — 100 pgs.
"Its cast of stooges, high-flyers, and maulers will, by turn, make you guffaw out loud, gasp with awe, groan with grief. This book puts the smack-down on poetry!"
   —Jim Simmerman, author of Kingdom Come

PUNCH AND PIE edited by Felizon Vidad and Todd Taylor   **$5 ppd.**
paperback — 160 pgs.
"These stories are great. The corporate publishing overlords could never put out an anthology such as this."
   —The Iconoclast

THANK YOU FOR YOUR CONTINUED INTEREST by Rich Mackin   **$10 ppd.**
paperback — 192 pgs.
"I can't believe they write you back."
   —Ralph Nader

RAZORCAKE MAGAZINE   **$3 ppd.**
bi-monthly magazine — 112 pgs.
Razorcake *is published by and includes most of these Gorsky Press affiliated rogues. Each issue features interviews, reviews, columns, and articles on independent culture.*

FOR A COMPLETE CATALOG OR TO ORDER ONLINE, VISIT:
    <www.gorskypress.com>

FOR OLD-FASHIONED MAIL ORDER, SEND CHECKS, CASH, OR MOs TO:
**GORSKY PRESS
PO BOX 42024
LA, CA 90042**

*("$10 ppd." means that the total for the book, including shipping and handling, is $10)